Kailas

THE INNER KORA

Contributions

Kailash with Mohanji Pilgrims

Gurulight

© GuruLight, 2017
All rights reserved.

No part of this publication may be reproduced, stored in a retrieval system or transmitted by any means, electronic, photocopying, recording or otherwise, without the prior written permission of the author

Cover design:
Mohana Hanumatananda

First edition published by Gurulight 2017

Email: info@gurulight.com
Web: www.gurulight.com

ISBN: 978-81-933091-6-2

Kailash - Tibet

Bhagavan Shiva

Mohanji

कैलासराणा शिव चंद्रमौळी | फणींद्र माथा मुकुटी झळाळी |
कारुण्यसिंधू भवदुःखहारी |
तुजवीण शंभो मज कोण तारी || १||

Oh, Lord Shiva, who is seated on Mount Kailash, whose forehead is decorated with the moon and the king of serpents as a crown, who is the Ocean of Mercy and the remover of delusion,

You alone can protect me. I surrender to thee.

Different Shades of Mohanji

Mohanji and Kailash

PREFACE

The Inner Kailash

MY BELOVED MOHANJI and a group of people went to Kailash this year. Eighteen of them did Inner Kora. Now they are writing their experience in a book form. I am deeply pleased to know that. All true pilgrims should write their experiences so that others are guided well.

Kailash cannot be defined. Each one gets from Manasarovar and Kailash according to their spiritual eligibility. Nobody leaves the abode of Shiva empty handed. Shiva is pure consciousness. Mother Shakti is pure awareness. They are the Shiva and Shakti of our life. Both complement each other. Shakti is aware of Shiva always. Shiva need not be aware of Shakti. And finally, all are one. Shiva, Shakti, you and I – we all are one. Through rigorous and uncompromising concentrated practices, we can bring our praana Shakti to our personal Kailash, our sahasrara. This is the true Kailash; each one of us should climb.

I am aware how deceitful the mighty Himalayan terrains are! When we look, the mountain ranges will seem close by and easily conquerable, but they are in fact miles away. Mohanji and his team went inside the most difficult terrains of Kailash and completed the Inner Kora. This is not an ordinary feat. And some of them physically touched Kailash beyond Charan

Sparsh (the feet of Kailash). Hence, this book will become relevant for the future generations who would like to go there. Take this journey seriously and go there to discover yourself, if you must go.

Those who have read my autobiography (Autobiography of an Avadhoota) would know that a few chapters of that book are dedicated for my unforgettable pilgrimage to Manasarovar and Kailash. How can I forget the event when Mother Goddess breast fed me and healed me when my legs were swollen and I was sinking into deep helplessness? How can I forget the experience of the great "Soham" mantra on the banks of Manasarovar? How can I forget my beloved mother, Avadhoota Tara Mayee coming out of Manasarovar, hugging me and wiping my tears of joy? How can I forget the meeting with the great Keenaram Paramahamsa, param guru (Guru's Guru) of my guru Tara Mayee? How can I forget him transferring me siddhis of doora sravan (ability to hear voices miles away) and doora darshan (ability to see things miles away) as well as Sankalpa Siddhi (wish fulfilling powers) to me when I least expected it?

And I can never forget my Mother, Guru and God Tara Mayee's command, "As I prepare you for 'Loka Sangraha' (living for the entire humanity), you should prepare any one of your disciples to carry out this work in the future." And I waited with my illness and failing body for the last 14 years to complete and fulfill this command of my Guru until they brought Mohanji to me, almost at the time when I was giving up hope. Hence, writing these few words are also an expression of fulfillment for me. This juncture in my life is almost like a successful completion of a great Kailash pilgrimage on earth for me too, as I hand over to Mohanji and step down to my shell and shelter. This is completion and release for me. Mohanji's Kailash journey is my journey too as I am with him always, now and forever.

I wish my Mohanji, his followers of this world and this book, Kailash with Mohanji, The Inner Kora, a great success. My blessings and the blessings of the entire Guru Mandali be with all of you always.

With Love

Avadhoota Nadananda.

The Inevitable Journey – Unlimited Grace

- Mohanji -

WE ARE BORN spiritual and we will die spiritual. Spirituality is nothing but our awareness of the spirit or soul, the very energy that maintains our existence without interference of any kind as long as karma attached to this incarnation exists. Being aware of our spirit is spirituality. Increased moments of this awareness will bring higher level of spirituality. This has nothing to do with religions, teachers, preachers or gurus. This is a simple awareness. Just awareness! And Shiva, the father of all souls is the inevitable destination of all beings. Kailash, the abode of Shiva, is the home of every soul. Hence, journey to Kailash is the ultimate journey of human incarnation. Kailash removes the obstacles, tears up the masks of existence, destroys relative truths pertaining to relationships, and makes man naked and pure, ready for the celestial home. It is usually a tough journey because of binding baggage from the past. Kailash! It is the ultimate journey of man and ultimate realization of mankind!

Kailash! It is a state in existence more than a mountain that stands in the horizons of human aspiration, as a challenge of will and endurance, reminder of the ultimate penance, ultimate destination, ultimate detachment, ultimate state of beingness, highest fulfillment in a human existence and the promise of final dissolution beyond the seemingly eternal bondage of births and deaths on earth. Every spiritual being craves for stillness of mind, the no-mind state to experience oneness beyond all diversities and diversions, oneness consciousness and associated awareness irrespective whether they have clarity about it or not.

Roughest terrains! High Altitude! Hypoxia! Unpredictable weather! Apart from all these, the looming uncertainties associated with travels into the unpredictable, unknown terrains. Nothing is predictable, even though elaborate plans covering micro details are discussed and rehearsed time and again. Everything can change in a moment. A hail storm, a cloud burst, rains or just the change in mind of the authorities can make the pilgrimage from ecstasy to agony in no time. This has nothing to do with the organisers or the sherpas. They are as helpless as the pilgrims are. Yet, the deep inner urge for completion within or a state of total oneness with oneself, urges the seeker to take this tough trip, destroying their usual comfort zones and plunge into the unknown and unpredictable.

Kailash never leaves anyone empty handed. This is my experience. Kailash removes the layer of superficial and unnatural from us, as well as numerous fake relationships around us. This could often be very painful because we are used to it, put up with it, through time. This is the celebrated abode of the Great Shiva or the symbol of Shiva-hood, the supreme consciousness beyond flavours and forms. Only one thing works here, the eternal 5 syllable merger mantra "Namah Shivaaya". Only one thing can ensure a successful journey – unshakeable faith which provokes unstoppable Grace.

Every pilgrim will be tested, one way or the other, to the hilt. Everyone gets to know themselves, their limits, their unmasked personalities, and capacity more than anything else in this endearing journey. Helplessness often hits between the eyes. There again, faith comes in handy. Only faith can help the journey. Total acceptance of oneself, one's limitations and environment becomes a necessity. There is no choice. Accept the truth even if it is bitter. There is no point in complaining because everybody experiences the same problems. Sherpas work hard to make our lives comfortable. But, terrains, climate and less oxygen test our mettle to no ends. Acceptance. No resistance. Surrender to the Lord with heartfelt, sincere gratefulness for allowing us to be at His abode will help the trip.

Kailash takes away the closely guarded pretensions and leaves us stark naked. It pushes us to remove layers of masked friendships, fragile relationships, false egos, pretentious and fragile images, as well as unfaithful connection with oneself. It forces you to accept and acknowledge your Self as the only reality. We realise the fragility of the body. We start feeling that the only reality is our soul even if the body withers away in time. It moves you to see your Self in the mirror of Manasarovar, the real and naked you. It is a choice less favour. Everything false must fall and drop off sooner or later. It will and it does. That is the experience of most of the pilgrims over the years. Kailash shakes you and stirs you in the most unpredictable ways.

When I had the first discussion with our tour partner in 2012 about our intended pilgrimage to Kailash with approximately 35 people, I told them not to compromise on quality of available facilities at any cost knowing fully well that once we cross over to China, facilities are very limited. I wanted to have the best possible options available to our team members because we can do nothing about the terrains, hypoxia and climate. Even though cost could vary, that is the only thing we can possibly gift to the fellow pilgrims in such a challenging journey. Nobody can change the climate, terrains or altitude. What we could possibly do is the best possible comforts within the available circumstances. Our tour partner always ensured that. Our group has been travelling since 2012. I personally travelled in 2012, 2014 and now in 2016. Kailash with Mohanji has been happening every year since 2012 even though I could not personally join in every year due to various constraints.

I consider it as a great blessing to step into the land of Shiva, the one who is pure consciousness and is the source and support of every atom as well as the entire universe. Shiva, the one who is both time and beyond time. The source of everything! The

The Inevitable Journey – Unlimited Grace

dissolver of illusory existence! The real, the true, the most beautiful and eternal! He is within every form and the formless.

Just like our home represents what we are, Kailash represents the state of Shiva. All His attributes are his mere expressions. Only through expressions, we can understand the being. The Trident (three-headed spear), three aspects of time, three states (waking, dream and deep sleep), three eyes (Sun, Moon and Fire) so on and so forth - complete expression of supreme, all encompassing consciousness. I felt deep gratefulness to have received the permission to be in a place of power, the place that through centuries attracted every genuine seeker in search of salvation from the continuous circle of birth and death. Countless masters live there still, away from the human ken. Countless masters have visited Kailash, daring extreme climate and terrains, some without even the basic clothes or footwear. In the book "Autobiography of an Avadhoota", the great saint Avadhoota Nadananda mentions his journey to Lake Manasarovar without footwear and without significant protection from the cold and here we are travelling with more or less every affordable luxury.

Kailash with Mohanji 2014

Performing a parikrama during the year of Deva Kumbh had been a dream. We did that in 2014. A memorable trip! We had many blockages, many uncertainties, confusions, and in the end a beautiful journey where 80 out of 86 people completed parikrama. When we all assembled in Kathmandu, all 86 of us, our visas were not ready. And in the same hotel where we stayed, we met some pilgrims waiting for visa to travel for almost 21 days. The Chinese authorities had clamped down on the number of tourists and were becoming more strict and stringent with visa regulations. Grace worked here too. All of us got the permit to travel within one day. We started our journey to the border after a visit to Pashupatinath temple and Buddha Neelkant temple. We stayed on the way, as we could not go all the way to Kodari border on the same day because we had lost one day due to the late arrival of visa. But, visa did come for everyone. Our happiness did not last for too long. Disaster struck. There was a landslide that night between where we were and the border of Nepal, the landslide broke a dam, went over some villages and close to 500 people died. A big question mark fell on our onward journey too. How will we, 86 people cross over as there were no roads to take us there. It was almost like our journey ended there before it even started.

Suddenly, our tour operator managed to get us three helicopters, to ferry across all the 86 people to Kodari border for an additional cost. This was a problem as most people were unprepared for it. Some decisions had to be made. There was no way that the roads would be opened for traffic within a foreseeable time. I took the decision. "Let's get out of this place. The rest we will sort out later". Helicopters relentlessly transported us until the last person. We all reached Kodari border and ideally, we should have crossed the Friendship Bridge and moved towards Nylam on the same day. But, by the time the helicopters ferried in all the pilgrims to Kodari, it was too late and Friendship Bridge had already been closed. We lost one more precious day. A scheduled day and this would have been perfectly useful for acclimatization! We had to spend that night at Kodari. One more day lost. Day's lost are better rather than not at all. We remembered the helpless pilgrims, who we met at the hotel where we stayed, sitting in Kathmandu for 21 days waiting for permits to go to Kailash. We were far better off. At least we were moving. This was the most important thing.

The next day we crossed over to Tibet. We lost two days of acclimatisation which is actually a very big loss as far as physical comfort levels of pilgrims are concerned. Yet, wonder of wonders happened. All the 86 people had dips in Manasarovar. Everyone had darshan (reverential view) of Kailash. Literally, everyone saw Kailash. And 80 people out of 86 completed the outer parikrama. It was sheer miracle and Grace of Lord Shiva. At one point in time, everything looked impossible. At another point in time, we successfully completed the journey. Some people including Devi (Biba), Rajesh Ramanaidoo, Swami Govinda and a few others descended about 1000 feet to the celestial Gauri Kund after reaching the top of Dolma-la Pass – the highest point in outer Kora, and drank the sacred water of the eternal pond. Everyone got what they came for. Everyone's wish was fulfilled. Shiva never leaves anybody empty handed. His Grace is unexplainable and unfathomable.

Shiva is pure. Shiva is innocence. If Shiva cannot be recognised as unconditional and innocent, Shiva cannot be understood at all. He is innocence. He is love. He is the supreme un-manifested powerful consciousness. He is the essence of everything, the subtlest of the subtle. This became clearer in this year's Inner Kora. In other words, I felt He revealed Himself to me more and more year by year.

At some point in time, I remembered a question that I answered there. Someone asked me if Maya is illusion, if everything is illusion, and if so, Kailash also could be an illusion. Then what is the purpose of this trip? Isn't Kailash an illusion that we can afford to ignore? It is such a tough and unpredictable journey.

I told him. The exact explanation of Maya is not illusion. Maya is relative truth. Illusion does not exist. Maya does exist. Relative truth does exist even as relative truth. Illusion is nonexistence of something. Relative truth is existence of something, but our understanding is partial. When we experience something in life through our level of awareness, we are indeed experiencing Maya. Whatever is not absolute truth is Maya. Whatever is relative truth is Maya. Absolute truth is Mata (the non-relative supreme force – Shakti - or the supreme mother). The trip to Kailash is man's internal quest for eternal truth. When we segregate consciously and discard all aspects of relative truth that we experience every moment, we will soon start experiencing the thread of absolute truth – this is our personal pilgrimage through the eternal Kailash terrains. Acceptance has a very important role here. Kailash brings us face to face with our stark realities. Maya also has its root in Mata. Without Mata, there is no Maya. Maya has come out of Mata and will dissolve back into Mata. Whatever rises and sets or whatever appears and disappears is Maya – relative truth.

Whatever is permanent and unchanging is Mata. So, calling Maya illusion is not exactly right. Everything relative is Maya and everything permanent is Mata. Hence the only truth for a perfect seeker is Mata. Mata is also the unchanging consciousness that works through the three everyday states of waking, dream and deep sleep.

The nature of complete awareness is that it has unfathomable depth. Just like the nature of a true yogi is his unpretentious simplicity or the nature of one who is fully aware is silence. The depth of silence is unfathomable. Shiva is that silence. Silence is the root of every sound. Every sound comes up and dissolves back into silence.

Our Inner silence has nothing to do with external silence. While externally active, a true yogi carefully maintains his inner silence effortlessly. Silence is inner stillness for a yogi. Stillness is nature and completion in being-ness. This is the symbolism of Kailash. This is what we see in Kailash. The Majestic silence of unfathomable beingness! This exactly is Kailash for me apart from the feeling of being at home.

The Inner Kora

85 of us assembled in Kathmandu. Unlike 2014, this time there was seemingly lesser problem with permits except for the bad news that Chinese Military had taken over Ashtapath and Saptarishi Caves after people died there. There was a big question mark in the minds of the Inner Kora pilgrims as to whether we would be able to go there at all. We surrendered it to the master of the land – Lord Shiva. The best thing to do when we know that something is beyond our capacity to change is to surrender to the higher powers and forget about it with the firm thought "let your will be and not mine". It helps. Then we must also be prepared to accept whatever the will of the Lord is, without complaints and judgments. Bhagavan Krishna says, "If you surrender all your actions and the results of actions to me, I shall relieve you from the baggage associated with it". Krishna, Shiva, Datta, Buddha, Baba, Father, Mother Goddess –

The Inevitable Journey – Unlimited Grace

all is one. One consciousness! Surrender to whoever you like. They all use same ears and same minds.

Most who travelled with me were those who know me, follow me, love me or want to travel with me. This year, there were three Swamis with us from Skanda Vale Ashram located in Wales in the UK, a highly respected ashram with dedicated saints with deep conviction and feeling (bhaav) living and practicing spiritual traditions there. Two Swamis – Swami Brahmananda and Swami Govinda accompanied us on our Inner Kora journey while Swami Karunananda successfully completed the Outer Kora, mostly by foot. They have been amazing examples of resilience, simplicity, conviction, unshakeable devotion and total acceptance. All through the trip, they were examples of how a renunciate should be. Their conviction was reciprocated as Grace as they could physically touch the impossible Kailash across the glaciers, beyond the Charan Sparsh. Their spiritual call was loud and clear when they were the first to win over the treacherous and dangerous Inner Kora terrains to reach Kuber Kund and perform their meditations there.

Only Grace can work on such terrains. Many people have died in these terrains earlier the year and there were strict warnings from the guides not to move out of the beaten tracks. The problem was there were no tracks. It was almost like the Lord who wanted to maintain his pathless path arranged to erase every trail that our predecessors might have made.

This was an interesting thought for me. I thought about it deeply. My whole life has been full of such terrains, unknown, unforeseen and unknowable. I had no predecessor to follow or guide. I did not come from a spiritual background nor did I have saints in the family. I had no Godfather either. Literally, nobody supported me in my professional career or life at any point in time. I had to struggle a lot in each situation to make the trail for others to travel. Time and again, destiny brought something or someone to destroy the terrains and I had to recreate it for the sake of who was with me each time. In January 2000, I was living with my wife and child. In January 2003, my child Ammu was already no more and

I was physically separated from my wife and had almost nothing. Gradually, one by one, I lost my income, savings, possessions and anything else which were reminders of where or what I have been. Wave after wave of tragedy hit my life. Time repeated the pattern. Many things I created were uncreated. I created again. Time uncreated again through some strange situation or someone until I understood the format. No attachment. No complaints. No expectations. No plans. Nothing! Just keep walking and if possible, do not leave any trails behind. If trails are left behind, if it is not supposed to be, time will erase it. If trails are not erased, it is ordained by the higher.

In existence, there is nothing permanent. Every stone evolves and changes itself. Every drop evolves and transforms. Then, how can we stop evolving whether we like it or not? We have to cope with pains only when we resist something in life. We have pains only when we have expectations from life. Otherwise, it is an Inner Kora into us each moment.

GOD's operating pattern is called Sanatana Dharma. GOD is operating on the basis of Sanatana Dharma (the righteous basic ground rules of existence which include Generation, Operation and Dissolution and this makes GOD who IT is. When man moves to the frequency of selfless existence where he wants nothing from anything, and senses and mind are at peace, his GOD element becomes predominant and he experiences subtleties of existence. Subtle or "Sookshma" is beyond time and space as only the gross and element oriented existence are governed by time. Sookshma or Subtle also has its own existence, seemingly separated from Parabrahma. Whenever there is a separation from the whole, there is separation in existence and a prescribed duration. There is also an automatic subscription to the law of relativity. Every bit will have its own time, effort and duration for complete dissolution. When sookshma itself gets nullified, the drop becomes the ocean. There is no seeker and the sought. Numerous beings invisible to human eyes existing in the Durbar, (court and courtyard) of Shiva at Kailash are in the process of dissolving their subtle and become the ocean called Shiva permanently. Here Shiva is supreme consciousness, the ultimate destination of every unit seeking wholeness. Millions of subtle bodies merge in Shiva every moment. Shiva remains unruffled without a ripple like an all-encompassing ocean unchallenged by gallons of water from numerous rivers joining it every moment. The quality of purpose makes the difference and sanctity of each existence, just like purpose makes each person.

Our own Milky way has many subtle realms which we cannot fathom through our element oriented existence. These realms are nearly accessible to humans only when one starts operating beyond the realms of one's crown chakra and transcend the ladder of the symbolic 18 stairs or platforms, where each stair signifies deeper and deeper levels in subtlety or deeper detachment from gross. Our senses are only programmed to understand and experience the visible or gross world around us. Our mind and intellect are tied to data filtered and perceived through senses. This is invariably far from absolute truth. Absolute truth is unknowable to the senses or mind. The energy called Shiva and His abode called Kailash has its roots and connections with all the subtle worlds of Milky way at least, if not beyond into the other galaxies.

The energy linkage between planets and power centers is also the essence of the science of astrology. Vedic astrology is a demonstration of the energetic connection between terrestrial beings and planets of the Milky Way. As a matter of fact, advanced astrology can trace back to the source and its receivable influences during lifetimes. The human brain does not possess that capacity. Great masters who operate on cosmic consciousness can easily decode the DNA of every atom if they want to. It takes man to be the universe to know the universe.

I am deliberately avoiding the inter-galactic aspect here because if we cannot perceive, it will remain as just a theory or information. This is absolutely useless. The inter-galactic energy highways link all such power centres scattered across the universe just like highways link our cities. The energy highways operate through propulsion and levitation. This is how the advanced beings from subtle realms travel. Propulsion is external and levitation is natural. So, energy requirement within each "vehicle" is only needed to illumine, pause and divert. This is totally different from the human vehicles where internal propulsion and navigation are usually to counter terrains. In the case of their vehicles, terrains assist movement. It is almost like water naturally floats the body. These highways are also the signs or state of expansion of consciousness of beings that are swimming in the oceans in awareness while choosing to experience being a drop or unit (seemingly separate from the whole in gross or in subtle). Existence by choice needs total awareness, otherwise, it is karmic, automatic and seemingly regular unconscious existence. There are inter-galactic beings who are operating only in the ocean of pure consciousness like water on lotus leaf.

The celestial snakes such as Ananta, Vasuki, Takshaka, Karkotaka, Sankha, Gulika, Padma, Maha Patmetyashta who remain as ornament to the perceived body of Shiva are representations of the deep link that Naga Loka, the world of Snakes have with the power mountain called Kailash. Our ancient memory or reminder of our inter-galactic connection too! Even though they appear as snakes to human eyes, they are not snakes in their realm. They are luminous beings of higher order that also uses mind and intellect. They also have different levels of awareness in their realm. They have the skill of energy/light travel and they transport themselves in non-frictional or round vessels which are energy conglomerates. Inside the vehicle, they exist in a relative womb state. This vehicle has no friction as it is round like a ball. And inside the vehicle also, the traveller is seated almost as if he is in his mother's womb. Fully insulated, safe and secure! All fluid objects naturally tend to become a globe in the sky. Hence this is the natural form that suits the mission. And they have the skill to travel almost at the "speed of the mind" because they operate on no-gravity and no-resistance technology. Zero gravity helps levitation. This is science and beside the point though.

Most of these beings who have the flexibility to attain the chosen form connected to the terrain usually assume the form which could create fear whichever world they visit. This is to secure them and do what they came for without hindrance from local beings ignorant of the stature of the visitors. This is a smart tactic. Assume the role of a villain and everybody will leave you alone. So, the beings of Nagaloka assume the form of snake and hence we call their world snake world. We may see them as snakes even if we visit their world because we are coming from the world where snakes exist. But, beings from another world, where there are no snakes may see them as a fear invoking species existing in their realm. So, like a chameleon, they can change their form suiting the terrains they visit. In order to understand the modus operandi of subtle beings, we need to attain their level of subtlety. And they accept everyone who "talks their language" or in other words, operate in their level of subtlety.

We must also be aware that not every being operates in linear time like we do. They operate in perpetual time or vertical time where past, present and future exist in one line. This means they can move up and down in time effortlessly. This may sound fantastic and unbelievable. Time machine is a truth in certain worlds and they do not even need a machine to travel. They travel at will. In other words, masters like Babaji are thousands of years old is a truth. They are immortal and unbound by time. In their realm, every being exists simultaneously beyond time. When there is no need of a body and senses; when there is no binding karma, if we still choose to be a unit, we are also not bound by time. Simple truth!

The power to dissolve the gross as well as subtle makes Kailash a high power centre relevant for all pilgrims to Kailash from every world that the sun presides over and beyond. Kailash has effect on every operating frequency which makes it universal. This also makes the Lord of Kailash, Shiva an enigma. All the beings visiting Kailash come to bathe in the energy of subtlety and dilute the layers of unseen gross that hardens on the surface of every existence. For every pilgrim, irrespective of every realm, Shiva represents total dissolution and the final destination where the traveller becomes the destination.

Lord Muruga, the son of Shiva, is also the master representing the knowledge pertaining to enlightenment as well as dissolution. He presents and represents the eternal knowledge of creation and beyond. He instructs the path. He is always young as eternal knowledge never grows old. He lives with every being in some form. He guides generations in the path of dissolution. He is formless. He talks through many mouths. He is relevant to all traditions. The best of His teachings can be heard only in silence. He is silence. He is all words. When the Supreme Shiva who Himself could not recognise Himself, Lord Muruga, the knowledge aspect of Shiva, who rose from Him, offered Shiva the knowledge of Omkar, the primordial sound, the sound of creation, the Pranava. In a way, Shiva manifested the knowledge aspect for the sake of seekers to get back into unity, as Muruga.

Mahavatar Babaji of Kriya path, Mahatapa of Gyanganj are all indeed Lord Muruga or Karthikeya, according to what I have perceived. Babaji is known to have been the disciple of the great Guru Siddha Bhoganathar. Just like Sage Sandipani knew that Lord Krishna was an avatar, Great Siddha Sage Bhoganathar, Guru of Babaji knew who was Babaji and how powerful He is. He knew Babaji as an avatar of Lord Muruga. Jnana Avatar. Knowledge incarnate. An avatar of knowledge! Hence it took Bhoganathar no time to decide who should be the model for the Muruga idol of Palani temple which he made with nine poisons, independently life threatening - when joined together became a powerful life-giving supreme, celestial elixir. Shiva, Muruga, Ganesha, and mother Parvati, the eternal consciousness that supports the entire manifestations of the universe are all multi-dimensional and inter-galactic. They cannot be arrested into any form or name. They appear as everything, everywhere, wherever they are needed to be visible.

Many Sages that we revere as great masters, Siddhas, Avadhootas and Rishis have inter-galactic connection. Who we consider as Gods such as Lord Muruga and Lord Ganesha are revered across the galaxy as supreme masters or representations of pure consciousness. Their appearance, name and form are definitely not the same in all dimensions as we, humans perceive in this realm. They are immortal and have eternal existence. They choose to display a certain character, aspect or characteristics in each dimension. In our realm of existence, Lord Muruga as Babaji chose to display his knowledge aspect on one side with the eternal, immortal master of the great science of Kriya (dissolution). Kriya itself means "nature". Being natural, being breath, being one with consciousness is the path of Kriya. For the sake of Human understanding, based on the nature of Humans, systems were created by these great avatars. And as Mahatapa Babaji of Gyanganj, he chose to display the free mendicant aspect of total detachment, with a begging bowl, a loin cloth and no other possessions or attachments – a perfect Avadhoota. Both are symbols of perfection in spiritual achievement; or as a search light for true seekers.

Lord Ganesha, the supreme destroyer of obstacles of life is also an aspect of Shiva where no obstacles matter when one is immortal. Obstacles are bound by expectations and mind. When there are no expectations, there is only total acceptance. There is only surrender with awareness - that is exactly all that will be! Everything is divinely ordained for the sake of entertainment called life or manifestations in existence to maintain the structure of relativity. The truth is that there is absolutely nothing to gain from or significantly nothing to lose, from this place and plane of gross existence. Experiences can create residual memories. Memories can build new lives. Memories can be binding. Experiences of various kinds are the causes of our incarnation. Memories are food for the mind. Mind is temporary and it is rooted in Maya or relative truth. Hence memories or mind does not matter in absolute sense. The appetite of the mind and intellect also need satiation. Mind has an appetite for experiences. Intellect seeks understanding and understanding can happen only through the senses. Hence all intellectual understanding also is relative and hence immaterial. Lord Ganesha has a strange form because there is no form suitable for him as supreme consciousness. Connection, contemplation and meditation on supreme consciousness create supreme dissolution.

Hence Lord Ganesha is meditated on to dissolve differences that mind perceives, which are the real obstacles in the path of spirituality and merges the man to the supreme. Thus he is the remover of obstacles.

Lord Ganesha represents the supreme beyond manifestation, one of the key aspects of Shiva. He represents the subtle and the gross, the macrocosm as well as the microcosm. The formless can have any form. All forms are representations of the formless. Ganesha is worshipped before all deities because He represents the beyond. Big head is the cosmic intellect that created relativity, which in turn created space, which in turn created time, which in turn created the whole universe. The big belly is the womb of the universe itself; the whole universe is the belly of Lord Ganesha. Two tusks of Ganesha out of which one broken represents the duality which is the source of relative existence. The high and low, the up and down, the left and right, the black and white, the gunas so on and so forth, which became the raw material for creation.

Kailash is truly relevant in the whole Milky Way, in all the subtle worlds or Lokas if not inter-galactic. Many beings from various levels of subtlety come to visit Kailash. Many have seen them coming as a globe of fire, light, brightness, luminescent beings etc, coming and going out of Manasarovar Lake close to Kailash. And why is Kailash situated on earth? Just for the sake of human beings. There are such power centres in most lokas, with a difference in the degree of intensity. They are like our metros connected by highways. These power metros are oasis or highway inns for inter-galactic travellers of various frequencies.

Most of us are bound by our personality. We are too pre-occupied by our human dimension which we walk, talk and express all the time. We do not know any other existence than the obvious gross and many of us are unable to connect to our subtle form in a lifetime. Other beings of subtler planes that understand and recognise the realm of Kailash also possess the skill to travel there if they wanted to. Many such beings are considered as Devas

(Gods) by humans because of their "beyond human" abilities. The Himalayas is such a portal for many beings that possess and operate in various capacities beyond human capabilities. Some beings that meditate or live in tough locations (for humans) like Kailash have nothing to do with a human kind of body created out of elements. Unlike us who are bound by air, water, fire, earth, and space, they have the capacity to shed the elements at will and exist in subtle as long as they want, even as a unit without dissolving themselves in the ocean of consciousness. They are unbound by time. Since they are unbound by time, they are also unbound by life or death. These beings have the choice to wear any form at will and purpose. Many higher masters who exist among us are also of this category of beings and for them, life on earth is just a joke where they willingly play the fool - for example - Avadhootas.

Shiva is worshipped as supreme consciousness by many beings from many locations within the Milky Way. Also, as earth moves, and reaches closer to certain realms or worlds (lokas) of the Milky Way, the flow of beings from those worlds to Kailash also intensifies. This is particularly the case of Deva Kumbh. During Deva Kumbh, which happens once in 12 years, earth moves closer to some subtle realms such as Deva loka and many beings of this plane finds it easier to visit the realms of Kailash because of spontaneous proximity. Thus Kailash provides access to all those who wish to connect, one way or the other. Not all connect to Kailash with awareness. Some come to see, feel and some come to merge. Nevertheless, Kailash attracts beings from every corner of the Milky Way. Kailash brings itself closer to various realms through the movement of earth and the wise human sages use this proximity to raise their frequency through co-existence and sometimes interactions with the visiting celestial beings. Each visiting being has their own vision and notion of Kailash, just like us, and they have their own connecting and worshipping methods. Kailash and its premises are always prepared to receive the constant flow of visitors who come as per their time and possibility. This is not easy for humans to understand because we perceive based on what our senses give us. This place, especially the durbar of Shiva, is the meeting place for many beings of many lokas including many inter-galactic masters. Lord Kubera created the pond for the benefit of these visitors, who are beyond elements, yet, sanctifies themselves in fire and water. This is why the space is so sacred. Many beings share frequencies there and help elevate each other in total selflessness. Many beings leave powerful energies there, which creates conducive environment for striving seekers to spontaneously achieve the higher. Hence Kailash becomes a womb to mature seekers to be incubated and delivered to the sought.

Once again, memories of Inner Kora 2016. Climbing the tough terrains of Inner Kailash trails, I reached the top. It was tough to conquer the glaciers. A veteran Russian climber who passed by us remarked: "I never saw the terrains so tough". Looking back, it is unbelievable that we did indeed climb the toughest recesses of Kailash. They said it is some 22,000 feet high. I felt exhausted and breathless. I lied down with my head towards Kailash. I had covered my head and mouth with my bandana. As I was lying down, a stone came into my mouth which is impossible as my mouth was covered. I took out the stone and at the same moment, subtle thoughts with extreme clarity started echoing in my mind, as if some invisible beings were talking to me; "This is the durbar of Shiva. We meditate here in subtle form since human centuries. We have no needs. We seek nothing, not even Shiva. We have no weaknesses. We are not bound by duality. Weaknesses need strength to survive. We have neither strength nor weakness. We are not bound by time. Shiva is truly timeless. In this state of subtle, unbound by the perishable elements, we are also timeless. But, still being a unit, we are not truly Shiva, the infinity. When we lose the subtle as well, as we have lost the gross, we will become one with Shiva and then, nothing will exist to know Shiva. Only when we become Shiva, we know Shiva. Even now, we can be considered as powerful in human yardstick because we are not bound by any matter of earth including death. Since we are not dependent on elements, we can rule over elements. Since we do

The Inevitable Journey – Unlimited Grace

not have any agenda of gratification, including the gratification of Shiva consciousness, we are absolutely still and powerful. When you need nothing, you are in absolute power. Yet, we do assist and support beings like yourself to walk the path to ultimate truth. We do guide and support the subtle amongst you who walk the path of liberation against all odds. You are our beloved. You are welcome here." I did not care who said this in my ears. It made absolute sense to me.

This brought me to the thought of the Gurus and disciples. We have seen, read and experienced various aspects of the relationship between a guru and a disciple. But, according to me, the highest aspect of a guru and disciple relationship is unconditional love and the awareness of a grand collaboration for a higher purpose. Lord Krishna is a complete Avatar and so was Lord Rama. Their teachers Sandipani and Brahmarshi Vasishta respectively knew very well the cause of incarnation as well as the true potential of their disciples. So did Govindapada and Sage Bhoganathar know the potential of Adi Sankara and Mahavatar Babaji. Hanumanji knew his purpose and role in the life of Lord Rama. Even though Lord Rama had the power to locate his wife, Sita who was kidnapped by Ravana to Sri Lanka, he requested Hanuman to do the deed. Hanumanji knew that he is just playing that role and was never egoistic or bloated out of proportions for what he did for his Lord. Both Rama and Hanumanji collaborated to complete the epic. It was a grand collaboration with full awareness. This makes everyone totally relevant in the story. Every guru-disciple relationship is collaboration. In effect, it is more of a role-play in many cases, especially with that of avatars like Rama, Krishna and Babaji.

The disciples mentioned above were clear about their purpose of life as all were avatars. Yet, they systematically went through their education under the tutorship of their respected teachers, except for Hanumanji who reached Rama when Rama was in the forest and not a king in power. Hanumanji met and stood by Lord Rama when Rama was not in good shape. Rama was not a king when Hanumanji met him. In a way, He was a helpless wanderer in the forests. In other words, this was a grand collaboration created to bring awareness to the world the importance and sanctity of the relationship between a guru and disciple. In today's world, the guru-disciple relationship has become contaminated to the extent that disciples judge, scandalise and crucify their own gurus and contaminate the guru principle that blows out the light in their own lives and reverses their hard earned frequency backward to many lifetimes. If we happen to consider a person as our Guru even for a minute, we should respect him as representation of the principle in order to maintain our inner sanctity and keep the guru principle in us alive. If we do not, we will lose heavily. Non-violence in its absolute perfection! This is the message that I received from the subtle masters of Kailash.

I was so overwhelmed to see the beauty of this relationship between the Swamis of Skanda Vale to their guru who left his body a few years ago. Their devotion and reverence to their guru, their dedication and commitment to his teachings were so palpable and inspiring to many. Swami Brahmananda was the first person to climb up the glacier into the durbar of Shiva, even before the Sherpas laid the ropes to hold on. This is no ordinary thing. Extreme conviction, unshakeable faith in himself and his Guru, path as well as mission was clearly written on his face and actions. He carried the stone that would eventually go to their new temple in Switzerland in his backpack. Swami Govinda also displayed similar will of steel. They never complained about anything. As perfect renunciates, they accepted what came their way and braved the terrains with faith and conviction.

I strongly feel that it is the blessing of gurus who have walked this path and helping us walk this path that has taken 85 of us to the extremely difficult pilgrimage of Kailash. My deepest gratitude and prostrations to all the visible and invisible (to human eyes) masters of the traditions that are uniting the world to the supreme consciousness.

All of us except one person in our group completed the Inner Kora. This was remarkable. Often, it was a life or death situation. Shifting ice sheets, melting ice, slippery terrain, high altitude, hypoxia, so on and so forth all adds up to a pilgrim's woes. Outer Kora is easier because of pony and porter facilities. Inner Kora is tougher without pony or porter. Everyone should do their own climbing even though our backpacks were carried by Sherpas. Despite all that, we had a reason to be happy. 79 out of the whole team of 85 completed the parikrama around Mount Kailash. And 10 of us actually touched the Mount Kailash off the Charan Sparsh. This is no ordinary feat. The tour operator said that this is the first time in their history.

We could not go to Saptarishi Cave and Ashtapath because the military had occupied those locations after people died there. As we were waiting for the permission, one evening, I had a remarkable experience. I was sleeping. Suddenly, I was with the great Rishis of Kailash, which I believe are the inhabitants of the Saptarishi Cave. They spoke "This is sacred space. One should not come here to go back. This means one should not come here in their body. They should arrive here in sookshma (subtle) so that they need not return. We do not tolerate people with arrogance coming to our place to boast to the world that they have come to Saptarishi Caves as well. When such unwelcome and ineligible guests come here, they meet with physical death. And they go backwards in evolution. In other words, if the merits and awareness that they earned over lifetimes allowed them to step here, their arrogance and ego will push back their awareness to that of numerous lifetimes behind. Each lifetime gives forth any being an increased level of awareness. That gets reversed because of bad action." When I met my fellow travellers the next morning for breakfast, I told them, "our permissions will not happen". And even though we waited for 2 days, our permissions did not come. I was deeply grateful to the great masters for allowing me their audience. The lesson one should learn is that egoistic actions as well as wrong actions or actions without clarity or out of arrogance always leads to fall in Grace and fall in awareness.

Many of my fellow travellers are writing explaining their journey in much detail. So, I refrain from doing that. With a heart full of gratitude and surrender to the Supreme Lord Shiva, pure formless form of supreme consciousness, I submit these humble words with all humility into the hands of the readers.

Thank you for your time and presence.

Yours,
Mohanji

Message To Kailash Yatris

- Mohanji -

Kailash is one of the major power centres on Earth. The Kailash journey is a life in itself. Kailash represents stillness. The state of Shiva is stillness. When we take an unsettled mind to a still environment, we need to empty it so much so that it can attain the state of stillness which the location represents.

Mind should be free - When I say mind should be free, it does not mean abandonment of duties and responsibilities. It means you have thought about your duties and responsibilities, recognised them and settled them properly and satisfactorily before embarking on this most sacred and transformational journey of a lifetime. Do not keep anything unfinished or unsettled and do not leave any loose ends before this ultimate journey any man can take in one lifetime.

In particular the following, :

1. If you owe anything to anybody, be it money, time, promises, etc,
2. If you have commitments of any kind which you had ignored or overlooked
3. If you have anger, hatred, enmity or ill feelings about something or somebody

4. If you are supporting somebody with money, time or personal care

Keep your body, mind and intellect clean and tidy.

- Eat healthy food - food that was exposed to the sun, non-dairy, non-animal products.

- Avoid unnecessary emotions, judgements, criticism, jealousy, hatred and opinions. Do not indulge in alcohol or any intoxicants as well as animal products

- Avoid the company that gives you stress and negativities. Opt for company of people who are positive in nature.

- Do not read materials or listen to that which is negative in nature. Avoid all kinds of negative impressions and inputs. Do not read or discuss materials that are negative in nature.

Before you embark on a journey such as Kailash and before you enter it's sacred space, make yourself eligible to receive the maximum by freeing, settling and concluding physical, emotional and mental activities or commitments properly.

Contents

Preface ix

The Inevitable Journey – Unlimited Grace xii

Message To Kailash Yatris xxxiii

Kailash – The Eternal Abode Of Shiva 1

THE INNER KORA

The Mirror Called Kailash 69

Kailash On The Wings Of The Master's Grace 95

Pilgrimage To Mount Kailash 117

Complete With Kailash 127

A Life In The Grace Of Kailash 135

I Am Always With You 151

The Homecoming 169

Surrender 183

The Grace Of The Guru 193

The Homeward Journey 197

The Touch Of Kailash 213

Eligibility – The Key To Unlock Grace 225

Why Fear When I Am Here 243
Faith Can Move Mountains 248
I Walk Where My Heart Leads 258

THE OUTER KORA

Beyond Miracles And Human Understanding 311
The Divine Call 328
Kailash - Still And Calm 337
The Journey Has Only Begun 340
Kailash - Heart To Heart 344
A Journey Of A Lifetime 350
An All-Encompassing Feeling 359
Outer Kora Experiences 366
Gratitude 380
The Journey Of My Life 384
Kailash And Badrinath – My Experiences 390
We Are Complete 407
Let it all go 418
Not A Soul Goes Untouched 429
Aum Namah Shivaya 437
Journey To Kailash 441
Glossary Of Terms 448

Kailash – The Eternal Abode Of Shiva

– An Introduction –

UP NORTH FROM the vast plains of the Ganges valley in India, beyond the kingdom of Nepal and north east of the great Himalayas lies the roof of the world, the land of snows- Tibet, home to the holiest mountain in the world- abode of Shiva - The Mt. Kailash.

Sacred to a fifth of the world's population, a journey to Mount Kailash is the ultimate pilgrimage for Hindus, Buddhists, Tibetans, Bons and Jains. Mystical, magical and sacred, Kailash and Mansarovar have a place in the human ethos, seldom given to any other pilgrimage destination.

Geographically, it lies at 6,638 m (21,778 ft.) above sea level in the remote south-west corner of Tibet, between three great mountains ranges of Asia, the Himalayan ranges, Karakorum Mountains and Naga Parbat. From here one can see Afghanistan, Pakistan, Hindustan (India) & Nepal. It rises beautifully above the rugged, desolate but enchantingly beautiful Tibet, a plateau of rainbow-colored rocks. Mt. Kailash is one of the highest parts of the Himalayas and lies near the source of some of the longest rivers in Asia including the Indus River and its major tributary Sutlej, the Brahmaputra, and the Karnali River (a tributary of the Ganga).

Around 40 kilometers from its southern base lies the beautiful Mansarovar (Sanskrit: ManasaSarovar; Tibetan: MapamYumco and Chinese Mapham Yu Tso), the world's highest freshwater lake. Geologically, Mansarovar is a piece of the ancient Tethys Sea. Set amidst Mt. Kailash and Mt. Gurla Mandhata, the Mansarovar is 55 miles (88 km) in circumference, 330 feet (90m) deep, and 120 sq miles (320 sq km) in total area. Famed for its exceptional beauty, its sacred waters change color from a clear blue around the shores to a deep emerald green in the center. It looks positively magical in the moonlight. The journey around the lake is 64 miles long and usually takes four to seven days on foot.

Together with Mansarovar, this mountain is surrounded by innumerable myths, stories and legends that add to the mystique of this most inapproachable place on earth.

Mount Kailash

There is no other mountain as revered as the Kailash. One of the most sacred sites, the least scalable, majestic and sacred Kailash towers over all the holy sites of the world in unmatchable glory as the eternal abode of Shiva.

It is known as the 'Axis Mundi,' the center and birth place of the entire world and the Crown Chakra of Earth. Other epithets of this sacred mountain are 'navel of the earth,' the 'world pillar,' the 'first of the mountains,' the 'still point in the turning world,' and Mount Meru rising from the descent of the seventh hell and rising to perforate through the loftiest of the heavens.

Different names of the mountain

Kailash, the name has been used synonymously with Shiva. It is known by various names, such as Meru, Sumeru (both meaning the highest point), Sushumna (the Spiritual central axis), Hemadri (Golden mountain), Deva Parvat (Summit of Gods), Rajatgiri (Silver mountain), Ratnasanu (jewel peak), and so on.

Mt. Kailash is known in Tibetan as Kang Rinpoche or Ghang Rimpoche (meaning 'Precious Jewel of Snow') or by its aboriginal name Ti-Se. In Chinese, it is known as Mt. Gangrenboqifeng or Kangrinboge and is called Mount Kailash by Indians. It has also been called Rinpoche Meru (meaning Sumeru in Tibetan) or Swastika Mountain or Mt. Astapada.

Ecology of Kailash

The ecological symbolism of Mt. Kailash is mysterious and awe-inspiring to many. Although not the highest mountain in the region, Kailash is distinct as it stands alone on the vast plateau surrounding it and its unique nearly symmetrical pyramid shape of a veritable Shiva-lingam. Its black rock face covered with snow is an amazingly symmetrical diamond dome with clear symbols on one of its face. For this reason it is also often referred to as the Mountain of Swastika.

The southern face of the mountain is marked by a long vertical cleft punctuated halfway down its traverse by a horizontal line of rock strata. This has been likened to a ladder or staircase rising heavenward through earthly existence. This scarring resembles a swastika-a Buddhist symbol of spiritual strength. Therefore, Bonpo, the ancient pre-Buddhist Tibetan religion refers to the Kailash as the 'Nine-Storey Swastika Mountain'. It is a fact that the Gurla- Mandhata range when viewed from above does appear as a massive swastika.

In myth and folklore it is said that Lord Shiva stays here, adorned with lotus flowers therefore the Kailash itself is surrounded by six mountains in the shape of a lotus.

The thousand different colours on the vivid landscape are magnificent in their sanctity and splendour. The expressions of the mountain change every minute; from blue, green and brown in the gentle sunlight to purple, grey and black in the shadows of the clouds and then again to a dazzling white crystal dome covered with snow.

The Four Directions

Its four sheer walls match the cardinal points of the compass and its four faces symbolize one spiritual aspect each.

According to mythology, south is the direction of death, hence the south face symbolizes the 'Rudra' or destroyer aspect of the deity. The Akora face, which is on the right shoulder of the Lord, is bearded with protruded teeth like that of an old man which produces fear and is black. This face symbolizes fire (Agni) out of the five elements and 'Sh' out of the five syllables of the Shiva's five syllable prayer 'Om Namah Shivaaya' (also called the Panchakshar- five syllable mantra). This face is also called Dakshinamurthy (one who is facing south or 'dakshin') which is an aspect of Shiva as a guru (teacher) or a bestower of supreme knowledge. It is represented by the cosmic principle of Buddhi and its deity is Bhairava. Gajasamharar, Virabadrar, Dakshinamurthy, Kirathamurthy, Vishapakaranar are the aspects of the Akora face. According to Tibetan mythology, this face shines like sapphire akin to that of ocean.

The west face (or the Satyojat face) symbolizes compassion and benevolence and symbolizes the 'Creator' aspect of the deity. In Hindu texts, it is the principle of 'Ichha' represented by the cosmic principle of 'Ahankar' and its deity is Nandi. Of the five elements, this face represents the earth element and out of the five syllables, it stands for 'Na'. While all other faces of the Kailash are convex, the Satyojat face alone is concave. Lingothpavar, Umamahesar, Harihara, Ardhanari are aspects of this face. According to Tibetans, this face shines like Ruby.

The north face of the Kailash is forbidding and daunting in its starkness. In Hindu texts, it is principle of sadvidya and is represented by the cosmic principle Manas and its deity is Goddess Uma. According to Tibetan texts, it is 'emitting rays of Golden Light and fire.'

The east face symbolizes the divine feminine and is the principle of 'Shakti Tattva' represented by the cosmic principle of Ananda. Its deity is Mahadeva. According to the Tibetan texts, is said to be filled with crystals.

The Mountain is said to have a fifth face as well which is invisible to mortal men and is said to be free from the limitations of space and time. There is no night or day on the mythical fifth face.

Each of the four faces of the Kailash reflects different moods. The southern face reflects majesty and splendour, the west is enveloped in an aura of compassion and benevolence. The northern face is stark and forbidding while the eastern, only visible from a long way off, is mysterious and distant.

The four faces of the mountain are also associated with colors and castes: White like a Brahmin, the priest, on its eastern surface; yellow like a Vaisya, the merchant, on the south; red like a Kshatriya, the warrior, on the north; and black like a Shudra, the menial on the western side.

According to Vishnu Purana, the four faces of the bejewelled mountain are made of lapis lazuli, crystal, ruby, and gold. No wonder even the Tibetan name for it is 'Precious jewel of snow.' One name for the mountain in Tibetan is Tise`, derived from titse in the Zhang-Zhung language, meaning 'water peak,' or 'river peak.' This is indeed the source of the four mythical rivers; the Indus (Yarlung Tsangpo/ Dihang) that runs towards the north and confers the courage of a lion, the Karnali (a major tributary of the Ganges) that flows toward the south and grants one the beauty of a peacock, the Brahmaputra that flows towards the east and grants the speed of a horse, and the Satluj that flows to the west and confers the strength of an elephant. These four rivers originate in the Kailash-Mansarovar region and flow outward in four different directions like spokes radiating outward from the hub of the wheel.

Energy Portal

Like there are energy portals (chakras) and acupressure points in the human body, the Earth too is said to have energy portals or vortexes of spiralling energy points. It is believed that this energy moves clockwise with gravity and anti-clockwise with anti-gravity. There are crystals within the Earth that receive and transmit energy, assimilate it and send it through the grids, all the while storing, amplifying and focusing it. They are aligned to our solar system, galaxy and the Cosmos, often aligning to a particular star system and are electric, magnetic or have both qualities.

Mount Kailash is one of the most important energy portals of the Earth as it has been consistently accepted as the Earth's crown chakra or Sahasrara chakra in many ancient historical references. The tantric Masters of India, through their correspondences of 'As above, so below,' state that the Supreme Consciousness in a human being or Lord Shiva resides both upon the physical Mount Kailash, as well as upon the "Mount Kailash" within the body, that is, the human crown chakra.

Supreme among the energy centers, the Kailash holds incredible energy and activates, and awakens those who travel here either physically or in soul travel. Many times, people who are not particularly spiritually inclined, may go there and then years later realize that this place had an undeniable effect on their energy field and their subsequent awakening process.

"In a thousand ages of the Gods I could not tell thee of the Glory of the Himalaya…" says the Skanda Purana, "just as the dew is dried by the morning sun, so are the sins of mankind by the sight of the Himalayas."

Religious Significance

The spiritual importance of Kailash dates back to the Bon and Hindu religions. Sacred to five major religions of the world, the Hindus, Buddhists, Sikhs, Jains and Bons, the Kailash is the physical aspect of the spiritual Mt. Meru, a tangible aspect of divinity on Earth.

Significance in Hinduism

Mt. Kailash holds great significance in the collective Hindu psyche, being the abode and the very personification of the Supreme Lord Shiva Himself. Journeying to this mountain is the most important pilgrimage a Hindu will ever take.

The pyramid shaped mountain is Swayambhu - the self-created one, and is considered as old as the creation. The Hindu regard Mt. Kailash as the earthy manifestation of Mt. Meru - their spiritual center of the universe, described in the ancient texts as a fantastic 'World Pillar' around which everything else revolves; its roots in the lowest hell and its top kissing the heavens. On the summit sits Lord Shiva along with his consort Parvati, the daughter of Himalaya. It is here that the Divine couple performed the Ananda Tandava – the Dance of Bliss that created the first Spanda – throb of cosmic creation. The mountain itself represents Sat-Chit-Ananda, the principle of Truth, Consciousness and Bliss. It is from Mt. Kailash that Aum the primordial sound emanates from the anklets of Mother Parvati and brings about the Universe in its variegated forms as the Nada (vibrations) spreads out.

It is also said that Kubera (or Vaishravana), the Lord of wealth and the king of 'yakshas' lives on the Gandhamandana mountain, near Mount Kailash. Sometimes Kailash itself is called Kubera's residence.

Significance in Jainism

For the Jains, Mt. Kailash is acclaimed as a site where their first prophet, Shri Rishabh Dev achieved enlightenment. The Asthapad (along the Parikrama) is said to be the place where Shri Rishabh Dev did Tapascharya. Then he went seven steps on a mountain and on the last (eighth step), he vanished. Only his slippers were found.

Significance in Tibetan & Bon Religions

According to the indigenous Tibetan and Bon religions, Kailash was the sacred Yungdrung Gutseg (Nine-Stacked-Swastika Mountain) upon which the Bonpo founder Shenrab (Thonpa Shenrab Miwo) had descended from the heavens. Shenrab predicted that there would be nine orders of Bon schools established near Mount Kailash and Mansarovar. Ever since, Bon believers have considered

Mount Kailash-Mansarovar to be the foundation of their religion. Followers of Bon call the mountain Tise and believe it to be the seat of the sky goddess Sipaimen.

According to Tibetans, Mt. Kailash is also the mythical palace of Chakra Samvara Demchok (Wheel of Bliss) or Palkhorlo Dompa and his consort Dorje Phagmo. Demchok is the powerful Tibetan tutelary deity who 'tears apart the elephant-hide of ignorance.' He is the wrathful manifestation of Sakyamuni (Sakya Thukpa) akin to the Hindu God Shiva. Demchok and his consort Phagmo together symbolize wisdom and compassion, making Kailash and Mansarovar the perfect complement: father and mother of the Earth.

The Tibetan Buddhists consider Kailash to be the place where heaven and Earth connect and divine energy replenishes the Earth, a place where Gods reside.

Legend says that inside this mountain is the rope (called dmu-thang) connecting the earth to heaven along which the first Tibetan king Nyatri descended. It is so light, it could fly. So it was staked in place by prayer banners and Buddha nailed it down with four footprints, so devils could not pull it underground.

It is also the retreat centre of Kagyupa Order started by the great Tibetan yogi Milarepa.

Significance in Buddhism

Buddhist cosmography, like Hinduism, identifies Mt. Kailash with the mighty Mount Sumeru, the central peak of the world. Where Kailash is 'The Father Mountain' representing the means to enlightenment, Lake Mansarovar is 'the Mother Principle,' which represents Buddhist transcendent consciousness. Three hills rising near Kang Rimpoche (Mt. Kailash) are believed to be the homes of the Bodhisattvas Manjushri, Vajrapani, and Avalokiteshvara.

Kailash – Myths and Legends

According to ancient legends, the sapta-dvipas (seven continents identified in the Hindu literature) are generally described with relation to Mount Meru with all the continents centered around this. Asia or the Jambu-dvipa (land of the rose-apple) is to its south; North America or Krauncha-dvipa (land of the heron) is to its west and so on. Some Hindu legends also place the first human beings appearing on the Earth at the base of Mount Kailash, and then spreading throughout the world from there.

According to the Linga Purana, the Kailash that we see with our physical eyes is different from the real Kailash. It says there is a city with eleven concentric rings, one above the other, which form the plains. Lord Shiva's palace rests on top of the highest ring, exactly at the top of the sacred mountain where Lord Shiva eternally dwells in union with Shakti (Goddess Parvati), daughter of Himalaya.

Ravana's Story

In one Hindu mythological story, Ravana was returning from Kubera's city, when suddenly, his 'vahana' (aerial vehicle) stopped. He was surprised and enquired about the reason. He discovered that this was the abode of Shiva, and that no one was allowed to pass that way, this enraged him immensely. He refused to change his path and arrogantly decided to challenge the Lord Himself! Getting down from his vehicle, he went to the foot of the mountain and began uprooting it with the help of his tremendous strength. However, some say that he attempted to uproot Kailash and move it to show Shiva's 'gana' Nandi, his love for the Lord.

Shiva, annoyed by Ravana's arrogance, pressed his little toe on Kailash, pinning him firmly and painfully under it. This was when he acquired the name 'Ravana', meaning '(He) of the terrifying roar,' given to him by Shiva. The earth is said to have quaked at Ravana's cry of pain when the mountain was pinned on him. Now he became penitent, and to undo his mistake began to appease Shiva. He plucked his nerves and used them as strings to compose music and sang songs praising the Lord for years until Shiva released him. Ravana in turn, become a lifelong devotee of Lord

Shiva. The foremost of the devotional prayers composed by him is the 'Shiva Tandav Stotra.'

A Buddhist legend says that in the fifth century, Shakyamuni Buddha went to Kailash along with 500 Arhats to prevent Ravana from taking away Mount Kailash. They say, there are four footprints of the Buddha in each direction around Mount Kailash and a rope's mark behind Mount Kailash left by Ravana trying to uproot it.

According to another Buddhist story, once there was a battle between the Gods and the demons over Mount Kailash. The demons wanted to take it to their place by using ropes and the Gods wanted to take it to heaven. Finally the Tibetan poet sage Milarepa stopped the battle between the two, declaring that the Mountain belonged neither to the Gods nor to the demons, but would remain to guide and elevate human beings in this world. The ring like shape on the upper parts of the mountain, they say, is because of that rope that they used to uproot and pull it.

Spiritual significance of Mount Kailash

The Rudra Shiva (fiery and destructive aspect of Shiva) in Kailash smears himself in ash signifying the burning of the lower desires. The higher significance of the destroyer aspect is that he cuts asunder the bonds of the ego, liberating the Atma within from the darkness of ignorance.

In other terms, the name Mt. Meru is also associated with 'Meru danda' or the spinal column of a person, along which the energy centers (chakras) lie. Therefore, esoterically speaking, Kailash (Mount Meru) is within one's own self. Ascent of Mount Meru means ascent of Kundalini, and the summit is nothing but the Sahasrara (crown) chakra. So, one could say that all fully realized beings, all jivan-muktas, have truly ascended that Mount Meru within!

Just as the physical mountain is considered the center of the known world, so Shiva is the center of the Self. Shiva is the Self (So'ham Shivo' ham).

Everything inside also exists outside because Atma has no inside or outside! It is just one's perception. Thus, Kailash exists in the universe as much as it does in the self. But until this state of oneness is attained, you will only see it outside.

Scaling the Mountain

In known history, no one has ever scaled this mountain, being a mountain of utmost spiritual significance for nearly a fifth of the population, its sanctity has been preserved till date. As the immortal advaitam remains uninterrupted and no mortal can disturb its perfection, so the eternal abode of Kailash must remain untrodden, with no mortal presence allowed.

However, from time to time, some mountaineers did contemplate climbing the mountain.

In 1926, Hugh Ruttledge and his partner Colonel R.C. Wilson had contemplated scaling the sacred mountain, but somehow, both could not make it. Ruttledge later wrote in his journal that the north face (approx. 6,000 ft; 1,800 m high) of the mountain was 'utterly unclimbable.'

Herbert Tichy was in the area in 1936, attempting to climb Gurla Mandhata. When he asked one of the Garpons of Ngari whether Kailash was climbable, the Garpon replied, "Only a man entirely free of sin could climb Kailash. And he would not have to actually scale the sheer walls of ice to do it – he would just turn himself into a bird and fly to the summit."

In 2001 the Chinese government gave permission to a Spanish team led by Jesus Martinez Novas to climb the peak, but in the face of international disapproval, China decided to ban all attempts to climb the mountain. Reinhold Messner, the mountaineer, adventurer and explorer, referring to the Spanish plans, said that trying to scale this mountain was like trying to conquer something in people's souls.

Who Climbed the Mountain?

Hindu Saints

In the Hindu stories, only four persons are said to have reached the Kailash in physical form.

1. Adi Sankaracharya, he brought the 'lingams' from Shiva and established the Shankara Mathams.

2. Avvaiyar, the ninth century poet of southern India. The story goes that one day, towards the end of her life Avvaiyar was in the midst of her daily worship of her beloved deity Ganesha when she saw saint Sundarar and the Chera King going to Kailash. Yearning to join her spiritual friends on the pilgrimage, she tried to rush through her puja rituals when Lord Ganesha appeared and said," Old woman, don't hurry. Let your puja be performed as usual. I shall take you to Kailash before they reach it."

   As she finished her worship and placed the sacramental offering at His feet, Vinayaka appeared before her and said," Old lady, close your eyes." That was all. When she opened her eyes, she found herself seated in Kailash in front of Parvati and Parameshwara.

3. Shaivite saint Sundarar Sundharamurthy Nayanar, while visiting the Chera King Perumal Nayanar expressed his longing for liberation from worldly ties. Lord Shiva responded to his cries and sent a white elephant to fetch Sundarar to His abode, Kailash.

   Hearing this, the Chera King Perumal Nayanar too left at once on a horse-back but how could he ever keep pace with Shiva's divine elephant? They say he whispered the Shiva panchakshara mantra "Om Namah Sivaya" in the ears of his horse and the horse flew, taking him to Kailash.

Milarepa

According to Buddhist legends, Milarepa, the champion of Tantric Buddhism, arrived in Tibet to challenge Naro-Bonchung, representative of Bon for bringing Buddhism into Tibet and also for the legitimate ownership of pilgrimage rights to Mt. Kailash. The two engaged in a great tantrik battle, but neither was able to gain a decisive advantage. Finally, it was agreed that whoever could reach the summit of Kailash first would be the victor.

At dawn on the morning of the contest, the Bonpo priest (Naro Bon-chung) started his journey to the summit riding on his magic drum, beating it all the while, leaving Milarepa's followers dumbfounded to see him sitting still and meditating.

Yet when Naro-Bonchung was nearly at the top, Milarepa suddenly rode on the rays of the sun and reached the summit in a flash. Bonpo looked up and saw him, so disconcerted and shocked was he that he dropped his drum and it fell and broke in two. It is said that the marks made from the falling pieces of the drum can still be seen in the mountain.

Enlightened beings live here

Not only Ravana, but sages and siddhas are known to be sitting near the feet of Shiva in Kailash. South Indian mysticism always say that their greatest yogi, Agasthya Muni, one of the seven direct disciples of Shiva who are known as the Sapta Rishis, who is the basis of South Indian mysticism, lives there in the southern face of Kailash.

The Buddhists believe that three of their main Bodhisattvas, Manjushri, Avalokiteshwara and Sandhyapani live in Kailash. The great Tibetan Yogi- Saint Milarepa meditated in a cave at Mt. Kailash and also at Lapchi Kang and finally attained perfect enlightenment. Hundreds of Arhats or elevated beings are said to live here. The Parashuram Ashram lies close to it near Mansarovar and many Gods and sages too live here.

Repository of knowledge

The belief that these Gods and sages live here does not mean that they are physically there but that all their knowledge, insights and work is deposited in this mountain. All the sixty-three Nayanmars from South India, the sixty-three major saints from South India, including one of the woman saints, came here because they could not transmit their perception directly to the people who might not be ready for it. Hence, it is a treasure house of knowledge.

In terms of inner dimensions, the summit of all knowledge is Kailash. If you know how to perceive it and decipher it, all knowledge of the self, the existence and liberation is all there for you to take. Every religion and tradition has deposited their knowledge here and it is available to the one who is elevated in consciousness and clear in perception. To him or her, it is distinctly visible.

According to one scholar, the world 'Kailash' itself indicates different things:

> 'Kila' means 'is' or 'being' (so). Indicating assent or emphasis (like saying "indeed" or "verily")
>
> 'kila' also means reason, agreement or communication of intelligence
>
> 'asa' means "not he," (what the Vedanta calls 'neti netina iti', "not this, not thus")
>
> Thus 'asa' is the unnamed Rudra who can only be known as neti
>
> Asa is also "the seat," so that KilAsa is "verily the seat."
>
> Asa also refers to "ashes or dust," so that KilAsa is "indeed ashes."
>
> Thus, KailAsa – the abode of Rudra-Shiva

And, they say Kailasa is within – the source of your own Manas (consciousness), which is your Mansarovar.

Mansarovar - Myth and Mystery

> *There are no mountains like the Himalaya, for in them are Kailash and Mansarovar.*
> —Skanda Puran

Mansarovar lies at a height of 4,577 m (15,015) and is situated 20 km away from Kailash. It is the most beautiful and sacred lake in the world. Believed to house the Kalpavriksha, the wish-fulfilling Divine Tree, the lake is considered to be the source of all Creation. This blue and emerald green lake has been attributed with healing properties. Kailash is reflected in its waters.

Legend says that the lake was discovered by King Mandhata. Mandhata had done penance on the shores of Mansarovar, at the foot of the magnificent mountains named after him. There was a big mansion down below on its bottom which was the abode of the King of 'Nagas' – the serpent God. Right in the middle of the arc-like surface of the lake, there once stood a huge tree whose fruits fell into the lake with the sound 'Jam;' thus, the surrounding region came to be known as 'Jambu-ling' or 'Jambu-Dvipa' in the Hindu Puranas.

In some Pali and Sanskrit Buddhist works, Mansarovar is described as Anotatta or Anavatapta – the lake without heat and trouble. Buddhists believe that in its centre there is a tree, which bears fruits of celestial medicinal properties that may cure all known physical as well as mental ailments.

Therefore, the Skanda Purana says:

"...just as the dew is dried by the morning sun,

so are the sins of mankind by the sight of the Himalayas."

Hindu

To the Hindus, the lake is mystically wedded to the mountain. Mount Kailash is Shiva, and Lake Manas (Lake of the Mind) is His

Shakti, His very Consciousness, in which all reality is reflected. Each stone in the lake is revered as lingam.

According to Hindu tradition, the name Mansarovar is based on this legend: Brahma had a mind (manas) to create a lake (sarovar). They say that Saraswati, the Goddess of thought, wisdom and the arts lives in this lake. She is called the Lady of the Lake (Saras), the swan symbolizing expressions of creative thought, mantras, music, arts, writing, speech, and teaching. It is also supposed to be the summer abode of the hamsa goose. Hamsa is a sacred bird that symbolizes beauty and wisdom. Since Mansarovar indicates the omnipotence of Brahma's mind (manas), to bathe in this lake delivers one to the paradise of Brahma and cleanses the sins of a hundred lifetimes. As per Hindu mythology, "anyone who touches the soil of Mansarovar will go to the paradise of Brahma and who drinks the water from the lake will go to the heaven of Lord Shiva."

It is also believed that the Devas – the Gods, descend to bathe in the lake at Brahma Muhurta – the auspicious time of the day between morning 3 to 5 o'clock and many Gods and sages are present at the lake in subtle from, blessing the pilgrims who visit it.

Tibetan

In Tibetan, Mansarovar is known as 'Mapham Tso,' meaning the 'Unconquerable Lake.' The name records a magical contest between the Tibetan poet and mystic Milarepa, and the Bon priest Naro-Bonchung, which is said to have occurred in the tenth century.

Buddhism

Buddhists associate Mansarovar with Anotatta Lake (the Pali name for Mansarovar).

Queen Maya (the mother of Shakyamuni Buddha) dreamt that the couch on which she rested was carried by the guardian Gods to the lake. This holy dip in the waters removed all human impurities so that Lord Buddha could enter her womb. He came in the form of a white cloud (or a white elephant) from the direction of Mount Kailash.

It is said that shortly after his enlightenment, Buddha used his super-normal powers to visit Lake Anotatta or Mansarovar near the foot of Mount Kailash.

Rakshastal

Next to the Mansarovar is Rakshastal or the Lake of Demons. The higher lake Mansarovar (one of the highest freshwater lakes in the world), is a sacred lake, and is round like the sun while the lower lake Rakshastal (one of the highest salt-water lakes) is the devil's lake and has the shape of the crescent moon. The salty water of Rakshastal, a stark contrast to the fresh water of Lake Mansarovar, produces no waterweeds or fish and is considered poisonous by locals. The two lakes represent solar and lunar forces, good and negative energies respectively, Mansarovar being associated with 'light' and Rakshastal with 'darkness'. So one can choose the Lake of Brahma's Mind (Enlightenment) or the Lake of Demons (delusion and destruction).

Lying beneath the symbolic temple of Kailash, Mansarovar and Rakshashtal represent the water tanks present at the entrance to every Hindu temple. These ideas are expressed in the names of the two lakes, to Hindus Mansarovar symbolizes the receptive, female aspect of creation, the yoni, while Mt. Kailash symbolizes the active male aspect, the lingam.

Parikrama

> *"Just as a white summer cloud, in harmony with*
> *heaven and earth freely floats*
> *in the blue sky from horizon to horizon following*
> *the breath of the atmosphere*
> *- in the same way the pilgrim abandons himself to*
> *the breath of the greater*

> *life that… leads him beyond the farthest horizons*
> *to an aim which is already*
> *present within him,*
> *though yet hidden from his sight."*
>
> —Lama Anagarika Govinda,
> 'The Way of the White Clouds'

For centuries, the faithful and the devout have abandoned themselves to the breadth of a greater life when they undertook the most difficult of all treks, the Kailash Parikrama. They dared the landscape of Tibet; utterly savage, untamed, raw, and yet incredibly beautiful. It's unforgiving, craggy heights utterly enchanting in their vastness. The pilgrim's sole purpose to walk around the holiest of all mountains, the Kailash, was as a prayer offering.

The 'parikrama' (circumambulation of the mountain) has for many centuries or possibly many millennia remained a vital pilgrimage, symbolizing life's stages of death, purification, and rebirth. The parikrama is done from a distance, walking around the mountain over a 53 km (32 miles) stretch.

Lama Govinda says, "To see the greatness of a mountain one must keep one's distance; to understand its form one must move around it; to experience its moods one must see it is at sunrise and at sunset. Mount Kailash has become a symbol of the ultimate quest for perfection and ultimate realization, signposts that point beyond worldly existence."

At 4,572 m (15,000 ft), the base of the mountain sits next to the holy Mansarovar. Starting at the town of Darchen just south of the mountain, the pilgrims progress up the western valley hiking to a meditative rhythm, then crossing the Dolma La pass at 5,669 m (18,600 ft) to the north of the mountain, and then walking down the valley to the east, all the way back to Darchen. The winding earthy trail is often interspersed with rough blizzards, precipitous climbs, landslides, and windy storms. At the same time, the sound of the Karnali river, the fluttering of prayer flags, salt traders hurrying their herd of goats, the crackling of prayer wheels, and Tibetan pilgrims chanting the ubiquitous mantra 'Om Mani Padme

Hum' under their breath, also engulf it. There are vast, sculpted red towers on one side and broken crags with huge scree slopes on the other. Every step taken on this holy land has been blessed by innumerable pilgrims who have trodden this very path in faith, prayer, and humility. The air reverberates with their vibrations.

The peregrination is made in a clockwise direction by Hindus and Buddhists. Followers of the Jain and Bon religions circumambulate the mountain in a counter clockwise direction. Normally, pilgrims do it in three days though some complete the entire walk in a single day. It takes a person in good shape, walking fast around it, fifteen hours. There are yet others, who venture a much more demanding regimen, performing body-length prostrations over the entire length of the parikrama route: The pilgrim bends down, kneels, prostrates full-length, makes a mark with his fingers, rises to his knees, prays, and then crawls forward on hands and knees to the mark made by his or her fingers before repeating the process. It requires at least four weeks of physical endurance to complete the parikrama this way.

The parikrama begins with crossing the 'Yama dwar' (the gateway of the God of Death) known as Chorten Kang Ngyi (two legged Stupa) in Tibetan. Mythological stories say that 'Yama,' the Lord of Death comes from this gate at the time of death of a person. By crossing this, the pilgrim seeks blessings from Lord Yama and leaves the fear of death behind. Further, it also means that they have now entered the zone of the Kailash.

On the ascent, one passes Shiva Sthal, where Tibetans leave the remains of the dead or their own blood. Nearer to the top is a rock, reputed to carry the footprint of Milarepa. Charansparsha is the closest view of Lord Kailash. The entire route is studded with sacred sites, marked by chortens. The land itself is sacred.

A single parikrama equals one turn of the Wheel of Life and will wipe away the sins of one's life. Twelve circumambulations will purify one's karma of all past and future lives and entitle a person to follow the hidden, special path of the Inner Parikrama. In 108 parikrama, one is liberated from the cycle of birth and death and attains Nirvana. Even one parikrama represents an extremely difficult task, since the mountain is difficult to access and is dangerous.

The parikrama is said to wash away the sins of a lifetime. Several religions believe that circumambulation of Mount Kailash by foot is a holy ritual that will bring good fortune and will wipe away sins for all past and future lifetimes.

The Inner Kora (Parikrama)

The Inner Kora is a special parikrama among pilgrimages of Hindu, Bon, Buddhist and Jain. Most popular and one of the hardest, the Inner Parikrama needs some mountaineering experience and equipment. This parikrama involves around 34 km walking journey including Asthapath, Nandi parvat, Atmalingam, Saptarishi Caves and Kuber Kunda. The landscape is entirely made up of rock, crevices, snow and ice. Apart from two small monasteries, no humans live along the inner Kailash region. The Inner Kora starts and ends at Darchen.

Charan Sparsh

On the Outer Kora parikrama, the closest that one can get to Mount Kailash is nearer the camp in Deraphuk. Here, one can have a beautiful vista view of the crystal north face of Mount Kailash. Located at a distance of 3 kms from Deraphuk at an altitude of approximately 18000 feet is Charansparsh (literally "touch the feet") - the snout of the Kangjam glacier at the foothill of North face of the holy Kailash mountain. There is a toe shaped flat stone projecting out from the bottom of a high ice wall which looks like the feet of the holy Kailash mountain.

One can reach Charan Sparsh after a strenuous trek of 3 to 4 hours (one way) requiring a steep climb of around 1000-1500 feet. Since it snows here often, the trails can get quite confusing and the services of a local guide is recommended. Typically, one has to set aside a whole day for this trip. Touching the base of the holy Kailash mountain is verily the same as touching the holy feet of

Lord Shiva himself. Further, one comes up close and personal to experience the grandeur of the beautiful perpendicular wall of the North face of the holy Kailash mountain. The sublime and serene beauty of this place awakens the latent faith and surrender in the pilgrim. Here, one can even pick up stones that have fallen off the majestic Kailash mountain.

Kuber Kund

Kubera, the God of wealth, is believed to have settled on Gandhamandana mountain near Mount Kailash. Kuber Kund is a beautiful pond built by Lord Kuber for the devas (demigods) to have a bath. This beautiful pond is dotted with sedimentary rocks with a cave like structure formed by a small projection on the banks. From far above, this pond appears like the crescent moon adorning Lord Shivas face.

To reach Kuber Kund, one has to cross Shivasthal, a rocky stretch lined up with mounds of rough stones that pilgrims drape with clothes. From Shivasthal, one has to turn left before Dolma la pass. After one passes Manjusri mountain, one has to turn right and reach the Kanda Sangla glacier. One reaches the pond by crossing the Kanda Sangla glacier with the use of ropes secured with help from the sherpas. This route is tough and challenging and one cannot avail of ponies.

On the way back to the Zuthulphuk monastery, one has to cross three glaciers and can partake of the natural beauty in the form of high peaks, streams, waterfalls and mountain caves. Here, we have a unique sighting of the East face of Kailash from the base to the top which is considered the entrance of Lord Surya (Sun). Pilgrims carry the sacred water from this pond back with them to keep it at home or use it in rituals.

Saptarishi Caves

The grand Saptarishi Caves looks like a balcony lying under the south face of Mount Kailash at a height of around 6000 metres altitude. The caves have small structures created by the Tibetans for their deities. Here there are more than thirteen chortens (Buddhist monument) that are managed by Gengta Monastery. These chortens are naturally protected from damage by snow and rocks by a long horizontal crack in the cave.

It is believed that Sage Agasthya and other great Masters live in the Saptarishi Cave. It is believed that Lord Shiva composed the 100 poems in praise of Goddess Parvati on these very walls. Adi Shankara made notes of these poems which were taken away by Lord Nandi since this secret belonged to Kailash. Adi Shankaracharya recollected the first 41 verses from memory (Ananda Lahiri) and composed the next 59 verses describing the beauty of the Divine Mother (Soundarya Lahiri).

The inside of the cave is painted red as per the Tibetan tradition. Pilgrims leave behind books and numerous other offerings to Lord Shiva inside the cave. To reach the Saptarishi Caves, one has to ascend a vertical wall that is almost at 90 degrees. This is one of the most challenging and difficult climbs on the Inner Parikrama.

Ashtapad

At an elevation of 4900 metres (17000 feet), Ashtapad (meaning eight steps) is a mountain on the western ring of mountains surrounding the holy Kailash mountains which has 8 mountain peaks. One of the peaks has a very high cave where the first Jain Tirthankara Shri Rishabhadev Bhagwan also known as Shri Adinath Bhagwan attained Nirvana (salvation). According to Shrimad Bhagwatam, Rishabhdev's father Nabhirai and mother Marudevi did hard penance at this spot following Rishabhdev's Rajyabhishek (coronation ceremony) and took samadhi (a saint's conscious exit from the body).

It is located about 4kms towards the south face of Kailash. Many saints go to Ashtapad to meditate in the many peaceful caves that are found in this area. This place provides a beautiful view of the entire Kailash area. From Ashtapad, one can have the beautiful view of the South face of Kailash which has the Meru

Danda (spine) running through its middle. One can see the Nandi parbat, Manasarovar and Rakshastal lakes, Yama dwar as well as most of the entire parikrama route.

Nandi Kora Parikrama

When viewed from Ashtapad or Saptarishi Caves, the Nandi Parvat (mountain) looks shaped like the sacred Nandi bull with its head raised towards the summit of Kailash akin to the way Nandi stands guard outside the sanctum sanctorum of Lord Shiva. The pilgrim does a parikrama of the Nandi Parvat. The Nandi parikrama is very challenging and has to be done on foot. After climbing down the steep slope of Nandi parvat from the right side one finally completes the parikrama.

During the parikrama, one arrives at Serdung Chuksum which, at around 20000ft, is the highest point of the pilgrimage. Here we can get excellent views of Mount Kailash. We also get a side view of the rock structures worshipped as Goddess Parvati by Hindus and as Tara Devi by the Buddhists.

In the words of a saint, "If you can really be with Kailash even for a few moments, life will never again be the same for you. It is a phenomenon beyond all human imagination."

THE INNER KORA

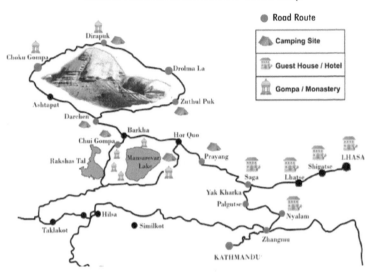

Map

The Parikrama

Monasteries around Kailash

Inner Kora Vistas

Inner Kora - on the Second day

A stone next to Mohanji in the form of a blessing palm from Shiva and Shakti

Mohanji in front of Kailash near Charan Sparsh

The Inner Kora group at Charan Sparsh

Approaching Kailash

Touching the Holy Kailash mountain

Kailash East Face

A Cave in Kailash en route to Kuber Kund

Climb up the glacier en route to Kuber Kund

Enigmatic Kailash

Listening to Shivakavacham

Face of Shamballa inhabitant visible (in red) above

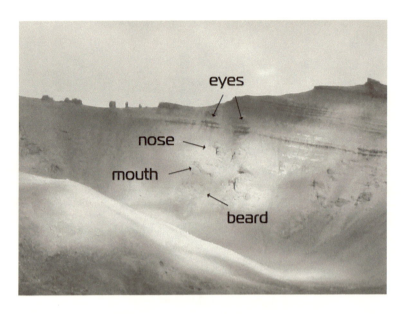

Hanumanji makes an appearance

Amrit from 3rd eye of Shiva

View of Kailash on the way back from Kuber Kund

Small Kailash

Laser beam stone structure

Stone Door to Shambala

North face of Kailash viewed from the parikrama

South face of Kailash during sunset

East face of Kailash

West face of Kailash

Devi offering water to the Sun in Mansarovar

Mother love

Devi Mohan

A Bare Embrace of Kailash

The long walk to touch the holy Mount Kailash

Rajesh Rammohan Kamath

Swami Brahmananda touching the Om stone to Mount Kailash

The last stretch across the glacier to touch the holy Mount Kailash

Swami Brahmananda

Havan at Lake Manasarovar

The group that managed to cross beyond Charansparsh before the ravine mishap

Swami Govinda

The ravine where few people slipped and almost lost their lives while walking towards Kailash

The ice Shivling in the middle of the small pool a few meters from Kailash. The small caves _ chairs embedded in surrounding walls are also visible

Dhritiman Biswas

Sumit and Kailash

North face of Mount Kailash

Sumit Partap Gupta

Hanumatananda touching the holy Kailash mountain

Akshata falling from the sky - a shower of blessings from Lord Shiva

Hanumatananda

The tiring steep trek en route to Kuber Kund

The prayer stones placed in Lake Mansarovar

Spomenka Dragojevic

The steep climb to reach halfway to Kuber Kund (bottom of image to past icy patch)

Mohanji and Orbs

Mitesh Khatiwala

Chai hugging with orbs all around

Posing in front of Kailash

Chai Lai Siong

Vijay and Chai touching the holy Kailash mountain

A golden dragon overlooking our residence in Manasarovar

Vijay Ramanaidoo

Walking to Charansparsh

Climbing the treacherous icy patch en route to Kuber Kund

Anjali Kanwar

Kailash Ganga

Grappling with ropes to get past the slippery icy stretch en route to Kuber Kund

Phaneendar Venkata Bhavaraju

Jayeeta Chakraborty

Mohanji with the Inner Kora group

North face of Kailash during sunset

Riana Gaspar

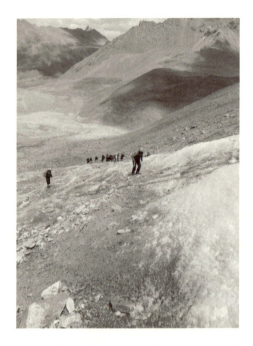

Walking across the final steep treacherous icy patch en route to Kuber Kund

The long walk back from Kuber Kund

The Mirror Called Kailash

- Devi Mohan -

THERE IS NO greater teacher than one's own experience. Especially when it comes to spiritual progress, theoretical knowledge is useful in satisfying the intellect, but lasting transformation cannot happen without one's direct experience.

Experience of Kailash yatra can never be fully explained in words, but this humble attempt will hopefully be used as an inspiration for those who read about it to strive to reach this majestic "crown chakra of Mother Earth" and achieve their own experience of the mighty Kailash one day.

It was a great blessing to experience Kailash Yatra with Mohanji twice, in 2014 and 2016. The greatest blessing of our colorful international groups of 80+ during both yatras was the opportunity to undergo this experience in the physical experience of Mohanji. When dealing with matters that are beyond the mind, only those who have mastered the mind can provide precious guidance in the right moment, the moment when transformation either happens or doesn't happen.

Mohanji had prepared us mentally that the journey to Kailash would be tough, a true test of our faith and surrender. He said that during Kailash yatra "Grace is more essential than oxygen." However, my mind could not quite grasp the true meaning of these words until the great teacher Experience appeared.

The experience of both Kailash Yatras taught me the following:

the energy of Kailash, just like the consciousness of a Master, is like a mirror – when approached with ego, expectations, concepts and doubts, it will reflect back to us just how small and fragile we are. But when we truly surrender, empty ourselves and with utmost humility allow ourselves to simply experience/feel Kailash beyond any of our existing concepts, it is then that we can behold Kailash in its grandeur and allow its energy to work on us deeply. As Mohanji said "Nobody leaves Kailash empty handed." But the depth of the experience depends on our receptivity and eligibility . . .

Another crucial question is – am I ready to face the mirror?

We got the hint of this profound truth while visiting the Buddhanilkantha Temple in Nepal just before the yatra. This is where one can behold the most fascinating 5m long statue of Lord Vishnu. As we admired its beauty and observed how the expressions on the face of lying Vishnu would change depending from the angle from which one would approach/observe it, there was one more observation that really left us in awe. The statue was being reflected in the water almost 180 degrees below itself!

We tried applying our reasoning while observing this sheer miracle, but logical mind had no explanation how the face of Lord Vishnu could be reflected in the water below itself. It was only later that I understood the subtle 'Divine mirror' message of this experience, a beautiful intro to the 'mirror called Kailash' experience that would follow. A physical mirror can only reflect back to us our perishable physical image, but no mirror can be compared to the mirror of Divine . . .

Kailash with Mohanji 2014 - Outer Kora

Before proceeding with my own "mirror facing experience" during the 3 days of trekking which were the most challenging part of the outer kora in 2014, I can't but mention the most sublime, most unexpected blessings received at Lake Mansarovar, the grand cleanser of negativities beyond this lifetime, the lake in which celestial beings bathe every day.

I must admit that I was dreading the experience of Mansarovar.

The Mirror Called Kailash

We were in the Himalayas, in our winter jackets with several layers of clothing – it's not all that easy to believe that we can just blissfully enter the ice cold water and take 9 or more dips in it, without any consequences to our health. During the long bus ride on the way to Mansarovar, my mind kept bombarding me with the fearful thoughts like "If I get an ovary inflammation due to that ice cold water, the whole yatra is gone for a toss. Is it really worth the risk?" At one point I got tired of these thoughts and decided to share the same with Mohanji. He immediately reassured me that I would be just fine. He said there is no way I could miss this opportunity of a lifetime – the cleansing at Mansarovar lake is too powerful, it penetrates and removes the negativities of many lifetimes.

When we reached Mansarovar, its surreal beauty left us in awe. While admiring its azure green shades and the divine sparkles of sun reflection on the water I suddenly saw a strong flash coming from the clouds. It was just like somebody flashed with the photo camera a couple of meters away from my face – except that this was coming from the clouds far away. I kept looking intently through the window of our bus but could not see anything after that strong flash. There was a strong intuitive feeling within me that this is something important.

I kept wondering what that was. A couple of minutes later, Spomenka shared with me the photos she clicked with her mobile and pointed at 2 balls of light that were visible on a dozen of photos, all in different locations (in the clouds, near the Mansarovar water, near one house, etc.) I was totally amazed – that was it! The celestial beings made their presence known to us in the most unexpected way. I was getting more and more excited about our Mansarovar dip!

When we reached the beach and the bus door opened, my joy was spoiled by many mosquitoes of huge size (at least 3 times bigger than the usual ones) that surrounded us all of a sudden. I kept waving with my hands in distress until one of the tour organizers said with a smile "Nothing to worry, these are vegetarian mosquitoes. They don't bite." I was not quite sure whether he was joking or not, but soon realized that they were indeed not biting us. "Vegetarian mosquitos" - how amazing was that?! I laughed and said this must be some good karma that I earned by being vegetarian ☺.

The overall feel on the beach was surprisingly great. The weather was perfect (22ºC), totally sunny and pleasant, and all of us rushed to remove our clothes and enter the water. I soon came to notice that most people were already wearing their bikinis or whatever they chose to wear for the dip, so they were ready to enter the water in no time. I was yet to change my clothes and had to wait for my turn in one of the two small tents allocated for the ladies. This took time and I was getting worried that I would be very late.

Kailash was at first not visible from the clouds and then, as if in Divine theatre, we saw only the base of it getting revealed beneath the white clouds, with an unmistakable small 'm' clearly written all over it in snow. What a beautiful welcome for Mohanji and all of us! After some time, the clouds parted and our joy knew no bounds as we beheld both, Mansarovar and Kailash with our physical eyes.

I finally got to change my clothes, took a deep breath and entered the holy Mansarovar - the cold water was strangely energizing and the feeling of diving into it and then looking at Kailash in between each dip was truly grand. After doing 9 dips and enjoying the view of Kailash some more, I suddenly felt a strong desire to perform abhishek of Mohanji with Mansarovar water.

I looked to my left and saw him turning towards the shore at that same moment. Since he entered the water much before me, he was just about to leave. I ran in his direction in strange desperation and shouted "Wait for me, wait for me!" Sumit and Spomenka also shouted "Biba is coming!" Some strange excitement overwhelmed me and my heart was beating like crazy! I briefly saw Mohanji's eyes and understood immediately that he was in an expanded state – the expression in his almost red eyes was very Shaivic, very powerful! My heart melted as I did the abhishek and then suddenly 'bham!' - a totally unexpected blow happened which almost knocked me off. Mohanji poured water on my head but energetically that felt like a mighty slap, as if the water thundered on me high up from a mountain. Shaken by this unexpected experience, I was squatting in the water and barely managed to fold my palms into a Namaskar when 'bham!'- another 'hit' came, so strong that it felt like it literally peeled a layer of skin from my face and body. There was no time to think, pray, breathe, or even remotely try to understand what was happening. With eyes full of water and tears, I looked at mighty Kailash in the distance, and then 'bham!', another hit and another layer peeled off. I cried and laughed at the same time, in total delirium, in total gratitude! The next thing I recall is Mohanji leaving the lake supported by Sumit and one more person and me following them somehow.

I still have not fully 'digested' this experience nor do I know how to name it. Baptism by Shiva? Astral operation in the lake Mansarovar by the mighty surgeon Shiva? Whatever it was, I am forever grateful to Mohanji, to Shiva, for granting me the blessing I could not have even prayed for because I never knew it was possible...

After we reached our accommodation next to the lake Mansarovar, I came to know that Sumit had clicked a couple of photos with his mobile while I was undergoing this experience. It was amazing that he even carried his phone into the lake and that he was right there at that moment clicking the photo. My heart skipped a beat when I browsed through the photos in his phone's gallery and noticed Shiva's third eye on my forehead. Not only is it clearly visible, but looks as if it is deeply engraved.

I just kept looking at it, totally speechless... Om Namah Shivaaye!

Celestial beings

That night I could not fall asleep - out of sheer excitement about this experience and the overall feeling of being totally energized.

A couple of us agreed that we would wake up at 3am and go to the wall that separates our accommodation from the Mansarovar beach in order to see whether any celestial being would come to take a bath in the lake. While agreeing about the meeting time, it was not clear whether that would be 3am Chinese, Nepalese or Indian time, so in the end Ami from South Africa and I ended up going to the wall 2h before the others came. It was so beautiful and auspicious to stand there in pin drop silence. Cold wind was blowing, but we didn't mind – the lake looked truly magical. Ami sang a beautiful Violet flame prayer with utmost devotion and our hearts were filled with love. In less than a couple of minutes we saw a light similar to that of a star on the sky, except that it was visibly mobile – it just appeared in the middle of the lake, as if floating on the water. Our jaws dropped! It moved a bit to the left, then to the right, then went under the water (took a dip), then surfaced again, changed color to pinkish, then to red – it was magical, to say the least. We stood there for more than an hour and saw at least a dozen of them.

As we were just about to leave, another light appeared but far brighter than the others. It was floating on the water and moving towards us. It looked like two twinkling stars on top of each other. I became breathless as I clearly felt it/them connecting energetically to my heart chakra. The sensation was incredibly beautiful. At that point in time two hours had already elapsed and I was eager to share this experience with others who just arrived to have their experience. Our little group gathered soon and we went to the wall again. At this point more people were waking up and some were using their flash lights. The sacred silence was broken and celestial beings would not come/reveal themselves. We stood there for 30 min. or so but nothing happened. Slightly disappointed, we decided to go back to our rooms. I almost felt that others did not really believe my experience. Monja and I stayed a bit longer, but since celestial beings were not to be seen, we started walking towards our accommodation. As we walked, I felt a sensation on the back of the heart chakra. My intuition said "Stop right there." I turned around and there it was, the celestial being with strong almost fluorescent light shining from the middle of the lake. We stood at the same spot and looked at it in awe. I opened my heart chakra in deepest gratitude, embracing its blessings... No fairy tale I ever heard could possibly come close to this.

The next day we saw something even more amusing – Mohanji's face (semi profile) on Mount Kailash, but this time with sunglasses and a white cap which he wore on the same day.

I laughed and asked Mohanji "How come you are wearing the sunglasses?" He smiled and said: "Shiva is pulling a prank. He has got a good sense of humor." Wow, all this had happened and our yatra had not even started!

Churning time

It is only natural that we compare ourselves to others and derive logical conclusions. When the trekking started, I recall somebody telling me "Oh, lucky you - you practice Yoga and pranayama, so yatra must be much easier for you." I looked around and saw so many people elder to me, and/or people whose bodies conveyed a sedentary lifestyle. In view of many years of Yoga practice plus my preparation in the gym, my mind accepted this comment as true. Oh you subtle traps of ego. Little did I know how soon these concepts and logical conclusions would be shattered to pieces in the mighty Shaivic energies of Kailash.

I started the 3 days of trekking (the actual Kailash yatra) overwhelmed by restlessness. I was told that morning that the weather could be very cold and thus added many layers of clothing to my body. However, by the time we were to start the trek, the sun was blazing and I started sweating a lot while waiting for the allocation of ponies and porters to be over. I was given a piece of paper with the name of the owner of the pony and was told to make sure I don't lose it. Before I knew it, Mohanji and the rest of our team started walking and I was still not able to identify the pony allocated to me (which I intended to use only in case I fell sick/weak and could not continue the yatra on foot). I requested some of the Tibetan porters to read out to me the name written on this piece of paper, but none of them could read the handwriting with which it was written - I was stuck! Sumit told me not to worry –the man who owns the pony will surely search for me as this is his livelihood. I thus started walking, even though I felt quite unsettled. Under the scorching sun I soon removed my heavy jacket and tied it around my waist. Then I removed my winter scarf and tied it around my waist. The next was my black sweater - it too found its place around my waist. I felt so heavy with all this clothing hanging from my waist, plus the two walking sticks that I didn't feel like using, water bottle, snacks - it all felt like a lot of luggage as the lack of oxygen started to make me feel increasingly weak. On top of it all, this inexplicable frustration, insecurity and restlessness kept building within me - in fact, I had never felt this restless in my whole life! I pretty much felt like a helpless child lost in a crowded market place. Other yatris kept passing me by, either on ponies or by foot, and I felt that I was the slowest and most miserable one among them. I could not recognize myself - I have faced far greater challenges in my life, but my inner state was never this bad. The scorching sun did not help. Then one of our sweet yatris Akshay came with a big umbrella and offered me most lovingly to share its blessed shade with him. That felt so great and I was very grateful. My morale was boosted a bit and soon everything seemed to be falling into place - the owner of the pony appeared and I was able to offload on him my heavy jacket and whatever else I could. What a relief that was! I kept blessing him. It seemed to me that all this was a powerful reminder of how important it is to "Travel light through life, drop the unnecessary luggage".

    Still, even after the offloading of clothes, I was feeling quite breathless and clearly lacked the stamina. This took me by surprise. I was quite happy that at the onset of the yatra my body was coping with the hypoxia (high altitude sickness) so well while many of our yatris were vomiting and falling sick. Another instance of sumptuous feeding of the ego, coupled with the wrong assumption that the same trend would continue till the end of the yatra.

    The straight path slowly turned into our first bigger hill. Due to hypoxia, what would have been a normal climb in the usual conditions, became a great struggle for breath after every couple of steps. I tried all breathing and concentration techniques known to me, but still could not keep the pace without stopping to catch the breath. My confidence was shattered and I felt totally miserable. After somehow climbing the first hill I had to admit to myself that I could no longer cope. With a heavy heart, I decided to use a pony. At that point, hypoxia already overwhelmed my system and the very act of climbing onto a pony made me gasp for breath. The scenery around me was stunning, but I could not enjoy any of it as all my energy was being spent on maintaining the balance on the pony and ensuring I took sips of water frequently enough to avoid dehydration that makes hypoxia even worse.

By the time we reached our destination, Derapuk camp, with the stunning view of the North Face of Kailash, I could not wait to crash into whatever bed I could find.

It was freezing cold, there were no toilet facilities, mud, chaos and noise all around – difficult to say what was worse, my inner state or my surrounding... It was ironic - the mighty Kailash that I dreamed of seeing for years was now right before my eyes, but I could not bring myself to even utter a prayer. I was just so miserable at all levels – physical, emotional, mental and spiritual, as disconnected as I could be from my Higher Self, Mohanji, Kailash, Divine.... I felt like finding a hole and hiding in it... When I entered the room in which Mohanji was seated with several other yatris, I witnessed myself being completely blank while they were overflowing with devotion, gratitude and joy, laughing and sharing beautiful experiences, massaging Mohanji's feet, soaking in love - DB managed to walk to Charan Sparsh, the point at which one could actually touch Kailash and came back with a big radiant smile. Others shared their own experiences... That made me even more miserable – I had nothing, absolutely nothing to share, zero 'bhaav' (feeling/flavor of genuine devotion), and I am the type of person who would never try to fake it. I felt totally numb, disconnected and miserable. At one point Mohanji looked straight into my eyes and said "You are in the illusion of doership. That is why you are going through this. You think you can do the yatra relying on your physical strength and stamina, that you are the doer. When you lose the bhaav, you lose the Grace – simple." This comment crushed the last inner wall that kept me composed – I knew that what Mohanji said was absolutely true and admitted to myself that I totally lacked surrender. I could not understand how this could happen to me though. I waited and prayed for years to come to Kailash and now that I had reached I felt nothing! I was agonized. To a person on a spiritual path, there is no greater pain than spiritual numbness, the feeling of being disconnected from one's Guru/Higher Self/Divine. After Mohanji uttered those words so bluntly, I had to agree – it was not about the hypoxia, the pony that was not to be found, or any other silly reason. This was all about me and my 'doership', my lack of surrender, while Kailash was right in front of my face! I drank a few sips of warm herbal tea and disappeared into my room, eager to sleep and rest from this agonizing turmoil, hoping that somehow sleep would make it all better.

But alas, what awaited me next was like a horror movie. We woke up around 5am to the prison-like sounds of loud whistling and rough male voices shouting 'Get up, get up!' as if some calamity happened. For a moment I thought I had regressed into some nightmarish WW2 holocaust scenario. It was cold and wet outside, mud, noise, crowds and chaos everywhere. With trembling hands and wobbly legs, gasping for breath, I somehow forced myself to go down the stairs and answer the call of nature (wherever I could find the right spot for it), and then brush my teeth using the last remnants of warm water that our sherpas (Nepalese caretakers who were assisting us most lovingly throughout the yatra) provided us with. It was then that I heard the beautiful sound of arati to Shiva – I looked up towards the balcony and saw Mohanji, Panditji and several yatris looking at Kailash and doing the arati with incense sticks. At that moment, I looked at the glorious Kailash before me, while my ego was drowning in the pool of helplessness, taking all the doership and trash with it. I started crying profusely, praying to Kailash/

Shiva/Mohanji from the bottom of my heart to take me out of this misery, to allow me to break the walls of illusion, to melt me in surrender. I cried and cried, allowing myself to go through the experience. I noticed that all the sherpas around me were pretty much staring at me, but couldn't care less (now that I think about it, that must have been quite a pathetic site - a white girl with a toothbrush in her hand, smudged make-up and goat-like cap with ears, crying like a baby and staring at Kailash! ☺) There was no shame. How else could one stand before Shiva but naked – there is no other way. We emerged from that consciousness naked and we can dissolve back into it only if naked, only after dropping all our masks. As Mohanji said "Kailash is Shiva, the state that you came from, but forgot as you lived. Be Shiva and you will merge with Kailash spontaneously. Shiva and Kailash are ONE." This was the moment when I truly felt the surrender . . . - the subtle inner wall got cracked.

By the time I composed myself, gulped some breakfast, chose the right clothes and packed my back pack, most of the other yatris had already started the trek. I hurried in order to catch up with them and tried walking a bit faster, but after 10 meters or so understood it won't be happening. I sat on the pony and kept quiet – whether I did the yatra by foot or on pony, it didn't really matter. What was far more important was that even though weak physically, I now started to feel connected spiritually - mantras and prayers deep from the heart kept flowing.

I spent the entire ride on the pony towards and up the steep Dolma Pass in a meditative state. At one point I totally lost the concept of time and can't even recollect certain parts of the journey. I just remember that I felt immense love and gratitude towards the pony that carried my weight up the Dolma La and kept caressing him. At one point, the image of surreal emerald-like Gauri Kund, the lake which, as the legend says, Lord Shiva created for Goddess Parvati to bathe in, appeared in my inner vision. Immense desire to go to Gauri Kund suddenly filled my heart. I knew that, no matter what, I just had to go there! The inner pull was very strong.

Touched by Divine – the purity of Gauri Kund

Once we reached the top of the hill, I got off the pony and soon came across Mohanji. My joy knew no bounds upon seeing the familiar glossy eyes full of love, the eyes that my soul had been connected with through lifetimes. Deep gratitude overwhelmed me. I knew he was watching on me, on all of us, and that the inner transformation was all due to his Grace. When I told him that I would like to go to Gauri Kund, his smile and gentle nod was all the confirmation I needed. I walked a bit further until my eyes could finally behold the majestic Gauri Kund in its full glory – it was even more beautiful than what I had seen on the photos!

I then noticed the big sharp stones and steep decline that led to the lake. Mohanji explained just how 'strategically' Gauri Kund was located – right after the extremely tough climb up the Dolma Pass, when most people could not even think of another climb. He also said that most of the time Gauri Kund is covered with clouds to hide it from the undeserving seekers. The stones around the lake are often wet and slippery to further deter unwanted visitors. Indeed, had there been even a drizzle, wet and slippery stones would have been too big of an obstacle. But that day the sun was shining and I felt the path to Gauri Kund was open. In my heart, I felt I was invited... I decided to wait for Sumit for I knew that he said earlier he would like to go to Gauri Kund. I walked for only a couple of meters and already felt breathless. For a moment a hint of fear came that I wouldn't be able to do it, but it wasn't even nearly as strong as my desire to go. At that moment I made up my mind that I would go to Gauri Kund even if I died there – and I meant it!

Sumit and Hein arrived soon, bowed to Mohanji and off we went down the steep path across many big stones towards sublime Gauri Kund. Rajesh from UK joined us as well, along with one of the sherpas. Great excitement overwhelmed me and my legs surprised me with their sudden speed and strength – it was as if they walked on their own.

When we reached the lake, I was surprised to see Panditji

already seated there silently and comfortably, with all the pooja paraphernalia, Mohanji's eye card, trishul and Shiva linga, all lovingly laid out in front of the majestic Gauri Kund. That site brought great joy to my heart.

The moment when I touched and tasted the water of Gauri Kund will remain forever etched in my mind and heart. It was like a long awaited flower that finally bloomed from my energy blueprint. I have never felt such a sensation – this water carried the secret codes far beyond this plane of existence. Its purity was indescribable, its sparkle divine, its taste sublime – the purest mountain spring would bow to it in awe. While washing my face with this water and placing some of it on my crown chakra and third eye, I felt nothing but pure bliss as I witnessed the thirst for intense purification, thirst beyond this lifetime, now being quenched . . . I looked up and on the mountain that was facing Gauri Kund I suddenly saw many faces of sages, mainly with long beards and expressions of profound depth. More than seeing, it was the inner sensation of utmost sanctity and purity that overwhelmed me. This lake and this moment in time did not feel like anything one could experience on planet Earth . . .

More than the beauty of nature, it was the vibration of purity of Goddess Parvati that created a deep 'click' within me – this is the aspect of Divine that resonates most deeply with my being. She performed unimaginable penance in order to reach Lord Shiva – hunger, heat, cold, nothing could deter her. Out of her pure heart and deep compassion she pleaded to him to share his wisdom with humanity. She was humanity's bridge to Lord Shiva, whose energy and presence was too powerful to be accessed by humanity. As our sweet Rima Yadav said during one of our conversations, "Even in our family life, when children cannot approach a strict and authoritative father, they always go through the mother."

I recalled the lines from Guru Gita that I enjoy listening to on You Tube describing the grand historical moment of eternal beauty embedded in the collective subconscious of humanity, the moment when Goddess Parvati bowed to mighty Shiva and addressed him with the following words:

"Om. Salutations O God, Lord of the Lords, Higher than the Highest, Teacher of the Universe,
O Benevolent one, O Great God, initiate me into the knowledge of the Guru.
O Lord! By which path can an embodied being become one with Brahman, the Absolute Reality?
Have compassion on me, O Lord! I bow to your feet."

And then Shiva answered, with words brimming with immense depth and Love:
"O Goddess, you are My very Self.
I speak out of My love for you.
This question, which is a boon to uplift the world,
Has not been asked before by anyone.

This knowledge is difficult to obtain in all the three worlds.
Listen, I will reveal it to you.
The Absolute is not different from the Guru.
This is the Truth, this is the Truth, O Beautiful One.

The ancient scriptures, religious books, texts of ancient legends, historical accounts,
and other writings; [...]
Without knowing the guru principle, people who engage in these are fools.

The Guru is not different from the conscious Self.
This is true, this is true, there is no doubt.
Therefore, a wise one should indeed make an effort to attain the Guru. [...]

He by whose light the true knowledge arises is known as 'Guru'.
The Guru who reveals THAT [...] who illuminates like the flame of the lamp,
The Guru whose feet are the visible form of the imperishable – one should meditate
on that all-pervasive, eternal Guru."

(Source: You Tube video "Shree Guru Gita"
with English translation, sung by Kumuda)

While all of this was happening in my inner space, Mohanji stood at the top overlooking all of us who had descended down to the Gauri Kund. I felt his presence and my heart melted as my mind acknowledged the miracle of everything that is happening in my life, all the unimaginable blessings... Indeed, the blessing of a physical presence of a Guru in the life of one who yearns for Liberation is truly the greatest blessing one can be granted in a lifetime.

In the midst of my bliss Sumit approached me with the most loving request – with endless devotion, he held the Prasad from Vaishnodevi temple in his hands and asked me to offer it to Goddess Parvati. He really touched my heart – what a beautiful gesture and what an honor it was for me to make that offering from one aspect of Mother Divine to another. All of us present prayed together. I prayed for the purity and selflessness of Mother Divine to become so deeply established in our hearts that nothing can ever taint it... The truth of the grand words "The Power of Purity" resonated in my being. We discussed later how it is indeed no coincidence that the first meditation that Mohanji received from the higher consciousness was not called The Power of Faith/Love/Surrender etc., but exactly the Power of Purity. When purity finds its throne in our hearts that is all that is required. We just need to maintain it and not allow anything impure to enter inside. Divine will do the rest...

The climb and the moment of transformation

When it was time to part from the Gauri Kund and the climb up the big stones started, I realized just how big of a challenge that was. Descending was fairly easy, but the climb was far from easy. After every couple of steps, I would have to stop and gasp for air in desperation.

My breathing was long and loud, resembling that of a lung cancer patient on a deathbed. It was extremely tough to do this, but I did not mind. It was worth it. With the loving help of Hein and the sherpa, I just went through the experience - totally empty, so filled with gratitude. This was, in a way, my penance in honor of the Mother and I was happy to do it. At one moment, I could feel a sort of a drizzle. It was not rain, but hail - very small pieces of ice suddenly started falling from the sky. I remembered Mohanji who always says how auspicious it is to experience rain after doing any pooja or offering to Divine. This beautiful hail meant that Goddess Parvati accepted our offering! My heart expanded instantly. After the next pause to catch the breath, I started climbing and suddenly realized that something had changed – as if touched by a magic wand, the hypoxia was removed from my system! I couldn't believe it! I could climb without any problem. What a miracle, what a blessing!

Sheer excitement overwhelmed me – I climbed the rest of the way with a big smile, and then blissfully continued the rest of the yatra by foot. (It was interesting to note from Monja's experience sharing that the same hail had the opposite effect on her and was the moment when she felt that the challenge of climbing the Dolma Pass was too much to bear – indeed, all of us had treaded the same path but had totally unique experiences, as per the divine drama created by Shiva for the purpose of our cleansing and elevation).

I continued the yatra with great joy and lightness.

I totally confused the man who owned the pony assigned to me. Knowing my condition till then, he approached me several times to ask whether I needed a pony, and I would always bow with a big smile and say 'No thank you'. Even if he spoke English, how could I possibly tell him: "I have been kissed by Divine. No further assistance needed." How could one ever find the right words for such an experience? Can anything come close to the experience of direct Divine intervention in one's life? These magical moments of immense blessing go straight into the soul's eternal treasure vault. They are reminders of the most revered inner Truth: "I am always loved for Love is what I truly Am."

Kailash with Mohanji 2016 – Inner Kora

The experience of Inner Kora in 2016 was completely different than the one in 2014. My life changed 360 degrees after the 2014 yatra – I left my office job and embraced the life of uncertainty but deep satisfaction as well, for I started living my dream by dedicating all my time to Yoga teaching, charity (ACT Foundation), Healing (Mai-Tri Healing, which just started at that time), our daughter Mila and all the work related to Mohanji's mission. I knew that the next Kailash Yatra would be yet another milestone in my life, because nobody leaves Kailash empty-handed.. This time I trained myself not to have any expectation whatsoever and just go with the flow. Some of us spent several days in Badrinath in order to acclimatize better and had many beautiful experiences before the yatra. I would like to share one profound experience that really stayed with me. I will do my best to put it into words.

It happened in the Pashupatinath temple in Nepal. I was hoping to be able to enter the temple this time since I have changed my name to Devi Mohan and have a certificate that proves that. However, that did not work and I joined the swamis from Skanda Vale and several other friends at one spot where we could see the entrance to the temple and do meditation. I could feel strong energy engulfing me and relaxed fully, diving into a deep meditative state. What happened next was somewhere between a vision and an astral experience. All I know is that I felt all of it very intensely. I had a vision of a person chanting Om Namah Shivaaya, with eyes in Shambhavi mudra (gazing upward towards third eye). Beautiful divine light could be seen and felt above that person's head. I was expanded and could feel and experience everything this person was experiencing because she was within me, i.e. myself as an observer and her as the object observation were one. Below her feet I could feel strange demonic flames which were something between flames and sticky tongues, resembling legs of an octopus. These 'flames' kept hitting the person all over the body, searching for a 'hook' on which they could catch its foothold in order to pull her down. But she kept chanting and looking upward towards the Divine light. They could not reach her. As the flames kept hitting, there was a moment when one samskara (a deep, painful impression stored within) popped out onto the surface in the area of the second chakra. For a fraction of a second, this impression caught the attention of that person and weakened her chanting. Even though this was very brief, it was enough for the hook to form. The next flame hit right there and made this impression bigger. The person kept paying more and more attention to this impression and the power of the fear/negativity soon grew to a point that she disconnected from the light above and got completely sucked into these demonic flames. The octopus sucked her in and she was gone! The sensation of pain and despair was strong . . .

At this point in time I came out of this experience and opened my eyes, but the impressions were still very strong. I have no idea how and why this experience came, but it was such a powerful message for me. I understood that at any crucial moment in life, when faced with duality of existence, it is us who choose where our attention will go and which side will win. No matter what happens one should never let the awareness drop and disconnect from the Divine Light. Just hold on and nothing lower can pull you down. One of the yatris, Swami Brahmananda from Skanda Vale ashram from UK, stood next to me while this was happening and noticed I was deeply moved by something. He hugged me and I cried, unable to say anything. This was the intro to my Kailash Yatra 2016.

A month or so before the trip, a friend of mine from Serbia gifted me the Serbian edition of a book called "U potrazi za Gradom Bogova – u predelima Šambale" ("In search of the City of

Gods – in the areas of Shamballa"), by Dr. Ernst Muldashev from Russia. This book brought a whole new perspective on Kailash, describing it as an ancient man-made complex of pyramidal structures called "City of Gods" built 850,000 years ago by a highly evolved civilization of that time, with an aim to take one through a process of spiritual awakening. I used every possible opportunity during the trip to read this amazing book. It left a deep impression on me, filled me with awe and added a completely new flavor to my second Kailash yatra experience. This time I saw and experienced Kailash in a completely different way.

When we starting walking the yatra, I noticed that my body handled hypoxia much better than during Kailash Yatra in 2014. Therefore, I could enjoy and observe the scenery around me far more clearly. I got really excited when I recognized some of the pyramidal structures that were described and depicted in Dr. Muldashev's book. There were right there, before my very eyes! My each step was a prayer to the Masters in Samadhi in the secret tunnels and ground around Kailash to bless me with the purity and emptiness which would bring me closer to them, closer to becoming a true instrument of Divine....

Dr. Muldashev said that all these structures were built in order to enhance the use and harmony of the 5 elements, the 5th being a pure human heart. In short, it all boils down to the "Power of Purity", the very first meditation Mohanji received telepathically in 2007. Purity of the heart and unconditional love that emanates from it is our true power that triggers the inner alchemy of Grace. Mohanji was saying the same thing from the very beginning. What a blessing it is to be on this path...

I would like to start my experience sharing of the Inner Kora by sharing some interesting images from this journey (taken by my phone and camera) with you, which were matching the illustrations I saw in the above-mentioned book by Dr. Muldashev.

During the first day of Inner Kora, I was overjoyed when I recognized the stone door to Shamballa (as per Dr. Muldashev, this is one of the doors to Shamballa, closed from within the mountain. The stone door can be opened only by those who have received the special mantra by the immortal Masters of Shamballa. It is big enough for a spacecraft to fly in).

What really touched me in Dr. Muldashev's book is the description of the small Kailash as the feminine part of Kailash, the most sacred part which corresponds to Kundalini. While the height of my experience during the yatra in 2014 was Gauri Kund, this time it was the constant inner pull towards the Small Kailash.

Dr. Muldashev described Small Kailash as a pyramid always covered with a 'white cap' (snow), regardless of the weather conditions and seasons. Even though Small Kailash is much smaller than the actual Kailash, energy-wise it is equally powerful and its nature is feminine. Small Kailash is like Mother Parvati seated on the lap of a mighty Shiva, always a bit lower than him, bowing to him in all humility.

As per Dr. Muldashev, the pyramid of Small Kailash is another portal to Shamballa. He said that a powerful Shantamani stone is kept inside the pyramid of Small Kailash. This stone is used by the Masters of Shamballa. It can strongly influence human mind and has a direct effect on Kundalini, which is why all precautions have been taken to ensure that it never gets into wrong hands. This is why Small Kailash has always been kept inaccessible from all sides and the beautiful white cap of Small Kailash is placed on a tall base which is impossible to access.

On top of that, I was overjoyed when I discovered another amazing structure that looked exactly like the illustration I saw in Dr. Muldashev's book – the laser beam base structure. He said that the advance civilization that built the City of Gods, created the structure that served the purpose of supporting a laser beam directed straight towards Small Kailash in case anyone who was not eligible attempted to reach it.

There are many other pyramidal, semi-pyramidal and other structures around Kailash, 108 in total, which serve different purposes. One of them is called "The Main Mirror of Time" and its purpose is to curve time and space.

One of the illustrations in Dr. Muldashev's book was especially interesting - that of a stone statue called "The man who reads." Dr.

The Mirror Called Kailash

Muldashev says that in the time of Lemuria (when the City of Gods was made), human beings were far more advanced spiritually. For example, they could read with their eyes closed, while gliding their palms over golden plates filled with knowledge and embibing that knowledge through the third eye. The illustration and image of "The man who reads" shows exactly that. This stone statue is clearly visible but, as per Dr. Muldashev, most of the time strange mist or fog conceals it so most people don't get to see it. He and his team were lucky to spot it. Whereabouts of this stone statue are not specified in his book simply because it is a very sacred place. Right below this stone statue, Masters in samadhi are buried deep in the soil in several layers and they are the protectors of all possible knowledge of our ancestors, our real history . . . Unfortunately, I did not see this stone statue but the story about it resonated deeply with me.

This is just a glimpse of a rich content of this book. Whether one chooses to believe Dr. Muldashev or not, whatever he has researched and proposed surely is intriguing. Deep within I feel it is true as the pyramidal and other structures all around Kailash surely do have unusal shapes and even the color and quality of the stone is different. All said and done, The City of Gods does sound like the right name for this sacred ground all around the sacred Kailash, the Crown of Mother Earth.

Charan Sparsh

After sharing the yatra experience with the first time yatris of Outer Kora, our Inner Kora started with the experience of Charan Sparsh – a trek to the point when one could touch the feet of Kailash. At this stage of yatra I was doing really great. Many people had various symptoms of hypoxia before and after Mansarovar and I was offering Mai-Tri Healing (healing method blessed by Mohanji just before Kailash yatra) to many of them, enjoying the supreme, extra warm and loving energy flowing through my body and palms. I felt so blessed and uplifted by this energy that I could perform the healing (that is, to be its instrument) for hours and hours at the time, without getting tired. Mai-Tri Healing suddenly appeared in my life and from the onset resonated with me very deeply. I could feel strange familiarity with it and could feel a new part of me being awakened. I have always felt that healing is my Dharma and am forever grateful to Mohanji on this sacred initiation and most precious gift of Grace.

All in all, when the trek to Charan Sparsh started, I was in awe and gratitude, bubbling with energy, cheerfully and steadily moving forward. When all of us reached the point of Charan Sparsh, a spontaneous decision came to go beyond the usual point, over a small hill and further towards Kailash. All agreed and we went ahead with the adventure. However, as we came to a point that somehow resembled a cradle (or a womb), at one moment Mohanji asked to play Shiva Kavacham and all of us sat for meditation. This was the time when I felt that a strange force literally glued me to the ground. I felt like a child in the lap of Kailash and simply witnessed what was happening within. Very soon a Divine essence of Amrit (nectar of immortality) overwhelmed my inner senses and pulled me into deep meditation. I was overwhelmed. At that moment some of the Inner Kora yatris opted to proceed further, to actually touch Kailash. Before I even got a chance to consider doing the same, strong pain appeared in my stomach, as if someone was stabbing me. I desperately searched for a body position which would ease the pain. It was almost as intense as contractions during labor. I was shocked and did not understand why this happened all of a sudden, but it was more than evident that I would not be proceeding with them. I surrendered to the inner guidance without any objection. It took me a while to relax again as the pain gradually reduced. Interestingly enough, Dr. Muldashev described almost identical experience at the location he called The Valley of Death. Surely a lot has been removed through this pain. After it was over, I felt very light, as if my body will start levitating any moment.

Before returning to our temporary accommodation, to celebrate this moment, I requested Raj Nair to click a photo of me doing Yoga (Parshvakonasana) at this ultimate location for any

The Mirror Called Kailash

Yogi(ni). It turned out that the hand flowed exactly towards the subtle crevice, pointing at the mighty Kailash.

The Crisis

The real challenges started happening on the second day of Inner Kora, when we were to climb the ice glacier in order to reach Kuber Kund. Hypoxia was getting stronger, appetite smaller and exertion far greater. During the long trek towards the ice glacier I suddenly felt that all the strength left me and that I simply could not proceed further. My feet were wobbly and overall I was getting dizzy. Mohanji was way ahead of me but he sensed that and stopped for a while, waiting for me seated on a big stone. I somehow reached him and fell at his feet. He pointed out that I made an egoistic comment the previous day about some of the participants who were not in shape, as I doubted such individuals would make it up the glacier. And now I was the one who could not proceed further. I immediately recognized the cunning traps of my ego and apologized for making silly judgements and assumptions. This was just like during last Kailash Yatra, as if I had to be reminded once again that physical fitness is not the main criterion on which the success of Kailash Yatra depends. It is Grace and Grace only, coupled with one's ability to surrender fully and transcend the body.

A sweet Sherpa was pushing me from the back when necessary to support my climb towards the glacier. After Mohanji blessed me and my ego got the blow it deserved, my strength slowly returned as I continued with the climb. This time the climb up the ice glacier was as tough as it could get. While using the rope to climb, each pull of the body up the glacier required a pause and minimum ten deep breaths in order to get enough oxygen to be able to proceed further. It was all taking a lot of time and the longer we waited, the weaker we got.

I decided to push myself to proceed as fast as I could, without taking any pauses to rest. Just as I thought the tough part with the rope and climbing of the glacier was over, an even tougher part came – a narrow steep passage through which we had to pass in order to climb to the top. This was simply agonizing. There were Sherpas helping us at each end of this crevice, but the exertion while doing this was so great that breathlessness was bordering panic and despair. After somehow passing that narrow passage, one would think some relief or easy patch would come – but no, it was just getting worse. Cold wind was blowing mercilessly through my thin jacket and there was nobody to direct me which way to go. The person behind me would probably take another hour to climb the glacier and I could not stand there on the cold wind. I felt completely lost. Finally, I saw two Sherpas, Mohanji and Rajesh, moving in my direction. Soon Vijay and Hanumatananda joined us as well. We were all in a state of semi-shock after surviving the climb and in one moment, as we looked towards Kailash, we saw an image in the rock that resembled eyes and a third eye from which a liquid was flowing. Mohanji said it is Amrit from the third eye of Shiva. This moment was indescribably sacred. Deep within I felt that something big and heavy is in the process of leaving my system, as if a subtle re-wiring is happening within me.

As it was already late afternoon, we had to hurry with the long trek towards our next accommodation. I was told we will have to walk down the hill onto a road which will keep curving and that our accommodation would be behind one of those curves. My Sherpa and I kept walking and many curves came, but as if caught in a nightmarish mirage, the final destination was nowhere on the radar. My Sherpa showed "2" with his fingers, but I didn't know whether this meant 2 hours, 2 kilometers or what. In the end, it took another 8 hours of totally exhausting walk, coupled with freezing in the cold wind and random hail before we reached our safe haven. I honestly have no idea how my body endured that ordeal. The exhaustion level was such that I barely managed to remove my trekking boots before crashing in the bed.

Revelations

The next day weather conditions worsened and we had to be transported to our slightly more decent accommodation in

Darchen. It felt great to get a hotel room again and feel the touch of white sheets on the body which finally got a decent bath. My legs got swollen and my body was undergoing strange sensations. Overall, I felt like a person who underwent an operation and is soon to be dismissed from the hospital. My body was yearning for rest, nourishment and recovery. But we were yet to go for the toughest part of the Inner Kora – the trek to the powerful Sapta Rishi cave. I opened a book in Russian language which some unusual Russian man whom we ran into the previous day gave me. Although he had nothing to do with Dr. Muldashev, he was also doing extensive research about Kailash and its secrets. I could not understand Russian fully but my eyes caught the part about Small Kailash. This man also figured out the connection between Small Kailash and Kundalini. He said that the Buddhists had a different name for Small Kailash and actual Kailash, but the division into feminine and masculine and parallel to Shakti and Shiva was the same. While contemplating about the sheer miracle of Kailash and the most profound play of Shiva and Shakti, suddenly something burst within me and I started to cry profusely. I had no idea why I was crying and sobbing, but I didn't want to suppress it. I just felt so deeply touched and so in awe of Divine that I couldn't hold back the tears. My face got all puffed, as if aiming to match the swollen legs. It was only later on, after returning to Serbia and visiting a friend of mine who has deep knowledge of energy meridians and main energy points of the body, that I got the confirmation that through this crying I released some heavy emotional trauma from the past which was stored in my subconscious. I felt endlessly grateful on this immense blessing.

In the end, the trek to Sapta Rishi cave had to be cancelled because 30 or so people died recently while aiming to reach Sapta Rishi cave and Chinese government would not issue permits. Besides, weather conditions worsened. I must admit that I was not too disappointed because deep inside I knew that my body was not ready for the blow of yet another super tough trek. Moreover, I knew that Sapta Rishi cave was in the vicinity of Small Kailash, which meant that only those who are ready for the full blown

Kundalini experience could go there. Since the path did not open, it was clear we were not ready – as simple as that. Sometimes it is important to admit what is beyond our limits...

Upon our return to Crown Plaza hotel in Nepal, I met another group of Kailash yatris whose Inner Kora was right after ours, only one day later. We engaged into a friendly conversation and I came to know from them that all they could do was Charan Sparsh, of course without going beyond the actual point of Charan Sparsh. Then the weather got worse so they had to finish the trek. The same happened to the group before us. The element of Mohanji's Grace thus surfaced in its full glory in my mind and heart as I understood how blessed we were to undergo the super tough trek to Kuber Kund and experience the most intense cleansing ever. The glass half full instead of glass half empty was evidently the lesson to be learned through this experience.

Whenever I see the majestic image of the South face of Kailash with Small Kailash/Shakti bowing to Shiva, I am reminded of the tears that cleansed me so deeply and endless awe I felt towards the unfathomable magnificence of Divine.

I have full faith that my Kundalini will find its way to reach its Kailash/Shiva when the time is right. Till then I remain in full surrender and gratitude to Mohanji and this beautiful Golden path.

I pray that I never take any of the blessings on this path for granted and always remain open for all that comes my way.

Reference:

U potrazi za Gradom Bogova – u predelima Šambale, Dr. Ernst Muldašev. Hema-Kheya-Neye, Beograd, 2009.

Kailash On The Wings Of The Master's Grace

- Rajesh Kamath -

KAILASH! To paraphrase Star Trek, it is the final frontier, a place where few men have ever gone before. Eight billion people on the planet and yet only a chosen few are privileged to undertake this amazing pilgrimage. And this privilege comes only through Grace. Nothing but Grace. The Grace of one's Master, the Grace of Lord Shiva, the Grace of the Guru Mandala (the Masters of the Tradition) and the Grace of our ancestors. It is this Grace that gets one an invite from Lord Shiva. It is this Grace that opens the doors to various experiences on the pilgrimage. It is this Grace that keeps one alive in the harshest of environments on this pilgrimage. It is this Grace that allows one to successfully complete the pilgrimage.

I have seen some pilgrims who feel that they are entitled to receive this Grace – wishful thinking that they are special in some way to deserve it. To mistake Grace with entitlement can only be termed as sheer ignorance and, without a shadow of doubt, ego and ingratitude of the highest order. I humbly seek to offer my experiences at the feet of Mohanji as an insignificant expression of my immense gratitude for all that He has done for me before I knew Him, from the point I came into contact till now and for the years to come.

By the Grace of Mohanji, I have been very fortunate to be on the Kailash pilgrimage twice – once in 2014 on the Outer Kora and once in 2016 on the Inner Kora. Like most Hindus, I had heard of the holy pilgrimage to Mount Kailash and Lake Mansarovar. Thanks to an amazing mythology attached to it wherein Lord Shiva stays atop this beautiful white snowy mountain in the middle of nowhere with His family and His army. It could as well be a fairy tale because not many even dream to undertake this pilgrimage unlike the Char Dham pilgrimage – a pilgrimage to the four holy sites in India widely revered by Hindus and considered highly sacred to visit at least once in one's lifetime. The Kailash Mansarovar is not even on anyone's radar, much less doing it. Even those that wistfully think about doing it feel that it is a pipe dream. And yet here I ended up doing a Kailash pilgrimage with a powerful Master a couple of months after vaguely thinking about doing it. If that is not Grace, what is?

Listening to a (now ex) colleague who had done the Kailash pilgrimages with the Chinmaya mission a couple of times, got me thinking about doing Kailash. I checked with his contact but they said that they did not have any pilgrimages planned and would get back to me if and when they do. Out of the blue, I received an SMS from the Mumbai Mohanji center that Mohanji would be in town. And guess the topic at the satsang when I entered the room – Mohanji asked Dhritiman (aka DB) to talk about his Kailash experience from 2013. At the end, DB mentioned that this year's pilgrimage would happen in four weeks at the end of that same month (July 2014). Talk about synchronicity! For me, it was like a huge flashing neon sign that I should do the Kailash pilgrimage with Mohanji.

Inspite of the last minute runup, the whole registration process was unusually smooth thanks to Sumit and the invisible grace of Mohanji. Someone canceled at the last minute opening a slot for me to join the group. The Chinese usually required the group permit to be applied a month or two before the pilgrimage (which would have ruled me out). However, that year, the Chinese delayed the group permit application process to just before the start of the pilgrimage. Finally, my mind started playing games. Do you really want to go to a pilgrimage where you don't know anyone? Wouldn't it be better to use the two weeks to do a bike trip to Leh-Ladakh (a holy grail for bikers to ride on the highest motorable road in the world)? Finally, better sense prevailed and I decided against the biking trip. So it was sheer grace that allowed me to participate in the pilgrimage.

Now onto the special moments of Grace on that trip. 2014 was a special year for the Kailash pilgrimage – the year of Dev Kumbh which comes once every 12 years. Dev Kumbh is special in that each Kora (circumambulation) counts as twelve. So for each Outer Kora, you get the benefit of doing twelve Outer Koras and equivalently the twelve whammy of transformation. As we will see later, this enabled me to qualify for the Inner Kora. So I "accidentally" ended up doing the Kailash pilgrimage during the best possible year. Amazing "accident" or infinite blessing? You decide.

I was expecting the group to be around 25-30 people. When I landed in Nepal, I found out that there were around 85 people from around 20 different countries. Such a diverse group with all the obvious differences of color, race, religion, culture, nationalities, etc. Yet, it felt like a special homecoming where long lost loved ones met after a long hiatus. It was an amazing group and, by the end of pilgrimage, they all seemed like family.

A landslide happened in the countryside the day we were supposed to leave Kathmandu. This took place exactly between Kathmandu and the Chinese border. The landslide broke a dam and almost 500 people died that night. The tour operators informed all Kailash groups that roads leading to the Friendship bridge had been devastated effectively cancelling the pilgrimage. No pilgrimage and the money paid would be forfeited. Mohanji told Sumit to find alternatives.Cancelling the trip was not a solution in Mohanji's tradition. Sumit acted quickly and took a decision, which was backed by Mohanji, to engage helicopters at an extra cost to pilgrims and fly over the impacted area to get to Kodari. After our last sortie, these helicopters were recalled back to assist with the emergency and were not available for general purpose usage. We literally made it through the skin of our teeth. Is this a sheer miracle? Remember, almost all pilgrims from other groups were still stranded in Kathmandu.

Back then in 2014, I smoked heavily. I made one feeble attempt to quit smoking in the afternoon at Pashupatinath but it was undone by the evening. Inspite of smoking heavily all the way through the pilgrimage in high altitude environments, I hardly faced any major mishaps save some teething acclimatization issues at Nyalam. The walk down from Dolmala pass was nothing short of an ordeal. One turn around the mountain led to another and then another and then a new mountain would appear and the scene would repeat all over again with no end in sight. I was stuck in an infinite loop like in the movie Groundhog Day. Mohanji once remarked to me, "You only think you walked Kailash. Someone walked through you." I have no choice but to completely agree. I know that if it had been left to me, I would never have completed the trek by myself. I zombie walked the whole way to Zuthulphuk. And this also happened partly on the last day (day 3) of the parikrama.

One highlight for me during the Kailash yatra was a deep anguish of being separated from the Divine that kept expressing itself several times at periodic intervals very strongly throughout the yatra. Like there is an awesome party happening in the neighborhood. You can hear the sounds and see the lights. And you want so badly to be there. But no one invited you and you don't know where it is happening so you can't gatecrash it. And you feel that they don't want you there. I felt a deep agony for the fall from grace that required me to be born on earth. I would sing devotional songs, be deeply moved to tears and call out to be taken back from whence I came though I have no clue where that was.

After the first day's trek, we reached Diraphuk which is the closest one gets to Mount Kailash on the Outer Kora. Mohanji wanted the priest to do a puja (ritual of worship) at Charan Sparsh (literally "touch the feet") – considered the feet of Mount Kailash located a 3-4 hour trek from Diraphuk. That year, the Chinese army were denying access to Charan Sparsh. A few members of our group went to request for permission. I didn't know it was Charan Sparsh and erroneously thought that we were going to the base of Mount Kailash. I stood by myself in front of Mount Kailash and strongly implored that I wanted to be let through and come closer (more like I deserved to). For some strange reason, I felt I was entitled to go there and touch Mount Kailash. I cried with a deep anguish both within and without. However, we were denied access. So we had to abandon the prospect of going there. It was not to be. I had deep feelings of betrayal and abandonment at that time. Like the Godfather "Fredo, you broke my heart" kind of let down. I still can't explain why I felt that way on that day. But the Master listens to all true cries of love and showers His grace to grant those wishes. This wish found fruition in my Kailash pilgrimage part deux in 2016. More on that later!

I remember the night vigils when we were staying right off the shores of the Manasarovar lake. We were told that divine beings come to take dips in the Mansarovar lake and appear to us as beautiful lights. Mohanji had warned us to watch and pray to them from a distance. He specifically asked us not to interact with them since their high energies could fry our nerves leaving us dead or worse in a vegetative state. Late in the night and in the wee hours of the morning, we would sit in groups just outside the gates of the compound and patiently wait for them to show up. And show up they did! Bright lights in multi-colored hues. They would radiate a bright luminous glow, increase or decrease in size, change colors, move in all directions – come closer or go farther, go up and down, left and right – flash on and off, come close to the surface and disappear for a while (presumably taking dips in the lake). You couldn't mistake them for anything else. In particular, I distinctly remember this group of three with one shining more brighter than the rest. They kept flashing in sequence and moving around as if dancing to unheard celestial music playing in the background. A truly blissful experience.

I got a first glimpse of the Master that was Mohanji. I was in awe of Him and maintained safe distance yet kept meandering close to Him. I was shadowing Him most of the way not really sure what was expected of me or what I expected of Him. I got to observe, first hand, some of the miraculous experiences like His face showing up on Mount Kailash complete with sunglasses and head dress. He told us, "Shiva is teasing me." Or when we were massaging his feet on Dolmala Pass, his thighs and calves became as hard as stone and he teasingly enquired if they were like Hanuman's (which they were!). In one of the stotras, Hanuman is referred to as Vajra deha Rudravatar. The avatar of Rudra (an aspect of Lord Shiva) whose body is as firm as vajra (the thunderbolt weapon of Lord Indra – the king of Gods).

Since I was a relative newbie to being around a real Master, I got acquainted for the first time with the different flavors of devotion to the Master. I observed public displays of fawning devotion from many pilgrims and naively took them to be real expressions of love. I felt sad that I lacked the deep devotion within myself compared to what I saw out there. A few months later, most of them disconnected from Mohanji for trifling reasons. They chose to weigh the words of others over the truth of their own experiences. I now realize that one's outward expressions are never a reliable measure of the depth of one's connection. However, some like Sumit who preferred to work silently in the shadows, left a deep impression and inspired me to dig deeper and achieve a greater degree of surrender.

The same goes for experiences shared by people at the end of the pilgrimage. Some pilgrims had amazing visions of Shiva and His family or other deities. Some pilgrims had reached a point of perfect peace, bliss, joy and other good-to-be-in states. Some were experiencing perfect stillness and silence. Some released a lot while others were feeling emptiness. Some had become enlightened (ok. nobody said that but you get the drift). I, for one, felt even more confused than I was before the pilgrimage. I now realize that experiences are just indicators given to seekers to suggest that they are headed in the right direction. Why they are given and the manner in which they are given have significance only to the seeker who is experiencing. Hence, it does not make sense to compare our progress based on other people's experiences. In some cases, the experiences are just elaborate illusions constructed by the mind to entertain itself. One's transformation is the only true metric of one's progress.

Life after Kailash was never the same. I attended the Rishikesh retreat later that year in December. Over the months, I had the grace to travel with Mohanji several times. I disappeared from office so regularly that people in my office started joking that I worked between vacations. Slowly but surely the spiral loop of my connection with Mohanji kept getting closer and closer. Exactly a year after Kailash, I decided to quit work, a day before my birthday, to be with Mohanji for good. The interesting part was it was a very natural process. Not easy but natural. Mohanji suggested that I continue for one more year before deciding but I had had enough by then and chose to cut the cord immediately. So the Kailash pilgrimage effected a major transformation in my life and set me firmly on the path. Hence, I have nothing but the highest respect for the Kailash pilgrimage. For me, the choice to do the Kailash pilgrimage is the clarion call that a spiritual seeker makes to indicate to the universe that he is done with playing games and is ready for the highest that evolution has to offer – total and complete liberation.

So cut to 2016 and the Mohanji team was organizing the Kailash pilgrimage again with both the Inner Kora and the Outer Kora tracks. Mohanji said that the Inner Kora was only allowed for pilgrims who had done at least 12 Outer Koras. Since doing 12 Outer Koras was a rarity, it implied that only those who did the 2014 Kailash pilgrimage would qualify, courtesy Dev Kumbh. Was it a fluke that I got to do the pilgrimage in 2014 or an act of immeasurable Grace? My eternal gratitude to Mohanji for bestowing His "chappar fadke" blessings on me (literally break the roof – shower so much that roof caves in). Mohanji only made an exception for Swami Brahmananda, the head of Skandavale Ashram in Wales. Mohanji said that Swamiji had the desired level of inner stillness. More than that, Mohanji was deeply impressed by his sincere and total devotion and dedication to his Guru. At the final count, we had 18 Inner Kora pilgrims and 66 Outer Kora pilgrims ready to undertake the pilgrimage.

As in the first episode, all kinks were ironed very smoothly before the start of the pilgrimage. Mohanji said that people cannot smoke in the Inner Kora. Lasting 14 days without smoking. A frightening prospect! In the past, I had been able to quit from several months to several years when I really wanted to but this time the habit was really rabid and I was at it with a vengeance. So quitting was a non-starter as far as I was concerned. But this is a story of Mohanji's unfathomable grace. So I ended up kicking the habit a month before the pilgrimage. Without a shadow of doubt, it was all His doing. But as is His characteristic low key style, it all happened imperceptibly without a seeming trace of His involvement. People and situations came together in perfect synchronicity to help me quit the habit. Same with my passport renewal. My passport was expiring that year right around the pilgrimage dates. The last time I got the passport renewed was a painful grating experience. But this time round, all the wheels were well oiled and it was smooth sailing.

Given the physically demanding nature of the Inner Kora, Mohanji planned a trip to Badrinath for acclimatization to prepare our group for the Kailash Inner Kora pilgrimage. As with all trips wth Mohanji, it was an amazing adventurous journey to visit Lord Vishnu's abode before visiting Lord Shiva's abode. It had significant moments of peril through the journey that were safely navigated thanks to the overwhelming protection offered for being in the shadow of the Master. In any case, I will leave the details of the Badrinath pilgrimage for a later day.

We arrived in Nepal and did the customary ritual of visiting Pashupatinath and Budhanilkantha Temple for taking the blessings of Lord Shiva and Vishnu respectively before undertaking the Kailash pilgrimage. The Rawal (chief priest) of Pashupatinath honored Mohanji and gave him a mala that was wrapped around the Shiva Linga. He also asked Mohanji to come back with water from the holy Manasarovar lake and he would do an abhishekam (ritual bathing) of the Shiva Linga.

Then, we proceeded to fly down to Nepalgunj and from there proceed to Simikot using domestic flights and then Hilsa by helicopter. From Hilsa, we crossed the Karnali bridge and finished with the immigration formalities at the Chinese border. We then drove to to Purang (Taklakot) where we had a day of acclimatization and were treated to an amazing satsang with Mohanji supplemented with talks from Devi. From Purang, we drove down to Rakshas Tal (the lake of the demons) and from there we drove down to the holy Lake Manasarovar. We drove along the shores of the lake to find a relatively secluded and clean spot that would be allow the entire group to alight, settle down and take dips.

The serene blue crystal waters with the backdrop of the majestic mountains including Mount Kailash against the amazing Tibetan landscape is a sight to behold. Mohanji has mentioned that pilgrims are considered to have completed the Kailash pilgrimage when they take a dip in the holy Manasarovar lake and have a view of Mount Kailash. The Koras (outer and inner) are optional penance that a pilgrim can choose to undertake. We found our positions by the shore and quickly got ready to take the dips. The water was unbelievably freezing. I have a decent tolerance for cold but this time the water was really mindnumbingly cold. Mohanji went in first and offered his prayers to Lord Kailash and took his dips. We had the ultimate privilege to do an abhishekam on Mohanji with the holy water of the Manasarovar lake in the presence of Kailash and to take His blessings before proceeding to do our own dips. I proceeded along with Sumit a bit deeper into the waters to take the dips. The river bottom in Manasarovar is soft and spongy and Mohanji had once mentioned that it is the body of Adi Shesha coiled around the lake.

Off the billions that have walked the earth, only a miniscule few have had the blessings of doing the Kailash pilgrimage. It is only an act of immeasurable grace that allows one to reach a place like Kailash. And this grace pours in from many sources – primarily starting with one's Master, the Guru Mandala (the Masters of the Tradition), the lineage, the best wishes of friends and family, etc. And it behooves every pilgrim to acknowledge that grace and express their gratitude by offering their most humble prayers on behalf of all these beings – known and unknown across dimensions, realms, time, space, etc. Mohanji had taught us to take 3 dips – one for the self, one for our ancestors and one for the Gurus – and then to offer dips to whoever we wanted. I took the 3 dips and then proceeded to take dips on behalf of family, friends, Masters and whoever I could think of. When I finished with the known, I decided to take 108 dips dedicated to Mohanji as an offering to all the unknown beings whom I needed to offer gratitude. As I went through with it, the cold water had literally frozen my brains. It was really hard to keep track of the count so I finally ditched the counting and just continued to do as many as I could. Standing next to me, Sumit was doing the same.

At some point, we both decided that we were done and headed back to the shores. As I got out of the water, my teeth were chattering involuntarily and I was violently shivering. The chill had hit all the way to the bones. I somehow managed to get into the warm clothes and just lay down for a while to feel my body. It didn't help much and I decided to walk a bit. Mohanji came out of nowhere and gave me a bear hug and I felt a whole lot better after that. He took the sting of the cold away and made it more manageable. After the dips, we headed to our bus and proceeded to Darchen.

The next morning, we left for Yama Dwar (the gates of Yama - the Lord of Death) which is the starting point of the Kora. It is a symbolic expression of the pilgrims' intention to be ready to leave everything behind as one does in death and start a new life towards greater freedom as they start the Kora. The ritual at Yama Dwar is symbolic of the above – where the pilgrims circumambulate the Yama Dwar thrice, enter Yama Dwar, leave something on their person behind, ring the bell and walk over to the other side without looking back. A beautiful ritual with a deep symbolism of dropping all that is not freedom before entering the holy land of Kailash.

The porters and the ponies and their handlers are a very important part of the Kailash pilgrimage experience. Mohanji says that not all of them are human and many are Shiva Ganas (members of Shiva's army). They tend to aggravate or smoothen the experience based on what Lord Shiva has planned for you on the pilgrimage. My porter in 2014 was mostly a no show. He and my bag made guest appearances once in a while but chose to keep out of the proceedings for most of the pilgrimage. But Lord Shiva and Mohanji either provide for their own or help sustain you beyond the suffering of doing without water, food, etc. This year looked to be (and was) similar and I got a porter who was in high spirits (reeking of alcohol :-)) Anyways, I didn't think too much of it and handed him my bag and tried to keep pace with Mohanji who was on a pony. Sumit got Him one for the first day to allow Him a bit of comfort. In any case, He was carrying 85 people through the pilgrimage. Very soon, we were joined by Nameshri on her pony. I was able to maintain a good pace and my porter was either too fast or too slow. But with the grace of Mohanji, I never had issues with water or food because it would find it's way to me when I needed it.

After a while, I began to slow down and gradually my pace was getting worse by the hour. I was slowly losing steam and came to a point where every step seemed like an eternity. I had read the disclaimers on how hard the Inner Kora was compared to the Outer Kora. And this was the first day of the Outer Kora which was supposedly the easiest. This was not supposed to happen. Not part of the plan. What in God's name was going on? If this was my condition on Day 1, what would happen on the Inner Kora? All these questions ran through my mind. I was devastated but at the same time I had to somehow complete day 1. I was drained mentally and physically. My body and mind were loathing the drudgery of every step. Slowly and slowly, I kept chugging along. Ashtamoorthy showed up along the way and he sensed that I wasn't doing well and provided me silent moral support. He walked behind me, walking when I walked and stopping when I stopped. He would offer me water, food and a few kind words of support now and then. It was as if Mohanji had sent him specifically to see me through this ordeal. The ego of having walked the Outer Kora in 2014, inspite of smoking heavily before and throughout the pilgrimage, was blasted to smithereens. Mohanji words flashed through my mind, "You only think you walked Kailash. Someone walked through you." That became obvious to me as the fact that it was only an act of compassionate grace that helped me complete it.

In any case, the realization helped me get to the point where I felt that this too shall pass.

Eventually, we stopped at a place where there was a direct view of the West face of Kailash. Madhusudan came around the same time and commented, "Nothing can prepare you for this." Coming from a person who runs 5-6 half marathons a year at a good clip made me feel better that I wasn't the only one struggling. I was in no hurry to reach the destination and sat down on a stone and gazed at Kailash. As I looked at it longingly, I forgot the pain for a moment and was happy to just be there. Tears flowed down my cheeks as I expressed gratitude to Lord Shiva and Mohanji for allowing me into these hallowed lands. I soaked in the feeling of being one with this space. Finally, I got up and slowly started walking and finally managed to reach our camp at Diraphuk. Once I had recovered, I located Ashtamoorthy and thanked him. He had tears in his eyes and I hugged him. But for him, I am not sure if I would have completed Day 1. I stood out of our camp building and gazed at the majestic North face of Kailash. This is the closest you can get to Kailash on the Outer Kora. I wondered if Day 1 which was supposedly the easiest was so tough, I shuddered to think what Day 2 would bring? I just decided to be in the now and sleep it off and worry about it tomorrow.

At Darchen, Sumit had told us that Prahalad (our lead guide) and Amar (one of the main sherpas) had actually touched the holy Kailash mountain and things were never the same for them again. In their whole history, no one from their groups had ever touched Kailash but they thought it would be tough but doable. He was very excited at this discovery and said that we will attempt and surely succceed at this task with Mohanji's grace. He repeated the oft-quoted chant from MahaKaaleshwar, one of the twelve Jyotirlings. "Akaal mryutyu se woh maray jo kaam kare chandaal ka, Kaal uska kya kare jo bhakta ho Mahakaal ka" (They die an untimely death who do the work of the devil, but even Time is helpless before a devotee of Mahakaal (Lord Shiva)?").

When I woke up, my body was tired and aching but thankfully no major pains and sprains. I had no idea what lay in store for us except that it would be way harder than anything we had done before on the Outer Kora. Not a very comforting thought. Today was an excursion to Charan Sparsh and a closeup view of the North Face of Kailash. We first bid adieu to the Outer Kora team early in the morning and left around 9:00am. The trek was steep and tedious but I was walking on autopilot only following Mohanji. The walk was amazing with the imposing view of the North face of Kailash in the distance. It looked so close that you felt you could just reach the base of the mountain anytime. Soon we reached Charan Sparsh after walking for 3-4 hours. We bowed down and paid our respects. But especially after Sumit's "discovery", some of us had decided along the way that we would attempt to go higher and touch the holy Kailash mountain. So this was just a pit stop for us and not the final destination.

Prahalad and Amar had climbed further up the glacier from Charan Sparsh to get a better view. They had used cloth tied together as a makeshift rope and Mohanji immediately climbed up using the rope and their help. They hadn't expected that Mohanji would climb up or the entire group to follow Mohanji and climb up. Now that we had all crossed Charan Sparsh, we all started walking in the direction of the holy Kailash mountain. Along the way, Mohanji would ask the group to stop and ask Phaneender to sing the powerful Siddha Mangala Stotram of Shripad Shrivallabh before proceeding. Finally after a couple of hours of walking, we came up a high point where Mohanji sat down and asked us to play the Shiva Kavacham. It was a divine experience listening to Shiva Kavacham with Mohanji in front of the holy Kailash mountain. Mohanji was looking intensely at Mount Kailash as if securing Lord Shiva's protection for our group. After chanting the ultimate protection of Shiva mantras, Mohanji got up and sat on a rock. Mohanji then told the group that whoever wanted to touch the Kailash mountain could proceed from here. He had created a protective cover around all of us with the Kavacham and then sat down watching over all of us. I took his blessings and set out towards the mountain.

There was a chasm across the glacier ahead with a boulder over the icy stream below bridging the chasm. To proceed, we had to climb over a slope, jump onto the rock and then reach out and pull ourselves up on the other side. The Swamis from Skandavale and Sumit crossed over first followed by me. It seemed quite simple until after we crossed over. The trail is always easy for the first few because of the rock covering the ice. Once the first few cross over, the rock gives way to ice which makes it slippery and difficult. When DB tried to cross over, he slipped and almost fell into the chasm but was pulled in time by Sumit and the sherpa. Next was Vijay bhai. He slipped as well and was pulled back in the nick of time perched even more perilously literally inches from the edge of the chasm. Both DB and Vijay bhai were literally snatched from the claws of death solely by the grace of Mohanji. They were reborn right there.

We were instructing people on how to cross over but the two near-death episodes weighed on people's minds. Hanumatananda was the only one to make it across and that too because of his firm belief in the Master. People from the group called out to him that it was too dangerous to cross. His reply! "Mohanji said I can go. So I will go." Pure trust and faith with complete surrender. He threw his walking stick on the rock and just jumped. On the rock, he was calling out to Mohanji to join him. When he realized that Mohanji would not be joining, he climbed up over the other side by himself. Mohanji couldn't join us because He was sitting on the stone chanting mantras to stabilise everybody. If Mohanji got up, others would fall. In this holy land, an act of faith and surrender is all the protection one needs to tide over all issues. By that time, it was quite obvious that this route could not be used by others. We sadly looked at the group that was stuck on the other side and decided to continue on our journey ahead. I then noticed Raj Nair walking up another route up ahead trying to chart out a different route. I was really inspired that people were not giving up and were trying with full faith inspite of the seeming adversity.

Since there was nothing that we could do for the group behind, we proceeded towards the holy mountain. Kailash looked so majestic and imposing and was beckoning us to come closer. The entire landscape was a beautiful combination of white and black. There were streams of water flowing through the glacier at regular points. This was the Kailash Ganga flowing through the matted locks personified by the rocky structures of the Kailash – the representation of Shiva. This is the water that we were drinking all the way from Charan Sparsh. The initial euphoria of getting an opportunity to touch Kailash soon gave way to the dread at the enormity of the task that lay ahead. We had already been walking for 5 hours and clearly there was way more to go. And fatigue had started to set in. Gradually, the distance between me and Sumit and between Sumit and the Swamis was increasing. I could see them in the distance inspiring me to keep going and at the same time worrying me about the distance that was left to be covered. The mountain looked so close but that was a mirage. As much as I walked, it seemed that there was still just as much to go.

After a point, the body just gave up to a higher power and I was walking on autopilot chanting "Om Namaha Shivaaya, Shivaaya Namaha Om" all the time. Somewhere my mind had made a contract that I would either go all the way or die trying. After all dying on Kailash was an immense blessing too. The pain was there but I had no thought of stopping or giving up. It didn't matter how far it was or how long I had to walk. I just kept going. I could see tiny figures of Sumit, Prahalad, Amar and the Swamis walking up ahead in the distance. The rocky surface gave way to an icy surface that was covered with numerous tiny streams that had to be crossed. It was getting more slippery and I kept sliding and falling down every now and then with regularity. My hands and body were getting bruised. But it did not matter. I just kept trudging along.

The icy surface then gave way to the final snowy patch that separated me from Kailash. Herein was the tricky part. A snowy glacier looks benign but can be very dangerous. Beneath the snow could be a rock or a crevasse. In the absence of any mountaineering expertise, the only way to find out what lies underneath is to step on it. That is the Russian roulette method of walking on a glacier and, for obvious reasons, it did not appeal to me. So I decided to surrender to the Master and follow in the footsteps of those that went before me. I have read that parts of the glacier can be very fragile and even the slightest rumble can have unexpected results. Further, this area does not receive any footfalls and is virgin in the truest sense. Hence, I tread as lightly as possible, tracing the footsteps in the snow, to avoid setting any unexpected activity on the glacier in motion that would jeopardize my safety.

From within, I had a strong feeling to take off all my clothes and embrace the mountain like I was within the mother's womb with nothing separating us. That was my natural expression of oneness with Kailash. I knew it was the final lap and my heart raced a beat. I could see our brothers in the distance standing near the mountain. Finally, I reached the spot close to the mountain. A short distance away was the short snowy ledge that connected the glacier to the mountain with crevasses on both sides. Sumit came close to where I was and asked me to stay back and wait till the others got off the ledge and walk back to where I was. He was concerned that it may not hold our weight. I waited my turn and finally had the whole place all to myself. I walked up to the ledge and proceeded to take off my jacket, tshirt, thermals, etc. By the time I got the upper body bare, DB showed up on the ledge. With my clothes on the ledge, there was just a little bit of room left for him to walk. So there was no room left for me to take off the rest of my clothes so I decided to leave my lower body covered and proceeded to touch Kailash. The moment that I had begged for two years ago was finally granted. It is a moment that will be etched for me for eternity. Yet, I can't think of how to write about this moment.

A "chance" meeting with Mohanji almost 2 years back and here I was embracing Kailash with my bare body. How can I express gratitude properly when I don't even know the full extent of the blessings that were showered on me? The holy Kailash knows. Mohanji knows. I only know that I won't do justice to that sentiment of gratitude so I won't even try to put it in words. To paraphrase Sri Yukteshwar's words from the Autobiography of a Yogi, "I choose not to bring out into the cold realms of speech the warm sentiments best guarded by the wordless heart." Deep within, I know I did not do anything. In the truest sense, I know that I had nothing to do with the outcome. And I would like to point out here that this is not to be mistaken with humility. It is perfect understanding that this was not humanly possible for me but was accomplished because of the sankalpa (intention) of my Master, Mohanji, who chose to grace me with this moment. It happened through me through the Grace of Mohanji. As Mohanji said, "Someone walked through you." Never more true. Hence, my only prayer is to be rid of the ego stored in the deep recesses of my mind that expresses doership or pride at the achievement.

From there, we retraced our steps back to Diraphuk. The walk back to the camp was really mind numbing. We walked back the snowy, icy and rocky patches. On our way back, we met the next group of Vijay bhai, Hanumatananda, Spomenka, Chai, etc. Finally, we seem to have lost our way and started heading in the general direction of the camp. Swami Govinda and I were together with Swamiji leading the way. He was Columbus the explorer leading us through uncharted terrain and unexplored territory. And like Columbus, he first ended up going to the Caribbean before he found the the route to India. A never ending walk up and down boulders and rocks. We finally made our way back to the camp after a long long long walk.

The next day, the body fared no better. The fatigue of the previous day was still there. I did not feel up to the task that lay ahead. Some part of me just wanted to give up and go home. But that wasn't an option. In such circumstances, the ego can be a good thing because it does not let you give up and suffer embarassment. We started walking uphill. The road was winding upwards and it was a long way up. At the very top of the mountain, I could a small cave at the top. There were mountains behind this one but I assumed that the cave must be our destination. I shuddered to think of how far up it was and then followed the time tested method of taking it one step at a time. My pace had slowed down to a trickle and I was lagging behind with Hanumatananda behind me. Hanumatananda was struggling with a swollen foot. I chanted and walked and walked and chanted until we reached a level space adjoining the cave. Devi, Spomenka and a few others checked out the cave and felt the energy in the cave was amazing. That is when I realized that there was another mountain behind this one where we could see tiny specks of people climbing up ahead. When I looked more closely, I realized that there was a snowy/rocky patch above the top of that mountain where I could see more tiny specks. Finally, there was an steep rock face which led to the very top which looked like the very top. And that was where we were supposed to go. My heart sank. I could not even begin to imagine how I could end up there. And the party had just started.

We met a veteran Russian climber, Alexey V. Perchukov, who had traversed these places for a long time and written a book on the Kailash Mandala. He happened to bump into us and remarked "I never seen these terrains so tough. I have never required a rope to climb these mountains." I continued walking one step at a time without thinking too much about the distance that left to be covered. After an excruciatingly tough trek, we finally reached the snowy/rocky patch. Prahalad and the Sherpas had setup the ropes to take us past this snowy/rocky patch. Towards our left, the mountain was slightly unstable and rocks were falling off to where we were sitting and along the route we were supposed to take. The rocks were flying off from high up the mountain on the left so even a small stone could become a fast moving projectile that could injure us seriously. To our right was a steep fall on a cluster of big jagged rocks. In Mohanji's words, "If you slipped and fell, you would not look very pretty." Finally, to add to the drama, the people walking ahead of us were releasing a fresh shower of rocks from the mountain in front of us. We were all sitting almost one behind the other and waiting our turn to walk up the patch. I was sitting with Hanumatananda next to me and Mohanji, Devi, Phaneender, Jayeeta, Mitesh, Chai behind me. Phaneender was a bit concerned about his safety. Mohanji told him point blank, "You have fear because you don't have full trust in me. If you trust in me fully, it is my responsibility to safely take you across." I wedged my shoe against a thin sliver of ice to lock myself in position. After a while, I had a feeling that the friction would make the ice melt. I called out to Prahalad that if this sliver melts, I would go down the hill taking Hanumatananda with me. Prahalad ignored in the beginning so I frantically called out to him again and showed him where my foot was propped. He agreed and asked me to climb up next using the ropes.

As I mentioned earlier, each person walking up the patch gets some of the rock off the surface with his shoes and exposes more of the ice underneath. So it becomes increasingly slippery for each successive person. I hooked my harness to the ropes and started climbing up. You had to pull yourself up using the strength of your hands and lock yourself in. Then you start all over again until you reach the promised land. Initially, the climb was fine. It was taking a bit of effort and energy but I was moving. Then I reached a point where there was mostly ice underneath. This was where my motion resembled one of the characters in children's cartoons – I was moving very fast but not moving ahead. Almost like walking swiftly in place. My energy was sapping really fast and my hands were getting tired. Finally at the midway point, the sherpas asked me to unhook the harness off the rope that was holding my weight, hook it on the another set of ropes that were a few metres away and set the locking mechanism in place properly so the harness does not come off and send me sliding and falling off the hill. I was stunned. I was supposed to be free myself of the only thing keeping me from falling off the patch. I had stand without any support because I had to walk towards the other rope. Further, I couldn't use my hands for support because I had to use both hands to set the locking mechanism on the harness. And I had to do this when I had barely any energy left and with rocks falling around me. Super! A perfect test of faith. I mentally affirmed, "Jai Mohanji", unhooked the harness, calmly walked over to the other rope and hooked myself in. It went like clockwork with the Master sitting and watching below. From there on, I really struggled to pull myself up. It didn't help that I had the sherpas shouting at me to move faster. I had to really dig in and use every last ounce of strength to get myself to the top. When I reached the top, I just collapsed with my back on the rock. My heart was pumping and I was gasping for breath. I just couldn't breathe and the sherpa was pushing me to get off and move forward. I just pushed him off and opened my jacket, tshirt, etc to free my lungs and get some air in. Mohanji later told us that you have to die to enter the durbar of Shiva. It really felt like I was dying at that spot. Once I recovered my breath, I got up to start moving forward. I was invited by a very narrow ledge just enough to get one foot in with no support except for crumbling rock on one side and a straight fall down the other. And to top it, it was winding.

I walked as quickly as I could and got to a huge open plateau where I saw our group standing – the Swamis, Sumit, DB, etc. Imagine my dismay when I saw Kuber Kund far ahead in the distance below. We would have to walk a distance almost equal to what we had traveled so far to get there. The plateau, as Mohanji explained later, was Shiva's durbaar (court) where millions of highly evolved beings lie in wait of a glimpse of Shiva. The wind was blowing very strongly through the plateau and it was very chilly (cold). Further, there was hardly any protection from the wind. Hence, it was hard to stay up there for long. The group had a discussion and felt that it did not make sense to wait there. They assessed that it would take some time for the whole group to get to the top since almost half the group was down below and the movement was getting slower due to the slippery icy surface. It was suggested that we should proceed quickly to Kuber Kund and everyone agreed. I felt that it was Mohanji who was working hard down there to ensure our safety. Proceeding onwards to Kuber Kund without Him did not seem right to me. There were some explanations going back and forth but I did not want to budge. At the same time, that was my personal belief and I did not want to dissuade anyone nor argue. So I quietly moved out and took a position behind some rocks that provided minimal relief against the biting wind. A few people called out to me to come along but I pretended to be asleep and just dug in.

I continued chanting to take my mind off the biting cold. Slowly, people started coming up one by one and finally Mohanji came in after Devi. Devi was really struggling that day so Mohanji was watching over her to get her up to this point. Phaneender and

Jayeeta were the only ones left below. Mohanji chose to lie down on the plateau. His head, ears and mouth were covered with a balaclava. He was in deep communion when he got up suddenly and opened the balaclava. A stone magically appeared in His mouth. He had a communion with the beings in Shiva's durbaar. As if on cue, we found a stone right next to Him which was in the shape of a blessing palm. The stone had a smaller palm shape inlaid inside the bigger palm shape. Like a combined blessing from Shiva and Shakti. Mohanji told us this place has millions of beings in deep communion with the Lord. We are actually sitting, standing or walking over them. They do not take offense because they think of us akin to little children ignorantly stepping on them. But we are not supposed to be stay on the plateau for long.

At this point, it was getting dark. Mohanji took the advice of Sherpas and decided to give Kuber Kund a skip and suggested that we head back to our destination for the night at Zuthulphuk. The road leading below was very steep and we were literally sliding as we were walking downhill. I was holding Mohanji and assisting Him and I observed that His hand and body had no weight. It was as if it just had the weight of the soul. It was a long walk back and most of us were very fatigued. The beautiful mountains were in the shape of various deities – Lord Ganesha, Lord Hanuman, etc. We were blessed to witness the abhishek of Lord Shiva up in the mountain ahead. Two half closed eyes clearly visible with the white milky snow falling as an abhishek to Him. Then we saw nectar clearly dripping from His third eye. It was an amazing sight. As we walked further, there was a shower of tiny hailstones. They were unusually small almost like akshata (uncooked rice grains that are showered on people as blessings). Mohanji told us that this was a real blessing and asked us to open our mouths and let whatever falls fall in. In India, rice coated with turmeric is sprinkled on the heads of people as a sign of auspiciousness, prosperity, good luck and blessing. Here, the ice pieces looking exactly like vermillion rice were sprinkled on all of us by the invisible divine beings of Kailash. Perfect blessings! What more can one ask for?

Soon we were joined in by the group that had set out for Kuber

Kund. Sumit had a bottle of water from Kuber Kund and offered it to Mohanji. Mohanji had some and offered it to the rest of us who couldn't go there. So we were also blessed to have the holy water of Kuber Kund. Coming down was also a very long walk which literally took hours. Sumit then went off and somehow managed to get Mohanji a jeep to avoid having him walk the entire distance back. Some people went with Mohanji. The rest of our group kept walking in the beautiful moonlight for the better part of the night and reached Zuthulphuk almost past midnight. I would like to end my experience sharing here. Of course, a lot of things happened after the last day of our Kora till the day we reached Kathmandu. And a lot of events happened in between as well that I may have glossed over. But I feel that they are not as important in my opinion to share with people.

For me, Kailash was a pilgrimage like no other. What happened at Kailash was just the tip of the iceberg. The transformation juggernaut that it set in motion has unravelled and will unravel slowly with time. Such a wonderful journey replete with experiences and learnings. Some part of me came alive there, some part of me died there. This was probably one of the hardest spiritual trips that I have done and, yet at the same time, one of the easiest as well because I did not do anything. The one underlying message from this whole pilgrimage was that everything is facilitated by Grace. Grace moves mountains. Grace is powered by eligibility which can only come through faith and surrender. And gratitude is the only thing that one can offer in return. So with all humility, I offer my deepest and heartfelt gratitude to Brahmarishi Mohanji for being the wind beneath my wings that helps me soar towards complete and total freedom and liberation. I offer my fervent prayer that I have the strength to cling onto the tail of the tornado - ready to go wherever it takes me, lose whatever I need to in its wake and allow it to power me towards liberation.

Pilgrimage To Mount Kailash

- Swami Brahmananda -

Editor's note: *Swami Karunananda, Swami Govindananda and Swami Brahmananda are from Skanda Vale, a Multi Faith ashram and monastery founded by Guru Sri Subramanium in Carmarthenshire, south-west Wales. Recently they had the chance of a lifetime to spend a few weeks in the Himalayas on a pilgrimage to Mount Kailash, the sacred abode of Lord Shiva, with Mohanji.*

According to tradition, one is eligible to walk the the Inner Kora only on completion of 12 parikramas of the Outer Kora. The Yatra to Kailash Manasarovar in 2014 was very significant as a parikrama during that year was equivalent to completing 12 parikramas. It was called the year of Dev Kumbh. Swami Brahmananda, the head of Skandavale Ashram, was specially permitted by Mohanji to be a part of the Inner Kora in 2016 despite not competing 12 parikramas. Mohanji said that the Swamiji had the desired level of inner stillness and was deeply impressed by his sincere and total devotion and dedication to his Guru.

Bathing in the Ganges at Devprayag

We started in the morning to take a dip in the confluence of two rivers, where it forms the Ganges, so you have two rivers coming together, *Alaknanda and Bhagirathi*.

Somebody had advised Mohanji on the way, and emphasized

how important it was that we got in the river at that point. We stopped there, and it was an extraordinary experience. Mohanji had been talking about the Ganges . . . the fact that it's a river, but it's also a celestial river. And that was our experience of it. I felt a tremendous Shakti associated with getting into that water. They have a metal railing where you can actually immerse yourself in the point where the two rivers are coming together.

We went in there, and each time I immersed myself in the Ganges I could feel my thoughts and my prayers really just being drawn out of self, in this really powerful way.

I felt that every prayer that we offered there was received absolutely and fully. It was a phenomenal experience. The whole river, whilst you're underwater, appeared to be full of blue light. It all sounds pretty cosmic doesn't it?!

Visit to Vashistha Cave

That was an amazing experience . . . and then we moved on after everyone had their baths, and we had an opportunity to go to the cave where Sage Vashistha meditated, where he lived.

He was Rama's guru and preceptor many thousands of years ago and since then a lot of great avatars and saints have used that cave as a place to meditate. And now it's protected as a little ashram by a very elderly Swami called Swami *Chaitanyananda* and we had an opportunity to meet this swami. He's now around 84 years, and it was an amazing boon to sit there in the room with him. He doesn't speak very much, and he doesn't move around a great deal.

He has a great rapport with Mohanji. Apparently he's usually very severe, serious and very intolerant. He upholds the discipline in that place, because he cares deeply about that cave, and he never wants the energy in that cave to be desecrated in any way. But when we had visited him he was very congenial and in a jovial mood. He allowed everyone to have their photos taken with him and he spent time with us. Although we couldn't converse very openly with him, it felt just overwhelming to be in the presence of this great soul. What a great man, what a great soul, to actually have that privilege was remarkable and humbling.

The sacred lineages of Skanda Vale & Vashistha Cave

One more interesting and important detail emerged during our meeting with Swami Chaitanyananda and looking at the photos in his book. His Guru was Swami Purushottamananda Maharaja and his Guru was our Guru *"Guru Sri Subramanium"* in his previous incarnation.

So that would be Swami Brahmananda *of the Ramakrishna Mission* as Guru's previous birth. Having pieced it all together we realized this, after we'd spoken to the Swami, and it was an extraordinary feeling of these Divine lineages coming full circle.

We realised the interconnectedness of our lineage in Skanda Vale, and that lineage which is pulsating here, throughout the Himalayas. The reality that we are this big Divine family and actually the operative force that is happening, governing our lives, is God is very humbling and very exciting when you feel that unfolding process taking place.

We then had another bath in the Ganges, and everybody sort of bathed each other in the end it would have looked quite funny if you weren't part of it. That was very refreshing. Then we went to sit in the cave and meditate in there. They also had, in the end of the cave, a Shiva Lingam – so we were also allowed to do abishekam to the Shiva Lingam and it was just thick with this amazing stillness and power. It felt like you could kind of spoon it out of the air and put it in a container and take it away, if you had such a thing.

It's very difficult to assimilate the whole experience now, but you come out of that cave not the same person that you went into it. And that was again an amazing blessing and privilege to be able to go in there and perform that pooja.

Spending time with Mohanji

Apart from that, just travelling around with Mohanji has been quite an experience, because you see just how dynamically he's works... continuously. You ask him something... a small detail, a small question, and he'll immediately act on it and resolve the problem. That's the way he's serving God in this really articulate, functional, disciplined useful way. It's a brilliant example to follow. There's a lot to learn from him, and it's been a massive privilege to spend that time with him.

Om Namah Shivaya!

We had embarked on the path Mohanji has been telling us that the only protection we have got really here, the only thing you can rely on is "Om Namah Shivaya" And that Om Namah Shivaya is present... you can feel it in this relentless wind that is coming... you can feel it coming through the whole fabric of the building. There is Om Namah Shivaya in that wind.

It was interesting looking at this whole group of people. Some of them were quite high, there was an excitement, but rest assured that the excitement would be followed by depression because of the altitude sickness. However, those who try to focus on that stillness of Om Namah Shivaya get the support they need. That is what this trip is about... about emptying yourself of everything. You can feel, the closer you move towards Kailash, that process is really happening now.

Taking a dip in Manasarovar was an amazing experience, a unique lake where the deities come to bathe.

Walking the Inner Kora of Mount Kailash

We started in the morning with a plan to go to visit the north face of Mount Kailash. Normally that journey stops when you reach the glacier. There is a glacier that flows out from Mount Kailash, and generally the sherpas are very reluctant to take anybody beyond the glacier, because it is potentially very, very dangerous.

We made the trek up to the end of the glacier, and it was very beautiful. We bathed the OM rock in the stream which was coming out of the glacier. We were a bit ahead, and when Mohanji came we sort of felt, OK, let us do a quick puja and then we can go home and go to sleep. But that was not the way it was going to work out. And much to everyone's surprise, Mohanji said, "No, let us go a bit further" and so the sherpas hauled Him up the steep part at the end of the glacier with an improvised rope – a five metre scarf or something that happened to be available.

It was really unprecedented, and then all the sherpas seemed to accept that we were going higher on this pilgrimage than more or less anybody else. We did not actually have authority to go beyond the end of the glacier, but somehow we did have authority because that is what Lord Shiva had planned for us.

So we climbed up, climbed over a few obstacles. There were a few areas which were potentially really very dangerous, where you had deep crevasses and water flowing at the bottom of the ice. So there were a few areas where it became fairly challenging.

Reaching the North face of Kailash

Then there was suddenly an amazing sense of purpose that we were going on this trek over the glacier to the base of Mount Kailash. Nobody could quite believe that was going to happen. I felt like we had come to a horizon and then it would not be possible to proceed any further, but amazingly there always seemed to be a way through. Either there would be a little bridge or a causeway and then finally we must have been about 5000 metres at this time, so it was pretty heavy going. Then we just came out onto this big open plateau over the top of the glacier. It led us right to the base of Mount Kailash.

The path led us to a little gap in the middle of the north face. It was absolutely in the centre of Mount Kailash. It was Lord Shiva's feet. It was just an extraordinary Grace that we had that opportunity. Unbelievable, Really unbelievable. So it got fairly challenging to get up there. We were fairly spread out by then.

I was chanting "Om Namah Shivaya" with every step. Something was carrying me up there.

Actually arriving in front of the rock face of Mount Kailash was utterly overwhelming. Prostration is something to do a lot here because it is a part of their tradition. But I had to prostrate. I had to lie on the floor in the snow, face down to worship Lord Shiva, because He created this amazing opportunity.

I lay there sobbing for quite a few minutes, and after that subsided we went a little bit further forward . . . another few meters, and another extraordinary thing happened. At the base of Mount Kailash, the glacier flows outwards, and normally there is a metre gap between the rock face and the glacier. And that is a very dangerous place to be, it would not be possible to actually touch the rock face, but a huge chunk of ice and rock had somehow been wedged in the gap, just at the point where we led to, and so there was space for one person, two people maybe, to actually go right across the crevasse from the glacier to the face of Mount Kailash.

So that is what we did. We actually had the opportunity to put our hands on the face of Mount Kailash, which is . . . something that cannot happen unless the Lord organises it personally.

People are very daunted by Mount Kailash – it is an overwhelming presence. But there is such sweetness and an amazing innocent, childlike love.

Absolutely extraordinary. Everything was organised for us to do that. So I was able to hold the OM stone against Mount Kailash and as I was doing that there was a tiny little shower of ice crystals which fell down on my head and on the rock at the same time, as if to signify as a little blessing from Lord Shiva, an acceptance of what we were doing.

I think everybody was overwhelmed by it. It is not something which can happen normally. Nobody gets to touch Mount Kailash directly, but when He calls you, anything is possible. So that was what the day was really about. There was a group of around ten of us I suppose who made that trip – some of them did not get back till very late, but really overwhelming, a phenomenal experience.

The Grace . . . and the Grind

Even Mohanji, I think is amazed at the Grace which had manifested on this trip, which gave us access to every deity and every opportunity . . . fully accessible to us. So it has been extremely successful and we all came back from that walk feeling, on one level, a lot lighter, although physically it was very challenging.

At breakfast time we discovered that we still hadn't got confirmation for the trip to Saptarishi Caves, so we all sat around having an extended breakfast. Everyone was still a little bit exhausted from their exertions the day before. At this point, it was very interesting because Mohanji came in, and He was obviously in a highly sort of energised state. He was describing to us His interaction with the Rishis, who are resident there in Saptarishi Caves, in a very sort of matter of fact way.

It was fascinating to hear Him because His interaction with those Rishis was that they were very offended by the increasing numbers of people who were going on treks there, not for any sort of spiritual purpose, and not with any sort of understanding of the spiritual importance of the place, but just to have a photograph taken, to say that they had been there.

There were remnants of beer cans and all sorts of indications that people had been for the wrong reasons to Saptarishi Caves, and in this year in fact 25 people had died whilst trying to reach that area, and for that reason as well the Chinese authorities had become increasingly nervous about giving any permissions.

However, that was something separate. What Mohanji was telling us was directly from those celestial beings, those Rishis, for whom that area is their home, and people had been desecrating that very, very sacred space and that was one of the reasons why many people had died there, because the rishis had pushed those inappropriate vibrations away, and the results of that would be that people would suffer heart attacks or die under very traumatic circumstances. Not dying in a sense of union with Shiva, but in a sense that they had crossed a boundary that they really had no right to cross. So this was one of the reasons why many deaths seem to have occurred there.

So this dialogue went on, and Mohanji actually asked the Rishis and got some feedback directly about our presence there (from Skanda Vale), which was fascinating and very reassuring. What they said was that they were extremely happy with the work that we were doing, and it was very much acknowledged.

The fact that we actually had the opportunity to physically put our hands on Kailash was an indication of that appreciation. So what they said was, "Keep on going, keep walking forward, our Grace is with you."

So we could not really want for more than that. In terms of what we have actually received from our pilgrimage so far, we have been given everything that we could have wanted and probably a lot more that we do not yet understand.

So this dialogue went on for quite some time. It was amazing to see Mohanji experiencing that kind of union with these Divine entities. Sometime after that, we got the confirmation that the permission was not given to go up to the Saptarishi Caves.

Saptarishi Caves

It was interesting to see . . . in myself I felt a deep sort of yearning to complete that pilgrimage and go there, so there was a deep element of disappointment – I cannot deny that, but then on reflection when you look at everything we had been given and you look at how amazing the whole journey had been to that point, you have to accept, "Well the Lord knows best for us."

There might have been a lot of reasons why we should not have gone there at that time. So anyway we had to just accept that that was the situation and it was beyond our control to change it. Whether we will have an opportunity to go there in the future – who can say?

So we had to make plans. After we had come to terms with

that initial disappointment, you realise that what you are yearning for is union with Shiva, that oneness with God, and that does not really depend on being in a particular location, although Saptarishi Caves represents a very, very unique and powerful place.

Lake Manasarovar

That is how it was, so what we decided collectively to do instead was to use the time that we had to go back to Manasarovar – we would have an opportunity then to perform a sacred dip in Manasarovar, and then perform Yagna there on the shores of the lake with Kailash in view on one side and Manasarovar on the other.

So that is what we actually ended up doing. It was a very beautiful way to finish the pilgrimage because it brought the whole group together. For us, it was a contrast because we had spent the previous two or three days facing quite daunting physical challenges, very intense and very demanding and then to move to this amazing tranquil environment on a full moon night . . . absolutely windless and cloudless conditions. We had a Yagna there with the 18 of us gathered around the yagna.

Mohanji was keen for me to lead the yagna ceremony with Swami Govinda. It was done quite freestyle, and it was such a beautiful event. Everybody completely lost track of time. I think the yagna went on for at least two and a half or three hours. We were all sitting there . . . once all the offerings had been concluded, then we all just sat there singing bhajans together.

It was something so familiar, so undemanding physically – it was such a beautiful, peaceful, tranquil environment – to see Kailash in the moonlight in front of us and the lake on the other side. It kind of rounded everything off in a very beautiful way. It is difficult to describe, but it was a wonderful experience to do that.

We then spent the night in a very strange little hotel, with extremely basic facilities, so we got about two hours' sleep and then most of us got up in the early hours of the morning to sit beside the lake and try and meditate. We were hopeful that we might catch a glimpse of the celestial forces that come to bathe in that area. I am not quite sure if that happened or not, but it was a very beautiful experience.

Being a full moon night, there were a few other groups there at that time. All in all, it was a really beautiful and very familiar, very warm kind of way to finish our trip. After that, it was a case of long journey, which gave a chance to begin to assimilate some of our extraordinary experiences.

Complete With Kailash

- Swami Govinda -

I was given the opportunity to look after my Guru's shrine, Guru Sri Subramanium, whilst He travelled to Switzerland for a week. While looking in a drawer for matches to light the lamps, I came across two pictures, one of a perfectly domed mountain, the other of a glacier, with what appeared to be a small river flowing out from underneath it. Enthralled by the domed mountain, on Guru's return, I asked Him what it was and could I have the picture for my shrine. He refused but then proceeded to give me the glacier picture which turned out to be Gaumukh, the source of the Ganges. I was not totally happy with the outcome, as it was the mountain that had sparked a deep resonance, but that is how it was. A year later, the same situation transpired. I was lighting lamps, looking for matches and again I came across the picture of the same mountain. I looked at it every night for the week I occupied Guru's room. When my Guru returned to Skanda Vale, I moved back into my own room and defiantly, the picture of Kailash joined me, and it formed the centre of my shrine, and still does.

The best part was that all this happened twenty years ago and ever since, Kailash has been the only place on earth that I desired, actually longed to visit. It was Mohanji who was to give me the opportunity to realise this dream. He inspired some devotees who visited Skanda Vale regularly to perform an act of seva for those in need. This small group chose food aid and subsequently every six weeks, Mohanji ACT Foundation travelled down to us to collect food. This was then distributed to the homeless in London and further afield to the poorer areas within Europe.

A year or so later it happened that Mohanji was organising a large group for pilgrimage to Kailash. On one of ACT Foundation's visits to pick up food, they mentioned this to a member of Skanda Vale Community who told them of my love for Kailash. Later that day, they bumped into me and I just said that when they come back from their trip, they have to tell me absolutely everything. Unbelievably a space for that pilgrimage became available and at the age of 45, I was suddenly on my way to Kailash; everything very beautifully arranged.

Visiting Kailash was the dream of a lifetime if not even longer. After feeling and drinking the waters of Manasarovar, standing in front of Kailash itself which was no longer just a picture on my shrine and visiting Gauri Kund, I felt all was accomplished. I returned home to Skanda Vale in Wales having satiated my desire for this great mountain, or so I thought.

Almost a year later when Mohanji was visiting Skanda Vale, He said that He was going to Kailash again and that I should come with him. I protested saying there are 25 people in the Skanda Vale community and it would only be fair for someone else to go. He replied again very clearly, "but you must, it is completion." My rather silly protests and lots of discussion lasted for some months until it somehow became clear that I was to travel again, this time not for the outer kora, but the inner, infinitely more challenging and right to the heart of Kailash. In addition, there was to be a week of acclimatisation in and around Badrinath..... incredible!

The Ganges at Haridwar prepared us for pilgrimage in earnest. However murky the water, its purification was very tangible and I felt ready for what lay ahead. We then travelled for days, mainly by bus up to Badrinath. At the back of the vehicle, my body was jolted relentlessly along the bumpy, crazy road bouncing so high that my head nearly hit the ceiling. It was rainy season and landslides were abundant with whole sections of our route completely disappearing. Again and again the way was cleared. Only one small section where the entire mountainside had been swept into the river below did we need to walk. Landslides continued to fall behind us, so when we finally arrived at Badrinath, we had the town and temple to ourselves. We were up at 3 o'clock the following morning in preparation for the abhishekam. First we bathed in the hot springs of Tapt Kund and then made our way up to the temple and attended one of the most beautiful and articulate poojas I have even seen. Rawal, (the title of the chief priest) also integrated the Om stone (see anecdote below), into the abhishekam; blessings for Soma Skanda ashram from a temple thousands of years old. Later that day Mohanji took us to meet Rawal in his home just below the temple. He spoke of many things, but one point that particularly stood out was that people only make it to Badrinath when they are ready to undertake a great change in their life. The following day we performed the same bathing ritual. We were cleansed in the hot waters of the kund and surrounded by sadhus in the dark hours of the morning. We then returned back up to the temple and unintentionally, I found myself near the front witnessing the same extraordinary abhishekam, again performed by Rawal with absolute concentration. So much happened in Badrinath, too much to describe here. It is perhaps only now as I write this a year later that I realise the significance of that visit, how transformative it was and how it paved the way to Kailash.

Just as the road was miraculously cleared on our approach to Badrinath, so was our return journey through those vast Himalayan valleys, even though there was evidence of fresh landslides everywhere. Travelling back to Rishikesh and then to Haridwar, so many remarkable meetings and events occurred, making me realise more intensely than ever before that I only have the smallest of inkling as to who really I am, where I have come from, and for what I am destined. There was such a harmony of experiences way beyond my control, even beyond my imagination and dreams. I came to the conclusion that the only thing I can vaguely attempt to control is my presence of mind; to be aware of what is happening right here and now and to attempt to do my duty, to perform my dharma to the best of my ability.

I travelled the last leg of that journey in the luxury of a car and Mohanji's company. At Devprayag, the confluence of the Alaknanda and the Bhagirathi, we stopped because Mohanji had received a message that the timing for a dip in the birthplace of the Ganges was now extremely auspicious. Three of us waded out to exactly where these two rivers meet, merge, and become Ganga Maa. Holding on tightly to some metal railings, I offered myself, my life, and the pilgrimage that lay ahead. I sunk into the swirling vortex of waters, the prayer racing from my mind to its destination. I made a second plunge as an act of gratitude to Guru and all He had done for me; again that prayer was received with lightning speed. I then brought every single member of Skanda Vale Community into my mind's eye and for the third time sank into that turbulence. The prayer shot from my mind, through these sacred waters, off to find its target. There was then a dip for my family. With each dip the prayers were formed, projected, and so tangibly received by Ganga Devi. Preparation for Kailash could not have been better.

Several days later, we were approaching Manasarovar and altitude sickness was back with a vengeance. Kailash was in full view as we took our first dip in the holy lake and again I experienced these pure waters working their magic. My mother was travelling with us and was not feeling good at all. Earlier that day, she had managed to dislocate her knee. This happens to her from time to time and normally she would require at least 24 hours lying down and resting before she can even begin to hobble. Mum could hardly walk into the water and had to take dips by falling backwards. Miraculously a few minutes later, she walked out of the water as though nothing had happened and proceeded to complete the rest of the parikrama effortlessly, despite being one of the oldest in the group. After taking my own dips, many of our temple artifacts were offered, some to remain at Kailash and some to take back to our three beautiful temples at Skanda Vale. The Om stone was bathed providing further blessings for Soma

Skanda ashram. All this was performed with Mount Kailash as our witness.

For the second time in my life, I arrived at Yama Dwar and after offering my life and all those who are a part of it, I walked forward into that valley of animate mountains. I was again in bliss with the sentient nature of these vast peaks that surrounded me, so alive. By the time I reached the west face, the same unbearable weight of altitude was beginning to get the better of me and by the north face, though in a slightly better state than my previous pilgrimage, I was still walking like a half conscious drunkard. By late evening, after some rest, I had recovered somewhat, could smile again, and begin to absorb the power of Kailash. I was so excited at the prospect of walking towards His north face in the morning.

Next day we walked to Charan Sparsh. As always, it was a battle to breathe, but the growing proximity of Kailash subdued the body awareness and the hardships it was facing. Even so, by the time we arrived at the snout of the glacier, Swami Brahmananda and I were ready to slowly descend and take a big long rest. After waiting a while, Mohanji arrived and with Him, a new lease of life.

When He asked, "shall we go further?" I jumped at the opportunity. Within a moment, He was helped up on the face of the glacier and we followed in quick succession. We all walked on across the ice for some time until Mohanji said that He was going to stay here and chant the Shiva Kavacham. He urged some to continue and some to stay with Him. At this point, I do not think any of us knew how far we would go. It was only when we had traversed a deep glacial stream, climbed the steeper sections, and reached the relatively level vast plane of ice strewn with stones, that I realised the potential of reaching and perhaps touching the north face. As I walked closer, Kailash completely occupied me; several times I was completely overwhelmed. These massive sections of rock were a part of me, every plane, every movement, each shape and formation, oscillating as one. A simple physical process, the mind was not involved. This experience grew until the very substance, the essence of Kailash could be felt. At the foot of this immense expanse, there was a tiny snow bridge that enabled me to step down, up close, and hold myself tight up against the sweetness of Kailash itself. I offered myself, Guru, the Community, my family, and many more. It was after those moments that I realised why Mohanji had insisted I come to Kailash again . . . "but you must, it is completion."

In stark contrast, I awoke the next morning feeling like I had been pulled through a hedge backwards and then buried in six foot of concrete. I could hear the words "chalo, chalo" (let us go) through this bleary state and my porter sharply telling me it was time to move. I managed to shut the door, get changed, stumble out along the corridor and down the near vertical metal stairs to have a wash. Then breakfast, a slice of bread and some chai and I became immediately sick. Cursing under my breath, I grabbed my things and set off. I knew it was going to be a very long 22-kilometre walk, a lot of it over 5000 meters high, up to Kuber Kund and down into the valley below. Every step was a massive battle and the slightest incline reduced me to 54 paces and then I had to rest, a bit steeper and it was 21, then only 9 on any real slope, and I was left gasping. The whole day my mind was saying, I cannot do it, I cannot do it. I had to fight every inch of the way in an attempt to be positive. As if that was not enough, after several kilometers of torture, we arrived at quite a steep glacier that was covered with stones. Swami Brahmananda was ahead of me. He was resting with two sherpas standing by him, but from a distance, I thought he had collapsed and quickly tried to reach him. Stepping onto the glacier I immediately started sliding. It was a long way down. Somehow I managed to steady myself and then wondered how on earth I was going to get across to him with no ropes, no crampons, and no ice axe. Armed with my trekking stick, little more than a toy, I jammed it into the ice and wedged my feet against the top side of the plastic, steadied myself and then jammed it in again. Amazingly I made it to Swami; ironically he was absolutely fine and just waiting for the sherpas to sort out the next bit of the route. The glacier got steeper and steeper till we arrived at a rock face. I stupidly declined the offer of a harness as it was taking people too long to put them on and was very aware that there were 20 people to come up behind me, some not very fit and time was racing. I wrapped the rope around my wrists and hauled myself up 3 steps at a time. I was gasping as if I had swum underwater for 30 meters. Rocks were flying down the slope narrowly missing us and the rope was being pulled from side to side by porters. My grip on the rope lessened with every step and there was no harness to fall back into. How I made it safely to the top I do not know and how all twenty of us made it safely to the top (some of our group members were really not built for any sort of climbing, even at sea level) is a miracle. Looking down the slope, I could see Mohanji quietly waiting, the last to ascend and silently working on us, every one of us, as He had done for the entire trip.

We reached an extremely cold windblown plateau, a waste land of stones and rocks, abode of many devas and great rishis, and walked down to Kuber Kund where the Om stone was bathed in the most sacred of waters. I was so imprisoned by the limitations of my body that these extraordinary places were only dimly perceived. At this point, I felt like I could do no more, yet I knew there were hours of walking ahead. I descended down a steep gorge, alongside and through a stream, into a larger valley before finally arriving at the main track, which I knew to be the way back; it was a never ending walk. I arrived after dark, meandering and stumbling down that road for what seemed like an aeon, barely conscious. Even now I wonder about this day and have no answers other than it simply had to happen.

I started this small account many months ago as I was travelling to Soma Skanda ashram, where for six weeks, I helped build the temple ready for its inauguration. On returning to Skanda Vale, work was intense and time was short, leaving no space for writing. I have now returned to Soma Skanda and I write this from what was and still is Guru's room (He passed into Mahasamadhi in 2007). I am sitting on His bed alongside His shrine. Amongst the murtis of Ganesh, Krishna, Brahma and Lakshmi, there are also pictures of Guru Sri Subramanium, Mohanji, and Sadguru Sharavana Bhava, and above them all, a picture of Kailash and in the foreground Charan Sparsh with the Om stone in one of its glacial streams.

Every day we perform the most beautiful abhishekam to Soma Skanda murti, three naags set above a lingam placed within a yoni. Kailash, Manasarovar, and the Ganges are all very present during these poojas. The three naags representing Skanda, are three intimate beings, my friends, perhaps three eternal companions. The murti resonates with a profound and absolute serenity, whole and complete.

Story of the Om stone

Several months before our journey to Kailash with Mohanji, Swami Brahmananda was high in the Swiss Alps at Soma Skanda ashram (our Swiss temple). Sadguru Sharavana Bhava was visiting. He walked a short distance from the temple, climbed up and sat on a large rock where a siddha had achieved moksha. He picked up a flat stone and started to inscribe an OM with another smaller chalky stone. When finished, He handed this to Swami Brahmananda. Closely following the drawn lines, we carved the Om out and inlaid the depression with gold, the gold coming from chains that had been offered to Ma Kali at Skanda Vale in Wales. This Om stone travelled with us to Kailash and received countless blessings, from many saints, temples, and waters including Manasarovar and Kuber Kund. The day when we walked to the north face, the Om stone was held against Kailash and at that exact moment was showered with snow crystals from high above. Later that year in October, Soma Skanda temple was ready to be inaugurated and both Mohanji and Swami Sharavana Bhava joined us. During one of those inaugural days, we made a procession back to that same siddha rock from which the Om stone came, and performed a beautiful pooja. The stone has now been permanently installed above the gopuram. Our pilgrimage to Kailash has and continues to be a fundamental part of Soma Skanda ashram and Skanda Vale.

A Life In The Grace Of Kailash

- Dhritiman Biswas -

THIS IS A journey that has neither beginning nor end. Kailash is not an event that occurs at a specific time. It's a journey that began many hundreds of lifetimes ago - just as the soul began its walk towards liberation. One that only ends when it finally merges with Shiva. On this physical dimension and in this lifetime, with the abundant Grace of Shiva and my guru Brahmarishi Mohanji, blessings have been bestowed on me to be with Kailash many times. Each time my physical body made the most sacred pilgrimage on this earth to Kailash, I shed many things to emerge with a new self. In fact, every time I have been called to visit Kailash, I go with the intention to shed things, not to gain anything. Because by shedding, I grow.

With every journey to Kailash, I have taken back with me much more than I had anticipated. And my yearning for Kailash has only grown, much like a lover yearns for an absent beloved. At end of each physical visit, my soul did not find any satiation or comfort. After each pilgrimage, I immediately start to prepare for the next. In fact, if I am to describe my life chronologically, it will be outlined between one Kailash visit to the next.

I can trace the first thought of this year's Inner Kora/parikrama yatra back to 2012 when a person informed me about Dev Kumbh (where one kora is equal to twelve koras around Kailash) and Inner Kora. I was immediately taken up by a burning desire to be part of Dev Kumbh in 2014. But the yearning inside me was flowing over. I could not wait for another two years to look at the face of my beloved Kailash. I finally got permission to come to Kailash in 2013. Till I actually reached Kailash, I did not quite understand the implications and meaning of Inner Kora. As I walked the outer kora, back in 2013, many things started to break down - my walls, understanding of the world, conditioning - in essence, the person who started the kora was dying. A new person had emerged by the time the three-day kora ended. At the end of the first day of kora on foot, I was face to face with my beloved Kailash for the first time in this life. Oh, how I wanted to run up and hug him. To melt in his arms. Touch it lovingly and never come back to this world. However much my mind wanted to do these things, my body was not. Looking back, I understand that I wasn't ready yet. That is the first time too I realized the meaning of Inner Kora. How one can, with Grace of Shiva, walk towards it and come closest to it physically.

The burning fire inside made sure that I was part of 'Kailash with Mohanji' in 2014 – the year of Dev Kumbh when all the Gods converge at Kailash every twelve years. The sacred of sacred. No human language can explain the significance of being with Kailash in this holy year. Even though the group was not supposed to go towards Inner Kora in 2014, during the first day of the kora, I 'lost' my way and ended up taking a path which leads me towards Kailash. I was blessed to see and be a little closer to Him. However, with the failing light of the day, I walked back with a heavy heart on not being able to hug my beloved this time too.

I smile as I think about my preparations for 2016 Inner Kora. This was almost immediately after I returned to India. No language is required for communicating with one's Master. And sure enough, one day as we sat discussing many things, including 2016 Kailash Yatra, Mohanji smiled and told me, 'You are coming'. Just that one sentence, nothing else. I had nothing more to ask too. The permission had been given. The universe was informed and I started my preparations. Mental strength is far more important than physical strength as only the Grace of Shiva and Guru helps one complete the journey.

All the intense yoga and physical training sessions that I underwent prepared me for what lay in store at Kailash.

The Inner Kora is unlike the better known outer kora trek. The Inner Kora is not actually a closer path around Kailash, but a series of lesser walked paths going nearer to Kailash than the outer kora. If one were to compare this with a Buddhist mandala painting, Inner Kora is like entering a circle closer to the central point at certain points and then exiting again to the outer circle. The biggest difference between the outer and Inner Kora is, however, the condition and difficulty of the path. In front of the Inner Kora, outer kora parikrama looks like a walk in the park. And yet, don't think outer kora is easy because it is difficult. For example, this year (i.e. 2016) we saw bodies of two people being brought back to Nepal who lost their lives while walking the highest point of outer kora – the Dolma La pass at about 18,600 feet.

Pilgrims usually go within themselves and remain in silence during Kailash yatra. This helps them to introspect and understand many subtle things that the noise of the world outside stops them from realizing. I did not have this luxury. For one, I chose to do seva and two, being part of the organizing team, there are hundreds of things, and sometimes unexpected ones, which crop up demanding for attention and resolution. I spent my time being a hare on wheels, till the time I started to walk the kora.

The first day passed like a breeze as I have walked this path before. It was the only day that pilgrims of both outer and Inner Kora walked together. As we assembled for dinner that evening, three of us - Sumit Pratap Gupta, a Sherpa called Amar and I - were huddled together sipping hot soup. We listened to a story in which Amar along with another Sherpa from our group had physically touched Kailash a few years back. A huge bell in our heads rang out as no one touches Mount Kailash! Sumit and I exchanged looks and smiled. Enough was said. Everything was understood. If we get the permission of Lord Shiva, we will surely try to touch his lotus feet!

Next day, the Inner Kora group of 18 pilgrims and Sherpas started off for 'Charan Sparsh'. Charan Sparsh (meaning touching the feet) is a wall of rock and ice (at least 8-9 feet high) to the north and is approximately 17,500 ft high and about 2 km from Dirapuk. I had springs under my feet that day and jumped from one big boulder to next like a mountain goat. There were just 3 or 4 of us who were ahead of the rest. We crossed rivers and ravines and we walked on rivers and inside ravines – and reached Charan Sparsh! In a couple of hours, we had made this trek. It was a difficult one but nothing spectacularly tough. So we all waited for the rest of the group to reach and in the meantime, sat under the intense sun by the brook carrying waters directly from Kailash to meditate. The rest of the group reached about half an hour later and rested, drank water and prayed by the brook which was falling like a waterfall. Most trips to Kailash end with this trip which, in fact, is considered very adventurous

And then like a dream come true it started. I saw Brahmarishi Mohanji nodding and telling the Sherpa to do something. I realized that He had asked the Sherpa to help the group to go up the Charan Sparsh. I wasn't ready to understand the full impact of this decision. My heart was racing. I knew that this meant that we will touch Kailash! But my mind was cautioning me to stay calm. I saw the Sherpa somehow scramble up the ice wall and he threw down a long piece of cloth. I was standing on right side of Mohanji. He turned towards me and said, "DB you go first". He knew my deepest wish. At this command, I realized much much later, that I had crossed a line in my head – and crossed over into a territory of fearlessness. I did not think about my family or anything of this world or even about the dangers on the path ahead nor had any doubt that I may not be able to reach Kailash physically. I was in a state of vairagya (this is a Sanskrit term that roughly translates as dispassion, detachment, or renunciation, in particular, renunciation from the pains and pleasures in the material world).

At this simple command of Mohanji, I jumped. Triggering a chain of events in my life, which would shortly bring me face to face with my death.

A Life In The Grace Of Kailash

I grabbed the hanging rope and jumped up. Jammed my trekking boots midway and then another step up till I reached a landing just short of the top. The Sherpa asked me to stay in that location and give hand to rest of the team climbing up. I did that for many, till someone else took over from me. Once the whole team was up, we trekked on. The landscape and by that extension, the trek became more difficult.

Suddenly Mohanji stopped. Looked intently at Kailash he asked for the Shiva Kavach (the mantra of protection of Lord Shiva) to be played. By chance, I had Shiva Kavach on my phone. As the powerful mantra started playing, we all took positions around Mohanji. I sat at His lotus feet on the left side and had his hand in mine. His grip was powerful, as if like a father he was about to help me cross the road while keeping me firmly in control. A surreal 17 minutes passed as the mantra played on. I still get goose bumps at the depth of the moment. Listening to Shiva Kavach in presence of Mohanji under the towering Kailash right ahead of us!

Just a few moments later, fresh after this recess, Mohanji sat down on a rock facing Kailash and asked those of us who wanted to touch Kailash, to go ahead while he waited for us on the rock. We didn't understand His worldly action then.

Right in front of us was a wide chasm which was almost like a line running from the left side (from the solid mountain) towards the right side. This was indeed a kind of a moat which would stop humans and animals from crossing into the land which then led to Kailash. There was solid ice right at the mouth of the chasm and a very fast stream that flowed over sharp rocks filled with ice-cold water. I saw few team members and a couple of Sherpas jump over to the other side. Then came my turn. I had no other thoughts but to touch Kailash. A burning desire which was consuming me.

As I jumped and landed on the other side (right leg forward), the ground where my feet landed collapsed before I could land my left feet. I started to fall into the chasm of ice water and rocks – towards a sure death. As my body was falling, two hands gripped each of my hands – that of Sumit and a Sherpa. And before I knew what happened, I was pulled up and on solid ground. In that spilt-second, I died and took re-birth.

Mohanji knew what I was going to face. On that rock, while I blissfully listened to Shiva Kavach, he had made sure His grip was strong and that I crossed.

I turned around and saw the whole group who watched this incident in shock. Sumit looked at me and uttered a couplet, which went like this:

अकाल मृत्यु वो मरे जो काम करे चंडाल का, काल उसका क्या करे जो भक्त हो महाकाल का |

(Translated, it roughly means: One who follows the devil, dies. But how can death touch the one who is a devotee of Lord Shiva!)

So true it was!

Then Vijay attempted to take the jump, but the soil gave away on his side this time and he was managed to get to safety before any damage. At this point, Sherpas told group not to cross anymore and asked the rest to stay back. What a privilege and honor bestowed for being able to touch Kailash! I felt the pain of my team members who were stopped from crossing over. Mohanji had told us that we don't do Kailash for ourselves, but for many beings and souls who are able to be with Kailash through us. I knew I was carrying them too on this trek towards Kailash.

Sad, yet elated, I moved on with the small group towards Kailash. The terrain became tougher and tougher progressively. First came the boulders, then the brook, then the maze of ice, then the slippery glacier and finally the waist deep snow. I trekked slowly. The mountain goat was tired. I was at the back of the pack and in fact saw the first couple of team members already coming back after touching Kailash. The sun was getting weaker. And the silence was getting louder and louder.

As I neared Kailash I looked up at the majestic, towering black facade of the north face of Kailash, I could have just collapsed and died there. The utter beauty, the sheer satisfaction of the dream about to come true. Did anything else matter in this world? Did this world exist at all?

All that existed was Kailash – throbbing, alive, yet so loving that one wanted to hug it and never let go. For the first time, I heard the sound of the continuous snow fall from its peak down its face, as if it is in a constant state of Abhisheka (consecration) on itself. As I took the final leap over the moat and started my final steps onto the heavily snow-covered area directly under it, I heard the sound of silence. The sound of the excruciatingly powerful machine barely running – a hum which is there, but just barely.

A couple of steps from the actual touching, I saw Rajesh Kamath and a Sherpa. They graciously made space for me to reach that natural little rock platform on which a pilgrim needs to stand to touch the Holy of Holies. I dropped my shoulder bag and stumbled towards Kailash. And sank, body and head on to the holy Kailash. The embrace... that moment of non-existence - timeless and unforgettable. The snow continued to fall on my head as a blessing.

After years of waiting just to walk around Kailash, this physical touching was paralyzing. My mind went blank and numb. I grabbed some snow and ate it like candy. Was I supposed to do that? I don't know! On hindsight, I could have meditated, chanted and done many things, but at that point of time, it's as if all programming in my head got corrupted and I flowed and behaved like a child.

My human survival instinct kicked in at this moment and made me aware that the sun was going down and I had a 4-6 hour trek through extremely difficult terrain back to camp. I took a couple of stones from Kailash and started slowly to return to the camp, feeling much like an Indian bride who doesn't want to leave her parent's home.

By this time, most of the Sherpas had gone back. There was another pilgrim, a Sherpa and myself. We started the trek back and somewhere lost our way. Although we continued to walk in the general direction of the camp, it was not the way we had come. This was no accident. We were supposed to receive a blessing from Lord Shiva.

My fellow pilgrim brother, who was ahead of me, called me towards him and showed a spectacular sight on the ground. It was a little pond of clear ice water. Inside it was a Shivaling made of ice. The Shivaling was completely submerged in ice water. When we peered closely, we saw small indents in the ice walls, as if they are small cave entrances or back of chairs. It looked like a court surrounding the Shivaling. Was this Shiva's court? What were we seeing? What was the blessing which was given to us? Our minds had melted by now. All we could do was take few photographs with my phone camera (and immediately thereafter my phone battery died). We also respectfully drank some water from the pond, gave it one last look and continued our journey.

It was night by the time we reached the camp. And I thought, all the blessings I was supposed to be given, was received this day. I was so wrong.

The next day, we started out early morning, right after the outer kora group had left for Kuber Kund – the pond of Lord Kuber, the lord of all riches. Way to Lord Kuber can never be easy, can it? Little did I know as we started that this day would reveal itself in layers and each layer would bring its own experiences. In fact, each layer was a journey and set of tests in itself! After each layer, I would end up thinking, that the excitement had ended, soon to realise there was a new one awaiting.

Anyway, in the morning as we started, it was an easy trek through green patches of level ground. But soon this gave away to ascending heights and bare mountains. We saw rocks jutting straight of the ground, which we had to cross over. Through a very steep path, where we had to stop every couple of steps due to the sheer height of each step and effort required, we reached the top of the rocky climb.

Only to realise that a massive climb through an ultra-slippery glacier waited for us. I was one of the early ones to reach the glacier. It was like a huge shiny sheath of ice falling over a mountain like a frozen river. (We met someone later in the day who told us that this glacier which formed every year was the most dangerous one he had seen in the last 7 years he has trekked on this path). As we walked closer and closer to the glacier, I began to understand the daunting climb ahead of me. I had never seen this kind of a monster glacier before (and I have traveled to many ice capped mountains in my life).

Before we had embarked on the journey, we were informed that we will need to use climbing ropes. This was the moment I saw the ropes being laid out by Sherpas. We had to cross the glacier horizontally first from end to end and then climb up vertically from the other side. While crossing horizontally holding the rope in one hand and my climbing stick on the other, I slipped a bit but managed to steady myself by quickly slamming down my walking stick against the hard ice of the glacier. But the moment the stick hit the ice, it snapped into two within seconds, giving me a split second to steady myself back. But in the process, I realized how hard the ice was and that walking sticks, which have served me so well in the past, was useless for this stupendous climb ahead. And now I was without my 2nd walking stick and would have to finish the rest of the journey only with one.

Shrugging off any fears and surrendering to Mohanji, I reached the other side of the glacier. The situation there was worse. Even standing still was an issue as the glacier was covered by loose dirt mixed with small rocks which would give away and fall down to an abyss below – a fall which meant a sure death. Just ahead of me was Sumit and behind me was Riana. The 3 of us were huddled together. Little did we know that the oncoming events of the day would tie us together for life.

As we huddled precariously on the hard ice holding a rope, waiting for our turn to be saddled with a harness for the climb, we realized that we are in the direct path of small rocks and boulders falling from the top of the glacier. The speed with which the rocks would hurtle down, each time bumping against the hard glacier, would only quicken their momentum and was enough to break open a skull.

We were completely exposed to these falling missiles. The one and only protection we had, was the name of Mohanji. I was continuously chanting His mantra. Stone missiles would cut through the space between the 3 of us but never hit us.

The almost 70-80 degree horizontal climb up the glacier was about 200 meters after which a person would need to climb unaided an extremely steep slope for about 20 meters only with help of their hands. The interesting thing about this aperture was that one missed step and the person would plunge down the glacier and into the long fall of the abyss to death.

When my turn came to climb the glacier, I was put on a harness and my body was hooked on to the rope. One had to climb by continuously pushing the hook of the harness upwards and keeping the body almost 90 degrees to the glacier so that the feet can get some support. This was the toughest part of my Kailash yatra. I just couldn't get my body angle correct for the climb initially. I used to climb for a couple of feet and then slid down the glacier. The saving Grace was the harness which could stop my fall into the abyss. I would then start again with the same result.

Half through this extremely arduous climb, my left hand got entwined in the rope and before I could take it out, about 4-5 sherpas had got behind me and was using the same rope to climb up. At one point of time, my left hand was crushed by the steel rope and was carrying the weight of about 4-5 well-built Sherpas. I thought, my hand would snap at that point of time.

By this time, I was already running low on energy after the tough trek. Suddenly I felt a surge of enlightenment on how to untangle my arm. It was as if it had been whispered into my ear. The moment I got my arm free, within 15 min I was at the top of the glacier. The loose dirt ground by now was beginning to crumble badly and even Sherpas were finding it difficult to remain steady at the top of the glacier to give us a hand to climb.

A wave of fear hit me as the harness was taken off from me at the top of the glacier. For few seconds, I was standing there with my back to the abyss, without the harness, only holding the jacket of the Sherpa. One and just one tiny rock slipping out beneath my boots could have caused a disaster. Immediately soon after this, I was pushed towards the mouth of the small aperture to do the next round of climb, and I looked down towards where the rest of the group was congregated for the climb. My mind was numb at this time, but still, I understood what I have managed to do – only with Grace! The scene is etched in my memory forever. I saw how easy it was for each one of us to fail. Yet we didn't.

Surrendering to Mohanji again, I started my climb up the aperture with my hands, not daring to stop for even a second or even thinking about the sheer fall if I have a misstep. My mind was completely focused on my steps. I really do not know how I got through that aperture. I remember it. But my mind doesn't acknowledge the feat. My body was like a stone. My mind was frozen with fear. Only my heart was uttering Mohanji's name. All I know was that I found myself at top of the glacier and that's when my mind came back to its senses. I realized what my body had just finished doing.

I wanted to sit down and weep in gratitude. There was only enough space for 2 people – one Sherpa and myself – at the top. But I was shooed away by the Sherpa on top of the glacier as I had to make place for Riana to come up next.

At this point, I thought I had achieved a big victory and could take it easy – till I realized what I had to do next. The Sherpa was pointing at a 'very narrow' path on the edge of the glacier, on which I had to walk. Space is relative term, so let me give you an example to illustrate. Have you ever tried or seen some video where a person had to walk on the edge of a building which is at least 10 floors high? Can you imagine how tiny the people look at the base of the building? This walk was like that. The breadth of the path was probably just 12 inches – I was glad I have a lean body! This path was about 300 meters till the top of the mountain.

The track was the literal translation of the English phrase of 'caught between the devil and a hard place'. On my left was the glacier and a slip down meant sure death. While on right side was ragged mountain side.

At few places, I had to completely turn and walk sideways while holding ragged and jutting pieces of rock as there was not enough space to walk with 2 legs side by side (even with my lean body). The highlight of this spacewalk was that I had to stop a couple of times to allow for the thin slices of rock walls on the track. This meant that I had to turn sideways, grip a sharp ragged rock, swing my left leg over the slice of rock, grab a jutting rock on the other side with my left hand and then bring my body to the other side of the track by swinging my right foot. For a second or two, one would be standing on one foot with one hand grabbing ragged mountain while the other hand and foot would be in transition in air – right over a glacier which will not show any mercy if one falls down.

As I executed a couple of these maneuvers, few rocks and small stones went over the edge and down the glacier. Now I realised, how the rain of stones was coming down the glacier while I was waiting below to climb it. This also symbolized life – sometimes one got hit by stones, and sometimes one kicked the stones.

Finally, I emerged to a small flat opening at the end the path. The scene in front of me was both joyous and daunting. I saw 5-6 of my fellow brothers lying down and some even sleeping, on the small clearing, completely exhausted by the climb. And more so by the mental exhaustion as all of them had realized that how with sheer Grace they had been able to conquer the almost impossible task!

I too lay down and passed out for a bit. By this time, the wind had become very strong and chilly. It was cutting through our heavy jackets. The sun was also weak and the prevailing cloud cover had further dipped the temperature. I woke up on hearing a sound. I realized I was shivering in cold even though I was sleeping in a fetal position to expose my body the least. I think most of the people had realized that this was a place where one could freeze to death and decide to move quickly. After the muscle ripping and sweaty climb, the body was being suddenly frozen. This was not a good idea and it would lead to painful muscle cramps. I saw many shivering and we all decided to walk out.

The only problem was – we didn't have any Sherpas. All the Sherpas were busy getting the group pass through the treacherous glacier climb. We were alone and didn't know which way was Kuber Kund. As we came out on the plateau, we saw a couple of locals. But they didn't understand our language. They were going down from the plateau on the other side. Just at this time, it started to drizzle very lightly. Just a hint of the rain in the strong wind. It was almost as if the rain was being blown away by the wind. We had to move as it was dangerous to get wet in this exposed part of the mountain.

We all followed the local people down from the other side of the plateau. I had given up seeing the Kuber Kund as I knew we can very easily divert from the track and before we know it, we may unknowingly walk away from it. But the story wasn't supposed to end in this way. In fact, the story was far from ending.

The sun came out bright and strong as we were climbing down a narrow and hardly defined path. It was a faint path running on edge of the contours of the undulating barren mountain. A faint line running on a dark brown mountainside. It was as if, we were being guided by the Sun God Himself, lighting our path, showing us the way. Grace all the way and in the little inexplicable ways of its working.

And then we saw it. Shimmering jade. Peaceful beauty. Right at the bottom of the mountain, flanked by a couple of others, almost like a pool weighing down the earth to create a funnel-like effect. Kuber Kund was waiting for me.

Our steps quickened and my heart was filled with happiness. I soon reached the glimmering jade green pond of Lord Kuber. I dropped my bags and knelt by the side and prayed. Cupped my hands and filled it with the clear and pristine water to drink to my heart's content. I sat down to wait, along with others, for the rest of the group to join. The weather was becoming worse again. Chilly winds had picked up and there was a heavy hint of rain in it. It was evident that the sun was about to go down and in the mountains, the weather becomes very dangerous during sundown. There was no sign of the rest of the group as yet. We began to understand that they might not be able to come to Kuber Kund that day. We even thought, that due to the crumbling earth of the glacier, it may even be possible that the rest of the group had been taken through some other path.

Most of the group decided to move on – to keep walking towards the only way possible as the other sides were high mountains, with the exception of the three of us – Sumit, Riana and I.

As the weather turned inclement and others were moving out, the three of us decided to stay and wait for Mohanji and the rest of the group. As people left, silence fell on the pond. The wind was still howling away. Sumit sat down to meditate. So did Riana. Something was urging me to do a parikrama of the pond. And I did. Walked slowly, almost doing Conscious Walking around Kuber Kund. The pond has a natural canopy made out of the mountain over it. It was a beautiful sight to look directly down while standing on top of this rock canopy.

After this, I too sat down in a little cave by the pond to take shelter from the strong chilly wind. Rising in front of me on the other side of Kuber Kund was a majestic mountain. As my eyes scanned it, I saw something amazing. But I should have expected it as we all have heard the rumors about it. The mountain was littered with caves – caves which were almost impossible to climb for humans as they were situated very high up the mountain on a sheer face. I sat and wondered about those beings who are in those caves. A smile crossed my lips in a moment of realization that I was in presence of higher beings.

In this happy state, I closed my eyes and drifted off in meditation. To be only woken up by intense rain. I saw all the three of us getting wet. Thankfully we had our rainproof jackets on and we kept sitting in these in the rain. The rain passed, after some time. We saw a group of people coming down the mountain from where we had come. I recognized Mohanji's red jacket and realised that they were not coming towards Kuber Kund but going away from it.

A final salutation to Lord Kuber and we started to walk towards the direction which the rest of the group was going.

As soon as we left the pond, the rain was back with force. Like it was telling us that we had hidden from it for too long and now there was no one to save us. In 2013, when I was about to embark on my 1st Kailash Yatra, Mohanji had told me that a little rain is good, as it cleans the karma. So be it. We kept walking through the rain.

Now it was evident that we were being tested. After the rain came the hail. Heavy hail pouring thick and fast. The wind was added as spice. We were walking and shivering. Sumit shared his dry fruits with us which we had while standing in the hail. Hail was replaced by sunshine. Strong and clear sunshine. It was as if we were living through a whole year of time in those few hours, reflecting the seasons in a year. Or maybe it was reflecting a lifetime.

Nevertheless, we walked on. Soon we saw another pilgrim, Chai from London, coming down alone with a Sherpa on the other side of a mountain. They were clearly lost and looking for the path to lead to the night camp. So then the party of five trekked on for about an hour or so, till we finally caught up with Mohanji and the rest of the group. Soon thereafter, we reached the main road which lead to Zuthul Puk, where we were supposed to stay for the night. By this time, sun had almost gone and evening had almost set in.

Three of us – Rajesh, Riana and I, decided to walk to the camp. We just didn't realise how far it was. Especially after the whole day for the walk over meadows, climb over rocky mountains, past the life-threatening glacier and 'space walks', and finally the walk in the rain and hail. We started walking when night was beginning to set in.

We walked. And walked. Walked a bit more. Some more walking. And some more. And another bend. And another light. And another rock. And another step. And . . . some more.

I was walking in full moonlight in and around Mount Kailash in Tibet. The scenery was surreal. Pitch darkness only lit by the silver of the moonlight. Dark shapes dancing around the mountain. Punctured only by the sound of the gurgling river flowing endlessly along the path. This is a very romantic way to look at the situation. In reality, I was a bag of very tired flesh and aching bones which were being carried by Grace. Each step, each breath was a labour. And an offering to Lord Shiva.

After walking for at least few hours, we reached the camp. By this time, the body had ceased to exist. I knew that I was walking only and only on Grace. I was witnessing the tiredness of my body and marveling at the miracle that a physical body this tired can still walk, hungry, thirsty and completely devoid of any energy, and not collapse and die of exhaustion. It was as if my legs had moved but someone had not let me feel the weight of the walk.

I had the most delicious cup-o-noodles in my whole life after reaching the camp. Soon the trip ended.

Or has it?

The journey to Kailash starts long before we are born in this world and transcends beyond this lifetime. The physical journey is just a manifestation of the karmic journey spread over lifetimes, to the privileged and few handful who can even in this world, come near Mount Kailash.

How many thousands hope and dream to see Kailash? Of these, how many do a parikrama around it? How many hundreds do the inner parikrama? How many few (out of billions of humans) touch Kailash?

Of the whole group, I was part of only half dozen pilgrims bestowed with the twin blessing of physically touching Mount Kailash and praying at Kuber Kund. Only with unfettered Grace, this was made possible. What more needs to be said?

I Am Always With You

- Sumit Gupta -

Before sharing my 2016 Inner Kora experiences, I would like to briefly touch upon my experiences from 2014 and 2015 to give readers an overview of the aspect called Mind, Fear and how Guru's Grace alone can offer an experience, which can never be expressed by mere words.

In 2014, I had literally died during the 1st day of the Parikrama and I very well knew that it was my Guru's Grace which saved me on that day. During this Parikrama, I was carrying Shirdi Sai Baba's Murti (idol) with me. After walking for a while, I realised that the Murti was no longer with me. Once I became aware of this, my Sherpa and I ran back and started looking for Baba's Murti everywhere. Sherpa finally spotted the Murti, however, it was broken, Baba's head was severed from the body with no other damage. At that moment, I realised that whatever had to come on me, Baba had taken it upon himself. I took Baba's broken Murti and continued with my Parikrama. This was also an indication for me that something huge has been taken off or a huge transfer has taken place. With every step, my discomfort was increasing. My first trip to Kailash was in the year 2012 and the 1st day parikrama was like a walk in the garden, but this time it was extremely tough on the very first day. Since father didn't see me, he was waiting for me and was enquiring about me with the people around him. The entire group had stopped for me while I came running and joined them. Father didn't ask me anything but HE knew very well what was going on. HE didn't interfere but yes HE intervened. We silently started walking again and with every passing moment, my headache was increasing. My feet were very heavy and my body was feeling very heavy. We reached the first official stop on Day-1 Parikrama, where the group had their refreshments. However, I had a splitting headache. I lied down next to Spomenka (Serbia) who applied some balm on my forehead and massaged my head. I will always be thankful to her. I felt I wasn't in my body and slipped into a deep sleep. When I woke up after an hour, Dr. Deepali Jaju gave me medicines and I realised that I was running temperature (Fever) too.

It was drizzling and I was walking all alone, didn't want to be part of any group as I would have slowed them down. I decide to walk alone. All kinds of thoughts were coming to my mind like my sudden headache, broken Baba Murti and weakness in my body that might result in me going back to the base camp and not completing my Parikrama. This chilling thought of not being able to go to Gauri Kund the next day (day-2 of the parikrama) stuck with me and made me very upset. I was crying and walking and after some time I started chanting Father's Gayatri Mantra. As I continued my chanting while walking, I could feel my fever coming down. I was praying to Mata Vaishno Devi (Divine Mother) to bless me so that I could complete this Parikrama.

I reached Derapuk, could see many fellow pilgrims overjoyed and happy to have made it. I enquired about Father's room and as soon I saw Him, just crashed at His Feet. I said, "Whatever it is, You are the one". I cried loudly keeping my head on his feet. He lifted me up and put me to bed in His room!!! These special loving gestures cannot be explained in words. Then Sanjay Sir, my friend Tarun, Dr. Deepali, all of them helped me by giving me medicines and taking care of me as I simply lay in the bed. Dr. Deepali was everywhere for everyone who was in need. Her presence in the group was a great blessing for all of us. She along with Spomenka were treating all the others in our group.

Later I was half asleep and I heard some noises coming from

outside that DB (Dhritiman Biswas) had gone and did Kailash – Charansparsh (part of Inner Kora) while there were few others (as a group) who were trying to go up but couldn't go. It was really special for DB and all of us that he could make it. This was the first time I heard about Charansparsh. However, I was in no position to get up from the bed and go there.

With Father's Grace, I woke up the next day early in the morning. Seeing Father sitting, I went and sat next to him. He was sitting facing Kailash. It was really a powerful scene. And then Father like Divine Mother kept his hand on my head and then on my back and said "Don't worry. You will complete the Parikrama". My Guru's words were like a command to the Creation. Parikrama got over for me in my mind that very moment. I had firm faith everything will fall in place. He also mentioned that don't worry about yesterday, something major left your system. Sitting in front of Kailash and getting this assurance from Father is a very special moment of my life.

He also asked Hein to accompany me at all times during the Parikrama. That was the beginning of a great relationship with my brother Hein. He held me whenever I was feeling weak in my body, gave me food, and matched his pace with mine. In that terrain, it's not easy to match someone else's speed as everyone walks as per their comfort. Hein followed Father's command and gave himself to ensure that I am comfortable with each and every step in completing Day – 2 Parikrama. I neither took a Pony nor had any intentions of taking one.

Hence, the Parikrama (all by walk) was physically challenging as I continued my walk. Father was sitting (near Dolma La Pass) on a rock and he was actually waiting for me. He had informed people around him that "Sumit has to go to Gauri Kund. I will wait here. Once he reaches Gauri Kund and has completed his prayers, I'll continue my walk". So, he was patiently and lovingly waiting for me. I was deeply touched and the feelings can never be explained or expressed in words. When I saw Gauri Kund, I literally ran down to do my prayers. There was not an iota of weakness or any trace of fever or physical suffering. It was my Guru's Grace that saved me from a near-death situation and blessed me with an opportunity to experience the Divine Mother at Gauri Kund in 2014.

Later, in 2015, I went with a small group of 5-6 for the Kailash Yatra. This year, Mr. Prakash owner of the travel company also accompanied us and I casually inquired if we could go to "Charansparsh". He said "Ok. If you want to go, let's go". So, this way, Prakash, Prahalad and I started our journey towards Charansparsh. Prahalad was ahead and we were following him. Somehow, we lost track of Prahalad as he went far too ahead of us. This is quite unusual as Prakash has been to Kailash at least 60 times till now and I could never imagine, with Prakash with me, we would ever lose our way. In fact, Prahalad had reached Charansparsh and we were quite far from him (and Charansparsh).

As we continued our walk towards Charansparsh, I started feeling really heavy and was finding it difficult to walk in that hilly terrain. Recounting my previous experience (2014) didn't help either as fear started getting better out of me. During this journey (towards Charansparsh), I was witnessing the grandeur of Mount Kailash. I was witnessing the most Majestic views that I had ever seen in my life. Kailash appeared very near (from distance). However, with every 10 steps, the climbing was becoming difficult. When I began my journey, I had a point in my mind (i.e.) I had a target location to reach from which I thought Kailash could be very near. However, I was proved to be wrong. Kailash appeared at a fair distance from that point and at that very moment, I started crying. I remembered Father (Brahmarishi Mohanji), all my ancestors, family members and I was simply thanking for giving me such a wonderful opportunity to witness the grandeur of Kailash even though I couldn't do the "Charansparsh".

I kept Father's picture there and few other possessions that I had carried with me. It was getting late and we waived our hands gesturing Prahalad to return. Mr. Prakash was unhappy with Prahalad and chided him for not guiding us to Charansparsh as we were stuck somewhere in the middle and didn't reach the Charansparsh point. I simply stood there, praying and thinking to myself that reaching Charansparsh isn't as easy as we think. Thus, a visit to "Charansparsh" remained an unfulfilled dream in 2015 too.

And so, in 2016, when the Inner Kora screening was happening, I knew deep inside that it's not that whoever pays money can go to Kailash. I always say it's a call, a call has to come from there, a call has to come from Param Bhakt Nandi Bhagavan, a call has to come from Bhagavan Shankar, a call has to come from all the Ganas and above all, the call has to come from that soil. Unless the call comes, no one can reach there. This time (in 2016), I was in my own shell, not talking much and deep down, I knew this (visit to Kailash) is something really big and special.

Special, because this time when I went for the Manasarovar dip, I invoked everyone, the way Father has taught us. Father always tells us that there is a debt we owe to the Mother Earth. We have received and continue to receive abundant love from many around us and so, I thought of using this body as a medium/channel to take a dip on their behalf. There were many whom I had not been in touch for a very long time. However, I remembered them, I remembered all my ancestors and I said: "Please come and I shall take a dip in Manasarovar on behalf of all of you through this body". Saying this to myself, I entered the Lake Manasarovar.

Father took the first dip and it was a great grand privilege to witness him taking the dip at Manasarovar with that intensity, humility, and love. At Manasarovar when Father goes for the first dip it's a very special moment. Taking his blessings after his dip, Rajesh and I went to the lake for taking our dips. I was deeply impressed by Rajesh's devotion. I was appreciating the way he was taking the dips there. It was extremely cold and when I was finding it difficult, I took the motivation from Rajesh who continued taking his dips and by then I had decided that let me connect with the Lake and continue taking dips. It is indeed a rarest of rare opportunity as not very often one gets a chance to take dips in Manasarovar. It was truly a learning moment to have taken dips alongside Rajesh Kamath.

Later in the evening, I started having burning sensations and acute pain on my shoulders. In fact, I had taken precautionary steps (applying sunscreen lotion, etc.,) in protecting my skin. Yet, there were severe sunburns. While we were traveling back to hotel, I got a subtle thought that these burns were more of a "loving kiss" from the people who had used this body to take a dip at Lake Manasarovar. When this thought arose, I could still feel the pain, but it was no longer uneasy. The whole process of invoking, connecting and then taking dips on behalf of many souls who have touched my lives was indeed a nice and a humbling feeling. I felt light and my Guru's Grace ensured my protection like always. I am sharing this because I strongly feel that when you get a chance or get a call to visit this kind of powerhouse (or) the most powerful place in the universe, if you can be in attitude of Gratitude towards all who have touched your life, it makes you light and fills you with love. It was a very spontaneous thing that happened and it really gave me immense satisfaction and happiness.

We started on our Inner Kora journey & Charansparsh was our first place, I had prepared myself to wear and carry things that weren't too heavy. The thought of Charansparsh occupied my heart and I was mentally very quiet and blank. The entire group had to walk as the ponies are not available and it's a very steep climb. Phaneendar, Rajesh, Hanumatananda, Jayeeta and I were walking with Father. A little later, I realised that there was no one behind us and it hit my mind that Father, by staying at the very end intentionally, was ensuring that everyone is ahead and walking comfortably. We reached a point to take a break and I wasn't surprised to see everyone in good spirits for I knew that when Father is physically walking with us, he protects us and it was as if we were all floating like a feather. We continued our walk for a while and finally, that moment arrived when we all reached Charansparsh. A dream that was not fulfilled in 2014 and again in 2015 is finally a reality.

In 2014, I literally died on the Parikrama and it was a rebirth of sorts for sure and came to know about Charansparsh for the first time. Again in 2015, when I was closer to Charansparsh I understood my capacity or the eligibility wasn't there to reach Charansparsh. In 2016, your Guru, he literally lifts you up and takes you to Charansparsh. I was witnessing these joyous moments and realised how fortunate all of us had been to reach Charansparsh ONLY because of his Grace. When this thought swelled, I bowed down, kept my head and surrendered everything at His Golden Feet.

Statistically speaking, let's assume 10,000 people are going to Kailash every year, only 1/10th (100) might think of going to Charansparsh. Of these 100, only <10 people might actually touch Kailash. It's impossible and has never been heard off. It wasn't in our program either. I don't know from where this thought came but everyone collectively decided to go further up from Charansparsh. And so, we all climbed a slope to reach a high point where we played Shivakavacham. As Father was about to sit, I slipped through a stole that I was carrying with me in 2014 and 2015 to make an aasan for him. Sitting In front of Kailash and listening to Shivakavacham in presence of Father it's surreal.

Out of nowhere, a Tibetan person came probably after touching Kailash and honored Father with a Tibetan Shawl and the same shawl he gifted to me, Raj Nair and then went away. I immediately wrapped my stole and shawl around my neck. In my heart now I knew that the call was there. After the Shivakavacham ended, I looked at Father, His intensity and stillness were indescribable. He sat on a rock and then commanded: "Now, whosoever wants to go, go and touch Kailash".

When the order came from him, we all could witness a transformed energy. I touched his feet, kept my head there, looked at Him and started my walk. The energy was surreal. I quickly figured out that there is this glacier that has melted thereby producing a stream of gushing water. We had to come down, take a jump over this stream of water to go to the other side before proceeding further to touch Mount Kailash, the abode of Lord Maheshwara!

Some people were successful in crossing the glacier, while some including Vijay Bhaiya slipped. When Vijay Bhaiya slipped, I don't know how, but somehow I managed to reach there just in time to extend my arms and held him. A major mishap got averted due to Guru's blessings. By now, Rajesh Kamath, Amar Sherpa, Prahalad, Swamis from Skandavale and I had successfully crossed while Chai, Raj Nair, Vijay and few others were behind. Rajesh Kamath was verbally giving them instructions on how and where to cross the stream but people were still struggling. Phaneendar called out my name in a deep (cry) voice and I said, "Phaneendar, it is very tough crossing this stream". However, I could clearly sense from his cry that he had this intense passion for coming and touching Mount Kailash. I just reiterated to him that it is tough for it was not my nature to say "please come" or "don't come" as it's not my call.

Hanumatananda didn't stop either and he was keen to get to the other side. I was moved to see his determination, his stick got washed away in the stream but he managed to cross it. By now, Rajesh, in a very loud voice was directing people to cross the glacier. I immediately told Rajesh "Don't talk too loud here now" as I said these words I felt a sudden shift inside me and I started walking towards Kailash. I was feeling very light like a feather. My heart was full of joy and I was thanking my Guru for giving me direction, courage, and belief to take this sacred path.

Sherpa Amar and Prahalad were ahead and I was the 3rd one. So, I was trying to make a sense of where they were and hence had to constantly keep an eye on them. But with every step came resurgence and there was no FEAR. It was a homecoming for me personally. The Monster called FEAR that had eluded me from Charansparsh got evaporated with every step I took. After crossing the glacier and walking further up, it was just me and my home. I kept chanting "Aum Namaha Shivaya! Shivaya Namaha Aum! and kept walking towards my Home. I had nothing to lose, no fear and felt very light and comfortable. Looking back, with every step I had no idea what was underneath my footsteps as it was covered with snow. There were stretches I could neither see Prahalad nor his steps. Yet, there was no fear or thought of what could be beneath the snow.

The journey became interesting as I moved nearer to Kailash. When I was almost there, my mind said, "Oh! After the Sherpas, I am the one who made it first". I was witnessing how my mind/ ego worked and said to myself, "Ok, Ab teri watt lagegi." (Oh, now you had it). When I was telling this, Senior Swami from Skandavale slowly walked past me. I was smiling seeing this and said to myself, "Thank you Bhagavan. One thought is so much and has so much merit in it. Mere ko koi number nahi chahiye. (I don't want to come as number one or two). What am I even thinking here?" At that very point, some divine arrangement happened. Swami was seen waiting and Kailash Ji was only a few steps within reach. The Sherpas called out my name and so I went, touched and I looked up at the magnanimity of LORD SHIVA in having all of us there at his abode. When I physically touched Kailash and looked up I could see snow was falling on top of Kailash and it clearly was Abhishekam of Lord Shiva that was happening continuously. It felt as if the entities were coming and performing the Abhishekam and that same snow came down on us as Prasadam. It was a beautiful scene to witness and experience.

God is never interested in serious movies. He always wants comedies. And so when I had finished my prayers and sparsh (touch & feel) of the majestic Mount Kailash, I looked at Kamath and asked him to wait as the stone which is so close to Kailash, the one that honored us to touch Kailash could not handle more weight. Hence the sherpas were guiding us to be careful, telling us to go light and not to crowd the stone. But Kamath was in a different world (obviously, everyone was) and he said, "I won't wait". I went to him and explained him the reason and when his turn came, I looked at Kamath and his clothes were off and he hugged Kailash with his bare body. I was wondering what he was doing and convinced myself that this is also a way to touch Kailash. All of a sudden DB and I started laughing. It was so innocent and a very beautiful sight to behold. Words cannot explain what I witnessed there.

Consecutively for 2 years, reaching Charansparsh was impossible for an insignificant person like me and there I was, touching Kailash. It was the Grace of my Guru who commanded me to go and touch. Maybe a master class from Shakespeare might help describe the experience in words. Even then, I still feel, I won't be able to articulate that experience. I neither had any thoughts nor any feelings/emotions when I touched Kailash. I was in total silence. It felt like I was in Alice in Wonderland. It felt like I was in a place where we don't even have the wisdom, mind or brain to understand. We cannot use our mind to describe or say anything about that moment. When I don't understand anything about me, myself, how could I understand Kailash? The eye, the brain, the senses, nothing can describe anything that happened in that space.

After our darshan, when we were returning we realised how many holes were on the path and wondered how did we walk this whole terrain. I also noticed that there were few other members of our team who were at quite a distance on their way to touch Kailash. I was impressed and touched by their devotion. It is Guru's Grace and Guru's Grace alone that such a call happens in life, not even one's eligibility but Guru's Grace alone. There is no other way around. So we both (Swamiji and I) were coming back. It was really a long walk. We didn't realise how much we climbed with Father. It felt like Father airlifted all of us to Kailash. My experience during 2014 & 2015 vouches for that.

I met Father. I gifted Him a stone from Kailash (from up there). When I came out of his room I saw a beautiful rainbow, just outside our guest house, covering our guest house. I also met Phaneendar and few others through whom came to know about how Chai almost lost her life up there and how Vijay Bhai and the group helped her come back. It was raining very heavily and yet; the group went up again and came back. It was amazing to know this. Hats off to the whole group for their support.

The third day on Inner Kora Parikrama, the tough journey begins again. As per the plan, we started walking to visit Kuber Kund. Some of us were on ponies and some were walking. We reached a point from where the ponies would not go any further and only porters were available. We waited there until the whole group gathered and started walking towards Kuber Kund assuming it was near. It was again a very long walk and there was no proper path. We were crossing small streams of rivers, climbing mountains or climbing big boulders of stones. It was a tough terrain. At some point during the walk, I was walking with Father holding his hand, to help Him. I know He was, in fact, helping us, but in physical body, I was trying to be of some help to Him. Father asked me, "Do you feel something? What do you feel about my body?" I looked at Him and said, "very light". His body felt very light, even though I was holding His hand.

Today, unlike yesterday Devi didi was struggling a bit. She was finding it tough. There was breathlessness and altitude sickness. But Father's body was light, very light, like feather-light. I was able to feel that lightness, especially when I was holding his hands. At this point, from nowhere a Russian came. We interacted with him and came to know that he has been coming to Kailash for the last 7 years and he always finds his own track. He tries to go deep inside to explore and understand the place. He showed us a straight mountain and a straight slope and said, "You have to climb that". I didn't realise the gravity of the situation. Meanwhile, Father was waiting for others to come up. Seeking His permission, I touched His feet and went ahead to see what the Sherpas and the others were up to because the climb did not look simple. When Father blessed me to "GO" I could feel the same kind of energy which I felt a day before on my way to touch Kailash, fully charged.

I walked very light and fast. I felt light but with every foot, the altitude was increasing. I met DB and Riana Gasper who were on their way to the steep/ straight mountain. We kept walking until we reached the foot of this steep slope. The Sherpas were trying to fix a rope in different places and I was also watching the stones that were coming down. I was unable to comprehend what was happening. The porter girl in front of me started walking on this slope. I also saw Swami Govindananda and Swami Brahmananda ahead of the group climbing the slope. They didn't use any rope as at that time there were no ropes. I also thought that this climb followed by very risky walk on snow was to be covered without any ropes. Also, Sherpas were so busy in making their arrangements that they completely forgot to guide us (Swamijis and me). We climbed the same way the sherpas climbed. The way the sherpas operate is- they fix the ropes throughout the track from the bottom of the slope to the top of the slope and they each one waits at regular intervals to push you up.

Unlike any other mountain, climbing this mountain did not feel easy. The terrain was mixed with ice and mud and was very slippery. But when climbing somehow with Guru's Grace this thought came to me, "connect to the mountain, don't try to conquer. Just try to be one with the mountain. Don't try to conquer, don't try to win anything here. Just try to be one or align yourself with the mountain". I also watched the sherpas as they climbed with no effort, very gently they were moving. I also kept my feet one by one, gently. There were some tricky places, but with the thought that this mountain is an ally, it is my friend, I just kept with the mountain and climbed.

I reached this point from where there is a small walk path in the snow and nothing beneath. One wrong step, it would be horrible. It cannot be described. It was so tough. We noticed how these stones of decent size were falling from top with great speed. I couldn't comprehend on why these stones were falling. The weather looked fine, but still, the stones were falling at a speed where, if it hits someone, you are dead. Now we reached a point where we had to do the real climb – rock or mountain climbing, the type of climb that I had never tried in my whole life. The Sherpas who were tying the ropes rushed us, which is when we realised why the stones were falling. The porters, who were ahead of us, were walking and playing in that steep terrain which is why the stones were falling. The Sherpas were shouting and telling them not to do that.

We now used the rope to reach the point which was full of rocks and the climb was extremely tough. Closer to the top of the mountain, there was no support and we had to use our hands to climb up and there was nothing below to support. When I reached that point, there was only one thought I had in my mind, "How will the rest of the team climb all this?" Because every step was very tough, it was like life and death situation. One small mistake of mine will result in someone else suffering or being dead. It was that tough; it cannot be explained in words. And for me, there was no other option. The only option was to climb because all the main Sherpas were down there to push people or pull them up and I had no one to support me. It was only the Grace of Guru that I climbed to the top. When I looked down, I was thinking that I did not prepare for this. Mentally we knew we will have to do a climbing, we discussed it, but no one knew how difficult this climb would be, we did not visualise such a hard terrain and it came as a shock to me. I was thinking how difficult it will be for Father to bring back all the consciousness into the body and do this to reach here. For the ladies and elders in our group, it was a real climb of life, I must say.

When I composed myself from all these thoughts and started walking on the top of the mountain, I was able to see that every miscalculated step of mine would result in stones falling down on the others who were climbing. I realised how porters kept walking without thinking about stones that were falling down upon us (at the start of this climb). I walked until a point where I saw the swamis lying and relaxing after such an experience. I sat there, took my jacket off and slept. I don't know how long I slept, but when I woke up, I saw few more people around me and it was horribly cold with severe winds. There were no main sherpas with us at this point. But the porters who were carrying our luggage forced us to leave the place immediately resulting in confusion. The place where we rested is called "Shiva's durbar" and we are not allowed to stay there for long. It is a huge open place and because we were forced to leave, the Swamis and the others prepared to start. Rajesh Kamath said, "I won't go. I will wait for Father. Until and unless Father comes, I won't go". None of the explanations from others convinced him. He said, "You guys go, I will come with Father". I kind of saluted him for taking that decision. I could see the care in his eyes, the concern in his eyes and firmness in his voice. Thanks Rajesh for giving me a chance to witness that moment.

I understood his noble intention and left with the porters who knew the way to Kuber Kund. So, along with Swamis and few others (4-5 people), we started walking towards Kuber Kund. It was a lengthy walk again, and a tough one too. The porters were walking very fast and here we had to match their pace. My mind was walking faster than porters, I was continuously thinking about rest of the group members and their journey further to Kuber Kund. We were at the scheduled time and porters wanted to reach well on time to the base camp. There was actually, neither any way nor any path, it was a tough terrain but somehow, we reached Kuber Kund. One can clearly see many caves inside the mountains around Kuber Kund. Just when we reached this place and started our prayers, it started raining again. The porters once again started rushing us to leave the place. This time, I was firm and I said "I am not leaving this place until Father comes here. I had enough of rushing and running. It is not happening now". As a result, my porter dropped my bag and left. So Swamis asked me what my program was. I said, "I will wait for Father and you all may leave". This was my decision. Db and Riana were there, they didn't leave with the group.

I just sat there and started praying and it started raining a bit heavily. A thought came into my mind, "What are you up to? It is raining here, there is nothing around, no hut, nothing, what are you up to?" I said to myself, "If this is my last day, let it be. I am not leaving without Father coming". I very well knew that it is very tough to climb for everyone and not very easy. Hence, I wanted the whole group to be safe. This thought stayed in my heart always. I was sitting, chanting, meditating, what not, but there was only one thought- The whole group should reach the base station safely. They should cross all these major hurdles and reach Zuthurpuk.

For the first time in my life, in that moment, I had the courage to face death. I felt no attachment to anything and I was willing to leave everything that very moment. I had only one thought, one prayer and that was for Father and the group to reach Kuber Kund or the base station safely. At one point, there was not even prayer.

I was just silent and connected to the surroundings totally. I invoked Avadhoota Nadanandaji and prayed to HIM to protect Father and all the group members. I received an answer from HIM as I felt lightness in my heart and a very clear thought that the whole group is fine and all the entities around them were blessing everyone and taking care. I felt everything is taken care of and everyone is safe. I received a cool breeze, which was kind of comforting, kind of bringing me back to the body or the senses, assuring me that "everything is being taken care of". Father didn't come there physically but came in subtle body and assured me all is fine.

Only then did I get up and looked around to see DB and Riana were sitting behind me. This was a turning point for me in my relationship with DB and Riana Gasper. There was a common cause for which we stayed and I felt a huge and deep respect for both. DB then got up and said that he did see Father coming this way, but did not arrive at this place and hence concluded that the porters might not have got them to Kuber Kund, instead went straight to Zuthurpuk guest house via some other route. Since I got an assurance sitting there, I could make sense of what DB said. So, I filled my bottle with water from Kuber Kund for Father and started with full energy. I was very happy and it was an unforgettable encounter. We saw Chai coming with her porter at a distance and so we waited. She informed us that Phaneendar and Jayeeta were still struggling to climb and Prahalad and other main sherpas were helping them. As it started to rain heavily and we had a long walk ahead of us, we left the place. When we were walking along the river, thinking about Phaneendar and other people, I nearly slipped and somehow was saved by Guru's Grace. I did fall into the river, but I was saved. At one point, from the top, we were able to see the whole group and Father. We were happy to see them and with more energy seeing them, we kind of walked fast, ran towards them. At last, I went to Father and offered/presented him the water from Kuber Kund. He took the first sip and shared the water with everyone else in the group.

I thought to myself, "In 2014 and 2015, even reaching

Charan Sparsh was so difficult, but today with his Grace and just one glance from my guru, the sacred darshan of Kuber Kund became a reality". We had a long walk ahead of us. I felt it was an unnecessarily long walk to the guest house. It must be about 10 km and it was already evening. I saw cars, pick-up trucks etc. on the way. As I did not want Father to walk further, I requested to stay/sit where he was and went further to see if I can arrange something like a GYPSY (model of vehicle) or a car that can drop Father and few other people with him (including Chai). I walked about 3 km and by Grace found this empty GYPSY and stopped him by going to the middle of the road. With nothing in common (language, etc.,) between us, he displayed anger and signaled me asking what my problem was. I showed him the picture of his guru and made some gestures to show my guru and also made whatever possible gestures I could, to explain that he will need to pick my guru and that I am happy to sit with him and show the place where my guru was waiting. After many back & forth gestures and arguments, I sat with him and reached the place where Father was waiting. (I had never done anything like this, ever in my life). Since Chai could speak his language, she explained the situation. He replied saying he is going to pick someone up and that I am behaving like a child by not getting down from the vehicle. I instructed Chai to explain to him that he must take Father and drop him at Zuthurpuk. Father convinced me saying, he will come back to pick Him up and that I should get down from the vehicle. The GYPSY driver finally agreed to come back after picking some people and dropping them at Zuthurpuk. He promised to come back after dropping them. I asked him to swear on his guru that he will come, which Chai translated to him. It was one of those light moments around faith.

As promised, the pickup GYPSY arrived and Father, along with few others left to Zuthurpuk. I started walking again without knowing the distance to cover. I felt like my feet were saying, "Why did I become your feet?" I was that tired. But I soon joined Mitesh who was along the way. Mitesh helped me walk by cracking some jokes and kept the atmosphere light and cool. On our way, we saw Hanumatananda struggling for reasons unknown. Seeing him, I was reminded of my 2014 walk when I almost died on the track. As it was getting dark and seeing him struggle, we turned on our mobile torches, held Hanumatananda on both sides (despite him saying that he would manage) and walked with him slowly.

Mitesh and I matched the walking speed of Hanumatananda so that we all 3 could walk together. It was again a wonderful experience to cherish when I saw Mitesh's concern, when I saw how Hanumatananda was reluctant to walk with us in the sense he wanted us to maintain our own pace and not be bothered/worried about him. He was willing to come all by himself in spite of his physical weakness. In those little moments, I witnessed the many expressions of love as we continued our long hard walk together, that was filled with many light moments including trying to stop every single vehicle that went past us as nobody bothered to stop. Even the ones who stopped were making fun of us in a light vein.

It was a day filled with so many experiences and emotions. I witnessed faith, I witnessed devotion, I again saw commitment of Father towards each and every member of group. I saw the zeal of sherpas to give themselves in order to help the pilgrims. I saw deep commitment of Rajesh Kamath towards Father. I saw DB and Riana's love for Father and the group. I saw the connection that the Swamis had at their age to the Almighty and to nature. I didn't see a single expression of fear on their face. They were being cared by the divinity. I saw unshakable will of Hanumatananda when he crossed that glacier. And above all, I witnessed what it means when Father says "I am always with you", he just lifts you up like a "rocket" irrespective of situation and venue.

Key takeaways from 2016 Kailash Yatra:

Subtlety is one of the key takeaways. After the 2016 Kailash trip, I realised that Seva, Subtlety and your day to day Work – all these are deeply interconnected. I mean – you will not enjoy your work until you connect with your center and to connect with your center, Seva helps. When you do the work as a seva without any attachments or expectations, living in the mode of Seva, you are bound to get subtle. You are bound to get the knowledge and wisdom that is needed at that point in time to move ahead or climb up.

I feel growth happened in a holistic way after this trip. I have always been a strong believer of "yes to love, no to bitterness at the thought, word, and action level" and this trip has further boosted this belief.

The Homecoming

- Hanumatananda -

Words will surely fall short in this humble effort to narrate my Kailash experiences, and I write only due to the flow of His Grace. Each letter of what I write, I offer as a flower at the lotus feet of Mohanji....

The Calling

The intention to return to Kailash once again had already been set two years ago. Kailash is magnetizing. The limitless peace and silence of the holy Himalayas, and the power and magnificence of Shiva's abode were calling out to me loud and clear. The 2014 pilgrimage to Kailash, was special in that it being the Year of the Horse, a single circumambulatory trek or parikrama around Kailash could be counted as equal to 12 ones. And that good fortune made it possible for the 2014 Outer Kora group to become eligible for undertaking an Inner Kora sometime in the future. I was yearning to get near and walk inside the heart of Kailash again.

I focused to prepare myself mentally, physically and emotionally for the trip by practicing yoga, pranayama, Consciousness Kriya, jogging and trekking. I was aware that in spite of all these, I could still fall short if the factor of surrender was missing. Mohanji has often said that none can enter Shiva's realms without His calling and His permission. And that the mind not being fully empty can become a blocking factor too - a challenge during a trip at altitudes as high as 6000m.

My wife's support was key to be able to undertake this journey, and I am forever grateful to her. Having the support of my closest family was invaluable since that would permit me to relax deeply, and experience this trip fully from start to end.

Proof that Shiva was indeed arranging the trip and dealing with the details, was the preponement of my flight tickets without any particular reason. Three months before departure, the airline company preponed the flight to three days earlier than scheduled. When I asked the officials the reason for this, they did not know, and said that it was very rare or it never happened that flights with three months still left for departure would get preponed! The clarity came to me much later.

On the evening of my day of departure, my hometown was catastrophically flooded. Such floods had not been seen in fifty years. There were more than twenty casualties, with thousands of homes completely destroyed. Had not my flight been preponed by three days, I would certainly have been stranded in my hometown and unable to leave. Shiva's Grace at work.

The journey starts

I arrived earlier in Kathmandu, relaxed and prepared myself mentally for a few days, before joining the rest of the Kailash with Mohanji group at the Soaltee Hotel for accommodation and briefing. The next day, we visited the holy temples of Pashupatinath and Budhanilkanth, and later that day we left for Nepalgunj. We stayed there overnight to fly out again next day by helicopter to Simikot, Nepal, and then on to Hilsa at the Nepal-Tibet border.

Finally we crossed the border to enter Tibet and drove to Purang where we stayed a whole day for body acclimatization to the rarefied air at 3770m altitude. The hypoxia was already hitting in, and I experienced from mild to at times splitting headaches, and occasional nausea. During the satsang Mohanji advised us not to use any medication for hypoxia, as the body has a natural mechanism of coping with altitude change and would acclimatize. I went with Mohanji's advice, determined to cope with the hypoxia symptoms on foot.

Early morning the following day, we headed towards the sacred Manasarovar Lake situated at 4590m altitude, to take the karmic cleansing dips and have the first darshan of Kailash from a distance. During breakfast that morning, Mohanji advised me to take at least eighteen dips: the first dip for ourselves, the second for our ancestors, and the third for our Guru. Any dips afterwards could be spontaneously taken for whoever we felt - friends, teachers, etc.

As soon as we arrived at the lake by bus, we all headed toward taking the dips, with Mohanji leading the way, Kamath and Sumit by his side. The rest of us followed. I waited for the crowd of people around Mohanji to clear so that I could take the dip at his holy feet. Once that was done, I moved away and started taking the rest of my dips. My goal was to reach 108 dips, which I accomplished only through His Grace. The feelings during and after taking the dips are indescribable. Purification happens on all levels. One dip after another I took for myself first, then my ancestors, Mohanji, all my past gurus, all the gurus of the Tradition, my family one by one, father, mother, wife, children, the Mohanji group in Macedonia, Serbia, worldwide... Faces kept coming up and I would take a dip for each being that came onto my awareness screen. I finished up with the last of the 108 dips for the Grand Tradition of Masters.

Once that was done, I stepped out of the lake and dried myself. Then putting on thermal clothing I sat to meditate, facing Kailash. It was a meditation I shall never ever forget, for there was no effort whatsoever necessary... I simply was already there. Aware as "I AM". It felt like I was finally home. A complete wholeness.

We spent that night in Darchen and had a good rest in preparation for the following day: the commencement of the Inner Kora pilgrimage.

The Pilgrimage begins

It was day one of the holy pilgrimage.

We assembled near Yam Dwar for the start of the 16 km long gradual walk towards Dirapuk, at the base overlooking North Face of Kailash. Ponies and porters were assigned through blind drawing of tickets for both Outer and Inner kora yatris. As soon as I was assigned a sherpa, I bowed down at Mohanji's feet, asking for His blessing for a successful pilgrimage. Father blessed me, and we moved towards Yam Dwar which we circumambulated three times clockwise. We were to leave some personal belonging behind symbolically, ring a bell inside Yam Dwar, and move on ahead without turning to look back.

It is a long walk but manageable. The weather was sunny and dry. My only concern and challenge was the sherpa being young and impatient, and nowhere to be seen. He was either running too far ahead, or lagging behind laying on grass, relaxing and dozing off in the sun! I was continuing to be patient, accepting everything as it came my way, especially regarding his frivolous nature.

A few kilometers into the yatra, I managed to keep up with the sherpa and ask for my 1L bottle of water which was in my backpack he had been paid to carry, so that I could refill my smaller bottle and extinguish my thirst. Well, he informed me that he had finished up all of it - there was no more water left. And, we had around ten more kilometers left to walk, now with no water. Hmmm, this pushed my buttons all right. So I was out on a mission to straighten up and discipline my sherpa or I was doomed for the rest of my trip. I gave him strict instructions not to drink or eat anything from my backpack anymore without my permission . . . or else I would be turning another page!

Not drinking water at above 4000m altitude can really makes things worse regarding hypoxia. Luckily, there was Vijay from UK with me, and he gave me a whole 500 ml water bottle. Vijay saved the day.

The sherpa, young and reckless as he was, continued to be nowhere in sight, and all my food, snacks, back-up clothing, and

The Homecoming

everything else was with him in the backpack. Anyway, I let him be for the day. Perhaps the day after we could get along better.

On approaching Dirapuk base where we would be spending the night with a view of the North Face of Kailash, I had a profound insight that would change my mind set completely for the rest of the trip, and onwards. At one point while walking, full clarity suddenly arose, and darshan of the pure, radiant, and formless being that is Mohanji, was revealed to me. I finally got it. All my doubts, conflicts and conclusions regarding Mohanji as a physical being, fell off. I was stripped off from all notions about him as a human. I saw who or what he actually is – a pure, uncontaminated, and indivisible consciousness, radiating unconditional love and driven only by higher purpose. I promised myself to remember this forever and pray for Grace to keep this revelation alive always.

I made my way towards the Dirapuk guest house and crashed onto the bed, for a good night's sleep. The following day we were to go for boulder climbing at Charan Sparsh where we would be allowed by Shiva to touch the feet of Kailash.

Touching Shiva's Abode

Day two of parikrama

The plan was to do a gradual walk towards Charan Sparsh and touch the feet of Kailash.

I was walking slowly at my own pace. I found that walking for a count of nine and resting for count of nine suited me, and I could keep up with the group this way. Finding a rhythm of alternate walking and resting was key at this high altitude, I realized.

Hanumanji's Breath

Soon, I caught up with Mohanji and half of the group. When Mohanji saw me he said, "Hanumatananda, breathe like Hanumanji. Try this: inhale fully through the nose, inflating your belly. Holding the breath, pump up the mouth muscles and make a monkey face. Release abruptly the air through the mouth. This is the Hanuman Breath. Now try it." I did as instructed for few breaths and felt a surge of new energy in the whole body. Mohanji asked me, "Now, how do you feel?" I responded, "Energetic, full of new energy." He said, "This breath is what Hanumanji did before he flew up in the sky. Now, keep doing this breath as we climb uphill."

Shiva Kavach

Finally, we reached the boulders of Charan Sparsh. We touched the feet of Kailash, feeling the blessing of being allowed to be there at Shiva's Abode. Soon enough, we started climbing the boulders with the help of the sherpas, to reach flat ground and sit for meditation. Mohanji asked for the audio recording of the Shiva Kavach to be played. We all sat in a trance-like state in front of the North Face of Kailash, listening to the chanting in Mohanji's voice. It was powerful beyond words. The ground was being prepared for more blessings.

As the chant ended, I noticed a small group of people continuing the climb uphill. I got up and started walking without much thinking. After a few minutes, we got to a place in the glacier where there was a slippery slope sliding into a stream and rocks. A few sherpas along with Prahalad, Sumit, DB, the swamis, Raj Nair and Kamath went ahead and managed to go on the other side of the glacier. Someone shouted to the rest of us in the back to stay back as it was too dangerous. I sat on a rock next to Mohanji, and asked him where we were headed. He told me that the intention was to touch Kailash, and that it was a big miracle that we were even there as the region had been closed up for entering by the Chinese army. I asked him if he was going forward to touch Kailash, and he replied, "Yes, I am going". Well, I was going too then, there was no turning back. At that moment I decided to go all the way no matter what. It was a force stronger than anything.

Ignoring the shouting and warnings, I moved forward to the crack in the glacier. I went near it, and saw Spomenka, Vijay and

The Homecoming

Chai sitting and waiting there on a rock. Looking back, I spotted Mohanji sitting on a rock as well and I start calling out to him to come over as I would make sure he crossed over safely. I was certain he could. I could hear the people around him tell him not to go as it was not safe. I saw him standing up and go down the hill to where a group was meditating. I was disappointed that he was not coming, but I turned back towards Kailash and started walking towards the glacier to cross it. Vijay shouted to me to not go as it was not safe. I responded, "Chill, Vijay, I am going." I evaluated the terrain, walked down the slippery slope, and jumped inside the crack beside the stream and rocks. I tossed my trekking sticks and gloves over onto the other side, and managed to climb the icy cliff. I managed to reach the other side safely.

Seeing this, Vijay, Spomenka and Chai got moving ahead as well. Spomenka's sherpa showed up from the top of the hill and pointed to another safer road for crossing forward. He was sent by Shiva to guide us until the end of the climb to touch Kailash. Treading the path, and guiding us through the terrain, the sherpa was so loving and gentle, giving us water to drink from the streams, and waiting for us to rest, never pushing us . . . just a loving, reassuring presence. It is such Grace that we had him to guide us.

After more than an hour of walking, we meet the first group coming back from Kailash. They discouraged us from continuing on as it would be dark soon and it was dangerous terrain. I said, "Thank you, but we have flashlights," and we moved on ahead. No one was taking away the blessing of touching Kailash from us at this point. We were determined to move on.

Moving ahead, I noticed a huge face in the rocks, and below it a triangle-shaped, snow-covered portal into Shambala. I just knew it, it was unmistakable. It was an entrance into another dimension, and the face above it was the face of its inhabitants. One could dismiss it as all a play of the mind from the hypoxia and the exhaustion, but I saw it and know it to be truer than true, and more real than anything. I cannot explain it, but feel it. It was not of this physical world, hence physical and logical explanations will fall short.

As we approached the magnificent Kailash, we could hear rocks falling off from everywhere. The mountain is huge, and the sound as that of small pebbles falling but in reality these were huge rocks falling off Kailash. The scenery was just breathtaking. The feeling was as if entering a womb since Kailash is not just the one huge piece of rock we see from afar. The mountain is massive, making a kind of half-circle shape, producing a feeling of entering a portal. There is indescribable peace and silence in that place. And the feeling that we all agreed on having, was one of homecoming. It was as if after lifetimes and lifetimes, we were finally back home where we belonged.

We had to now take the last few steps towards Kailash. The snow was deep here that we needed to tread carefully. One by one, we went near the rocks to touch Kailash and have communion with the holy mountain. The feeling was one of eternal gratitude to Mohanji for making this encounter possible, and to Lord Shiva for allowing us to get near His abode and touch it. I moved closer and placed my forehead on a round rock in the mountain, resting both arms on the surface and merging into Kailash. A moment of blessing I will never ever forget. I remain forever grateful for being allowed this incredible privilege of physically touching the Bindu of the Universe.

We picked up some smaller stones from Kailash as power objects, leaving behind a few personal belongings as symbols of the letting-go of old karmas, and then bowing down to Kailash, we headed back towards Dirapuk base as it would soon be dark. Retracing our steps and descending through the hill was so much easier. We glanced back often to have Kailash darshan. It was all happening as if in a dream. Soft hail started falling on our faces with the wind, and soon it began raining. None of it mattered, though and we were all looking forward to getting some sleep and resting from the super difficult climb uphill.

Once we reach Dirapuk, I immediately looked for Mohanji's room. I found Father resting, and I entered just to hug him and touch His holy feet. I am drenched in endless gratitude.

The Re-birth

Day three of the Inner Kora pilgrimage: the plan was for an 18km long trek towards Zutulphuk.

I woke up with a stiff swollen left thigh. My mind was in panic, that my journey was finished then and there. I touched my thigh and did not feel anything - it was numb from the long tedious uphill walk to Kailash from previous day. At that moment Mohanji showed up at the doorstep of the room to ask me how I was feeling. I told him that I could not feel my thigh and was not sure what to do. He spoke in his calm and reassuring way, "Just drink more water and it will be fine." Drink more water? At that moment in time I did not believe it would be better merely from drinking more water but Mohanji just reaffirmed by repeating that it would loosen up. I reminded myself to just have faith in Mohanji's words. I got up, my thigh hard as stone, but managed to walk with full faith that somewhere along the way it would all be magically better somehow.

It was a steep uphill trek, and I was trying to get into a rhythm of walking and resting so that my energy was evenly maintained throughout the whole day. My sherpa was very unhelpful and distracting me from preserving the energy for walking. He was again either running in front or hanging out somewhere behind, out of sight. The memory of Spomenka's sherpa from the previous day who had been extremely helpful, was making me very jittery towards my own sherpa who was pressing all of my buttons. I managed to find him and tell him very strictly that he needed to always be within ten steps from me, and be asking me if I needed something and giving me water to drink. He couldn't care less. He just nodded, but did his own thing again. What was even worse was that he was even teasing me and asking me sarcastically if I needed something, like I was some kind of royalty. And he then also told all the sherpas about what a pain I was. They were all then talking about me in Tibetan behind my back. Hit after hit to my royal ego!!

I give up on the whole sherpa thing and tried to concentrate on the trek and drink enough water as Father had suggested.

I could sense that there was a big reason for all the drama that was happening but did not have a clue as to the reason at that moment. After a few hours' continuous walk uphill, my thigh was already half way better and I started feeling it. Drinking lots of water seemed to have made a difference. But, to be fully honest, I feel that it was really Mohanji's healing words that were the 99% of the magic. I relaxed, and became confident that the journey was not finished for me after all.

We soon arrive at a huge plateau and at a distance, I could see a steep icy glacier and people climbing up like little ants on top of the hill. At first, the idea of climbing this hill seemed crazy. But we had full confidence in the experienced sherpas who were treading the path, setting up the ropes and making sure that all was safe for the climb. At this point, I noticed that my left leg thigh had miraculously recovered completely. Nothing but Mohanji's Grace.

The highest point of the hill was somewhere around 5800m of altitude, and to reach there we needed to use ropes, helmets and harnesses to climb the steep icy glacier. One by one we started climbing to a spot in the glacier where we needed to be locked with harnesses to the rope, which lead to the top. It was getting very cold and windy, and most of the people were progressing very slowly, as there was very little oxygen. We needed to use a lot of muscle power to pull ourselves along the rope to which we were safety locked.

Every few minutes one of the sherpas would shout "Roooooooock", as rocks fell down the hill, flying towards us. Most of the rocks continued swooshing down, missing us. But some of the rocks did hit us. Luckily the bigger and sharper rocks were missing us. I was gazing, almost hypnotized at the top of the hill from where the rocks were shooting down, awaiting a rock to fly past by or hit me. Soon, I start shouting "Rooooooock" too and warning the rest of the group. Soon enough Father turns around to me, looks me in the eyes and says, "I told you. Don't worry. I am taking care." OK. I relax, and let go. Still, my gaze is fixated on the hill above, and I am super-attentive for any rock that could hit me and finish my journey!!

I was among the last in the group to climb through the rope. When my turn came, there were no harnesses left and I had to wait for half an hour more for a new harness in the already freezing weather. At last, the harness was on, and with helmet on, I started pulling myself up the hill through the rope. I thought that once I finished the climb it was all over and I could relax. But oh, how I wrong was.

Second birth

There was one point where we were instructed to unharness the safety belt from the rope and climb a steep passage holding onto a rope with bare hands. It was almost a 90-degree climb and I was completely without a breath. Around 7-8 sherpas had positioned themselves in the passage on both sides. The right side was a full fall down, and one could not hold on to anything for safety. Once the sherpas saw me they started making fun of me when they noticed I was struggling for air. I shouted, "Stop, stop, waaaaait, I need to rest." They started laughing even more. In the struggle for breath I started panting and screaming, and the sherpas laughed even more. I felt my heart was going to explode from beating so fast. It was a moment of truth. I then and there realized that my ego was being provoked by my sherpa, and then by all of the other sherpas in the passage, so that it dies in the passage. Struggling not to die, with all of them laughing, my ego said goodbye to me. I felt so helpless.

The whole scenario was very much like that of taking birth. The feeling was of going through the womb, through a narrow passage and passing through it up to the hill outside, which represented a new life. I was struggling to get to flat and safe ground. It was painful but inevitable. I managed to climb the passage, but it was not over. One of the sherpas gave me a hand and guided me to safety.

Later, they told me he was not one of the sherpas, and Father commented that it had been Shiva himself guiding me to safety. I had glued myself to the rocks, still struggling for air. Bit by bit, holding this hand, I had been brought to flat ground. My old ego had died. I was born anew. I will never be the same again.

I looked around to see where to go next. Spotting someone in the distance, I started walking towards them. The area was piled with stones placed one on top of another, and the feeling was like being in a field of death and birth at the same time.

My sherpa's role had now become perfectly clear to me. I felt only gratitude towards him at that moment. He was not even aware that through the nature of his character he had provoked my ego leading to its slaughter in the narrow passage. Shiva had arranged it all. It had been His orchestration. It was Mohanji's Grace. I feel eternally grateful to Mohanji for I am re-born because of Him and his Grace.

My sherpa came to ask me if I needed water. Haha. Sure, I already loved this guy so much, I could hug him the whole day and night. I then offered him the entire lunch package that the sherpas had given me that morning, and he accepted it wholeheartedly.

I left behind Mohanji's eye-card on the field and turned towards the most beautiful mountain scenery ever. I asked my sherpa a few times where Kuber Kund was, so we could visit it, but he shrugged as if he did not understand what I was saying. Pointing downhill, he then uttered his most favorite word, and the only word he said to me from the moment we met, "Chalo! Chalo!" Which means "Let's go!" in Hindi. He is hurrying me because soon would be the pitch blackness of night.

We continued the trek downhill towards Zuthulpuk base. Along the way we soon caught up with Mohanji, Devi, Mitesh, Kamath Bhai, Spomenka, Vijay, and their sherpas. We moved ahead together as a group seeing a lot of miracles along the way.

One of the miracles was the darshan of Shiva Abisheka in the mountain behind us. His two eyes visible in the rocks, and amrit falling from his third eye. We prostrated and thanked Shiva for the blessing.

We also had darshan of aged bearded Hanumanji meditating and blessing us, on the mountain ahead of us.

Along the way, hail started falling. Mohanji said that we should

The Homecoming

open our mouths and what came in from the little frozen droplets was enough, and the right amount. He said it was not hail at all, but purely Shiva's blessings. We were all standing there with open mouths ready for the blessings. It must have been quite a scene.

We needed to move fast as there was still a long way to go, and it was soon going to get dark. As we trekked, Mohanji pointed out to me a stone on the ground, asking me to pick it up. It was a brownish stone, mountain-shaped. He then told me to keep it for protection like an amulet, and as a reminder of something that he then forewarned me about.

Mohanji spoke: "Always be at the feet of Shiva no matter what happens in the outer world. The next few years will be very challenging for you. You will soon face many obstacles, doubts and losses that can displace you from the path. Many will try to malign my name and talk ill about me. But you must always strive and stay with what is true for you. This is why you took the Inner Kora call. The remembrance of this can save you, otherwise you may miss the opportunity for liberation in this life, as I am not coming back."

I took the stone and placed it on my heart, and promised and prayed to remember these words always. Along the way, Mohanji showed me two more stones to pick up. They were black smaller stones. I keep these power objects on my altar to keep me safe and protected on the Path of Liberation. Mohanji's blessings are engraved on them.

Our group soon split in two. One group left for Zutulphuk in a car, and the rest of us continued walking. It was the end of the day and I was completely exhausted, my legs not able to move any longer. I was walking with two beautiful souls, Mitesh and Sumit Bhai. It seemed like a never-ending walk. It was already pitch-dark, and there was no sign of Zutulphuk being near. At one point, I could not keep up with Mitesh and Sumit. They noticed this, so both took me by hand from both sides, and supported me in walking. I am not a person who shows weakness or helplessness, and I hide it well and avoid being helped. But as my old ego had died up there on the hill, I even enjoyed the help and support with the walking. It felt so good to be vulnerable and helped by my two wonderful soul brothers.

After each ten meters I had to stop and rest. My body was giving up and I was starting to fall asleep as I walked. At last, we reached Zutulphuk base and stopped in the canteen to eat some noodles before hitting the bed. That night, Grace was at play, so I even stayed in Mohanji's room and slept beside his bed. What more to ask for? What a beautiful ending to a long miraculous day. I fell asleep even before my head hit the pillow. I slept like a baby beside my beloved Father.

Full moon at Manasarovar Lake

After having one day off at Darchen, the Kailash trip concluded with one more visit to Manasarovar Lake. We found one nice place on the shores of the lake, and went in to take more karmic cleansing dips. The ambience was serene.

Later that evening, a full-moon homa was performed by Mohanji and the swamis from Skanda Vale UK Ashram on the shores of the lake. We sang bhajans late into the night. Early morning at 3:00 am I woke up to hopefully see the Celestial Beings take dips in Manasarovar Lake under the mesmerizing full moon. I meditated until 4:30 and practiced Consciousness Kriya. There were a lot of noisy people beside the lake shouting and calling upon Mahadev as if He would respond to shouting, or commune with minds filled with noise. I realized that to have communion with higher beings one has to match their frequency and level of operation. One has to still the mind and be so utterly tranquil that the Higher will have no choice and descend by itself. We only have to prepare the ground with purity, faith and patience. The rest is up to Grace.

I remain eternally grateful to Mohanji, Shiva, Hanumanji and the Grand Tradition of Masters.

Surrender

- Spomenka Dragojevic -

Kailash. The moment I heard during one meditation session that there was going to be an trip organised to that place with Mohanji in the spring of 2012, it crossed my mind that I wanted to go. A few days earlier I had received an email, a wonderful story about that place, with photos (from our lovely Hana) and I was enthralled. Otherwise, before that, I had barely been aware of Kailash's beauty and importance. Kailash is the "Crown Chakra of the Mother Earth", and home of Lord Shiva. The pilgrims circle around the holy mountain, chanting sacred prayers and meditating. The pilgrimage lasts for three days, the time it takes pilgrims to make one 52-kilometer-long circle around the mountain. It is believed that after making one circle around the holy mountain, an individual is cleansed from all the sins committed during his or her lifetime.

The meditation started, and I was contemplating about Kailash. Something unusual happened to me. I had a feeling as if my legs had been paralysed, but in a good way. Something like a deep connectedness – rootedness. The decision was made: I would sign up for that trip. And of course, I did just that. But that year our group from Serbia could not manage to get the visa, so I gave up on the trip.

Now Mohanji was going again, and I signed up again. The day of departure came, everything ran smoothly, and there were no particular obstacles. A few days before the departure I noticed that everything was somehow going smoothly for me - it simply flowed. A wonderful feeling. It continued in the next few days. After arriving at the airport, the feeling only intensified and I became aware that I was surrendering to the flow. Nothing surprised me and nothing annoyed me - I accepted everything as it was. The experience of being in the present moment. A magnificent feeling. The beginning was nice and pleasant. Izabela was a wonderful co-traveller. Even if there was something that bothered us, she resolved it. I was just travelling and smiling.

Kathmandu - I was thrilled by everything around me, all my senses were alert. I wanted to feel and experience as much as possible. Being for the first time in a part of the world which is so different from everything I had seen before, I wanted to absorb as many things as possible.

The next day, Mohanji and Deviji arrived, and till the end of the day, all the remaining members of the group kept arriving to make up the group - 84 of us in total.

We left Kathmandu and continued on our way through the marvelous landscape of Nepal. All this was new for me, and I was trying to take in as much as possible and lock it inside of me, not to forget ever again. We arrived at Hilltake where we marvelled at the tallest statue of Shiva, which is 44m tall and which is also called Kailash Mahadev. The next day we were supposed to continue by bus towards the border. It was past breakfast, and Mohanji told me I needed to massage Sumit (one of the main trip organizers, who was holding two phones at that moment) since he needed it (by the way, I often massage my Guru in Novi Sad, it does him good). After that, we found out there was a landslide and the only road which could lead us further was closed. But the Grace of Shiva and Mohanji took us on. There were no obstacles for us, and we continued our trip by helicopters. Our organizers managed that morning to rent the last two available helicopters. The Grace and blessings followed us during our journey - the journey towards transformation.

We reached the place Kodari on the Tibetan border where we

waited for the remaining part of the group to arrive. I decided the best thing for me was to lie down a bit on the wonderful grass carpet and just enjoy myself. Filled with wondrous impressions and happiness, nothing bothered me, everything was splendid and I felt well. As the journey progressed, more and more friends from the group start feeling sick (altitude sickness), and I was helping them, of course, as much as I could, with homeopathic medicines and massage.

Almost everyone took the medicine for altitude sickness, some people even two or three times a day. I didn't need it, only feeling something mild in the forehead area, a light pressure which occasionally faded away or increased.

When we arrived at Nyalam, the number of people I was trying to help was quite significant and it kept rising, though of course, I was not the only one helping. I have to admit that I was surprised by the number of people who were ill, as I was feeling ok and was not thinking of how hard all that was. Izabela was there, and she was helping me wholeheartedly. That night I felt for the first time the symptoms of altitude sickness. I was woken up by the struggle for air, and that was the first time I took the medicine for altitude sickness.

Gratitude

Even though I massaged him every day, Sumit didn't feel all too well, which, of course, never showed because he was so attentive and eager to listen to and help everyone, regardless of how occupied with worries and problems with organization he was.

I can't remember exactly where it happened, but I think it was Nyalam. While I was massaging Sumit, I felt an incredible energy. Even though I had done it on several occasions before, that day was different from the others. I can't describe in what way, but something was different, even though the participants were the same. After the massage, Sumit thanked me in such a way that I just wasn't able to receive all that gratitude. I have never experienced something similar in my life. In order to distance myself from it,

I told him there was no need to thank me, since I had nothing to do with it, that Shiva was working through me. Only when I uttered that did I realise the true meaning of those words, and then scolded myself. Who was I for Him to work through me, so I was ashamed of my words.

But here: Dear Sumit, I'm using the opportunity to thank you once again from the bottom of my heart for that incredible experience I had.

Unusual Welcome

The trip was still a real joy for me in the full sense of that word. I was enjoying and absorbing. I was simply basking in the energy of those magnificent landscapes we were going through and in Mohanji's energy. I had no expectations, I enjoyed every moment.

We arrived at the foot of Kailash and approached the wonderful lake of Manasarovar, purgatory of all negativity, transcending life and to which celestial beings descend and bathe. I felt amazing and full of enthusiasm among the energies, something that was to be experienced, not described. I rarely took photos during our trip for two reasons: the first one is I didn't have my camera with me and the second one is that I had left my phone charger at the hotel. My battery was almost empty, but I was thinking: what do I need it for, I'm not expecting any calls anyway, I can just take photos. While we were approaching, I picked up my phone and started taking photos. I couldn't see anything unusual, I was just thrilled by that place and all the sights and wanted to capture all that. At one moment, I glanced at the photos I had previously taken, and remained surprised, to say the least, by what I saw. Three circles were present in almost all the photos I took. I showed them to Devi telling her - look what a welcome we've got. She was as surprised as I was. I was the only person who captured that, or in other words, they were visible only in my photos. It was a fantastic feeling and again proof I was not alone, there was someone to help me. There was only one question I couldn't answer: how come I deserved that?

Swimming in the lake was unforgettable. I wasn't cold, not for one moment, though we were at the height of 4500 m, with snow on the surrounding mountains. I took 9 dips and remained swimming in the lake, collecting pebbles. I was among the last ones to get out of the water, and thank heavens I had the opportunity to witness Mohanji doing *abhisheka* to Devi. A wonderful feeling of calm and peace which I had had during the whole journey, was only intensifying as we were approaching our goal. During the night I woke up with the same feeling of not having enough oxygen, so I took the medicine for the second time. With that came the unforgettable experience of holy beings at night over the lake. They appeared as light forms flying above, dipping and disappearing. I wanted to thank Devi for being with me.

Arrival to the Threshold of Lord Shiva

Parikrama began, and even before we arrived, I had decided to go on foot. I was even thinking of carrying my own backpack, but gave it up the moment I felt its weight on my back!

I didn't know what to expect further, and what could happen to me, but I knew that the only things that mattered were Grace and surrender. Was I going to make it? Did I manage to surrender myself? Did I manage to achieve at least one bit of what our Gurudev had been telling us? The profoundness of the experience depends on our openness and readiness to let go of our ego. Difficulty or easiness of the trip is proportionate to that experience.

So far, everything had been going perfectly for me, and I knew then it wasn't because of my fitness, since it is actually irrelevant at this place. After all, I was at the Grace of the two great ones, Lord Shiva and Mohanji. The first day was a light walk through heaven for me. The energy made me feel as if I had been on a different planet. All that happened there had nothing to do with being in everyday life, at least that was my feeling. I saw Kailash from up close for the first time. Happiness, thrill, joy, all that together followed by the feeling of immense gratitude to Lord Shiva for allowing me to be in that place and on that path. By the way, it is said that only those who are allowed, arrive at Kailash. I had the wonderful company made up of our Jelena, Mitesh, Zoran, Hein, Zagy and all the other ones kept adding to it. We were at quite a high altitude at that moment and a lot of people didn't feel well. It's not easy to be on the path of Shiva and stand in front of his door. But that was exactly why we had come, for him to release us of our burden, and no release is easy. Mohanji's presence was invaluable. As he said: "Kailash is Shiva, the state of your origin, which you forgot during your life. Be Shiva, and spontaneously you will be in unity with Kailash. Shiva and Kailash are ONE."

Arrival at our accommodation marked the end of the walking for that day which went flawlessly. The day concluded with a great number getting sick, and I was trying to help as many as I could. The only thing I couldn't do was eat, though it had been said that we all had to eat, no matter how we felt. Oh well, I managed to evade that order saying I had eaten when asked, because nobody was really able to check it. I was literally running from to room to room to help the ones feeling sick. When I went to bed that night, a well-known feeling woke me up - the lack of oxygen. I took the medicine for the third time.

I love you, Shiva

We were all excited that day because of the thing that was awaiting us – the hardest section of the road. That day we were supposed to pass 22 km and reach the highest point of our journey, Dolma La Pass at 5700 m. Everyone was in a hurry that morning, and maybe a bit worried. I was still feeling very well. My dearest Jelena and I moved on, with the rest of the crew of course, and everything went just fine until we started climbing seriously. My heart began pounding and I had to take breaks more often. At that moment, we had already been seriously divided as a group and everyone was trying to catch their own pace which was, actually, the most important thing. Among the last ones, Mitesh also split from us. I was slowing them down with my frequent halts to catch my breath. Jelena and I remained with our inseparable sherpas who were now glancing at me with more and more concern, while I was just smiling and saying I was fine. Naturally, by the way, we encountered numerous Tibetans who were on the same path as us, the only difference being they looked like they were walking over a plane, unlike us. I noticed curiously that a Tibetan woman in a big hat had been walking close to us for quite a long time, and the two of us were exchanging glances every now and then. It seemed as if she had been asking me how I was, and I had been answering with my eyes I was okay, that everything was alright. At that point we had already got quite far away on our journey. At one moment, I stopped to take a rest and realised something unusual was going on behind me. I turned around and saw an incredible scene. The sunrays were falling on Kailash in such an extraordinary way, a magnificent sight. I told Jelena to turn around and see it herself. While the two of us were watching enchanted by that spectacle, someone stopped next to us. I saw a young man who was telling me he loved me, and completely astonished, I told him I loved him too. He turned from me to Jelena and told her the same, and after she answered him, he disappeared. The two of us looked at each other, astounded, wondering what had just happened. Then I laconically answered - Shiva was telling us he loved us and again, I scolded myself because of that thought, asking who I was to deserve that.

We moved on, and after a few steps, I had to stop again, asking Jelena if she thought our pace was too fast. She thought it wasn't, it was just right. I told myself that it was okay, she was younger and I had no right to impose my tempo on her, but I had to follow hers, because the young are the future of the world. However, we had barely crossed 100 m, when she complained about not feeling well, and that she was feeling faint. Good people around us helped me to catch her in time and put her down, so she wouldn't fall and hurt herself. Of course, I had the medicine I needed at that moment at hand, but a few Tibetan women also offered help with something they had, some kind of chewing herb which we gladly accepted. In the meantime, our sherpas had reached us and when Jelena convinced us she was better, we moved on. However, we didn't get far, when she started fainting again. The sherpas began to get really worried at that moment, and said that we had to take ponies or Jelena would have to go back to camp. The two of us were at first taken by surprise, because we had been told before it was impossible to rent ponies during the *parikrama* itself. We accepted that, and when we actually looked around, we saw three ponies were in our vicinity. Again in action, our dear guardians negotiated the price and at the next moment, the two of us were on the back of those lovely animals. We were joking along the way that Shiva decided to send us help, commenting the character of those marvelous creatures, since they were quite different in behaviour. I'd rather not share our comments.

And so the two us safely reached Dolma La Pass where we were welcomed by light sleet, but regardless, the feeling was magnificent. We were sitting and enjoying ourselves for a long time. I wanted to go down to the Gauri Kund, but I was aware it would have been too much for Jelena so I didn't mention it. Leaving her was simply not an option. Only the desire to wash my face and take a sip of that water stuck in my heart. While I was thinking about it, I was watching Swami Govinda lightly descending and reaching the wonderful lake.

The rest of the journey was quite smooth. We rejoined Mitesh and moved on. In the meantime, a lot of other people had also reached the top. The curious thing was that I hadn't seen the woman with the hat who followed us again. But the really strange part of it was that the same person had also helped Mohanji when he wasn't feeling well. The story about an unusual woman who showed up at the exact moment when he was feeling sick, made a great impression on me. And I would not have thought it extraordinary had I not seen the photo and realized that this was the very same woman who had spent a good portion of the journey with us. But again, why should that be so strange? Actually, there was a difference of couple of hours between us. Mohanji was so much ahead of us. How was it possible for her to be near him, when she should have been far behind him?

We arrived thrilled, at our accommodation where we were

welcomed by Izabela who was hugging and kissing us and at the same time asking what took us so long! I was overwhelmed with happiness and fulfillment.

The third day was really a light walk through heaven with incredible sights I'll never forget.

The rest of the trip was the most beautiful thing in my life. I felt as if I had been floating through some out-of-the-earth time. During the whole trip, I was wide awake, eager to experience everything incredible and ethereal. I spent that day with the fabulous feeling of love which was really intensive. I would glance at the sky and clouds quite often, and I only saw messages of love. I even saw the head of my beloved dog Čupko in one of the clouds, and that really moved me.

Grace and Surrender

I was often wondering what had actually happened on that journey and I think I've found the answer. When they asked Mohanji how to know if someone was ready for Kailash, he answered: Grace is the thing you need, and faith is the key for ensuring it. This is a rough journey. It will test your courage, faith, belief and devotion on your path of liberation. This is a supreme pilgrimage! Thus the Grace is crucial, it's more important than oxygen. When you face all your troubles with faith and surrender (to the highest force), the journey will go smoothly and pleasantly. When you approach it with expectations and doubts, you will only encounter problems and difficulties. We can decide for ourselves that we'll go to Kailash. But if the Lord does not allow it, we won't make it. That is why faith, belief, silence, prayers, surrender and observation are so important. Kailash has to be experienced, felt, witnessed, and not "seen".

Now, when I'm thinking about it, I can only say that my journey was as easy because I managed to surrender myself completely. There were no expectations, not anything, only the empty space ready to be filled with all that energy. I'm still wondering, at how Shiva chose to help the others through me, and I don't have the answer to that question. I'm only certain that His energy was more than present in me, because how else could I have overcome with such ease all the challenges carried by such a journey.

The trip was ethereal and elevated, being in front of God's door in the presence of Mohanji. The feeling is incredible, but I don't have to describe it to all of you who have been there. And to all of you who are reading this, but haven't been there, I don't know how else to describe it. There are things we experience which are simply said to be indescribable, in the best sense of that word. This journey was an absolute confirmation of that for me.

Is there anything greater in life than receiving the Blessing and God's Grace?

I feel immense gratitude and love for my Guru. Thank you for helping me live and experience all this.

The Grace Of The Guru

- Mitesh Khatiwala -

I OFFER THIS WRITE up at the feet of my Guru - Sri Brahmarishi Mohanji, as without Him my journey to the Inner Kora would not have been possible and how far in my life I have come.

The journey to Kailash started sometime in 2013, I met Mohanji for the first time (physically) in March/April 2013 at his Datta Tapovan Ashram near Pune. I clearly remember each moment of that visit, but the one that still strikes me the most is when I asked Him if He is going back to Kailash, I will join him. We were walking towards the havan area when I had asked Him and He just looked at me and gave His trademark smile. Next year with His Grace I was able to complete my outer kora on foot without any difficulties – it was a walk in the park when I look back.

Late 2015 or early 2016, the Mohanji team announced the Kailash trip once again (but just the outer kora). I, like the others who completed the outer kora in 2014 were more interested in the Inner Kora but there wasn't any announcement around that. I applied for the 2016 but with the conviction that I would be doing the Inner Kora this time. I normally don't attend many meditations due to work commitments, but during one of the meditations (just after I had applied) I could see myself back at Kailash and also could feel the fabric of the clothes I was wearing – it was as if I was there – that's when I knew, this year thru Mohanji's Grace I will be able to do Inner Kora.

Later that year, Mohanji visited SA and I again got the honour of driving him to different venues. During one such trip to a devotees house, we were just chatting and suddenly Mohanji asked "Khati what's the plan for Kailash", I replied it's all on you – he then said, please contact the Kailash team for Inner Kora

I also remember that while on our Durban trip, Mohanji said that he is going to Badrinath before Kailash and asked me "Khati, come to Badri – it will be fun". I changed my tickets and then went to Badri with him before Inner Kora.

We started our parikrama in the month of August and I had heard that there are many saints, sages etc meditating which we cannot see with our naked eye but are all around Kailash. So ,before I started I prayed to all the beings out there to please forgive me as I would be walking over them during my parikrama.

The first day of the Inner Kora is the same as the Outer Kora and I precisely remember that in 2014 the first day was like a walk in the park – but this time I was struggling and thought that if I am struggling today how was I endure Inner kora which was to begin the next day. I met my fellow travelers of Inner Kora and they mentioned the same thing which actually made me feel less miserable.

19 devotees got the chance to do the inner parikrama, but one could not do it after the first day and we were left with 18 people = which makes the count as 1+8 = 9 (as per Sripad SriVallabha Charitaamrut - The number 9 indicates the 'Parabrahma Tatwam' which is not affected by change).

The second day we left around 6 am or so and headed towards the feet of Kailash (north facing side of Kailash). This part of the parikrama is also called as Charan Sparsh as we will be touching Kailash's feet. During the entire walk, there is a river flowing on our right which is known as Kailash Ganga

Once we reached the feet of Kailash, we bowed down, drank the charnamrit and then Mohanji decided to walk further beyond the Feet and so we started climbing a small but very slippery climb / hill due to the melting ice. We all sat and meditated there while the Shiva Kavach was played.

Once we finished our meditation, some of us started walking ahead to see if they could reach Kailash. The terrain was very dangerous due to melting ice which caused the rocks to slip as we walked.

Mohanji then sat on a rock while 9 pilgrims went ahead to do Kailash sparsh. The reason Mohanji sat on the rock was to support the 9 pilgrims to cross over from where we were to reach Kailash safely as the terrain was difficult to cross. As soon the 9 pilgrims crossed over he got up from the rock and we started our descent back to our camp. We were back at the Charan sparsh and saw that Mohanji had a cut on his palm. He said that someone had fallen down and he had taken the injury upon himself so that person could complete his/her parikrama.

So, day 1 was complete by touching the feet of Kailash (and for some lucky ones touching Kailash).

On day 2 we started again early and this was one of the toughest day in our entire parikrama. After a long walk, we reached the point where we had to climb a steep mountain of 70 to 80 degrees amidst falling rocks and melting ice. Some of us climbed the mountain without any assistance of line ropes however, by the time I reached the base of the mountain the ropes were ready and I started my slippery climb.

Midway during the climb, I had to wait for the people ahead of me as the Sherpas were helping them to climb up. As I waited my turn, a big rock came straight towards me – I was shouting look out for this rock... I could not move away from the path of the rock as nobody knew when it would turn its course and be back for me. I waited for the stone until it was a few meters and moved just before it could hit – Jai Brahmarishi Mohanji.

When my turn came to climb from the midpoint, I started my ascent a bit faster as I did not remember the technique to pull the rope and was also fearful of falling rocks - this was a very bad idea, I was totally breathless and my heart must have skipped a dozen beats – Once again, thanks to His Grace (Mohanji mentioned that the way I climbed looked like watching a Tom and Jerry cartoon) I reached the top.

Once I reached the summit of the mountain, there was no one around. I looked down and could just feel stillness and then when I started to go ahead – I couldn't as I couldn't see any path and one slip I would have go straight to heaven or hell (depending on my karma balance sheet). Fear gripped me as I did not know how to proceed. Suddenly, I saw a Sherpa but this one was totally different. He looked gigantic and I can still see him clearly while I write this. He came from nowhere and asked me to stay there and he would be back for me. He came back in a few minutes and holding his hand I crossed the cliff and was on the other side of the mountain. There I met my brothers and my Sherpa and we started our descent back to our camp.

A few of our fellow devotees were still struggling to come up the mountain, I reached with other brothers just after midnight, the last person to reach the camp was around 2:30 am and one person stopped over at another camp.

The third day was a parikrama to the Saptarishi Caves and this climb was almost a 90 degree climb. As we were waiting for our approvals at the camp that night we had a satsang with Mohanji. During the satsang, Mohanji said that some of the sages/saints look very fierce just to avoid people contact. I recalled that while taking the bus to reach the first day of the parikrama, I looked up into a cave and had seen a very fierce looking huge person and wondered who he was. Now I knew.

Unfortunately, we could not get the permission to go to the caves and left for our hotel in Nepal. Hopefully, I will be able to journey to the Saptarishi Caves sometime in this life.

The Homeward Journey

- Chai Lai Siong -

IN 2014, I did not even know what a pilgrimage was or even where Kailash was. I met Mohanji in person and attended his first retreat in Dubai in April. I shared this experience of meeting a very special spiritual master with my friend, Dhanya from whom I learned that Mohanji would be going to Kailash in July. We managed to participate and complete the Outer Kora parikrama and were fortunate that completing a parikrama that year was equivalent to doing it 12 times, as it was the auspicious year of Dev Kumbh. (Coincidentally, it also happened to be the Chinese Year of the Horse also a remarkable year). We came to know later that this trip had made us eligible for the Inner Kora in the future.

The news of Kailash with Mohanji in 2016 flashed to my mind when Mohanji asked, "Would you like to come for the Inner Kora?" As much as I wanted to commit, I was discouraged because of my financial condition, of travelling and living between two countries, and the family situation. I began thinking of all the hassle and difficulties involved. Though I knew I couldn't go, I couldn't stop myself from going through the registration process either. I submitted the application close to the deadline, and waited. My attitude was to wait and see what would happen when the time came. Until the point of time of the Kailash trip, my daily life was in a big mess, and I was depressed. But somehow, at the very last minute a helping hand appeared to finalize my journey: the Grace was present.

After meeting all the pilgrims in the Kathmandu hotel, it already felt like I was returning home, especially the reunion with the pilgrims from 2014. I did not envisage a visit to the Pashupatinath temple as I knew foreigners were forbidden from entering. Dhanya and I decided to shop around while waiting for the Indian group. Suddenly, Mohanji turned around and said, "Chai, quickly put your shoes inside. Don't keep the others waiting." I wondered out aloud, "Can we really go?" The reply came, "Ask Sumit," Mohanji headed towards the entrance of the Pashupatinath Temple. We ran to Sumit to repeat the same question. Sumit said we could give it a try. Positioning ourselves at the rear of the group, we tried to blend in. Rima gave me her scarf and I covered my head. Grace! We were able to enter the temple with the others. During our previous visit, we had tried to enter, but Dhanya was spotted and brought out from the temple. I was the only foreigner who went into the temple in 2014.

The arrangement of transportation was an amazing experience. We caught a domestic flight, and halted at a beautiful village called Humla in Simikot. We then flew to Hilsa by helicopter. Besides the one-day rest for acclimatization, it took us only a day to reach Manasarovar Lake. Along the journey to Manasarovar from Kathmandu, the pictures of Kailash 2014 flashed in my mind again and again. That time I cared only about myself. It had been all about me and I did not think about others. This time around I felt some kind of heaviness and experienced '*myself*' in a different way. It was not just me travelling. The Goddess, my ancestors, my family members, friends, enemies, animals, beings and so many people; they were with me throughout the whole journey. Later, all their faces appeared one by one in my mind again when we took our dip in Lake Manasarovar. I did not count how many dips I did. I stopped to connect with Dhanya. We held each other's hand and dipped again for our Guru, Mohanji. We continued the dips for the Goddess and anyone that appeared in our minds until our bodies couldn't bear the cold water anymore. We had no appetite

The Homeward Journey

at all but forced ourselves to eat some, as Mohanji and Sumit kept reminding us those who did not eat were likely to fall sick. The energy of Manasarovar Lake was overwhelming - my whole body was burning and I felt the energy moving up and down from head to toe. We stopped for the night at Darchen, to get ready for the first day of parikrama the following day.

We were told that though the Inner Kora group had to walk through the parikrama, Sherpas would be available. Thus, I would not be alone even if I were to walk slowly and there would be someone with me always. The Outer Kora group travelled together on the first day of parikrama. Both Outer and Inner Kora groups were to rest for the night at Dirapuk, and the Inner Kora would continue the stay for one more day at the same place to acclimatize. I was still taking it easy before we started. We gradually started walking after the porters and ponies had been allocated. My sherpa was a strong middle-aged man with a friendly smile.

My memories went back to the 2014 trip. Reaching Yama Dwar made me recall the purpose of my journey. After making three rounds of Yama Dwar I walked through the gate of death, rang the bell and shouted out loud, "My only purpose of life is LIBERATION." Mohanji had told us to walk straight ahead and not turn back. I continued on the trail. Everything in front of me was so familiar. The mountains, the streams, the beautiful views, the Tibetan pilgrims with their full prostrations, the sounds of the bells tied to the yaks. I was deeply immersed in the scenery and sounds of nature. As usual I walked at a slow pace because of my short breath. At every step I chanted Om Namah Shivaya and Om Shivaya Namah. I managed to clear the flat part of the trail. Before we could see the west face of Kailash, we had to ascend uphill. I was struggling to breathe and had to constantly stop to catch my breath. I tried the *'Hanuman's Breathing'* (Read about the Hanumanji breath in Hanumatananda's experience on page 173) but failed. Dragging myself, through stopping and walking this way I kept on until I saw Mohanji's face on Kailash. I recalled a breathing technique that Mohanji had taught us during the UK program. I used that and chanting *Om hoom joom sah*, I continued walking. Eventually I reached the guest house for the night at Dirapuk, where Mohanji asked me if I had seen him on Kailash. Smiling amidst tears, I nodded my head in assent. He asked me to share the picture with others.

This second time, the first day of parikrama had not been as easy as I thought it would be. I had still struggled to complete it, being unable to finish 16 km in 5 hours. I had fallen far behind. Many people were quite sick because of high altitude changes the first day. Dhanya arrived late in the evening, her body cold and trembling. She was very ill and threw up a few times. I helped her clean up, and changed her clothes. Giving her some water and warm soup, I sat next to her to make sure she had calmed down till she went to sleep. The same thing had happened to me in 2014, when I had been seriously ill and had passed out. I had to take three cylinders of oxygen, with the doctors and sherpa constantly rubbing my cold body. Dhanya had held my body and helped me through. What was happening now was like a history repeating itself, only our roles had reversed.

(P.S. I called it *'Hanuman's Breathing'* because in 2014, when I was about to collapse due to short breath, I saw Hanumanji looking at me, and recalled a breathing technique taught by a yoga teacher). It looked like Hanumanji helped me finish the walk on the first day of parikrama.

The next day we said goodbye to the Outer Kora group. Few pilgrims who were seriously ill had to return to Darchen, including one from the Inner Kora group. Looking at Dhanya in the morning, it seemed like nothing had happened to her the night before. She was absolutely fine and continued her second day parikrama without pony and porter. We were asked to meet up at 11 am to have a short trek. When I came from the room, almost everybody had left. I met Vijay then quickly grabbed my bag and joined him. I was confused with the Chinese time and Indian time. As that day was a rest day, most of our sherpas were asked to rest. Only a few sherpas were leading us. We were heading upwards to the North face of Kailash which we could see right in front of us clearly from the guest house, to trek up to Charan Sparsh.

The Homeward Journey

Charan Sparsh is actually a glacier mountain covered with rocks and stones all the way towards Kailash. The trek was an upward climb all the way. We had to trek very slowly, stopping often to catch breath. The view was stunningly beautiful along the way. We drank from the glacier stream, taking the holy water with our hands and touched our foreheads. The water was cold and refreshing and I could feel the energy of Kailash flowing into my body. After a few hours of walking, we stopped at the point where we needed to ascend with ropes. Mohanji said those who were tired could stay behind and rest. The sherpas started to climb up without any tool and rope, they then twisted a cloth to make a 'rope' for us. Mohanji and most of us climbed up. The view of Kailash was much closer, the stream of glacier wider, and the ice turned to glossy snow. Nevertheless, the air had become thinner, and we had to inhale deeply.

After walking for a while, Mohanji stopped and asked us to pray and turn around 360 degrees standing at the same spot. We chanted the Shiva Kavacham together to ask for protection from Lord Shiva for the Inner Kora group. Mohanji then sat on a big rock and said he would rest there. I followed and sat down on a smaller rock next to him. He asked us to look at Kailash, saying that someone had just offered abhisheka to Kailash. We saw a light flurry of snowflakes fluttering down the walls of Kailash. Mohanji then said that those who wanted to trek closer to Kailash could move on ahead. He repeated that should be only for those who really wanted to. I was thinking of resting but when Swami Brahmananda passed by and asked me to join him, I just followed. The trail became steeper until we came to a big gap in the glacier. It was a deep stream with fast running icy-cold water. A big rock sat like an uneven bridge in between the glacier banks of the stream. To cross that we had to slide down carefully from one side, climb onto the rock and jump up to the other side of the glacier bank. The sherpas had crossed through and helped six of us cross. I was focusing on sliding down and waited for my turn. Vijay started to set his foot on the big rock, when I heard a scream and looked to see two sherpas holding on to Vijay. Later I learned that Vijay had lost balance and nearly fallen into the dangerous deep bottomless stream. The big rock was actually a glacier covered by stones. As each person stepped on and crossed, the stones would wash away, with both the big rock and the bank of the glacier exposed and melted to form a slippery surface. Vijay returned and sat down on the side. Those who had crossed to the other side shouted out loud "No, don't come." Spomenka was standing next to me - we looked at each other, unsure of what to do. Vijay told us that it was not safe for anyone to cross anymore. Mohanji still sat at the same place watching us.

The six people who had crossed started to move ahead. Vijay, Spomenka and I silently watched them walk away from us. My mind was empty and disappointed that I could not continue the journey. Suddenly, Hanumatananda (Zoran) moved quickly and jumped on the same big rock. One of those that had crossed, returned warning that it was too dangerous for him. But he replied that as Mohanji said he could try. We all shouted at him to stop again, but he ignored us saying, "Father said I can try." He then called loud to Mohanji. I was frozen for a moment at watching his determination. I saw Mohanji moving to a place from where he would be able to watch him from afar. Hanumatananda started tossing his trekking sticks and gloves one by one onto the other side of the glacier. One of his gloves fell into the stream. Our hearts fell with it too. He then jumped and somehow managed to climb onto the glacier, to join the others who had crossed. The three of us, Vijay, Spomenka and I had not decided on whether to go, still waiting. Spomenka's sherpa suddenly appeared from behind and called us to follow him. We took it as Lord Shiva's calling and started our journey.

After the detour, we would need to jump over the glacier gap which was narrower than where we should have been crossing earlier. Vijay and Spomenka easily jumped onto the other side. As I tried to hop on I slipped and fell. My body hit the glacier which was covered with stones. I used my left palm to support myself but it got cut by a few sharp stones. Then my right leg slipped again and my right knee banged on the ground. The sherpa ran to help

The Homeward Journey

me get up. As I stood up I looked at my left palm and was surprised to see that nothing had happened. It had just turned red. I shook my wrist, rubbed my right knee and felt that they were alright too. I quickly walked towards the two of them without delay, and soon we caught up with Hanumatananda. Then the four of us trekked together. We were way behind the first group and had lost sight of them totally. Upon crossing the glacier gap, my stomach started filling up with air. Almost every step I walked I was constantly burping. Every step was so heavy. I had to stop frequently to burp and catch breath. Each breath was so so deep. Sometimes I was dizzy, I had to stop and stand still, and close my eyes for a short while. Each time I opened my eyes, everything in front of me was completely different. The view seemed to be changing itself. It was blurry for a second then turned into bright and clear vision. The feeling was so, so strong. A kind of energy that can't be described in any words. When I had to stop I felt I was passing away. When I continued walking I felt I was arising. It sounds very weird but I can't deny that I had experienced it.

I had not been paying attention to how far we had trekked or how far we had to go. We just carried on walking. The view eventually shifted to black and white, which was only snow and the exposed mountains. The North face of Kailash in front of us at a distance was beautiful. We spotted the first group moving like little black dots in the snow cover. They had gone all the way to the steep walls of Kailash and to the base of the mountain. We were not sure we would be able to make it to the base since the sky was growing darker. We were far behind them. Though we doubted, we kept on walking. After about an hour's trek, we finally met up with the first group which was returning back. The sherpa with the first group did not encourage us to move on any further as the sky would have had turned dark on our return. Unless we had flashlights, but none of us did. They were concerned and said they couldn't take responsibility for us. We still continued walking. Later on we met DB on his return who told us it was an amazing experience to touch Kailash. He said we should go no matter what, and that if we just followed their footprints, we would be safe. What he told us gave us the strong determination to go on.

We were moving on full of excitement. Kailash sat right in front of us. It was so close and clear, and the scenery was absolutely beautiful. To view that unique scene is not possible unless you are that close. As we walked closer to the snow cove, we needed to cross a wide and deep pit which was covered by a thick blanket of snow. I was unaware how deep the crevasse was. Vijay had jumped over and crossed before me. I cautiously took a step to find firm ground to walk on, but as I stepped across, my entire left leg sank into the snow and reached my waist. I quickly balanced on my other leg going horizontal to prevent myself from sinking further. It was an instinctive reaction. One leg was inside the deep pit of snow and one leg outside. I used the trekking stick to try and pull myself out from the trap and shouted for help. Vijay turned around but he was on a slippery slope himself and trying to stabilize his own feet. He lay on the ground and shouted at me trying to reach out to my trekking stick. I extended it and held onto it very tightly. Though I was nervous I had to stay focused. When the sherpa saw us he rushed to pull me out from the pit and pushed my body forward. By then I was able to move towards Vijay and grabbed his hand, pulling myself out from danger. I could easily have lost my life and was really lucky. Hanumatananda and Spomenka crossed easily.

We continued on our snow trek. The snow got deeper until it reached above my knees. Each step we walked seemed harder. Eventually we reached the cove, where we could see the track of footprints left behind by the first group moving up and we just followed the prints. As we went closer we could see the deep walls of Kailash right in front of us. There was only a very narrow path we could actually cross to touch Kailash. This mule path was in between the ravine. While looking up to Kailash, I saw Vijay go near and touch Kailash, followed by the sherpa. I was waiting before the mule path for my turn, as the space was narrow and only two people could stand. I saw that the sherpa was chanting and was very moved. When I asked him about it later, he told he was overwhelmed with Kailash energy and deep gratitude to Mohanji. Because of our group he had had a chance to touch Kailash in his lifetime.

After they returned, I slowly walked to Kailash. I touched Kailash with my hand. I placed my forehead to Kailash. The energy of Kailash flew into my body through my forehead. From icy cold to boiling hot. It was overwhelming. I felt Mohanji's presence there with me. I prostrated my gratitude to Mohanji for bringing me to Lord Shiva. I felt I had come back home. I felt my journey was complete. I felt gratitude towards Lord Shiva for calling me home. "Only when Lord Shiva calls, can one reach the surrounding of Mount Kailash."

It seemed like a long long time when I realised that the others were still waiting for their turn. I picked up two stones for Vijay and returned. Hanumatananda and Spomenka were having the feel of touching Kailash. Vijay was taking their photos. I wondered if anyone had taken my photo of touching Kailash, since it was a very important moment for me. No one was sure about that. So I decided to go back. While I was crossing through the mule path, Hanumatananda was also returning and we needed to pass by each other. We stumbled and held on to each other to stop falling down the ravine. When I stumbled, the warning of the Swami from Sivananda Ashram flashed in my mind. He had told us that Kailash could be a very dangerous place and to not even think of taking photos, and that the only thing we needed to bring back from Kailash was bhakti (gratitude), nothing else.

We had trekked for nine hours to reach here as Vijay reminded us. We had to turn back now while there was still daylight. Trekking downwards was comparatively faster but still strenuous. After passing the crevasse in which I had been trapped earlier, I turned around to look up at Kailash again. The whole mountain had turned into pure white and was shining bright like a diamond. I remembered Mohanji had once said that Shiva is innocent! I noticed a shower of snowflakes on the top of Kailash. I shouted to the others, "Look! Someone is offering abhisheka to Kailash again!" I was so amazed to see that again. Vijay urged me not to delay any further.

As we set out on our journey again, hail was falling like crystal rain. Devi's experience at Gauri Kund in 2014 came to memory, of Mohanji coming to her in the form of hailstones to save her in her moments of breathlessness. Mohanji was there for us too. This was in my mind at that moment. I felt so blessed. Closing my eyes, I turned my face up to the sky and let the hailstones fall on my face. It was like an immersion in Grace. Soon I realised that I had to catch up with the rest of the group. I tried to quicken my pace but was feeling exhausted and could barely walk. The hailstones began getting heavier and heavier. I was very dizzy and sick, my chest was starting to hurt a lot, and my stomach felt bloated. I was having to stop constantly. It was a horrible feeling.

I am not sure how long I went on that way. Suddenly, I felt my feet drawn to the ground as if by a powerful magnetic attraction. My whole body was tightening. A kind of strong energy, heavy like a thousand tonnes of waves forced open my mouth, flowed down through my throat into my stomach and moving toward the ground. I could feel it rebounding from my sole, and going back up straight through the center of my body, through the spine and the chakras. The energy forced up and stretched both my arms, then went and touched my throat to come out from my mouth, caused a sound like a heavy exhalation. This was repeated twice or perhaps more. Something was stopping that energy from going up to my crown. I struggled to move my stiff and locked neck by shaking my head as if signaling it to stop. The energy then diverted the movement to the crown of my head like an electric flash, and from the top began descending down to the bottom chakras. I suppose this was Kundalini energy. It then began the ascent up to the crown, spiraling through the body continuously. I was absorbed by this super powerful energy. When I finally came to, it felt like a lifetime.

Later I came to know that Vijay had again supported me from my back and helped me through. When we slowly trudged on, I started to throw up along the way until my stomach was emptied.

The Homeward Journey

After that I felt much lighter and could now walk together with the others. We staggered along the way, covered with mud and soaking wet. My sherpa appeared out of nowhere. We assumed the group had sent him to look for us. By now we could see the moon in the dark sky. Not long after that we finally reached the camp.

We went straight to Mohanji's room. Devi let out a sob when she saw us. She had been so worried, waiting for us. Mohanji was laying down on the bed. He blessed three of them and asked them to rest well. I knelt down in front of Devi, and we hugged each other, both crying in relief. She told me Mohanji was not well. His left palm was bleeding, his right wrist was hurting and the right knee was swollen. I burst into tears again and told Devi that I had fallen down and cut my palm, and hurt my wrist and knee. Mohanji had taken all the injury on to himself. I slowly crawled on my knees towards Mohanji and thanked him. He asked me not to hold his hand tightly because it was still painful. I hugged Mohanji. He touched my head and blessed me. I felt sorry and had no words. Everyone else had returned to their rooms.

I came out from Mohanji's room, extremely cold and exhausted and stumbled to my room. Swami Govinda helped me to the bed, dried my hair, and asked someone in the room to help me change. Then he brought some hot soup, but my hand was shivering so much that I couldn't hold the spoon. Swami carefully spoon fed me. But I could hardly eat much. My body began getting warmer when I was covered with two blankets and went to sleep. Swami now assured, left to go back to his room. The rest day and short trek had ended up being 13 hours long.

I woke up in the middle of the night. The energy of Kailash was still flowing in my body. I could not understand what had happened during the trek. And I did not have an urge to ask Mohanji or talk to others about it either. I just felt like being silent. Before dawn, we heard the sherpa coming to serve us ginger tea in bed. I woke up feeling well. What had happened the previous day seemed like from a long long time ago, but the memory was fresh. Today was going to be our third day Inner Kora parikrama.

We started on our walk early in the morning after breakfast.

Carrying our packed lunches, we moved on with our sherpa. We needed to trek uphill all the way. It was even tougher. The rocky path made it slower and more dangerous. We could easily fall and twist our ankles. We were stopping very frequently to catch our breath. When Mohanji stopped, he would face down and looked down to us to ensure that everyone was safe. Vijay was always there reminding me to stop and breathe. Mohanji was looking at me. That provided me so much of energy to carry on.

At a rest point, I went over to where Mohanji was sitting. He asked me to help Devi as we could spot her lagging far behind us and hardly moving forward. I had no idea what to do since I had been struggling much myself. He then asked me to push her up or send Devi a sherpa. I asked Devi's sherpa to give a hand, but he said he could not. Her sherpa was not helping much and only carried her bag. I requested him to swap with Spomenka's sherpa so that he could help instead. I trusted Spomenka's sherpa fully after yesterday's trek. But Devi's sherpa refused to do so because after the swap, the bag would be heavier for him. I thought if Mohanji asked them, they would follow. So I told them it was Mohanji's instruction that if they swapped, everything would be better for both of them. He believed me finally. It took me some time to communicate because of the language and I had to tell a white lie to comfort one of them. Spomenka's sherpa now started to push Devi from the back, they both walking very slowly to eventually reach Mohanji. Devi was absolutely exhausted and was crying to stop there and wait for our return. Unfortunately, we would not be returning back the same route. We had to walk all the way to Zuthulpuk and set our rest there. It was a one way trek with no return.

Devi now had a Sherpa she could rely on. She continued her trek with his helping hand from back, until we saw a cave which was formed by a glacier. A small stream was running out from the cave. We stopped to rest and take some photos. Devi went into the cave which energized her enough to keep on ascending uphill.

As we moved upward, we reached a narrow space where we had to wait and climb one by one with a rope. There was barely enough room to stop and sit. We waited in the limited space that was almost vertical. Some rocks which sat on the mountain were holding us, saving us from sliding downhill. Jayeeta, Phaneendar and I were at the rear still climbing up to the space. The path was getting slippery for the people behind because the stones on the loose surface were slowly getting displaced by our feet. Phaneendar and I started sliding downward but no sherpa was able to help as they were busy setting up the ropes and helping those who were climbing up on the rope. We slowly managed to settle ourselves in the only small space available, waiting for our turn to climb.

Mohanji sat still, watching us. I then sat next to Mohanji. He patted me on the leg and asked how I felt. I replied that I was exhausted. He said, "It is only the body that is exhausted, not you. Remember that. You are not your body." Mohanji then climbed to the other side with the rope. I was looking at him, he had moved from sitting next to me then swung far far away. It seemed very easy, I thought.

I was set on the rope getting ready to climb but there was no grip on the feet at all. The surface of the mountain was only loose stones and sand. As I moved I slid straight away. I was hanging on the rope and my hand couldn't even reached the harness tied on the rope. They had forgotten to measure the length of my arm. Now I was hanging in between. A small landslide had occurred and rocks from the top were falling down towards me. I had to swing away to avoid injury. One of the sherpas quickly swung to me, adjusted the harness, then climbed up together with me. Yet, it was not at the top when my feet touched the ground. After the first part of the vertical rope climb, we were free from the rope. The amazing part was now we had to climb the iron rope vertically without any safety equipment. I struggled and somehow managed to reach the top. It was so dangerous, and yet even with the limited climbing tools we all climbed to the top without any injuries. Only amazing Grace could have made this happen.

At the top, I rested for a while. I walked alone, stopping to take in the view from far. I realised how very small a human is - so small in terms of size, only one little tiny dot in Mother Nature.

"Where do we keep our anger, jealousy and hatred?" "Where could we find that room?" "Where am I?" "Who am I?" I asked myself. I took some photos and continued walking.

The trek was relatively flat. I saw a small Tibetan temple. I prostrated to the goddess and carried on walking. I was walking fast and the sherpa put some pieces of cloth and bags on the trail for us to follow as markers. I was not aware that they did not lead us to Kuber Kund. Most of us missed Kuber Kund and went down straight. While I was trying to find the way to go downhill, my sherpa appeared. He was moving straight down from the hill instead. At this time, I did not find any problem following him. I found myself gliding down as fast as him. He was smiling at me. I replied with smile. We continued gliding until we spotted three people far away from us. Later we met up with them - Sumit, DB and Riana. Then we continued our journey together, followed by the sherpa. We walked the path along the clifftops. The stream was underneath us. I was still gliding down effortlessly. The others were tired. Sumit slipped and fell to the side of the stream. I shouted to the sherpa for help. He pulled Sumit up and tried to find an alternative way. But it was even harder to climb up to the top. We decided to continue on the same path and moved on. Eventually we met up with Mohanji and the others. It was not the end of the day. Later, Sumit managed to flag down a four-wheel Land Rover and brought six of us to Zuthulphuk. That included Mohanji, Devi, Spomenka, Anjali, one sherpa girl and myself.

We settled down in the Tibetan rest house. Mohanji and three others were not feeling well. I was very worried, bringing medicine and warm water to them, checking for fever each one. I requested more blankets but was refused by the rest house. I made sure they were covered warm and could rest. I was not able to rest and stayed by the restaurant waiting for the others who were still walking in the dark. I kept praying in my mind that they would definitely come back safe. A Tibetan boy came and played with me and that helped relieve my tension a bit. After about two hours, the others arrived one by one very late into the night. Everyone was worn out after another full day of hard trekking. Most of us had some

The Homeward Journey

Tibetan noodle soup and tea to relax after the long tough day which was finally over. Phaneendar reached the rest house about 3 am. Jayeeta was not able to reached that night - she stayed at the sherpa camp and came back to join us early next morning. The sherpas reached their camp very late at night and they all were dead tired too.

The morning of the fourth day was cold with heavy rain. We all had rested well, and the sherpas did not rush us that morning. We were supposed to trek down a gradually winding track to Chongdo and continue travel by truck back to Darchen, the Tibetan village where our Kailash parikrama had begun. Due to bad weather, we decided to ride the trucks all the way down to reach Darchen. Our real rest day set off when we reached the Darchen hotel. We waited for the Kailash working team to confirm the permit approval to trek to Astapad and then moving forward to Saptarishi Caves. While waiting, the group eventually had time to sit down and talk to each other for sharing experiences of the journey. Every meal became an unofficial satsang with Mohanji, the swamis and the group. I was really enjoying those moments of exchanging feelings. A long table was set up just like 'The Last Supper' of Jesus.

Despite the Kailash working team best efforts for the permit approval, we had been rejected due to too many deaths that year. But the group was not disappointed. The three full days of parikrama had made us feel complete. We had immersed fully in the expericnce. We had touched Kailash! We had reached home to the abode of Lord Shiva! The Inner Kora parikrama had been completed! We had contented with the energy of Kailash! What else do we need!! Instead we went to Manasarovar again for a second dip. We did a puja in the evening by the sacred lake facing Kailash and stayed overnight on the shore. The parikrama was considered finally complete when we left Manasarovar.

The next morning we retraced the same route we had taken to arrive there. We crossed the border through the Friendship bridge of China and Nepal. We took the helicopter back to Humla, a beautiful village on the hill in Simikot. We did have to stop for a night's stay in Humla due to the bad weather conditions. We were lucky enough to experience a very special celebration of all the villages in Simikot which only happens once a year. The people wore their best clothes and gathered in the centre, dancing and singing. Swami Govinda and I joined the celebration in the rain. We took some photos of the children and the beautiful faces of the women. We met a young Tibetan monk from the nearby village, who had walked three days to reach here to meet his relatives. He is a Tibetan temple's abbot. He told us about his master and the building of the temple. He took us around the village then accompanied us back to the guesthouse. The next day, we continued our journey by plane and finally returned back to Kathmandu.

In the process of writing this, I have felt the energy of Kailash continue to flow within me. Mere words cannot describe everything we experienced. This unusual journey can only be understood through personal experience. Reading or hearing about another's experience can only be another bedtime story. No amount of gratitude would be enough to express to Mohanji who took 'me' there. I can never thank enough the Kailash working team for all their hard work. And everyone that walked together in this journey. The connection with everyone who made this happen was amazing. How much Grace I have had to join this trip! I feel so much deep gratitude, Grace and love.

The Touch Of Kailash

- Vijay Ramanaidoo -

My eyes slowly opened. I could hear a high-pitched ringing sound. The type of sound you hear in deep silence. Where was I? I could see a sink in front of me and a white toilet to my left. The strange thing was that I could see the underside of them both. I slowly realised that I was lying down on the floor of a bathroom. Why was I sleeping in a bathroom? Slowly my memory came back. I was in Darchen on the Inner Kora Kailash trip with Mohanji. I had been suffering from altitude sickness and had been sick in the night. When I had gone to brush my teeth in the morning, I started being sick again and the next thing I remember I was lying on the floor.

As I slowly and carefully got up from the bathroom floor, my head still spinning, Swami Karunananda, who I was sharing a room with, and Dr Harpreet Wasir appeared and came to my aid. Swami Karunananda later explained that he had heard me being sick in the bathroom and the next thing he heard was a big crash. I had fallen to the floor unconscious. He rushed to find Dr Harpreet who fortunately was in the room next door and when they entered the bathroom a few minutes later they found me getting back to my feet. They helped me get back into my bed and Dr Harpreet checked my pulse and gave me an anti-emetic under the tongue with the instruction to rest for one hour. Dr. Harpreet then informed the organizers of the trip who informed Mohanji.

As I lay down I started to feel for any aches and pains on my body from the fall. I must have banged my head on the concrete floor. I felt my head all over but could not detect any bruising or pain. It seemed as if I had fallen to the floor unconscious but did not suffer any injury. Surely an act of the most amazing Grace.

As I lay in bed I came to the conclusion that the Inner Kora parikrama, which I had been planning for so long and was due to start that morning with a 14 km trek, was over for me. As well as passing out, I was feeling very ill, weak and nauseous and remembered that Mohanji had on previous trips stopped people from going on the outer parikrama if they were seriously ill. The Inner Kora trip was even more difficult. I realised that I would probably have to stay back in Darchen for the next few nights until the Inner Kora group returned. Various thoughts came to mind. What was I going to do in Darchen for the next few days? Where would I have my lunch and dinner, as there would be no sherpas to cook any food? Why did Mohanji select me for the Inner Kora trip if I was not going to make it? Why did I need to go back to Kailash again having previously been here in 2014? Why on earth did I agree to go back to Kailash knowing the cost, the harsh living conditions, and the likelihood of suffering from altitude sickness which I had experienced last time? These random thoughts were going through my head as I lay there.

After an hour, the doctor returned, checked my pulse and said that in his view I should be okay for the parikrama! I looked at him in astonishment. How could he say I was fit when I had had no sleep, been sick all night and passed out in the morning? I had difficulty in believing that I would be fit enough, but decided to get up anyway. As if in a daze, I shaved, showered, got changed and somehow managed to pack my rucksack for the Inner Kora trip.

Mohanji had said previously that those who did not eat would not go on the parikrama as they were bound to fall ill. I therefore went to the dining hall to see if I could manage some breakfast. I was surprised to find that I was feeling better and managed to eat some toast and drink some tea. Initially I decided not to tell Mohanji about the incident, as I was afraid that he might tell me that I could not go on the trip. But as I was leaving to go back to my room I passed by Mohanji, who asked me how I was feeling. I found myself confessing that I was not well in the morning and had passed out but was now feeling okay. He did not say anything. I felt that Mohanji already knew this and with his immense kindness had removed most of the sickness from me. I felt deep gratitude for this evidence of Grace and compassion.

Later that day as I waited at Yam Dwar, the gateway to Kailash, helping to organise the porters and ponies for the 80 plus pilgrims, I marvelled at the Grace which had enabled my recovery. A few hours ago I had been flat out on the floor and here I was now, helping to organise ponies for pilgrims and about to start a 14 km trek at over 16,000 feet altitude! Our group waited patiently as chits were drawn to see which porter and pony were selected. There were about 65 participants for the outer kora, and 19 selected for the Inner Kora trip. A few participants were not well enough to continue. The Inner Kora group consisted of those who had previously gone in 2014, the year of Dev Kumbh, when one parikrama was the equivalent of 12, making them eligible for the Inner Kora trip. The one exception made by Mohanji was for Swami Brahmananda, who is a renunciate and head of the Skanda Vale ashram in Wales.

The Inner Kora group had to walk, as ponies cannot be used for the more difficult Inner Kora trek. On the first day of the parikrama, both groups travelled together. Before starting off I went to take the blessings of Mohanji. As I took blessings he said to me. 'Do well. The second day will be tough'. I thought to myself that he must have meant the third day as the second day was a 'rest' day. Little did I know that he would prove to be correct! To my surprise, my porter was a woman accompanied by her young daughter who could not have been more that 13 or 14 years old. They shared the job of carrying my rucksack. I could not but admire the strength and toughness of the Tibetan people. They would be my porters for the first day, after which the Inner Kora porter would take over.

The first day brought back memories of the 2014 trip. The amazing landscape and vistas. The views of the west face of

Kailash, the snow-capped mountains, crystal-clear streams, herds of yak carrying large blue water barrels, Tibetans making their own pilgrimages, and the porters singing in high-pitched yodeling voices. I walked at my own pace, joining up with different people along the way. The first day was a long walk of about 14 km which was relatively flat but on the occasions where we had to walk uphill it was a real challenge, especially with reduced oxygen at altitudes of over 16,000 feet. Eventually we reached Dirapuk where we rested for the night.

The next day we bid farewell to the outer kora group. Some of the pilgrims who had only hired porters had to get emergency ponies for the second day as they were struggling physically. A few people were more seriously ill and had to return to Darchen. This included one of the Inner Kora team. The remaining 18 Inner Kora pilgrims would spend the day and an extra night at Dirapuk. We were asked to get ready by 9 am as we would be trekking to Charan Sparsh, which is a very auspicious spot where we touch the foot of Kailash. Charan Sparsh is actually a glacier covered by stones and rocks which extends all the way from Mount Kailash itself.

Just after 9 am we set off for Charan Sparsh at a slow pace as it was mainly an upward trek towards the North face of Kailash. We rested frequently to catch our breath and to adjust to the high altitude. As we trekked upwards, we looked back to see in the distance the Dirapuk monastery that we had just left and the amazing scenery below us. Eventually, after trekking for about three to four hours, and stopping frequently, we reached the holy spot of Charan Sparsh. We drank the water from the stream flowing from Kailash and placed our hands and forehead on the glacier to absorb the energy of Kailash and offer our prayers of thanks and gratitude. At this point we were meant to head back to Dirapuk in good time to prepare for the long, tough inner parikrama journey the next day.

Mohanji then turned to me and said that those who were feeling tired could rest here but whoever wanted to, could climb up onto the glacier and trek further along to get a better view of the North face of Kailash. He said that he would like to do this. The sherpas made a makeshift rope up which he climbed. Of course, the rest of us also climbed up too. We trekked further along to see magnificent views of Kailash in the distance, the ice and snow melting in places to form rivulets which trickled down to form larger streams. After trekking for a while Mohanji asked us to say a prayer for merging with the consciousness of Shiva and turn around 360 degrees on the spot. After doing this we all sat down, and Mohanji asked to play the holy Shiva Kavach – the prayer for protection to ensure our safety for the Inner Kora trip.

We trekked further towards Kailash until we came to a big break in the glacier, separated by a large stream with fast-flowing icy water. The banks of the stream were made of solid ice. In order to proceed further we had to carefully slide down one part of the glacier onto a large brown boulder which was in the middle of the stream. We would then have to climb up onto the boulder and jump up onto the other part of the glacier to carry on our journey. The sherpas helped six people make the crossing. As each person slid down the glacier, the path for the next person was made trickier, as the thin layer of stones covering the glacier was brushed away exposing the slippery, icy surface. As I started to slide down, I found that there was no more grip on the ice and I started to slip out of control, and away from the large boulder that was to stop my slide down so I not fall into the dangerous fast flowing icy stream. Luckily, a couple of the sherpas immediately grabbed my arms to stop me sliding into the stream, and saved me from suffering a potentially serious injury.

Spomenka and Chai were supposed to cross after me but decided that it was not safe enough for them or anyone else to cross. We signaled to the rest of the group to not come any further as it was too dangerous. I watched the group of six: Swami Brahmananda, Swami Govinda, Sumit, DB (Dhritiman Biswas), Rajesh Kamath and Raj Nair proceed along with a couple of the sherpas towards the north face of Kailash. I had mixed feelings. Sad that I was not going with them to get closer to Kailash, but also relief that I would not be putting myself in further danger.

As we watched the group walk away, we suddenly saw Zoran

(Hanumatananda) heading towards the same boulder in the stream which I had been trying to reach earlier. We shouted at him to stop as we knew that he was putting himself in danger. He ignored our cries and shouted back, "Father said I can make it!". We watched with trepidation as he slid down to the icy stream and managed to climb up onto the boulder. I was convinced that he would slip into the icy stream at any time. He stood on the boulder calling out to Mohanji to join him. The rest of us signaled to Mohanji and the rest of the group to not come any further. Zoran then tossed his trekking sticks and gloves onto the glacier and with superhuman effort managed to climb up onto the other side of the glacier.

As we watched Zoran walk towards the others who had already crossed, Spomenka's sherpa suddenly appeared. He was gesticulating wildly to the three of us to follow him along a different route. We hesitated initially, then took it as a call from Lord Shiva. He had appeared almost like a messenger of Shiva, his persistence overcoming our hesitation. We followed him up another part of the glacier towards a higher point, and he found an easier crossing for us. We crossed the break in the glacier at this point and as we trekked along the other half of the glacier we caught up with Zoran. The four of us slowly travelled together towards the North face of Kailash. By now, the first group were way ahead in the distance. Given the contours of the landscape we lost sight of them but continued to follow our sherpa. At this point I had no idea what the group ahead had planned. Were they just going to travel as close to Kailash as possible and return, or were they going to go all the way? Looking at Kailash in the distance, I thought it would be madness to try and reach it. However, we just carried on walking.

We trekked on for a few more hours. Eventually the terrain changed from rock-covered glacier to ice, and then to snow. We saw the first group far in the distance, and realised that they had gone all the way through a cove covered with snow to the sheer face of Kailash, and had actually gone to the base of Kailash. We were at least an hour behind them. We carried on walking until eventually we encountered the group who by this time were on the return journey back. As we approached them I could see the look of concern on their faces. The sherpas with them asked us if we had flashlights as it would be dark by the time we returned. They said that they could not take responsibility for us. However, we were happy to carry on by ourselves with Spomenka's sherpa. As I passed DB he said to me that it was an amazing experience to touch Kailash, and that we should do whatever it took to reach there and touch the holy mountain. He told us to beware of a few crevices in the ground which were covered by snow, and that we should only follow their tracks to be on the safe side.

We watched them disappear back down the mountain, and then carried on. As we approached closer to Kailash I could see the sides of the mountain and realised that this was a view that no one would ever see unless they were this close. The scene was one of absolutely breathtaking beauty. The blue sky and white snow framing the black, beautiful mountain.

As we got closer I came across one of the crevices that DB had warned us about. I carefully prodded the snow, put my feet down where I felt some support and managed to jump over the wide crevice. As Chai approached, she tentatively took one step which found firm ground. However with her next step her leg sunk deep into the snow until the snow reached her waist. She perched precariously on the edge of the crevice. One leg outside which was stopping her from falling deep into the crevice and one leg inside. I turned back as I heard her shout and realised that I was on a slippery slope myself, which inclined downwards to her. If I slipped down I would knock into her and she would fall deep into the crevice. I therefore lay on the ground, and inching my way towards her, I shouted at her to reach out with her trekking stick. I grabbed the stick which she held tightly and I tried to pull her out. Luckily the sherpa had seen what happened. He rushed behind her and helped to push her towards me. I grabbed her hand and pulled her to safety. That was a really dangerous moment. We had no idea how deep that crevice was underneath the snow and ice but luckily she was now safe. The others crossed carefully with no incident. We went across a couple of other crevices. The snow got deeper until it was up to our knees. Each step was a step into the unknown. Eventually we approached the snow-covered cove. We could see that the others had entered the cove and made a circular path up to the sheer face of Kailash. As we got closer we realised that there was a deep drop just next to Kailash preventing us from reaching it. But at one spot there was a natural bridge of ice and snow that gave us the opportunity to cross the gap and reach a small ledge on Kailash where we would be able to stand. I slowly made my way up to this snowy bridge.

As I was about to cross the ice and snow bridge, the sherpa indicated that I should take my hat off. I removed my hat and very carefully walked across the bridge and stepped onto the ledge of Mount Kailash. I had reached Kailash! I was stepping onto Kailash! I removed my gloves and put my hands and forehead onto the face of Kailash. As I touched Kailash it felt like touching an energy field which was cool and vibrant. It was a welcoming and loving energy. My head, hands and body drank in that wonderful vibration and energy for a few minutes. I thought of Mohanji whose Grace and blessings had enabled me to reach this point. I also thought of Sathya Sai Baba and Lord Shiva whose bountiful Grace had allowed me to reach this point. I thought of my family, my ancestors and my whole lineage on behalf of whom I was doing this pilgrimage. Friends, relatives, and the rest of the group came to memory and everyone else that I could think of, so that as many people as possible could get the benefit of my touching Kailash.

I was elated. I had reached Kailash! I had touched Kailash! I had experienced Kailash! At this point I felt that I needed nothing more. I had reached the ultimate! If the trip ended now I would be happy. There was nothing more to achieve. I had touched Kailash, this wonderful divine abode of Lord Shiva, the subject of so many scriptures and legends. The imposing mountain that we see in pictures and usually only from a long distance. We were in the lap of Shiva. As I looked more closely at Kailash, I could see that the divine mountain was made up of lots of smaller rocks and stones which seem to be bound together almost as if someone had gathered an enormous mound of stones and fused them together. I had always imagined the surface of Kailash to be like a huge slab of rock, relatively smooth and black in colour. On closer inspection, the stones making up Kailash were mostly light grey of varying sizes with some stones slightly pink in colour, all bound together by grey earth acting like cement. Chai clambered onto the ledge next to me. We both appeared like spiders on the side of the mountain. Next to the ledge was a deep gorge the opening of which was covered with long icicles, like an open mouth with icy white teeth. I slowly returned to the bridge of snow and ice to allow Zoran and Spomenka to come onto the ledge and touch Kailash. As I stood on the icy bridge I realised that I should have taken a stone. I scanned the ledge and my eyes fell on a particular stone. I asked Chai to pick it up for me and also get a stone for Mohanji (which was later given to the Swamis for Skanda Vale). Zoran and Spomenka climbed onto Kailash and took their fill of the divine energy emanating from this powerhouse.

When Chai returned, she asked if someone had taken a photo of her while she was on the ledge. As I wasn't sure, she started to make her way back to the ledge so I could take a photo, passing Zoran who was also now on the ice bridge. On either side of the bridge there was a sharp drop. As they tried to pass each other they both stumbled and had to hold onto each other to stop falling down into the drop. As I saw this, the memory of a swami we had all met at the Sivananda Ashram came to me. He had told us that Kailash could be a very dangerous place and that we should not try and take photos while we were there. This came to my mind in a flash and Chai later told me that the same thought crossed her mind as she stumbled. We immediately decided to turn back and make our way back to Dirapuk. We had trekked for nearly nine hours to reach this point. Although going back would be easier as it was mainly downhill, it would still take us a few hours to reach Dirapuk.

As we turned back and walked back down, the weather started changing. The blue skies disappeared as a fog of cloud quickly descended on us. Small hailstones were showered upon us and the atmosphere became dark, cold and clammy. We could hardly see the ground ahead. Lord Shiva had bestowed the most amazing Grace on us. Right up to the point where we were able to touch Kailash the weather had been absolutely beautiful with clear skies so we could reach safely and see Kailash in full glory. If the bad weather had come upon us earlier, we may well have had to turn back without touching Kailash. The hail turned to rain and we got soaked through. The ground became more slippery and we had to watch our steps more carefully. We were exhausted. Chai could hardly walk and was starting to feel very sick. She kept on stopping and holding her stomach and chest. She was feeling worse and worse. Eventually at one point she stopped and I supported her to stop her collapsing on the floor. She suddenly arched her back, threw her arms out wide and exhaled loudly, mouth wide open. I held her to stop her falling. I seriously thought she was dying in my hands. I held her not knowing what to do. I thought that she was definitely dying and my next thought was how were we going to bring her body down the mountainside! I then thought that perhaps I could give her Shaktipat so Mohanji's energy could save her. I put my hand on her head but she slowly shook her head so I removed it. This was a good sign. At least she was able to respond to my hand on her head. I continued to hold her while she inhaled and exhaled deeply, still with her head back, mouth open and arms outstretched. Little did I know that she was going through a deep spiritual experience where she could feel the energy of Kailash moving within her. After about ten minutes, she seemed to recover enough to carry on walking and we slowly carried on our journey back to camp. However, she now kept on stopping to retch and vomit periodically.

We carried on, slipping and sliding, soaking wet until we got to Charan Sparsh. As there was no rope to help us get down, we tried lying down on the glacier and sliding down feet first, using our hands, feet and trekking sticks to slow our descent. We all somehow managed to make it down safely although the sherpa slid out of control down into the icy stream, but I was able to grab his hand to stop him falling.

We carried on down as night descended, punctuated by the

light of the moon on the occasions when the clouds allowed it to pass down to us. As we walked, another sherpa appeared who I assume had come to look for us as the group had worried about what had happened to us. Slowly we made our way back to camp. I looked at the time. It was past 10:00 pm. We had left just after 9.00 am for what was meant to be a 'short trek', but had ended up trekking for nearly thirteen hours!

As we reached camp, relieved and exhausted, we made our way up the iron steps to the living quarters and straight to Mohanji's room. Devi let out a cry when she saw us. She was so worried about the four of us and tears of relief poured down her face. Mohanji was lying down, not feeling well. He had taken so much on himself to protect us. Soaking wet, we all hugged him while he was still lying down. He blessed us all but did not say anything. He probably was in an expanded state. With immense gratitude, we thanked him and took our leave.

We met the rest of the group, changed, drank some hot soup, ate whatever we could and then sank into bed, exhausted. I could not sleep - the images of the day were just too fresh in my memory. I thought of all the things that could have gone wrong and all the dangers we had experienced, and marvelled at the protection and Grace bestowed upon us.

The third day of our Inner Kora trip was even tougher. We were also completely exhausted. We needed to use ropes to climb up a mountain pass to cross over the West face of Kailash and down towards Kuber Kund. I could not believe the almost vertical path we had to take over the pass. This was even more frightening and exhausting than the previous day! Mohanji's protection was on us. He sat on the mountain intending to wait for the group to cross first before crossing himself. With the divine Grace the whole group completed the second day arriving late at night at the next camp. Phaneendar did not reach camp until 2.30 am! Jayeeta could not reach camp that night and with the help of a sherpa managed to find a place to camp on the way, before continuing early the next morning.

On the fourth day we went back to Darchen. We had all

completed the Inner Kora successfully! We were due to go to the Saptarishi Caves the following day, but were not able to get permission to go as there had been so many deaths this year that the Chinese authorities, unsurprisingly, were not issuing any permits. Instead we proceeded to Manasarovar, where we had another dip in the holy lake and had the most amazing puja by the lake facing Kailash. We spent the night on the banks of the lake. It was fitting that the Inner Kora trek had started with a dip in Manasarovar followed by a puja, and we were finishing the parikrama in the same way. Somehow it seemed auspicious to end the parikrama this way. After spending the night on the banks of Manasarovar we made our way back to the beautiful village of Simikot by helicopter, where we had to spend one night due to poor weather conditions for flying. Here we were privileged to witness a special celebration of dance by the villagers before making our way back to Kathmandu by plane the next day. In Kathmandu, we met up with some other members of the Outer Kora group, and had some much needed rest and recuperation before flying back to London.

Looking back on this trip, I can say that this has been the most amazing journey of my life. Mohanji has taken me to places where I never imagined I would ever go, and helped me achieve things which I could have only dreamed of, one of which was touching Kailash and completing the Inner Kora parikrama. I bow down to Mohanji, Sathya Sai Baba, Lord Shiva, the Divine Mother, and to Lord Ganesha to whom I was constantly praying to remove all the obstacles on my path, and to all the other facets of the divine, and to all the masters. I offer you all my immense love and gratitude.

Eligibility –
The Key To Unlock Grace

- Anjali Kanwar -

IT ALL BEGAN in Oct 2015 when I went to meet Mohanji at Phaneendar's house. There seemed to be a buzz about Kailash and a Guru buddy, Jayeeta, asked me, "there is talk about Inner Parikrama the next year, are you going?" I took a moment before I smilingly replied, "Have not decided, let us see."

Over the years of my discipleship with my hallowed line of Gurus like Mahavtar Babaji, Lahiri Mahashaya, Swami Sri Yukteshwar, Paramhansa Yogananda, like a refreshing waterfall, Their Grace has flowed towards me and Their wisdom-guided will and instructions that I received during my meditation has made me mostly obey doing certain things on the material plane that I was asked to. So, a decision to go for the Inner Parikrama of Kailash could not have been mine, unless I got the go-ahead from the divine inner voice.

Then after a couple of weeks, around Nov 2015, I heard from DB that Mohanji had recommended my name for the Inner Kora of Kailash in 2016. I wrote to Mohanji asking the same and He responded saying He surely had and I should go only if I feel like it.

In Jan 2016, I and a friend named Pooja were performing a hawan at my home reciting the Mahamrityunjaya mantra and when I did the mantra 45th or 47th time, in a flash, Mt. Kailash appeared before the screen of my closed eyes and God said, "you have to come for the Inner Parikrama this year" and I was like, "really?" and He said, "Yes" to which I said, "Oh well then You got to arrange the funds!" I felt His presence so strongly and I said, "bless my parents, my brother and sister-in-law" and a clear response came, "whatever spiritual practices you are doing, the blessings are automatically flowing to them too." I also prayed for all my trainees – past, present, and future -- that they be blessed always. After the hawan was over, I messaged Mohanji and told Him about the guidance. Mohanji said, "If Shiva is calling you, then He will arrange everything." Later on, I informed my parents and brother about what had transpired during the hawan.

A bit of flashback here to Aug 2014 would be interesting. When we came back to the hotel in Kathmandu from doing the Outer Kora of Kailash in Aug 2014, then I mentioned to a couple of friends (Jayeeta and Rima) that I had told Shiva on the last day of the parikrama, that I had done it on behalf of everyone in my family – all generations – and that he kindly accept it. Also, since sanitation had been a major problem there, further, I mentally told Shiva that especially I would not send the women in my family till the time the sanitation problem remained, and I for one had undergone tapasya on behalf of all, so nobody else needed to come and attempt the parikrama. I had gone for my parikrama as a blank slate; was so blank that had been unaware about the sanitation situation. When I reached back in Gurgaon, the second day, in my early morning meditation, I again told Shiva the same thing to which I received a response. A sweet voice, lovingly said to me, "If I call you again even then you will not come?" There was so much love oozing from that voice that I melted and immediately replied, "If you call me with such love, how can I say no, I would come!" and I smiled. I did not give much thought to this later on.

Now the moment I completed the hawan in Jan 2016, I recalled the above conversation that I had had in 2014.

Then Mohanji messaged me to inform the Kailash team to include my name and that He would want to speak to me. One morning Mohanji called me to explain that the Inner Parikrama was a very tough one that involved doing an arduous climb of an almost vertical mountain slope with the help of ropes. He gave an elaborate description of what challenges lay ahead in the Inner Parikrama. Mohanji (Baba) is like a parent to all who receive Him and so He takes deep interest in the welfare of each one. I intently listened to all that He explained and assured Him that I shall prepare myself mentally and physically and also again confirm in meditation if I have to make Inner Kora pilgrimage this year. Post that, I confirmed my going to Kailash 2 more times in meditation and every time there was an affirmative answer.

After receiving the confirmation inwardly, I began preparing myself for this thrilling pilgrimage! I was also excited because for me it was a deadly combination of going for an adventure in a divine space.

Mohanji had guided us to inwardly keep our hearts open, enhancing our devotion and bhaav for the divine, tune ourselves to Shiva (chanting Om Namah Shivaya) and to do our sadhana more and more. He also guided us to ensure we fulfill our duties before we proceed for the pilgrimage and seek forgiveness from anyone we may have hurt and let go of things.

In the meantime, my father had to undergo prostate gland removal surgery as he was detected with cancer and Mohanji blessed him and Mohanji was with my father in His subtle form right through his surgery and beyond. I write this with the conviction of my personal experience. Earlier it was thought that my dad's surgery would be over in 5-6 hours, but as the day progressed, the surgery carried on and this got us concerned. When my brother informed me, at around 1 pm I immediately started meditating and then I felt the presence of The Creator (God) with my dad – all the forms in which God had been invoked, He was there, I perceived Mohanji, Mahavtar Babaji, my father's Guru, Divine Mother, Sai Babaji, Yukteshwarji, Paramhansa Yoganandaji, Swami Kriyananda – all these Illumined Ones present were blessing my father during the surgery. I felt my father's karma and it was heavy. While meditating at the same time as his surgery was going on, astrally I could feel all this. I expressed my gratitude to Mohanji and mentioned all of this to Him later. We all felt His blessings and kripa.

I continued with my sadhana as preparation for the Inner Kora of Kailash.

As it was taking a bit of time for the money to be arranged, in my meditation, I asked my Guru, Paramhansa Yogananda. He said, "Funds will be arranged, you just go, remember you are not doing this pilgrimage for you and your family alone, you are doing it on behalf of a lot of other souls, even from previous lifetimes to whom you had promised you would, they are counting on you to do this." I was silent after this – no more questions! And I carried on with my meditations and prayed that my Gurus do this pilgrimage through me and that I would only be a humble instrument.

The time was approaching and the packing was being done in full fervor and a feeling of joyful anticipation of not just being at Kailash Manasarovar, but of meeting the previous trip's Kailashis and being in the ever-loving, ever-caring fatherly presence of Mohanji was exciting!!!

The fabulous day arrived when we were to reach Kathmandu and by God's Grace, my Guru buddies Rima and Jayeeta were on the same flight as me, though we had not booked the tickets together. On reaching our hotel in Kathmandu, we eagerly met the other pilgrims for Kailash who had been with us in 2014. I met Mohanji, felt His limitless affection and care being showered on all. That evening, all the devotees gathered in the hotel conference room for satsang with Mohanji and a presentation by the tour operator. All of us got our kits to be used during the parikrama.

It is said that the Kailash pilgrimage begins with paying obeisance at the Pashupatinath Temple and so the following day Mohanji led all of us there.

Mohanji at Pashupatinath

Post this, we reached the Buddha Neelkanth Temple also known as The Sleeping Vishnu Temple; this is my personal favourite of the two. We had little time since we were supposed to have a quick lunch at the hotel and then take our flight to Nepalgunj. So we had to make it brief here. However, when I reached the sanctum sanctorum and stood right before Lord Vishnu, my heart swelled up with love and devotion and I didn't know why, but tears started flowing and I continued to cry for the next 10-15 minutes while I mentally conversed with Him. I did not want to leave, but I had to. I took a quick look at His reflection in the water and hurried towards the waiting bus.

All this while, with surrender and love in my heart I had requested my Gurus - Babaji, Paramhansa Yogananda and Anandamayee Maa to do this pilgrimage through me, I was only to be an instrument.

The following morning we had a delicious breakfast and clicked pictures and left from Nepalgunj airport for Simikot. Simikot is a lovely picturesque village of Nepal. The helicopters came and it was our turn to be transported to Hilsa. As we flew away from Simikot and began approaching Hilsa, the magnificent green mountains gave way to arid mountains with small shrubs and bushes. We reached Hilsa, which is 8000--8500 feet and felt a difference in the atmosphere and temperature. After eating our fill, we walked towards the border which was a pontoon bridge made of steel plates and wires over a rushing, roaring river. While the villagers walked on the bridge as if it was a park, some of our team members were scared as the wind was strong and the bridge moved from side to side. Well it was amusing to see how some of us were crossing it!

After crossing that bridge, we were in China and after the check done by the Chinese Army, the buses took us to the Immigration Office. As all the formalities were being done, Mohanji was sitting and overseeing things and His fatherly care and concern towards all was palpable. Taklakot was our first high-altitude station. Later on in the afternoon, Mohanji conducted a satsang. All were glued to the wise words that flowed from Him and His overwhelming love and care. Apart from answering other questions, He guided us about the sanctity of Lake Manasarovar and how to approach the dips in Manasarovar. Also, he highlighted the significance of how our taking dips on behalf of others could benefit those people. He also mentioned that this time He would be in the lake only for a few minutes and those devotees who wanted Mohanji to bless them with Manasarovar water in the lake and those who wanted to do His abhishekam would have to hurry, once they all were in the lake.

There was an incredible story Mohanji related of a female devotee of Shirdi Sai Baba who gets visions of Sai Baba and Baba talks to her, she sees Him as if seeing a television screen. So back in 2014, when Mohanji was leading the Kailash trip and was en route to the Manasarovar Lake, this lady devotee was in the kitchen cooking and Baba suddenly appeared before her and told her, "Mohan will die now." She was appalled on hearing this and Baba continued, "Mohan is doing such great work of leading so many souls towards liberation that the dark forces are trying to stop him." The devotee asked Sai Babaji to protect Mohanji and Baba said He will protect, but Mohanji would have to die in a sense. And then Baba showed her the scene of buses moving towards Manasarovar Lake and the bus in which Mohanji was sitting, there were lot of disembodied restless spirits moving along with the bus and after reaching Manasarovar when Mohanji ventured inside the lake and took dips, all those spirits too dived in and they became free and moved up towards the sky. And Sai Babaji continued to be concerned about Mohanji and protected Him as the scene showed dark negative entities trying to harm Mohanji. Soon after that year's Kailash Yatra got over, Mohanji faced character assassination. Mohanji has always maintained, "Those who have the eyes to see, will see the truth, others who are superficial or not eligible will not be able to, they will get carried away by the lies and rumours." He also maintains, "If anyone had a doubt about me or a question or a problem with me, why they did not come and freely ask me, they should have as I would have clarified everything."

I feel those people never had the courage to directly face a perfect Master. The one who is connected to the Source is scared of nobody, He will not shy away, and out of unconditional love for all, He may even go ahead and choose to clear everything or even anticipate and prevent things that may harm Him. The Masters of the White Path generally as a norm do not use their Siddhis for Their own well-being until and unless They get a directive from the Source. I too had gone with Mohanji in 2014 and I too heard all the rumours, but did not react to any of those. Mohanji manifesting The Absolute has been known to me since March 2014, I never doubted it then and I do not doubt it now and I will not doubt it ever. Mahavtar Babaji has been the glorious Guru who blessed Mohanji with the flowering of Cosmic Consciousness and Oneness with The Absolute and I know that He guides Mohanji. Each one of us, if we follow an inward practice with devotion and surrender, we will be able to discover our true nature and identity and the practice will also enable us to discriminate between the ones who fool us in the name of God and the ones who are true.

Coming back to 2016 and the satsang, all the pilgrims were filled with devotion after drinking from the well of Mohanji's inspiration. Mohanji mentioned that that satsang maybe the only one in which pilgrims for both Inner and Outer Kora were together and there may not be a chance to hold such a one later. After that, Swami Brahmananda from the UK ashram gave uplifting guidance on how one should approach one's path and how devotion plays an important part in our spiritual practice.

We proceeded towards Manasarovar. As one approaches the holy lake and its surroundings, there is an automatic natural change that happens; one starts to withdraw and begins to go inward. For the dips in the Holy Manasarovar, Mohanji says, "After taking the dips, it is your eligibility, your karma that takes you forward to the Kailash parikrama."

I got down from the bus and proceeded towards the lake and saw Mohanji along with a few devotees was already inside taking the dips. This time I wanted to do Mohanji's abhishekam with the holy water and I hurriedly walked towards the lake. Anandamayee Maa has said that when one approaches a sacred water body, then first one should humbly bow to the lake/river and then put one's foot in. I shared this wise counsel with a few other devotees and did this and entered the lake. The first step and the water was ultra-cold!

Well, there is no other choice but to keep chanting "Om Namah Shivaya" and the chill would take a backseat. I reached that zone in the lake where Mohanji and a group of devotees were already taking the dips. Mohanji was splashing the "holy jal" on everyone and they were doing Mohanji's abhishekam. I too had desired to put some jal on Mohanji, but I saw he had started to turn around and walk out of the lake, so I rushed and Rajesh saw how eager I was to do Mohanji's abhishekam, he encouraged me to move in closer, I did and managed to splash some jal on Mohanji while chanting Om Namah Shivaya. We had to be fully immersed, our heads need to be submerged in water to make the dips count. The water was above the waist level. The first 3 dips are for one's own self, family, and ancestors and then we can take as many dips as we want on behalf of our friends and Gurus. The water was biting-cold and I would visualize the person for whom I was taking the dip and then dive in and take 3-4 dips in one go and then would stand up for a few seconds chanting "Om Namah Shivaya" and feel the warm sunshine and then again go under water.

All the devotees in the lake were paying obeisance to God in the form of Shiva in their own devotional manner. It was a thrilling experience! I managed to count up to 24/25 dips, then I felt that I should now turn around and as I was about to do so, I remembered Mohanji's words saying that we could also take dips for Lord Shiva and his family and so I did the same. I happily turned around and while I was coming out I saw Shirdi Sai Baba's idol also in the lake and I inwardly bowed to Him. I was feeling content after having done Mt. Kailash's and Mohanji's abhishekam with the holy water. After the dips, I sat by the lake shore, facing Kailash, chanted and meditated for a while. I took out my phone to pray on behalf of all the people whose names were in the list on my phone. Then I clicked pictures. Some of us were meditating, some were softly chanting, some clicking pictures, and some were simply sitting and gazing at Kailash – each one had his or her private conversation going on with Lord Shiva.

"Shiva is a state," Mohanji explains, "Shiva is not a form, it is a state of absolute stillness, and when you do Kailash Yatra, you are announcing to the world that you are choosing to move towards this state of stillness."

There was elaborate preparation done for a hawan and once the sacred fire was lit, the hawan commenced with Mohanji starting with Ganesh Avahaan. The Swamis from the UK ashram and Devi ji were sitting along with Mohanji while each of the devotees came and offered pure ghee three times into the sacred fire as the mantra chanting went on. After the hawan, facing Kailash, all of us did the abhishekam of the Shiv linga. Each one was feeling the powerful blessings and the vibrations of the holy lake and were communing with the Divine.

Decorated Horses

Each of us was excited about this and we were inwardly connecting with God, some of us did charansparsh of Mohanji and He lovingly blessed us all and continued to lead us on the pilgrimage. We came to Yama Dwar, the point where the Parikrama begins. It is believed, that at the Yama Dwar we need to leave our ego behind before we enter the sacred space of Kailash. So symbolically, pilgrims leave behind any of their belongings at the Yama Dwar, it is best to surrender one's lower self to Shiva, any desires, fears, doubts, pessimism, it's best to drop it at the Yama Dwar and surrender to Shiva. We are supposed to do 3 parikramas of the Yama Dwar and then go through the narrow passage as we ring the bell and after moving out, we have to walk ahead and do not have to look back.

After doing this, my Parikrama began. I kept clicking pictures here and there, and my mental chanting of "Om Namah Shivaya" "Om Yogananda ji", "Om Anandamayee Maa" continued. This time I had mentally asked my Gurus to do the parikrama through me and I had surrendered and offered myself as an instrument for whatever my Gurus wanted me to do. Chanting silently, we kept on walking, some with Mohanji, some ahead, some lagging a little behind though Mohanji was aware about each and every pilgrim under His wing and He would respond to the mental prayers of each one.

Finally, I came to the West face of Kailash and Lord Shiva was very kind to give me His darshan, His face appeared on Kailash and I like a small child was beaming with smiles and my heart danced with joy. I bowed down and paid my respects and prayed, not just for myself and my family, but for all those who had asked me to and for all whom I was meant to – after all, I was only a humble instrument. What else could one have asked for but to get darshan of the Lord Himself. I was immensely grateful and then a kind of contentment set in, the knowing that indeed God, like my closest buddy, was traversing with me every minute of my life.

I was glad that I could make it safely to the guesthouse at the end of day 1. From my bed, I could see through the balcony and could look at the mountain adjacent to Kailash when I saw 5-6 huge faces of Saints, I kept looking at them and just had enough strength to mentally pay my humble respects to them. At the time of Brahma Mahurat, I woke up and sat in meditation. After a while, I felt the presence of one of my Gurus – Swami Sri Yukteshwar and God in the form of Shiva with me. I acknowledged Their presence by conveying my "pranaams" in my heart. They were there with me for some time and some transmission and transformation happened post which, they were gone. Mentally, I expressed my thanks and then went off to sleep. Sleep after meditation is the best in quality.

The instructions for us the previous evening had been that Inner Parikrama devotees could sleep a little extra as they would leave at 11am the following day for Kailash Charan Sparsh.

We started the climb and after every 7 to 9 steps, I would take a pause. As the incline increased and we kept trekking, my conversation with God continued, I also invoked Hanumanji and asked Him to bless all devotees and help them in the ascent. Strength poured as Hanumanji's jaap was carried on besides also mentally calling out to Mohanji. He would keep checking every now and then about the well-being of everyone in the group. As we neared the Charan Sparsh, I would keep taking breaks, and once I jokingly told Hanumanji, "kahaan fasaa diya?" (Hanumanji, what have You got me into?). All this while, my porter was very kind and affectionate and every few steps, she would ask me if I wanted water or if I wanted to stop and she would remind me, "Walk slowly, take small steps." It was as if Divine Mother was affectionately taking care of me though her.

Kailash Charan Sparsh

In the meantime, the sherpas and held a rope, we all were supposed to climb up an inclined wall of snow – it was a part of the glacier and snow on Kailash. It was also covered with gravel and stones and hence it was slippery to climb. Once all of us were up, then we had to move further up another 500 metres to reach a higher ground, so that we could be closer to Kailash.

By this time, my stamina was dismally low and I wanted to do nothing else but sit and relax. I had touched Kailash, I had lovingly bowed to Shiva and Parvati and prayed for all, now all I wanted to do was sit down. I was feeling very drowsy. My porter asked me not to sleep and I was like "Ok, I will not," but I knew that I would end up doing it. Everyone else had reached the higher ground while I decided to take a break and I sat down, made myself comfortable on a spot and soon after I put my hands behind my head and stretched on my back and lovingly told Divine Mother that I was lying down in Her lap. My porter who was sitting with a friend in the plain area below me, saw me, and she again cautioned me against sleeping. I waved and nodded my head but my eyelids were very heavy and before I knew, I was asleep. It was cloudy weather then. After 3-4 minutes I think, suddenly the sun came out and broke my nap, it seemed as if Divine Mother woke me up.

Well, we started our trek back down and going downhill for people from the plains is even more trying! So the initial descent was a bit slow and I prayed to Hanumanji and Mohanji to give strength to the body. I was chanting all the time and admiring the scenery around me!

The next morning, we woke up early and freshened up to start our third day of the climb. The sherpas tested our oxygen levels. Those with less than 60 oxygen level would not be allowed to proceed. I kept mentally chanting and prayed to Hanumanji and Mohanji to give me the strength to keep walking and am sure the help came.

Eventually we came to a pass and from there we could see a glacier at a distance. By now, the altitude had increased a lot, there was very less oxygen, and due to breathlessness, I was walking very slowly and by now, was at the tail-end of the group. Then, I came closer to where Mohanji was walking and I saw Him conversing cheerfully and amiably with a Russian mountaineer who was coming to Kailash for the 7th time and he mentioned that he had written a guide-book in Russian about all the paths that he had trekked on in Kailash. He gave a copy of the same to Mohanji. I had continued walking on slowly and before we knew it, the mountaineer was way ahead of us and had reached the far end of the pass – it seemed as if for him it was a walk in the garden!!! We continued moving ahead and Mohanji came closer when He mentioned that the Sherpa accompanying Him had been especially sent by Mahavatar Babaji for taking care of Him. As we came closer to the glacier, it seemed even further away and higher than what it looked when I first set my eyes on it.

Like a guardian, Mohanji would lovingly and patiently wait for all the devotees to be together at various spots and I am sure silently, He must have assisted each one innumerable times. At one spot, I told Baba that I would carry on walking as my speed was slow. We saw a big cave beneath the glacier and a couple of us went to check it out. I only had limited energy and my aim was to use it up in climbing. I was surprised to see that our team of sherpas was so agile in the snow and gravel terrain, that they had already crossed the glacier and gone up to fix the ropes and pickets for enabling and easing our climb.

After crossing I had hoped to be on solid ground but lo and behold! It was all gravel and loose rock on a ground of snow!!! Well, somehow, I balanced myself and faced the steep upward climb that lay ahead while my back was towards the drop. By now, the picket had been again dug into the snow of the glacier and I saw it was Mohanji who had came across after me, He and Deviji, Vijay,

Eligibility – The Key To Unlock Grace

Mitesh, and a couple of others were dexterously seated about 5 feet above from where I was. I tried to crawl up, but could not as there was no foothold and the gravel and the snow made it dangerously slippery. I tried a couple of times, but then decided against it. At the other end of the glacier, it was Phaneendar, Chai, and Jayeeta waiting to be helped across. Mohanji was caringly watching over all of us and He said twice to me, "Wait, Anjali! Prahalad will give you the rope!" Then He directed Prahalad to throw me the rope and get me up. Prahalad tried to take a strong swing towards me along with the rope, but the first attempt failed. He tried the second time and reached next to me. Then he instructed me on how to pull myself up with the rope. The nerve-chilling cold coupled with high altitude breathlessness had driven the strength out of me and as I began the few steps upwards, I paused after a couple of them and heard Mitesh encourage me out loud, "Come on Tiger!" and I managed to pull myself up and found a spot, turned around to face the downward slope and sat down on the snow and gravel. Oh! What a relief it was for the body to get a break from all the trekking and climbing.

Slowly, one by one, the others were moving up using the clip and harness and the mountain ropes. From our group, up went Rajesh, Jay, and then Deviji and I saw everyone experiencing some or the other minor slip/loss of balance or lack of strength in the arms and this made me prepare mentally for what I might come across. Breathlessness was happening to all due to the high altitude. This was the most adventurous thing that I had ever attempted, but I was not scared even for a moment because I had full faith that if I had been guided to do this pilgrimage by the Source, then the Source would take care of me and all that I was meant to do would get done.

As I began the ascent up the glacier, I paused every 3-4 steps to catch my breath. According to the sherpas, we were running behind schedule and they wanted us to hurry up. Now my body would not have any of the hurrying-up thing and I was not able to proceed higher and higher without taking a 15-20 second pause for proper breathing! As I reached almost at the top and paused our Sherpa Amar asked me to continue moving further up and the body was so exhausted and gasping for air that I again stopped. I saw Mohanji was coming up after me and I mentally prayed to Him to come up a bit slowly as I needed the pause. Amar again told me to keep moving up and my mind was screaming that the body needed the pause and in an almost crying voice I forcefully blurted out, "I need to stop, I cannot breathe, do not say anything to me!" and I stopped. The body and brain just did not care, the body needed a break, and it would not move without a breather. What else could we have expected at almost 22000 feet, from people from the plains who had had only a handful of days to adjust to high altitude?

The remainder of the climb was a narrow slippery path with snow and finer gravel, the path was only as much wide as one foot could be positioned on it and there was no foothold and so at various points, 4 sherpas were sitting to give their hand and pull us up and here there was no scope to pause, but I was very thirsty and I needed water. When my porter who had my bag and flask was sitting at the topmost point, got to know this, he threw the flask towards me which the able Sherpa placed at the lower foothold caught and then I took the much needed draughts which made me feel somewhat better. My Sherpa tried throwing back up the flask which the porter at the top could not catch, then the flask was thrown up again with such force and at a wrong angle that none could catch it making the flask go sliding down the glacier. Now it must be there like a souvenir from me to Shiva.

So I kept moving up and then one Sherpa guided me from the top to go left on a very narrow trail that curved along the side of the glacier, a slight loss of balance on the left and one would slide down. I was dazed by the cold and my only saving Grace was the incessant mental chanting and conversation that I did with Shiva. It seemed to me that the trail going around the mountain was unending, eventually it opened up into a vast open space, and we saw the East face of Kailash, we were in Shiva's durbar as Mohanji called it where He gives Darshan to all beings – terrestrial or celestial . I bowed there, paid my loving humble respects to Lord

Eligibility – The Key To Unlock Grace

Shiva and Maa Parvati. My body did not seem to have any energy left, I was thirsty and hungry and my backpack was with my porter who was nowhere close to me. Vijay offered me the little water that he was left with and an apple. We were tired and we sat on a rock for sometime to recharge ourselves. I saw that Mohanji and His porter and Deviji had been walking on and had reached far.

It seemed that Shiva wanted us to get up and continue the walk too as there was a hailstorm that began. There were mini-hailstones, small in size but came down like speeding bullets. We got up quickly and walked, my pace gradually slowed down while the hailstorm continued intermittently. It was biting cold. By now, after offering everything to Shiva with my heart and soul, and hearing His answer that my effort and pilgrimage on behalf of whomsoever I had to do and all that I was supposed to do had been accepted, there was a new kind of contentment that filled me.

Now, my sole interest then was to go down the mountains and back to the guest house and eventually tuck myself in bed. So I followed Mohanji. Like the pole star, He was way ahead than me but as long as I could see Him, it was fine. The body was tired, my mind dazed, the legs were gone, just the heart kept me going on. As we went down, after sometime I caught up with my porter and gulped down the last bit of water that was in my bottle. At a distance, we saw that 3 of our team members were at Kuber Kund (I was already clear that I would not go there – it was way too far). Mohanji was proceeding downhill and we followed Him. Later on, I got to know that He was very thirsty and nobody had any water left. Suddenly, I remembered that my backpack had a small bottle that had water from Kailash Charan Sparsh, I told my porter to take out that bottle and pass it on to Mohanji. Mohanji was way down and my porter threw the bottle towards Mohanji's porter, unfortunately he could not catch it and the bottle fell and some water spilled out and I was like, "Oh! I do not know if there is any water left and that Mohanji's thirst may not be quenched." The next instant Mohanji picked up the bottle and drank the water that was left, He offered some to Deviji too and to His Sherpa and others. The body was terribly tired and all the while I was telling Yoganandaji and Anandamayee Maa to do the remainder of the trek down through me. And how sweetly Divine Mother did take care of me, my porter and his daughter with their warm encouraging words held my hand and walked along.

By now our friends Sumit, DB and Riana from Kuber Kund had caught up with us. Rajesh, Deviji, Mitesh, and Vijay were walking along with Mohanji. Mitesh had been clicking a lot of pictures. The body was so fatigued that it did not want to walk any further, so I asked a fellow devotee, Mitesh to give me his hand and walk along with me. Mentally I kept telling Yoganandaji and Hanumanji to carry the body forward, to make it walk! At times, I would mentally tell Mohanji to walk a bit slow.

After sometime when we looked back at Kailash, Mohanji said that Shiva was giving us Darshan and we all saw two eyes and the third eye of Shiva from where nectar was oozing! We all bowed in reverence and devotion. Mohanji asked us to pick up any stone from that sacred space of Shiva, He said we had been fortunate and blessed to have been in the durbar of Shiva and He asked Rajesh and Mitesh to click a lot of pictures.

All said and done, my only target now was to get down as soon as possible to the main road. We all were very tired and wanted to reach our guest house and rest. We reached the guest house after 45 minutes and we all went to our rooms to retire.

After reaching Darchen, I meditated and thanked God, Gurus for everything! The next morning after we were ready, we went to the dining area and saw Mohanji seated at the table with a few of the devotees. After a while once we were seated, Mohanji informed us that the Chinese Army had not given us the permission to go to The Saptarishi Caves, in fact no permits were being given to any group to go there. Adding further, He talked about His communion with the Saptarishis in meditation the previous night. The Rishis told Him that in the past few years, the sacred space of Kailash has been violated frequently, and people have been coming there as if for a picnic rather than with a sincere thirst for seeking the truth. The Rishis said that hence the irreverent ones were being pushed back, which means that those people were not just losing their lives in Kailash, but were also being pushed back on their evolutionary path. We heard this in rapt attention.

We were scheduled to leave for Manasarovar Lake in the afternoon and the night would be spent in a lodge next to the lake. The buses came and we departed from Darchen for Manasarovar and reached the area of the lake where we could take dips expressing our gratitude to Shiva and Parvati for blessing us and making the Inner Parikrama a success. It was almost evening and when we ventured in the water, it was very cold, but the sun remained for sometime and gave us warmth. We took dips facing Kailash. Apart from being grateful for such a blessed trip, it was also a chance for us to take dips on behalf of those whom we missed doing when the pilgrimage started.

There were arrangements being done for a homa by the lake side. It was dusk and a cold breeze blew. Some of us gathered with Mohanji and the Swamis from the UK ashram to do the hawan. Mohanji asked Swami Brahmananda to lead the hawan this time. Swamiji invoked Ganesha and then the holy ceremony began. We were seated around the sacred fire, wrapped up in our blankets and jackets, chanting along the mantras with devotion as the ahuti was poured into the fire. Towards the end, various bhajans were sung by the devotees and then the purna ahuti was done to conclude the ceremony.

Grace, straight from the Source had flowed all throughout the pilgrimage. All of us were carrying inside our hearts the blessing and transformational touch of Kailash. Now the days and months coming ahead would show the overhaul that would happen at the astral and material levels. That evening some of us went to explore the market and shopped.

As the grand finale, an evening satsang with Mohanji was scheduled. Post the dinner, each one of us waited eagerly for the wisdom and warmth to flow through Mohanji to all of us. He mentioned about His morning trip to the ancient Shiva temple situated in the higher reaches. It is difficult to access area with less transport facility. By road, it would take 3 days to reach that spot. The priest of the Shiva temple showed them the footprints of Shiva, when Shiva escaped from the Asura – Bhasmasur who attempted killing Shiva to whom Shiva Himself had granted the boon. Then Mohanji was given a Rudraksha Mala by the priest. The mala had adorned the Shiva lingam for many years. Swami Brahmananda too spoke about his perception and experience of the Shiva Temple.

Mohanji asked each one of us to speak about our experience of the Inner Parikrama. His love and blessings permeated the whole atmosphere as each devotee shared his/her experience. Each devotee is special and connects with the Source in an endearingly unique way. At the end of this, Mohanji blessed us all. Mohanji gave us the Rudrakshas from that mala as prasad and said that He felt the powerful energy in the Rudraksha beads. He wished us a safe flight back home. We dispersed and retired for the night. The next morning saw us bidding good bye to each other, everyone carrying the special benediction of Lord Shiva- Parvati Maa deep in one's heart, knowing well that in the days to come, the transformation and transition in one's self would unfold.

Why Fear When I Am Here

- Phaneendar Bhavaraju -

Why the Inner Kora?

It's an extremely sacred journey to traverse the divine path in the sacred space of Kailash, the divine and mystical abode of Mahadev. I have been blessed by Brahmarishi Mohanji to take part in the Yatra. This couldn't have happened without blessings of his Divine Consciousness as I was completely unfit from not only physical perspective but mentally as well. I am overweight and my mind has also been weighed down with lots of thoughts as I resigned from a cushy job to take an entrepreneurial leap.

I was fortunate to perform the Outer Kora 3 times, most notably in the year 2014 known as Dev Kumbh. So, I was really looking forward to the Inner Kora sans all the preparation that was required for it!!

Dip at Kailash Manasarovar

The Yatra always starts with the holy dip in Manasarovar. As we approached Manasarovar I saw the repeat scenes of the previous 3 visits, i.e. cloudy sky as if the rains are going to lash out. I have also seen the previous 3 times that as soon as Brahmarishi Mohanji gets down and walks towards Manasarovar the clouds disappear!!! Will it be the same this year? Absolutely, as soon as we got down the bus and started walking towards Manasarovar, the clouds meandered ominously but once we reached Manasarovar they started fleeing as if someone was shooing them away; revealing the majestic Mount Kailash!! We were awestruck with the turn of events while I was smiling at the familiarity of it!! The Sun was shining in full glory as if to heat up the super cold water of Manasarovar. I along with my friend Mitesh walked into the water, chanted Siddha Mangala Stotra, Mohanji Gayatri and took a few dips in the holy Manasarovar

Day 1

The day 1 which is same as the day 1 parikrama of the outer kora is always a breeze, so I started my walk enthusiastically. The trek on day 1 gives one a glimpse of Kailash!! The parikrama despite being in a group is as good as being on your own. So, within a couple of hours, I was on my own (physically!!) along with the Sherpa who was walking at least 1 km ahead of me. As I glided through the initial part, at about mid-way I completely collapsed at the rustic cafe where everyone stopped by. My friend Mitesh Khatiwala and Divine Mother in the form of Milu took care of me for a few minutes till I felt better. The next half was arduous as I was unable to walk more than 25 steps at a time. I had to stop at least 3-4 minutes after every 25 steps thus slowing me down considerably.

Right from my childhood, I have been quite attracted to pictures of Gods with various animals and birds surrounded by them. It has been an ardent desire to naturally attract a bird to play with me and stay by me!! Little did I know that the divine consciousness of Brahmarishi Mohanji will satisfy that desire during this trek. I was followed by a beautiful orange coloured bird, which would come and sit right next to me whenever I stopped to take a few breaths. After watching it for a few times sitting next to me on the same rock, I prayed that now it should come and sit on my lap!! Lo!!! The bird flew straight to my lap when I rested on a large rock!! The bird was on my lap for many seconds and then flew, but continued to follow me. It was a divine feeling and cannot be described in words!! In that satisfactory moment, I continued my trek to reach the destination of the 1st day! I slipped into the bed with high fever but had a very peaceful and restful sleep.

Charan Sparsh

I woke up and had the Darshan of the majestic Kailash, and we started the Inner Kora with a trek towards Charan Sparsh!! As the name denotes this is the feet of the Divine Kailash, the trek took us on a long yet breath-taking path towards the closest point of Kailash!! We walked on large boulders, quenched our thirst with water of Kailash Ganga!! Yes, Kailash Ganga the origin of river Ganges!! The flowing water of divine mother Ganga from the eternal father Lord Shiva was pure, fresh & supercharged us with divine energy to take the onward journey towards Charan Sparsh. Brahmarishi Mohanji was walking ahead of us, leading us in his own home!! Father Mohanji would stop after every couple of hours and ask me to chant Siddha Mangala Stotra, it was a delight chanting the mantra while looking at Kailash. I guess it is father's way to remove unforeseen obstacles in my Yatra. We walked several hours before we reached Charan Sparsh!! We sat for a couple of hours at Charan Sparsh, soaked in bliss!! A few members of our group took the decision of going ahead and touching the divine Kailash!! Alas, my energy levels were not up to it, so couldn't join them in the ultimate journey towards Kailash!! Blessed are those souls who touched Kailash, embraced it and came back with a loving smile!! Har Har Mahadev!!!

Day 3 - Kuber Kund

The 3rd day turned out to be not only adventurous but also a faith-testing experience. The trek was long, convoluting, steep and breath stealing!! I walked endlessly along with the group through the streams of water and damp soil to reach a huge ice mountain. This is the mountain we needed to scale before we got on to the other side towards Kuber Kund!! I was right behind father Brahmarishi Mohanji throughout as I always knew that his divine consciousness is the only saviour for my fearsome mind. My mind entered the fear zone right on the ice mountain!!!! Father said, "Phani, we will be doing this once in a lifetime and don't fear when I am here". These words still ring in my ears whenever I recollect this particular day. As I scaled the ice mountain, I was falling off, again and again, I was making large noise "amma "calling for my mother's help and blessings!! After scaling the mountain, at the fag end I realised that it's a narrow 10 mt distance that has to be covered in one breath. With the help of father's Divine Consciousness, I lunged at it, which is otherwise impossible for me!! Entered a large open area that was looking like a courtyard of a great King!! I called father several times in the hope that he may be close by, I did get a response in the form of cool breeze which carried with it the blessings in form of ice pellets!! I sat in the courtyard for several minutes bathing in the cool breezy blessings of the Ultimate i.e. Parabrahma!!! and then proceeded towards Kuber Kund. The Sherpa had no clue about Kuber Kund, father arranged it through the Nepali sherpas who gave a huge shout for me!! I had the Darshan of Kuber Kund, had many sips of the holy pure water from the Kund!! As we started walking towards our next camp, I realised this is a long one. My torch had run out of light and I had only my mobile. It got pitch dark but as father ordained it was a full moon and the entire trek was dotted with moonlight. I started chanting Mohanji Gayatri for the next few hours as I did not want to stop till I reached the destination. I was walking all through the night along with the Sherpa chanting Mohanji Gayatri and finally reached at 3 am!! (started the day at 5 am) so a 22-hour trek with the help of father Brahmarishi Mohanji's divine consciousness and Mohanji Gayatri!! While the trek at night was scary and treacherous, father said as soon as he saw me "Phani, you have spent the longest hours in the Kailash region"!!

With deep gratitude to Brahmarishi Mohanji & his Divine Consciousness!!

Faith Can Move Mountains

- Jayeeta Chakraborty -

God comes to all of us in various forms. Sometimes we recognize Him, sometimes we don't, but He is there – ever watchful, ever present, waiting for us to open our eyes and heart.

In 2016, we took a pilgrimage to the Holy Mount Kailash once again. There was excitement as well as apprehension. Am I eligible? Does Shiva want me there? Will this body hold up the physical exertion? And many more! Firmly putting my faith in God's will, preparations began; more mental than physical. Mohanji always says, "Faith can move mountains" Keeping this thought firmly in my heart and mind, the journey began well before the actual physical journey. During this phase, there were plenty of doubts; mind doing its job and playing constant games, but who is to tussle with the might of God and Guru? In the end purely by Their Grace, things started falling in place.

I remember, during the first day of the Kailash Parikrama in 2014, I walked right behind Mohanji, following His footsteps. His blessings engulfed us and helped us move forward even when we were physically exhausted. I was in a daze just thinking that a "no physical exercise" person like me could walk all of those kilometers and willing to walk more right till the day ended! I have my limitations to physical exertion and a certain amount of unwillingness to walking; I could never imagine that this body

Faith Can Move Mountains

would be able to do that! It was only and only Grace that made it happen!

Therefore, this time from the very beginning, I resolved that I will walk right behind Mohanji (honestly, without Him, there was no way I could go on).

On 9th August 2016, we arrived at our hotel in Katmandu and in the lobby. The first people we met were Mohanji and Deviji. It felt like homecoming. This, I realized was what I was waiting for with bated breath; returning home to family. We all rejoiced at this togetherness, which carried on right through our Yatra and still continues on a soul level.

That evening we had a Satsang with Mohanji where he spoke to us about the Yatra and gave us guidance on how to conduct ourselves both physically and mentally. His specific instruction about Manasarovar was, "Leave all your baggage. Throw it out (get rid of it) before you take your dip. Think that you are diving into the Divine Mother's womb." That was an emotional moment for me; I had tears in my eyes. Let me tell you, for the past few years, I have been trying to connect more with Divine Mother; ongoing mental conversations, sometimes complaints, sometimes tears and all the time a lot of love, and here Mohanji was showing me how to be in Her Womb! How could it get any better than that? My soul was singing! The Master knew my heart and showed me the way! Never would I have in my wildest imagination had this insight. I resonated with it, but along with it came this niggling thought . . . what baggage would I need to discard and the next few thoughts – What does it feel like to be in the Mother's womb? I do not remember! How will I know? In spite of these questions, the soul was very happy! And thus began the first leg of the journey to Kailash.

Being with your soul family makes up for everything. They somehow know you, your eccentricities, strengths, shortcomings, and of course your requirement. With amazing ease, the family took care of all, like they have been doing this all along, when perhaps many of us may have just met once before. The connection with each other was unfailing and extremely reassuring, especially when you embark on a momentous journey such as this!

On our way to Manasarovar, I encountered my "getting rid of the baggage" challenge. Ego flared, almost leading to an altercation with two people. The first got resolved soon enough, but left me on guard for what was yet to come . . . . ..and the second one was huge! I could not sleep at night thinking about it. I wanted to quarrel and tell the person off, badly. I knew it was a strange emotion that I was going through, especially considering the fact that I only just met this person who was not likely to travel with us for the rest of our journey. Yet I was extremely upset, but Thank God, He put me on guard so I was trying my best not to give in to the emotion. I tried innumerable peace and harmony prayers, which would relieve me for a few minutes, but the anger and ego would come back in no time. I was being eaten alive by negative thoughts. It was really terrible as I realized that my soul was suffering in the process. What could I do? I kept praying to God and Guru to help me through this. Of course, they have their "right time" for it to get all sorted out! So They let me fester on this for a day and night right till the time I reached the banks of Manasarovar. I was determined to drop this baggage before the dip and that is when God stepped in and took over – my anger was gone, there was no judgment in my voice, I was strangely calm – I walked over to the person and the issue was resolved; never to bother me again.

I realized, in hindsight; when we go to a high-energy place like Kailash Manasarovar, any thought form, positive or negative, magnifies many folds and manifests. If you go with love, that is what will overwhelm you and if you go with any negative emotion . . . well you saw what happened! So getting rid of the baggage was sound guidance!

The thought of Mother's womb revisited my mind. What is it like to be there? Perhaps the feeling of a protective and nurturing fluid around me like in the womb protecting the baby? The mind tries to reason and can only relate to the physical aspect. The mind in its limitedness tries to draw similes and logical understanding. I did not fight. Hence I went along with the thought.

Now I was ready to take the dip. Mohanji had already set the stage for us. By the time we got ready to get in the water, He had already finished His dips and abhishekam and was out of the water. There was a cold breeze blowing. The sun was shining bright. Was the water cold was my first question. Bracing myself for the onslaught of cold, I waded into the water and kept thinking "Mother's Womb! What would that really be like? How would I feel if I was in the Mother's womb? I want to feel my Mother's womb. I want to feel Your womb Divine Mother." As these thoughts played in my mind, the water around me felt warmer and warmer. There was a gentle whirlwind of this warm water surrounding me beneath the surface, keeping me in its protection and comfort. I deliberated whether I would start feeling cold on the upper part of my body which was not submerged, but to my wonder I was nice and warm through and through. Even after taking many dips, my body temperature was being maintained. Not once did I feel the chill. I was perhaps as content and comfortable as one would be only in the "Mother's Womb." For the first time, I realized that Divine Mother was all around me, in Kailash! Another perspective which was new to me, I always thought that Kailash being the abode of Shiva would have more of male aspects, but I could not have been more wrong. This is the place where Shiva and Shakti resides – both Father and Mother. That day, Kailash instead of being my father's home, became my parents' home! What joy! The day ended with a beautiful havan on the banks of Manasarovar. The following day our parikrama was to commence.

As much as I was looking forward to the parikrama, I was a bit unsure of how this body would fare with all the walking. Leaving it all to God, the new day began. I had envisioned that I would walk with Mohanji, just behind Him; however, as Gurus would have it, Mohanji asked that Rima and I to walk together as He would be doing the first leg on a pony.

We walked at a comfortable pace and this time I got the God-sent opportunity to spend a lot of time in the presence of Kailash, gazing at it, appreciating its beauty. It felt like I was walking with my friend, chit chatting and I just did not want it to stop. I must have been the last person to reach our guest house in Diraphuk and I was not worried at all. I felt like prolonging this experience. I was totally enjoying myself. Kailash, "my friend," gave me the most amazing day I could ever wish for and perhaps because I was allowed to have an uninterrupted prolonged interaction. Mohanji allowed that to happen. I am so grateful.

The next day our group was divided. One group went for the Outer Kora and our group stayed on to continue with the Inner Kora. We started late as that day we were going to do Kailash "Charan Sparsh."

This day, I got the opportunity to follow Mohanji throughout. Not once did I feel out of breath or tired. There was a spring in my step and the energy level was high; not my doing; all Mohanji! Where He takes you, if you follow, Grace finds you! The Master is always there to encourage you, watch over you, and protect you. That day, we all returned to our guest house feeling fantastic, in spite of the long walk. Some amongst the group, with Mohanji's permission, ventured further on, through a fast moving glacier, ravines, frozen ground; in short - perilous terrain, where losing a limb or even life would be "normal, as they had no mountaineering equipment apart from a walking stick. However, each one of them returned with not so much as a scratch. That night when this small group returned late in the night after a particularly difficult and life threatening trek, one of them kept saying on and on, looking at them as though in a trance – "I fell and cut my hand, not a scratch! Mohanji took the cut."

And true to her word, I remembered from earlier that evening, while we were on our return from Kailash Charan Sparsh, Mohanji's hand was bleeding. He kept each one of us safe taking it all on Himself.

God and Guru's Grace is ever present for all true seekers. Mohanji said that those who went on the Inner Kora had 10,000 years of good karma to bring them there and their unyielding loyalty to their Guru.

The Inner Kora Yatra day approached. We were walking to Kuber Kund that day. We were to leave very early at around

4am as we were going through tougher routes, which would take us quite some time; however, we all were delayed by almost 4 hours due to our exhaustion of the previous day. We all slept in. When we got ready, I realized that I was not feeling too well – blurry vision and my legs seemed to have lead weights attached to them and movement was difficult and clumsy. By the time I went downstairs, the rest of the group had already started their trek. I was one of the last ones. Dragging my feet for more than 3 or 4 steps at a time was proving to be difficult and no matter how much I tried, I could not move fast enough to catch up with Mohanji and the rest of the group. The only thought that was persistent was, only if I could walk behind Mohanji, it would get better. I kept mentally asking Mohanji to sit somewhere and wait for me to catch up. And guess what! A little ahead I saw His red jacket! Mohanji sat on a boulder and waited. As soon as I reached close by, He got up and started walking. I got my energy boost. My speed doubled, tripled even, and soon I was walking right behind Him.

Upon introspection, I realized that God and Guru watches over all devotees, whether the person is fast or slow, bright or dull, a winner or not. God and Guru love us and protect us equally and do everything necessary as per our individual need, to help us improve and move forward. Mohanji could have walked right ahead with the others who were walking fast. Instead He walked slow, waited, gave us a chance to catch up and gave us the boost of energy and continued. At every step He ensured that each one of us was following and that each one of us was safe. He never lost sight of any of us. In the Bhagavad Gita, Krishna says, "He who perceives Me everywhere and beholds everything in Me never loses sight of Me, nor do I ever lose sight of him."

We kept walking and up ahead I saw a huge snow clad mountain, which some of our group members had already started to climb with the help of our Sherpas. From far it looked like a gradual icy climb, but as I got closer the difficulties became more prominent. The incline was very sharp and the ice and loose gravel were giving us no hope of being able find a strong foothold. A Tibetan Sherpa and his daughter came to our rescue out of the blue. The man took hold of my hand to give me support and when I looked at him and smiled, I found myself looking into a pair of crystal clear smiling eyes, full of love, compassion and understanding. His daughter's eyes also had the same expression expect for the addition of a twinkle of fun in them! I did not expect that at all. I felt that the presence of these two beings beside us eased the climb.

Up ahead, Mohanji was sitting on a small rock waiting for the last of us to reach Him. There was already a line of climbers before Him from our group. Mohanji wanted to ensure that ALL of us were fine before we carried on as this was the most difficult part of the climb. The terrain was near vertical which had to be covered with the help of ropes and not much of any other climbing gear.

I promptly sat down at Mohanji's feet. I "believed" that this was the only place to be. Phaneendar was right behind me and to his utter dismay, for some reason his shoes were not being able to provide a good grip on the treacherously icy landscape which made him slip and slide a lot making him feel uncertain of his balance. There may have been some amount of fear too and he could not relax at all. Mohanji knew what was going on inside of Phaneendar and told him, "Do not be afraid. Remove the fear. Have faith. I am with you."Mohanji kept giving Phaneendar this same message repeatedly to help him overcome his fear while Phaneendar tried to tell Mohanji why he was feeling afraid and the condition of his shoes. As I was sitting right there, I became a part of this conversation. To add to everyone's distress, suddenly there was a small rock slide. We all were already tired due to the altitude, the difficult climb, fatigue, etc., and this rock slide further added to the difficulty. Three of the rocks came and hit me one after the other. The first thought was that some karma must have been dissolved now.

However, since I was exhausted, this felt like another difficult thing to handle. I felt Divine Mother was reprimanding me (beating me) for something I may have done. This made me feel very tearful as I had no clue what it was. Such childish thoughts! I started crying and telling Divine Mother that since she was beating me without any reason, now she absolutely has to show herself to me and I just did not care how.

It is only now while I am writing this, I realize that on that particular day this was just the beginning of the many of my childish demands which I would make!

One by one the group members started climbing and soon were out of sight. Now it was time for Mohanji to go ahead. We were waiting in line as only one person at a time could climb. Phaneendar and I were the last two left of the group when he was asked to go before me. I was quite alone. I looked around properly for the first time to gauge the yawning chasm down below and how far I would go if I fell! Well I could not see where I would land if such an incident took place as it was way too deep, so why worry!!! Instead of feeling frightened of the peril and the unknown, strangely enough I was feeling excited and exhilarated about the adventure ahead of me!

In front of an overweight, fitness and exercise challenged, and inexperienced me, was this frozen vertical wall and extremely slippery and equally frozen ground and a kind of climb which I had never attempted before. However, something was very familiar about all of this as though from some other life. Also there was a total lack of fear! All thoughts of body weight, fitness challenge, etc., went away in a flash and all that remained at that time was God and Guru! Everything physical and logical made no sense at that time. I or anybody in my position could never imagine walking and climbing this difficult terrain of the Inner Kora without Their Grace and constant blessing. They provided the strength, the stamina, and also the able Sherpas. In spite of being of petite physique, they were a powerhouse of energy and strength.

My arms and legs were aching, but the Sherpas did not give up. They pulled and pushed and helped until they got me up that wall. During this process at one point I accidentally pulled on the rope which was tying me to the Sherpa in front (Amar bhaiya) and caused him to almost tumble down, yet there was no fear of peril, neither in him nor in me. Mohanji while speaking to Phaneendar about fear took mine away as well. He erased that thought process completely. It felt as though I was meant to be in that place, at that time, sitting at Mohanji's feet while he spoke to Phaneendar. Those words out of the Guru's mouth released me of the baggage of mortal fear. Yes I was tired, yes I wanted to just lie down and not move, but fear was not one of the thoughts that crossed my mind even once.

When you go through these experiences in life, you realize how protected you are. I am amazed at the love that God and Guru showers on us unconditionally. Only their Grace sustains us. Many, many pranams at the holy feet of Mohanji for watching over and taking care of this struggler. Without Him, this would not have been possible. Millions of "thank you" to Mohanji.

Kailash, the abode of Shiva – The Male Energy as perceived by most of us changed for me that day. As the journey continued, I got to see the Mother aspect too in the form of a male member in the group, Sherpa Amar bhaiya. He portrayed the nurturing love, compassion, and care of Shakti – the Mother Divine. From the vertical climb up the wall, to reaching Kuber Kund, to the tedious journey back, Amar bhaiya was there at every step. For some reason, he assigned himself to take care of me. He held my hand through the journey with infinite patience and care. I made his life miserable with childish demands and my Divine Mother in the form of Amar bhaiya complied.

I would walk two steps and stop. I would ask him to tell me how much further we had to go. I would whine and cry like a baby and ask after every 5 minutes, "Have we reached yet? How much further"? And very gently, with the utmost care and compassion, Amar bhaiya would answer my questions every time. At times, I would refuse to move any more, but never for once did he get impatient with this kind of behavior from a grown person. His soothing and encouraging behavior towards my petulant demands and impossible whims was one only the Divine Mother could have. At one point without our knowing, we were being stalked by a huge wild dog who was attracted to me because of all the moans and groans escaping my mouth and of course I was shuffling around like an injured person . . . hence to the dog, I looked like DINNER! Amar bhaiya took care of the imminent danger by throwing stones in the dark and scaring the dog away and said, "Do not worry didi, I am your bodyguard." This "man" with his ready smile, soothing voice, even temper, and genuine loving care, guided the way to safety. You see, that day, Divine Mother did come! in the form of Amar bhaiya.

The physical Yatra went on for some more memorable days till we arrived back in Delhi. The Yatra in my heart and soul still continues. I am eternally grateful to God and Guru for preparing this mortal to witness the love and care of the Divine Mother and Heavenly Father. Blessed was this Yatra by Their constant guidance. Many are the learnings which keep unfolding in surprising ways even to this day. Mohanji says, "Shiva is Silence. Shiva is Innocence." Let us all dip ourselves in Him and become Him!

I Walk Where My Heart Leads

- Riana Gaspar -

*I walk where my heart leads.
Every journey and friendship is a story of
unexpected transformation.
When Kailash called to walk the Timeless Path,
I was ready, all because of Mohanji.*

Everyone has a favourite story to narrate of their Kailash yatra – a specific time, day or event - which they fondly remember. My story which I love sharing is of day three. The day I gave up and nearly died, but for Grace and Mohanji.

Day three started crisp and cool. Standing on the balcony of the 'hotel' where we stayed after the 1st day of Parikrama, experiencing the awakening of the early morning and listening to so many sounds (and the shouting of the Sherpas to hurry up as we have far to go), I wondered what that day will bring. I heard Mohanji's voice in my head "have no expectations" and in that moment my heart and mind melted together and gratitude flowed through me. The universe creates what you focus on and for more than a year, every day, I focused, prayed and gave all of myself in everything I did, to be here in this blissful moment.

My only prayer is that today I will stay conscious throughout and face the challenges. Yesterday had come and gone. Today might pass me by if I don't give my all. Humbly I stare at the majestic Kailash right in front of me and gratitude overwhelm me to be here while the world awakens. While gazing at the face of Kailash, my soul became merged in a mystical union with love, and I experienced a love so complete, a love so absolute. This all-embracing love transcended all physical experiences I had of life. I stopped existing in that moment..

As we started our journey I became totally enchanted by the flowers on the path. The most amazing flowers everywhere. At first glance the earth was barren. Rocks upon rocks upon rocks and rivers. But now in this wonderful morning, I noticed flowers everywhere, the vibrant colours of these little dwarf flowers standing proud, some less than 2 centimetres from the ground. The first part of the morning passed with me engrossed in watching flowers, laughing and crossing rivers.

I chanted the name Lakshmi over and over again. I had started the chanting a couple of days before when I was thinking which name I would be like to be known by, if Mohanji gives me a name. Every time I try to pronounce a long name like Hanumatananda I really have to concentrate hard and wrap my tongue around it. Please don't laugh! The name Lakshmi popped into my head and I thought yes, maybe I can be called Lakshmi! As I chanted, I wondered - who is Lakshmi and what does her name mean?

The morning passed by blissfully listening to the silence, keeping my heart open so the light can shine through. As time passed and we slowly made our way up the mountain, tiredness started creeping in. Remembering to drink water and to stay hydrated became a constant reminder in my mind as I scaled boulders. My legs became heavier and I started to look for pathways round the rocks. Trampling and stumbling through the rocks, I realized that these boulders are just like obstacles we encounter within ourselves. This thought kept looping over and over again in my head. The only way I could keep focused and keep going was by chanting *Aum Lakshmi Aum Mohanji Aum*. My brain started misfiring.

At this point we reached a deceptively easy looking uphill stretch. I thought this would be easy to cross and even an unfit person would take a couple of minutes to reach the top. On closer inspection, I realised the hill was covered with ice and loose rocks which could at any given time start moving at a great speed and cause grave danger and even death.

Later the hill became so unstable and treacherous that not all of us could cross that day.

I recalled my own condition Just after Kailash 2014. I had become seriously ill and was battling with cancer. Mohanji had guided me through this time and he assured me that with time and proper care I will bounce back. I will never forget his messages where he told me to take care of my body as it is the canvas on which one paints life. After months of healing I started walking one kilometre a day. I will never forget the first day when I sat on the side of the road, wanting to throw up. My only aim was to prepare for the Inner Kora. It was a burning flame of desire to walk the Inner Kora.

I knew that I could not go in the state I was in as it was essential to build strength. It was such a strong conviction to be fit and healthy to go to the Inner Kora that it started overshadowing everything I did.

When the Inner Kora list came out, my name was absent. I was devastated. I put my running shoes on and went for a couple hours walk. I was angry with Mohanji. Why could he not see that I am healthy. I know he was still worried about my health. I went back to the doctor and the doctor told me in the state I am in, he would not allow me near any mountain, even half that height. I did not lose my determination. I increased my exercise, prayers and chanting (okay also begging, pleading and maybe a tantrum or two in the meditation room!). When Mohanji came to South Africa in early 2016, he looked at my aura and only said: okay you can go.

How Master tests! How did I miss the fact that I was being tested to see my determination for Inner Kora. I had to prove myself worthy, burn in its desire, not lose focus in face of adversity – to be able to walk the sacred spaces of Lord Shiva, under Grace of Mohanji.

Coming back to the present moment, I stood in front of a

puny hill made of ice with strong legs. After I was strapped into the harness my legs became a useless part of my anatomy. There was no traction on this icy surface and I had to pull my full body weight, up by my arms. After walking for hours, already exhausted this is where Grace appeared. All hours and ways of preparation meant nothing on this hill. Mitesh was in front of me and I could see his dance while hanging onto the rope when a rock slide started and he was right in the middle. While I was watching Mitesh, not breathing from fear, I heard Mohanji's voice floating up from behind: "Don't worry I am with you". As I dragged myself up the hill through the first phase, I became totally depleted of energy. With less than a third of oxygen I was used too, something happened. First I fought with God, scolding Him that he could have told me to exercise my arms. Then I fought with Mohanji because it is his fault I am here and he could have warned me. Gosh! I cannot stop laughing now when I think about this.

By the third phase of the climb, I was on the wrong side of the rope, no harness and did not have any more stamina. I still remember when I let go physically, mentally and was prepared to die. The thought still crossed my mind that at least I was dying on the best spot ever on earth and nothing could top this. As I let go of the rope, I pitched backward and started falling down the glacier. Yet, I was at peace. The very next moment, a pair of strong hands grabbed me and sherpas came down the last part of the hill and pulled me up, passing me from one to another.

Reaching the top, I started shaking and could not breathe. Tears were rolling down my cheeks. I wanted to sit down and just catch my breath, rest a bit. The sherpas did not allow me and I had to move immediately as there was no space on the ledge when the next person arrived. I could not move as I have a bit of a problem with heights and when I looked at the narrow path in front of me and the straight down cliff on the side of it, I froze.

Here a very strange incident happened. A young boy I did not notice before or saw afterwards again, came to take my hand and lead me round the hill. Rounding the hill, I came across everyone who made it, no one was standing, everyone was flat on their backs and looked out for the count. My legs collapsed and I fell were I stood and just laid there till the group decided to get a move on. Who was this young boy? I never got to say thank you.

As we reached a beautiful pond, I asked someone the name of the pond. I thought I heard him say Gauri kund but I was not sure as he spoke very fast. I looked at the pond and thought to myself - no way this is Gauri kund as I have seen it before in 2014 during my last Kailash yatra. I had no idea where we were, but it was absolutely amazing and I fell in love with the pond on the spot. Unknown to my mind, I had reached Kuber Kund, the pond of Lord Kuber, the God of riches – which I found out later. Strange it is to be chanting the mantra of Lakshmi and landing up at Kuber's pond. When I finally made this connection much later, I was left stumped. This was sheer Grace!

I was busy scanning the line for caves and finally picked one (on the mountain overlooking the pond) where I would like to live in. Everyone did their pujas and decided to leave immediately as it looked like rain was about to fall and the evening camp was still far to go. Dhritiman (DB) and Sumit insisted that I leave with the group but I was adamant. I told them that I would wait at the pond for Mohanji.

After everyone left, silence settled back and I walked to the edge of the water. I sat down and looked into the cave, for a moment I thought I glimpsed people sitting. Smiling at myself and my fanciful thoughts, I listened for Mohanji arrival. I could not wait to ask him where we were. It felt like home! Looking over my shoulder I saw Sumit chanting with malas and DB much further back already deep in meditation.

I started hearing voices in the distance and bent forward to listen better. The sound changed to wind, sounding like whistling through a flute. Starring at the reflections in the water and trying to capture the sound my mind fell into a black hole. I cannot describe the nothingness of which I have no memory. Moving back into my body with a jerk I looked behind me and saw Sumit and DB also getting up.

We had no idea how long we were waiting there and we discussed that Mohanji probably took another path as it was getting dark and hail was starting to fall. We decided to leave, but with no guidance we were totally lost and had no idea which direction to go. We decided to go down hill. Down hill turned into an uphill and so it went on. It was surreal walking in the mountains with snow flake and hail falling all around us and we were lost. My mind told me I should fear but I was so euphoric that I did not care that we may have to spend the night on these rocks. In fact, I was secretly hoping to go back and stay the night at the pond.

Thankfully we spotted Devi's white hat very far in the distance and knew we were going in the right direction. A couple minutes later Chai and her Sherpa appeared over a hill and we rejoiced. She told us that Mohanji was in the front and not everyone could get over the hill as it became way to dangerous and unstable.

We made haste to catch up with Mohanji. We rushed down the slopes slipping, sliding and climbing over rocks and boulders to reach Mohanji. When we caught up we could see that he was not well. After a long time of walking, we reached a road. It was decided that we would wait here and get a vehicle for Mohanji. Sumit and Chai managed to organize a vehicle with someone making deliveries to a camp and while we waited for the vehicles to return, I quizzed Mohanji about the beautiful pond and told him what I experienced. I will never forget when he started smiling at me and told me we were at Kuber Kund and told me about the Lord abiding there. Many were waiting in this inner court.

I was worried that we travelled over such sacred ground and may have disturbed the peace of dedicated seekers waiting for eons. Here we come along with our loud mouths and stumble around like drunkards at a pool party. I started feeling my chest closing up as I contemplated how inappropriate my lack of knowledge was and an insult to Lord Shiva. I wished at that moment for the earth to swallow me, the embarrassment was so acute. Mohanji laughed and said not to worry. The beings see us like little children who stumble into the courtyard, play around a bit and leave. Why would they be upset with a joyous child?

The vehicle arrived for Mohanji and we started walking towards the night camp.

The Sherpa assured us we only need to walk for two hours. Two hours later he assured us only two hours more, two hours later he started laughing and said 10 hours, luckily he was joking. We had been walking for hours in the dark and all that was propelling me forward was Grace. No amount of exercise had prepared me for this excruciating exhaustion and pain. I spoke to mountaineers afterwards and they informed me that this point of exhaustion is the time when people walk straight out of their bodies and don't return.

When we eventually arrived at our seemingly heavenly tent with food and heat, I could not move my body for a very long time. Could not eat, drink or take care of body functions. Slowly I managed to start feeling my body again and went to bed. As I laid down on the bed, I could just stare up at the ceiling and could not command my eyelids to close. With force slapped my hands over my eyes and so I fell asleep, grateful that I was blessed to stay on this earth for another day.

Nearly a year has gone by, but I still reflect and contemplate about day three of the Inner Kora Parikrama. Every hardship and trail I encountered was part of the journey, every step I took was an exploration of inner self. Day three has become my inner sanctuary where I go to in my heart. My heart has become Kailash and I only have to go inside of myself to be at Kuber Kund.

To continue the amazing story of Kailash, a couple of days later arriving in Nepal, I started seeing the Green Tara everywhere and decided to buy a mandala painting of her, for no other reason other than I thought she is beautiful. The salesman told me she is Goddess Lakshmi in the Hindu tradition. I was stunned and frozen. He could have pushed me over with a feather. By then I had been informed about Goddess Lakshmi and today she is part of my daily spiritual practices and home. Goddess Lakshmi who I met in Kailash is now my mother goddess.

In the same week arriving home back from Kailash, still trying to acclimatize, I got an unexpected call informing me that I have a couple of days to prepare a presentation for a company from Amsterdam which funds shelters (I run a shelter for abused, destitute and abandoned girl children at Johannesburg, South Africa). It was totally out of the blue as I did not know the funding company at all and never had contact with them.

Our shelter is situated in the most dangerous part of Johannesburg in a locality called Hillbrow, in the inner city of Johannesburg. We are surrounded by hijacked buildings, drug dens and illegal immigrant crime activities. As I finished the presentation, the Chairperson of the funding company turned to me and said: I give you two million rand to relocate, I saw his lips move but could not take it in. Apparently this was the first time they had given such a big amount to a facility they were funding for the first time. I knew to the core of my being that this was nothing to do with me, but it was Kailash, Kuber Kund, Goddess Lakshmi and Mohanji's Grace flowing.

As one travels this sacred path, it seems to go on into time without an end and one walks with other travellers becoming their companions dedicating yourself to them. Your spiritual journey becomes shortened when you share the way (walking together), with another. They help you fight the illusion that holds you back and help you escape from fear. If you walk this Timeless Path of Kailash together, you will unlock the secrets of inner peace and love. The love and joy in their hearts will brighten your path and shorten a seemly long difficult journey.

My sincere gratitude to every traveller, who walked this journey of the heart, with me.
We walked this sacred journey under the guidance of our Guru.
May your heart be your Kailash.
Our destination is liberation.

THE OUTER KORA

Badrinath Temple

Pashupatinath Temple, Kathmandu

Buddhanilkanth

Shiva foot in the background

Beautiful view of Kailash from Lake Manasarovar

Blessings from Lord Ganesha

Intensity of thousand suns

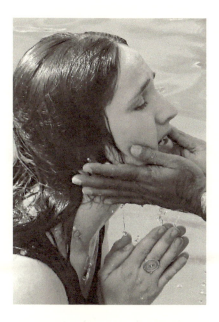

Third eye appearing on Devi Mohan

Mohanji offering prayers at Mansarovar

Havan at Lake Manasarovar

Mohanji performng the Havan

Sai and Kailash

Day 1 of the Outer Kora

The multi senses of the terrain in Kailash

Gauri Kund

Rakshas Tal

Climbing Dolmala Pass

Mohanji and group in the Halesi Mahadev

Outer Kora Group

Ananth Sankaran

Havan at Manasarovar

Looking at Kailash

Lake Manasarovar

Mohanji at the Deraphuk guest house

Arun Vathavooran

Ashtamoorthy Kurur

Mohanji and Animals

Mohanji

The parikrama track

Aviral Srivastava

Mohanji and group walking to Rakshas Tal

Parikrama Day 2 vistas

Dr. Harpreet Wasir

Merging with the serenity of Lake Manasarovar

Tibetans doing the parikrama one prostration at a time

Jay Jeyaseelan

Priya Maharaj

Spectacular views of the parikrama track

A yak grazing on the mountain slopes

Mohanji in contemplation communing with nature

Shirdi Sai Baba eyes in the sky

Rakshita Ananth

Mohanji starts the parikrama with the group

The bridge across the border from Nepal to Tibet

Shyama Jeyaseelan

Golden birds in Lake Manasarovar

Mountains on the parikrama

Vesna Bogdanov Stark

Kailash view from Dolmala pass

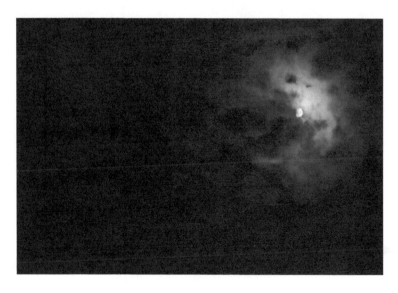

The moon peeping through the clouds - the silent witness lighting the way for the pilgrims

Vidya Rajagopalan

Yohan Pathmanathan

Saptarishi Kailash

First rays on the South face of Kailash

A double rainbow welcoming us on a long yet beautiful 2nd day

Kailash view from Yam Dwar

Milica Bulatovic

Nameshri Chetty

Sunrise on the pilgrimage

...and Sunset

Rashila Pankhania

Mohanji at Pashupatinath

The group circumambulating Yam Dwar

Tina Arya

Mohanji reaches Hilsa

Helicopter ride to Hilsa

Beyond Miracles And Human Understanding

- Ananth Sankaran -

I HUMBLY SURRENDER TO my Father (Mohanji), every thought, emotion and underlying TRUTH that came to me while penning this article.

A visit to a place like Kailash is like revisiting the Mother's Womb. It can never be explained, and only experienced. However, I would like to share the incidents that happened prior, during and post journey which will give readers some understanding on how Grace flows eternally and how the Masters operate for our betterment in uplifting seekers when they truly surrender with FAITH.

The trip also happened to coincide with my birthday (Gregorian calendar and asterism as per Tamil Calendar) with the second day of the *parikrama* happening to be my birth date. We just cannot plan for such things unless the Divine bestows its Grace and love upon an individual.

As Father always says, the only baggage we need to carry to Kailash is faith and complete surrender. This was evident right from the time we sent in our applications for this epic journey.

Prior to Kailash

Before meeting Father in 2015, I was just another family man. I was methodical, constantly planning and replanning, anticipating worst-case scenarios in life, and saving for the future as someone who does not enjoy surprises.

However, since the time I have met Father, this has changed completely. He has brought in changes within me that have made me slowly start accepting things the way they are and prepared me to 'go with the flow'. Father had inculcated this habit in me, a pre-requisite for a trip like Kailash. Kailash will break all rules, concepts and if you don't go with the flow, you are bound to suffer.

I have no doubts that it was Father who had sown the seed of Kailash in our (my wife and I) thoughts. The moment we saw "Kailash with Mohanji – 2016" on our webpage, we decided to go with no second thoughts. With God's Grace and Father's blessings, there were no financial hurdles in raising the necessary funds. However, Father had other surprises in store for us.

Job loss

My wife had been associated with a not-for-profit organization for over three years. The trust and support of her peers and seniors had made her feel that it is the place she would retire from. But within two months, her entire department was made redundant (change in management) and she was the only one left behind and that too with a diminished role. She was told that a new manager would step in, and would evaluate her role, performance and eventually decide on her position within the organization. She was hurt and felt that she shouldn't continue in an organization that did not value the work she had put in all through those years. It should be added that since the time she joined, the performance of the department she was associated with had shown significant progress due to her analysis and recommendations.

Health: My wife has had a history of abdominal pain since the past eight years and it had aggravated since Jan 2016. She was literally surviving on painkillers (4-5 a day) for 20-22 days a month. Frequent visits to doctors and naturopaths did not alleviate the problem.

Having decided to undertake a journey to Kailash, it was

important that she remain pain-free if not fully fit and we were now against the wall. When she contacted Father, he recommended her to visit a place in Kerala for treatment (naturopath). My wife proposed multiple options including one of surgery after the Kailash visit but Father reiterated that she first visit Kerala for treatment.

We had decided that we would travel together to India via another country where we had lived a few years earlier, meet friends, and do some shopping before heading home. Here we were, a month before Kailash, cancelling her tickets and booking new ones in hurry and that too at twice the cost. 'Going with the flow', 'surrender' and 'complete annihilation of fears' were the mantras that kept us going during this phase.

This was also a test of faith as the treatment in Kerala involved complete fasting (only water allowed) for over a week which included complete rest (no walking, talking or any energy-consuming activity) and another week of a diet of only tender coconut water before slowly introducing solid food into the system. While a trip to Kailash requires a preparation of walking at altitude for 50 odd km spanning 3 days, she was here in Kerala instead fifteen days before the trip taking COMPLETE REST (Yet, she was able to complete the *parikrama*). The only thing that made her cross the line was FAITH in Father, ACCEPTANCE of his words as final and SURRENDER at his feet, ignoring the constant chatter of the mind.

Six months before the Kailash trip, I had taken up a contracting job in a government firm, entrusted with the responsibility of a digital transformation on one of their applications. After joining, I realized that what I was promised during the interview was quite different from the reality. This included the work that was expected out of me, and challenges in effecting a change. A month into the job, it became clear that I was going nowhere. I was still determined to continue at the work at least until I completed the Kailash trip, and then make a call on my future upon my return. Exactly a month before the Kailash trip, my boss was laid off while he was on holiday in Sri Lanka. A week after the sacking, I was called into a room and served my notice period as well as the department did not want to do the transformation, citing spiraling costs in executing the change.

The only thing I did was to SURRENDER at Father's feet. My mind kept analyzing all possible options but every thought surrounding the uncertainty was surrendered at his feet. I had firm FAITH that it was his *leela,* and that he was preparing me to ACCEPT things as they were for they happen only for the good.

Two weeks after being sacked and two weeks prior to Kailash, I was able to land a job. I attended an interview at a firm I had worked before, and right after stepping out of the interview room, I received a call from my consultant confirming the offer. What else do we call this if not GRACE?

I should also add that this job had a lower salary (<20%) compared to what I had been earning before. Also, I had attended another interview with another company that was keen to hire me (pending a final meeting with the resourcing manager) and they had a better offer. While I was confident that I could have secured the other job that offered the better pay, I have started accepting the attitude that 'whatever comes my way in life is what I am destined for' and neither the pay nor the position/role attracted me.

Exactly one hour before leaving home to catch the flight to India, my wife woke me up from sleep to tell me that my baggage allowance was 20kg. I had originally packed for 30kg as until then I had always carried 30kg as check-in baggage. This was the first time that I was traveling a different airline. Soon I rearranged my bags and reached the airport barely in time with baggage weight within acceptable limits.

Settlements

Father always says that we should do all 'settlements' before embarking on a journey like Kailash, where you are BORN AGAIN. This includes any commitments, any promises made, money owed, settling anger or hatred with anyone, etc. While I was busy listing the settlements I had to make, Father took it upon himself to surface them, execute and achieve the desired outcomes. This included:

- An extended family reunion after 8 years at the house of an ailing uncle who is counting his last days. He felt so happy seeing all of us that he had removed his oxygen mask for a while and started conversing with each of us as he used to do in his early years.
- Saying 'sorry' to a friend in a dream for my betrayal 14 years ago. That may sound so unreal, and I didn't even have it on my to-do list! I sought a sincere apology with my friend's soul and left it at that. However, one fine night, Father (taking another friend's body in a dream) brought both of us together, made me say SORRY and my friend left the place with a smile. The setup was EXACTLY the same setup where I had betrayed him (in college/university premises)
- Introducing my wife to the extended family and seeking blessings (I married against the wishes of my family, and for six years none had seen my wife prior to that day except for my immediate family).
- Saying 'thank you' and touching my ex-boss' feet for his helping shape my life and career.
- Meeting scores of friends and reaching out to family members who I had never liked before.

The list goes on, but in essence I am thankful to Father for doing everything for this soul which doesn't even know if it deserves all the love, Grace and care from him. As Father always says, "Connect to my Consciousness. You need not come to me for I shall come to you and protect you always!" Words can never express a disciple's feelings for his Guru.

Apart from meeting families, friends and spending valuable time with them, my wife and I also were blessed with an opportunity to do some temple-cleaning tasks. We used to often go for a gentle stroll around a temple and park near our home. The area around the temple was littered with plastic and in a spur of the moment, we decided to do a clean-up. We completed the task to the best our abilities with a friendly reprimand from my sister for venturing into cleaning without enough protection. I pray and wish my Father give me many more such opportunities, as it gives me immense satisfaction to serve.

Kailash

With so many events already taking me by surprise, I only told myself that this was just a beginning of many more to come. I would like to humbly point out that I had decided not to take 'expectations' with me to Kailash. I had no expectations whatsoever and was filled with Grace to the extent that Father felt I could handle. He was my Kailash and I strongly felt that doing a *parikrama* of Father is equal to doing Kailash *parikrama*. Meeting him, surrendering my feelings and letting my emotions pour as tears at his feet was the ONLY thing I had on my mind.

Missing photo

Upon reaching the hotel in Kathmandu, we were asked to share our passport size photographs to the volunteers. Prior to the travel, I had taken the photos as per dimensions and clearly recollected placing them in my check-in baggage. But they were 'missing' now. A good search by removing all items from the suitcase didn't help. I surrendered the situation to Father, and was preparing to go and get a fresh photo. That's when I stumbled upon my waist pouch where I discovered a few passport-sized photos that had been taken a few years ago. I should state that these photos were originally kept in a wallet which I left behind at home but vaguely remember moving the photos alone to the pouch as a backup option.

Pashupatinath temple

A visit to a sacred shrine like the Pashupatinath temple means that we have definitely accumulated some good karma in previous births. Right outside the temple complex, Father was feeding the cow, pigeons and other animals with grains. The cow was so beautiful and was eating out of everyone's hands except mine. When I closed my eyes and prayed for a few minutes seeking her attention in eating at my hand, she readily obliged and consumed the grains from my palms.

Mohanji was walking towards the temple complex with the *swamiji*s from Skanda Vale, deeply immersed in conversation. There was this dog which was wagging its tail, barking continuously and jumping out of joy. Father stopped walking, blessed it for a few seconds before continuing on. I was keen to touch the dog and seek its blessings. It wouldn't let me touch him and was nowhere to be found a few seconds after receiving Father's blessings.

Inside the temple the chanting of verses from Sri Rudram was going on, hearing which tears flowed uncontrollably from my eyes. The group split and we were left on our own without a guide. I walked past 184 *shivalingas,* soaked in emotion from chanting Om Namah Shivaya. Upon entering one of the *shivalinga* shrines within the complex, I was given a string of *rudhraksha*s by the priest. It's a practice that the priest hands over a string or a single bead and asks for money. I told the priest that I didn't have money and offered to return the string to him which he resisted and said "*paise nahi hai to theek hai. Yeh bhagvaan Shivji ka prasad hai*" (it's all right if you don't have money. It's Lord Shiva's gift).

When I was about to exit the 184 *shivalinga* temple, I was strongly attracted by the sight of a *Naga Baba*. His eyes were so powerful that I could not take my eyes off him and wanted to go and surrender at his feet, which I did. When I got up, he asked for my name and when I told him that, he kept his right thumb on my third eye and chanted some mantra before blessing me. He walked away without seeking anything, and I felt very bad for not offering anything to a saint.

While walking back to the bus, I encountered another aged *baba* on the streets. At first I ignored him as I was walking a few meters away from Father. I had the thought in mind that if the aged *baba* was indeed powerful or genuine, Father would prostrate to him but he didn't. I kept walking behind Father when the old *baba* beckoned me towards him. I went and with no second thoughts touched his feet. He blessed me, and giving me holy *tulsi* leaves, asked me to eat them. When I had finished eating, he offered me one more *tulsi* leaf to eat. By then others had started seeking his blessing too and I made way for them. Later my wife and a few others said they could feel that this old person was none other than Shirdi Sai Baba. Another classic example of the mind analyzing while Grace flows eternally!

During the entire time at the temple complex, emotions were running high and I kept weeping for no specific reason. I felt an urge to ask Father who those two *Naga Babas* were but refrained from doing so after telling myself that they represented the same consciousness and that their identities didn't matter.

We reached Hilsa (Tibet-Nepal border) on August 11th which happened to be my 'birth star' day (as per Tamil Calendar). It was here in Hilsa that I went closer to Father to finally converse with him. Until then we had just shared few glances but I had not made any effort to speak to him. Looking back, I never really had anything to say to him, or to ask him. What can a disciple ask from a Guru apart from silence of the mind, and to liberate him from the cycle of birth and death? Again, the Guru knows and gives a disciple what he deserves. All a disciple can do is surrender at his holy feet and allow him to take over for the rest of the lifetime with Guru's teaching always in mind and with every heartbeat.

Father seeing me walking towards him asked, "How are you doing?" and before I could respond, he said, "From here on, everything will only be good." My wife informed him that that day was my birthday. Father rubbed my heart, wished me good luck and blessed the *eka mukhi rudraksha* that my wife had gifted me on my birthday.

Beyond Miracles And Human Understanding

On August 12th, we sat to a *satsang* at Taklakot where Father spoke about Kailash, Manasarovar, the significance of the place and how a true seeker should approach the pilgrimage. Every word, every sentence uttered by Father brought tears to my eyes and this continued for the entire 30-45 minutes of *satsang*. By now, I was becoming blank at mind. It made me feel that I had taken this entire journey only to take the holy bath in Manasarovar to remove the karma of the past and that of my ancestors, especially my father.

Like many others, I too suffered from high-altitude sickness. I developed severe migraine from the time of reaching Taklakot and it only worsened. It didn't help when I sprinted about 50-100m in order to call someone which was when the pain came crashing through my skull.

En route to Manasarovar, I sighted clouds shaping up as a half-moon crescent which I immediately brought to my wife's attention. We both looked at it in awe with tears rolling off our eyes before the clouds rolled on.

The very sight of Manasarovar brought all kinds of emotions to the surface for me and visibly for others as well. As soon as we got down from the bus some of us followed Father who braved the cold water to immerse in Shiva's consciousness. People were so completely lost in thought. Father waded in wearing his wristwatch, my wife walked in wearing sunglasses, and a few others holding their wallets in hand. We were oblivious to everything except two: 1. Kailash 2. Father. In essence, Shiva (Father) was merging with his (Kailash) own consciousness.

While Father took his first dip in the lake, the air was filled with the chants of *Om Namah Shivaya*. There was not a pair of dry eyes as all stood gazing upon Kailash while standing in the lake.

Father's eyes were red as he finished his dips and we started offering *abhisheka* to him while getting immersed in his Grace. Father was visibly shivering (physically) but his eyes were fixed on Kailash, the Ultimate Truth!

Sumit Bhai did a full prostration while many others including me, touched Father's feet inside the water and he blessed us by placing his hands on our head. Father later took the water and sprinkled it on everyone standing around him and at that instance many sensed the water as warm. It remained so until they completed their dips.

As Father advised, I took the first dip for myself, the second one for my deceased ancestors and the subsequent ones for those living, all gods, goddesses, Kailash, Shiva and for all living and nonliving beings of this universe.

I don't remember how many dips I took, nor did I wish to count them but for the entire time I was there, my tears kept flowing and merging with the lake. It was as if my emotions were disappearing and I felt a deep void inside when I stepped out of Manasarovar. Every mantra chanted, every thought of beings (living, dead, non-living) were filled with *bhaava* and you realize at that instance that all that you are left with is gratitude, surrender and faith towards your Guru and Shiva, for they are both one and the same.

Stepping out of the Manasarovar, I went straight to Father (who was in the Shiva state of consciousness) surrendered at his feet and fulfilled my wish of doing a *parikrama* around him. He is verily Kailash, he is Shiva and he is everything to me and it only made sense for me to do a *parikrama* around him first before doing the *parikrama* around Kailash.

My other desire of chanting *Sri Rudram* on the banks of Manasarovar came true thanks to my fellow family members from UK (Jay, Vigneshwaran, Yohan, Vijay, et al). I surrendered every word of the great mantra at the holy feet of Kailash. This was followed by a powerful *homa* performed by Mohanji with the *swamijis* from Skanda Vale taking turns, and making our offerings to Kailash.

Prior to the trip, we were warned about the wild dogs in the area, and to form a group when going out for nature's call. However, I did have an encounter with a dog and it was truly a *hamsa* of Lord Datta. I sought blessings from them and it was heartening to see them eating the food that was offered to them at the end.

Parikrama

On day one of *parikrama*, I woke up with a severe, splitting headache. With every step I took, it felt as if someone was pulling the nerves through my head. With Father leading the way, I told myself that he would take care of everything (which he did) and I need not worry about a thing.

I had an opportunity to press Father's holy feet the night before *parikrama*. There were around ten people present, and Father was interacting with each one of them. Father looked at me and said the following things:

- You will have no problems in completing parikrama.
- When you feel tired take the pony, otherwise keep walking. I will be with you.
- Don't worry – I may not be physically present with you, but help will come when you need it.

I never needed any more assurance than Father's words and I kept walking chanting *Om Namah Shivaya* and the *Mohanji Gayatri*. I walked almost in a semiconscious state for most of the day and even with eyes closed for some time. I had also exhausted my water supply within the first few hours thanks to a leak in the camelback bladder I carried. With determination to complete the *parikrama* by foot, and with no water or porter/pony in sight, I literally struggled during the last one hour of *parikrama* on day one.

The mind was fully at work throwing out all kinds of fears including that of collapsing or getting hurt. I would pause after every five steps to gasp for breath. That's when 'help' arrived in the form of a sherpa. He held my hips and had me wrap my hands around his neck and we both started walking. He would keep talking to me just to ensure that I didn't feel the pain and stayed focused on the walk.

I literally viewed him as Father holding me and helping me complete the *parikrama* and couldn't think of anything else. This was one of the many instances where Father kept his promise to a seeker. I should confess that without his assistance, I wouldn't have completed the first day of *parikrama*. Once we reached the end, I touched his feet for he was like Shiva to me helping me in completing such a daunting task.

Throughout the first day (and for the rest too), we had dogs accompanying us. Whenever I was finding it difficult to walk or wondering where they were, a black dog would cross us. It also gave me (and others) a sense of awe that Lord Dattatreya himself was accompanying us. It also reminded me of Father's words: "I may not be with you physically, but help will come whenever you need it "

Day Two: This day happened to be my birthday but I didn't wake up to any joy. The headache had gotten so severe that I could barely take a step. We were supposed to be up early and get going with the *parikrama* as it was the day of the longest walk.

My wife had a terrible cold and cough and had trouble breathing. She was contemplating on returning to Taklakot, our base camp. By now, even I was almost at the point of giving up on completing the *parikrama*. After breakfast, people slowly started out. My wife, being a fighter decided to give her all and began her day two. I wasn't even there to see her off as I was too preoccupied with my headache. I couldn't even brush my teeth since any movement of my head could cause a fresh attack of nerve-wracking pain.

That's when Father breezed down to see-off the remaining people. With pain overtaking me, I went and fell on Father's shoulders in a hug. Tears started flowing and he said, "Bless you. I'll always be with you". As if I was waiting just for that assurance from him, I surrendered at his feet. Handing me a *rudraksha mala*, he asked me to carry on and assured me that all would go well.

Surely it must be the GRACE of the Guru Mandala that must have brought me onto this journey, with my receiving a rudraksha mala as a birthday gift from the Father on that day two of *parikrama*.

Standing on my feet, I felt revitalized and that's when I had caught sight of my porter with my pony. He assisted me in getting on to the pony and we kept moving. I closed my eyes and started chanting *Om Namah Shivaya* and the *Mohanji Gayatri* mantra.

Though I felt guilt that I wasn't walking, I comforted myself by telling myself that a few minutes ago I had almost given up on the parikrama itself. With Father's Grace, I was continuing and he knew what was right for me.

The sight of Gauri Kund at Dolma la Pass was pleasing to the eyes. My heart wanted me to climb down and submerge myself in the divinity of the place. However, the mind resisted any such moves violently and I gave up going to Gauri Kund. I sincerely wish Shiva grants me permission to travel to his abode once again and that He will be with me throughout when I complete my *parikrama* on foot. Shivoham!

The climb down Dolma la Pass was steep and difficult. In spite of the walking poles, the soil was so loose that I slipped a few times before reaching down safely. My wife was not so lucky and stuck midway not knowing how to climb down.

It was here that Father came to her rescue in the form of a sherpa. He held her hands throughout the steep climb and got her down. Later, I heard stories of how people sighted the dogs even at the Dolma pass. Everyone could sense the presence of Father throughout the *parikrama* and there was the strong feeling that he was literally carrying us on his shoulders. Otherwise, there is no way a group of 60 people can all complete *parikrama*. Doing it 'on our own' was out of question.

Just like in day one, the last two hours on day two were tough. My legs were giving away and I slipped repeatedly. It was then I spotted a few people doing their *parikrama* by actually prostrating around Kailash. How silly of me to complain about my headache and bask on the luxury of travelling on a pony, while they circumambulated by prostrating throughout the way! The amount of surrender, faith and love they had for Kailash can never be fathomed by the logical mind.

Day three of *parikrama* started once again on a rocky note with severe headache. But I was determined to make it count. With plans of completing the immigration and crossing over to the Nepal side a priority, many of us started our pony ride. Almost one hour into the ride, I grew restless and started walking.

I felt a sudden rush of adrenaline rush and my steps became steadier.

That was when I observed something about myself. On Day 1 and Day 2, I had used pole sticks to assist my walk. On Day 3, with the use of pole sticks, the steps were far closer to each other as if I were walking on ice. The moment I walked without assistance, my steps were firm and confident. It was once again a note to myself about the play of the mind and the importance of not caving in.

With Father's Grace, all 60+ of us completed our parikramas and it goes without saying that it was HE who walked, and not us. After having our lunch at base-camp (Taklakot) and clearing the immigration, it was a race against time to move people to Simikot as facilities in Hilsa were next to nonexistent. Added to it was the fact that there were already two other groups waiting at Hilsa for their fellow *yatris* to join them before embarking on their journey to Great Kailash and Manasarovar.

About 50 people made it with 14 people staying back in Hilsa as the helicopters wouldn't operate beyond 6 pm local time. Also, news was coming in that the weather at Nepalgunj and Simikot was worsening (rain) and hence no helicopter would operate beyond that time. Around the same time, some of us sighted the symbol 'Om' (in the Devanagari script), the Hindu *swastika* symbol, the letter M and a few other alphabets on the mountains.

That night was one of the most amazing nights we have ever had. Jokes, pulling each other's legs, Aviral's nose transformation story, and my *pada-seva* to my wife had the group in splits. We also had a *satsang* of sorts that went on for hours where each one of us shared our connections with Father, the miracles he has performed in our lives and those we had heard of from other. We could see people wiping off tears at multiple instances. Moments like these are ones that make our life complete. Stories about Father's association with Swami Mohana-Bhaktananda Bharati were also shared and everyone listened with utmost astonishment and joy. There comes a realization that Father is beyond physical dimensions and by simply staying within his consciousness, we are benefitted to a large extent.

Even with no electricity, and with water from the toilet seeping through the floor and wetting all the bedding, just one functional toilet for 50-60 odd people, one room for 9 people, I should admit that it was the best time of our trip. Nobody complained about anything and we were laughing our hearts out.

A gloomy morning welcomed us but the entire group was once again in chuckles thanks to the 'snoring stories'. The sound of the chopper around 10 am brought out the child within us, and we ran towards the airbase carrying our bags.

Our happiness was soon cut short when we realized that the choppers weren't for our group, but for a different group making their entry into Hilsa. Soon minutes turned into hours and we decided to seek Father's intervention.

We must have chanted *Mohanji's Gayatri* for not more than 15 minutes when we heard the sounds of two choppers coming together to take us to Simikot. This is purely his response to the SOS call made by his *bhaktas* and there is no doubt at all about it.

Things went extremely smoothly from thereon and everyone reached Nepal safely without any further delay or trouble. This was followed by a good night's rest on the 17th and preparing to bid goodbye to our family members.

Saying goodbye has always been my weakness. I tend to get emotional saying 'bye' even if I am sure to meet the person in the near future. One such difficult goodbye was to Vigneshwaran. He was easily one of the elders of the group but his enthusiasm can challenge even a 20-year old. One other reason why I was attracted to him was that his appearance closely resembled that of my uncle who was almost like a banyan tree to our family in every aspect. His opinions were highly revered and his would be the final say when there was confusion prevailing. Maybe I was seeing my uncle in Vigneshwaran that day.

On the 18th, my wife and I wanted to revisit the Pashupatinath temple as I was harboring a desire to meet those *Naga Babas* again and give them my offerings. Since it was full-moon day, the temple was flocked by thousands of people. With no sight of the *Naga*

Babas, we were wandering like lost children amidst the crowd before we were attracted by the sounds of *conch* and *damaru*.

It was a narrow hall with images of various Masters displayed on the walls. About ten people were sitting praying at a *dhuni* in front of Shiva's *trishula*. It was only after we entered the hall did we realize that there was a *aghori baba* sitting inside the hall with his eyes fixed towards the sky, in a divine state, swaying to the mantras glorifying Lord Shiva.

Our glances were fixed upon him and he nodded his head at us as if blessing us while we offered our prayers from a distance. Upon the completion of the rituals, we prepared to leave the place and prostrated at the feet of the *aghori baba* who blessed us with ashes from the pyre lit in front of Shiva's *trishula*.

We returned to the hotel happily, feeling our trip had indeed been a fruitful one. Now comes the important part on my 'takeaways' from the trip. A few things I can say for sure:

- The term 'I' is nullified. The realization has set in that there is a larger scheme of things that takes care of every atomic movement in this universe and it will be silly to think that this body-mind is doing something.

- No matter how well-prepared an individual is, Kailash will test his faith. If you surrender completely, you will be taken care of.

- Father is beyond physical dimensions. He is everywhere and will never desert his children.

- Go to Father & Kailash with complete surrender and faith and you shall return with GRACE taking over you for lifetimes.

- It is very important to 'go with the flow' at all times to stay in perpetual bliss.

- You will NEVER understand what you are really destined for. TRUST in Father and he will make your life smooth. Hold onto his feet to cut lifetimes of karma.

We all have read stories of Hanuman and his devotion towards Shri Ram. Should you wish to see him this lifetime, you can see him in Sumit Bhai, Rajesh, DB and other organizers. I would like to single out Sumit Gupta in particular. His every word, every action, every movement and every thought are all dedicated towards the well-being of Father, and the group that has made it to Kailash. Without Father's blessings and without completely selfless devotion, it is totally unimaginable for an individual to oversee a trip of such importance. Nobody had the slightest of discomfort and it was all due to the amazing work by volunteers, the sherpas and of course FATHER.

I once again prostrate at his lotus feet, seeking nothing but Stillness in Mind – SHIVA's CONSCIOUSNESS. Om Namah Shivaya. Jai Mohanji!

The Divine Call

- Arun Vathavooran -

On my return from the Maha Shivaratri celebration at Skanda Vale, I felt strongly about something. I didn't realise at that time that one of my long time wishes would be fulfilled very soon.

Following Maha Shivaratri, I attended a retreat with the Skanda Vale swamis in Gilwell Park, London. It was not a coincidence that brother Vijay and I were assigned the washing-up duties after breakfast. While cleaning the plates, brother Vijay shared that he was going to Kailash again this year. I was pleasantly surprised at that and he added humorously that he was also going to get liberation there this year! While laughing at Vijay's joke, I told him that I too wanted to go but would not be able to this year, since I had already purchased non-refundable flight tickets for a family holiday in Sri Lanka for the entire month. Vijay, someone I have known for nearly ten years as a Skanda Vale devotee, was definitely aware of my love for Lord Shiva and the Divine Mother. He probably knew of my spiritual need and development requirements at that time as well. He said, "You can try, Arun, there is a possibility if you wish so." He added "There are three *swamis* from Skanda Vale who are also going this year." This message ignited the fire in my mind. I had been looking forward for several years and possibly several lives for such an opportunity. However going with Mohanji and our *swamis* to Kailash is something I wouldn't even have imagined

The Divine Call

as a possibility. In my mind, I have been connected to Mohanji through Skanda Vale.

I was in a dilemma at this point: on one hand I wanted to go to Kailash and on the other, I had booked family holidays for the entire month of August, spending almost all of my holiday budget on that. As usual, I discussed this with my wife, during a refreshment break at the retreat. The answer was crystal clear. In her words, one may plan and prepare everything yet one may not get the opportunity at that time. She said, "You have received the invitation now so you must respond positively. You try your best, if there is a divine will everything will fall in place. I took her words, and applied when I got home. My application for 'Kailash with Mohanji 2016' was approved almost instantly with brother Vijay's recommendation.

Preparation

At this point, I felt that the upcoming pilgrimage had already started to make changes in my life. In short, I became a vegan (from vegetarian) within a few weeks of the call from Kailash. I increased my daily yoga routine from 20 minutes to 45 minutes. Waking up early in the mornings, I walked for an hour almost every day. Most importantly, I started to worship Lord Siva and Mother seeking their approval to touch their abode 'Kailash'. Even though I have worshipped at home daily ever since I can remember, I could now clearly feel more energy during my daily worships at my home shrine. I also started to meditate in the mornings. In short, I strongly felt that I connected to Mohanji and that he worked with me on my preparation.

Travel to Kathmandu

Time passed very quickly. I flew to Sri Lanka with my family and spent a week with my parents and parents-in-law. Then I left my wife and son at our native village with my wife's family, and travelled to Kathmandu. To my knowledge, no one from my family has ever been to Kailash before. Therefore, in my mind, I was travelling as a representative of the entire extended family. I had no expectations, other than that of completing the *parikrama*. The journey to Kathmandu was smooth, but I was tired after the travel which included a long transit at Mumbai airport. At the hotel, I heard that Mohanji and the rest of the UK group were delayed due to bad weather. I thought to myself that there should be some strong reason for this, perhaps some of the hardships that we would need to face during the coming weeks have been 'taken' by Mohanji now to comfort us. With this thought in mind, I decided to take a nap in the early afternoon.

At around 9 PM Mohanji and the rest of the UK team arrived in a bus, and all of my tiredness disappeared instantly at their arrival. We greeted each other, had dinner and retired for the night.

Blessings from Lord Ganesha

In Kathmandu, we visited two Buddhist temples, Pashupatinath temple and the Budhanilkantha (sleeping Vishnu) temple. After spending two nights at Kathmandu, we travelled to Nepalgunj.

Despite the severe weather, many flight cancellations and other issues (we learned that several groups were stuck in Kathmandu due to visa issues) we managed to cross the border on schedule and reached Taklakot for acclimatization stay. Several pilgrims started to feel the altitude sickness but I was all right at that point. Mohanji insisted that we save energy for the upcoming days and advised us to take plenty of rest.

I was trying to sleep after lunch on the second day at Taklakot but was not feeling sleepy. My eyes were closed but I was in full awareness of the environment. All of sudden, I could see different colours (purple, blue & violet) in front of me. Then I saw my own face clearly: it was like looking at a mirror. This was then followed by Mohanji's face and then I clearly saw a temple of granite very similar to my *kula devata* temple in my native village in Sri Lanka. Then I saw a beautiful idol of Lord Ganesha (*kula devata*) followed by the idol of Lord Shanmukha (with six faces) similar to the idol

The Divine Call

at Skanda Vale Ashram in the UK. I then saw some rocks, hills, rivers, trees and finally the mighty Kailash in my vision. I was so overwhelmed by the thought that this must be some blessings for my *yatra* from my *kula devata* (Lord Ganesha) and *ishta devata* (Lord Murugan). I later asked Mohanji about this experience and he explained that it was a blessing and confirmation that I have been on the correct spiritual path.

Manasarovar and the first sighting of Kailash

On the following day, we all sat up and listened attentively to the *Siva Kavacha stotram* and boarded the buses for the most important *yatra* of a lifetime. At this point, I went and touched Mohanji's feet to seek his blessings. We travelled in four buses escorted by Chinese police officers. We first got down at Rakshastal and then continued towards Darchen as our next step. On the way to Darchen there was another big lake and I thought this might be Manasarovar. In no time Swami Govinda (Skandavale) who was also travelling on my bus confirmed me that this is indeed Manasarovar. At that point I was in bliss, unable to speak or look at anything, and enjoying myself in silence with closed eyes.

At some point, brother Sumit said, "There is Kailash!" I opened my eyes and could not believe what I was witnessing and experiencing. I was full of bliss and tears rolled out of eyes for a long time. In my very first view, I could clearly see a face and the 'Vel' on the Kailash itself. Brother Rajesh and I tried to take some photos with our phones but I was unable to hold my phone. The feeling of being so close to Kailash had made me feel so completely out of the material world that I was unable to do anything for some time, other than enjoying the moment.

We stopped for a break, and then continued our journey to take a dip in Lake Manasarovar. We reached the shores at around 3pm and immediately got down to take our dips. The water was freezing cold and my body was shivering a bit at the start. I walked into the water until I reached the point where the water was up to my waist. I worshipped mount Kailash standing there and offered a *trishula* and an *Aum*-shaped figurine that I had brought from home as offerings.

I started performing *abhisheka* to Mohanji along with the other pilgrims but Mohanji was is in a full meditative state within the water. After that I started taking dips for myself, for my ancestors, gurus, family members, friends and several Skanda Vale devotees. I also took dips for those who were born in my village, every single soul that has taken birth in Sri Lanka and lost their physical body as a result of decades of civil war, every human being on the planet and for every single living being on earth.

I didn't count the dips but when I count the number of people that I have taken dips for I realise that I may have taken more than 30 dips. I then sang a *thevaram* by saint Sundarar praising Lord Siva's men (*thondar*) and then the *Shivapuranam* along with my fellow pilgrim Vigneswaran. At the end of the *Shivapuranam* I took three dips keeping Lord Ganesha, Lord Murugan and Siva and Shakti in mind. After almost 30 minutes in the holy water, I asked permission from the Lord of Kailash to take some pebbles (*lingams*) with me. At this point I realised what was going on around me and joined other pilgrims in performing an *abhisheka* to the idol of Sri Shirdi Sai Baba and the *Shiva Lingam*. I then collected the holy water in a plastic container to take home with me.

Then I came out, changed into fresh clothes and meditated at the shores while some of the pilgrims chanted the Sri Rudram. Vigneswaran and I started singing the *thevaram* (Tamil hymns praising Lord Siva's abundance) sung by saint Thirunavukkarasar on mighty Kailash in the 7th century. We all then assembled for a very powerful yet simple *yagam* (*havan*) at the shores of Manasarovar. The *yagam* was performed by Mohanji and our three *swamis* from Skanda Vale. All of us were able to offer grains to the holy fire. I was able to feel a very high energy flow and was full of bliss at a number of times during the *yagam*.

After the end of the *yagam*, we had our lunch (freshly cooked by our sherpas at the shores) but I developed a severe headache after lunch. Shortly after, I was sick and vomited everything that I had eaten. I felt a cleansing happening at every level. We then boarded our buses to reach Darchen by around 8pm. I was in a drowsy state during our journey from Manasarovar to Darchen. At Darchen, we realised that none of us would be able to travel back to Manasarovar in the night to see the celestial beings taking the dip in the early hours. I felt a bit sad but realised that it would be good to get some decent sleep prior to starting the *parikrama*.

Parikrama

On the first day of *parikrama*, I was very enthusiastic and full of energy. The dip in the Manasarovar and the night's sleep had washed off all of the tiredness from me. I started the *parikrama* around lunch time by passing through the Yam Dwar. It was a gentle but tiring walk on the first day but I felt so overwhelmed at seeing and experiencing the mighty Kailash so close. We spotted many caves and naturally occurring sculptures on our way. At some point, Swami Karunananda (from Skanda Vale ashram) and I were walking together and clearly identified the appearance of Lord Ganesh (as a natural sculpture) on one side of Kailash. I also saw clearly the face of Lord Shiva and Mother Parvathi as we see in pictures within the snowlines of Kailash. Another noticeable observation were three friendly dogs following us for a long time without any disturbance to us. I felt that these dogs must be some sort of protection for us from Lord Siva's army of millions of helpers. We finally reached close to the north face of Kailash and went into our accommodation after a very powerful *darshan* of the north face.

Morning Star / Blessing of Celestial beings

I was extremely tired and went to bed straightaway. The sherpas insisted on us having some food and I did have some soup and a very light dinner, but had very sound sleep that night. Early in the morning, I woke up around 5am to attend nature's call. I went out of the accommodation with brother Rajesh accompanying me. Black clouds had completely hidden the moon and made it a very dark morning. I went outside and with my hands in Anjali mudra towards the Kailash, made a prayer before starting my day (of course I was a bit uncomfortable mentally about polluting the area so close to Kailash in order to attend nature's call). I had no other choice so that I requested the Lord to pardon me. At that time I could not believe my eyes and my entire body was shaken as I saw a bright star appearing from Kailash and going up in the sky. I followed the star with tears in my eyes, being able to follow it for a few seconds. Then the star vanished into the dark sky. I was so overwhelmed that I was able to see the celestial beings leaving Kailash in the *Brahma muhurtham*.

Later around 6.30am I was sick again while brushing my teeth, and all of my previous night's dinner came out. I decided not to have any cooked breakfast but to carry a cereal bar with me that I had brought from UK. We were all preparing to leave when Mohanji gave each one of us a *rudraksha mala* that had been dipped in the Manasarovar waters. I touched Mohanji's feet and he blessed me. Mohanji then said," Walk slowly, I will walk with you." I started the second day of parikrama with this powerful blessing and started to go up towards the Dolma la Pass. However, after a point I decided to use my pony as I was exhausted from being sick in the morning and not having eaten. The horse ride was a bit tough as I had never ridden a horse before. However I reached the Dolma la Pass without any issues with his Grace. I am sure that Mohanji walked with me in some form as a guardian even though he was undertaking the Inner Kora in his physical form on a separate track.

Gauri Kund and Divine mother's Grace

Once I had reached the Dolma la Pass, I got down from the horse and enjoyed the presence of being there and close to Gauri

Kund. I wanted to walk down to the Gauri Kund but my body's condition was not so great and I felt that I may struggle to return from there. I had brought a *trishula* all the way to be offered in Gauri Kund but was now unable to go down. It was drizzling lightly and I spent around twenty minutes waiting there, enjoying the wonderful feelings. I was looking for someone that may go down to give my *trishula* to offer. However no one known to me went down at that moment. I was a bit sad, closed my eyes and prayed to the Mother saying that I have bought this *trishula* for her, unable to offer it now. I begged for her Grace so that I could offer it to her somehow. When I opened my eyes, there was a man standing next to me (a stranger) who asked me whether I wanted to offer the *trishula*. When I affirmed that I did, he took it from me. At the same time another guy who was in between (half way down towards Gauri Kund) asked this guy something (I didn't know their language). He said something in reply, and tossed the *trishula* towards the other guy. The second guy caught it and ran down quickly and offered it in the Gauri Kund water within minutes. It was all completed like magic in no time. I was full of bliss for a moment and then wanted to thank the guys but they had moved on by then. I thanked the Divine Mother for answering my humble prayer instantly and started descending towards the trekking path.

I walked down along with brother Rajesh and Swami Karunananda and we were able to see the east face of Kailash at some distance. We enjoyed being there, walked the rest of the trek and reached our accommodation around 8pm. The toughest day of the parikrama was effectively completed effortlessly with Mohanji's blessings.

We all left early in the morning on the third day and I completed the entire *parikrama* by around 9.30am. I was full of energy and had not even slight tiredness from not having had proper meals for three days and from trekking 52 kilometres, despite having walked more than 80% of the distance. I didn't suffer at all from my longtime body ailment of knee pain.

I was full of bliss and enjoyed being in the bus with my pilgrim friends, returning from a journey of several lives.

Once I reached Taklakot, I was able to contact my wife and parents. I was speaking to them after a week to inform them that I had completed the *parikrama*, and had nothing more to say. We were all over the moon.

Kailash - Still And Calm

- Ashtamoorthy Kurur -

THE SPARK FOR the journey was lit when Mohanji spoke about the scheduled trip to Kailash when he visited the US in 2015.

The wonders and blessings of the trip were manifold. They began as soon as Mohanji welcomed us at the hotel. I had often wondered what His sound coming from one's own body would be like, and in the welcome hug, I could feel that sound coming from inside of this body. A few months earlier, I had read Zoran's blog, and had a thought as to where he was. And as it was His wont, Zoran was assigned to be my roommate! Then next day at breakfast Mohanji only reinforced that by saying, "So you met Zoran!"

During this trip, I was somehow able to spend a lot of time in His shadows. Most of the time He let me walk with Him and be near Him. A big difference from earlier retreats was that I was not expecting anything, or thinking or trying to know what was happening. The words, particularly 'Just Be', were finding resonance and meaning.

One was enchanted with the beauty of Manasarovar in the afternoon and it was enhanced by the intensity of His presence in its waters, and while the *homa* was on. The spectacle of the ever-moving clouds forming various known and unknown figurines over Kailash was a sight in itself. It is the biggest of big screens and one can immerse in that sight forever. Mother Nature's beautiful play in the sky with moving clouds, with Kailash in the background and Manasarovar in the foreground could be felt in every part of one's body. As I recall and write about it, it sends tremors up my spine.

When we reached Darchen, I was nauseous and threw up. But just as suddenly, the sickly feeling ended, as Mohanji did take upon Himself all of this. The next day, we embarked upon the *parikrama*. At the Yam Dwar, I was thinking of receiving Mohanji's blessings before going through the door. Just as the thought occurred, I spotted his card at the entrance assuring me that the time was right. The walk along the flat trails with all-encompassing: mountains on the sides, and glimpses of the majesty of Kailash. It seemed like one was only floating by. The thin air seems to be by design, since after every few steps one is forced to stop, and so take in the whole vista, particularly that of the various formations on the rocks and on the clouds, catering to the eyes, and the flowing river and wind catering to the ear's delight. They all fill one with a deep sense of gratitude as their blessings are taken in. In between, Kailash shows a majestic face as the Rocky Mountains part. Clouds cascading on top of the ice-capped head and then moving on fill one's heart to the brim. The stillness and calmness of Kailash amidst all the movement, helps the *panchaksharam* to take root deep inside.

I began to realize how the Master had been working on this being in the past few days. Without that Grace, it would not have been possible to reach there, let alone feel anything. I had shared or offered most of the lunch packet except for an apple. As soon as the tents at half way were reached, Mohanji made me sit by him and offered me his lunch packet saying that he had eaten only the apple. That left me speechless. In the evening when we reached the closest to Kailash, for no rhyme or reason the dam burst, and I wept out my heart. Sitting on a rock there, it took forever to compose myself as the tears would not stop. The short walk to the camp from there was a breeze as I didn't feel anything.

The second day was the toughest. The fact that one has to have good thoughts was reinforced. Perhaps the thought that Mohanji and the Inner Kora team were going, or perhaps it may have been the great trek of the previous day, both may have contributed to bloat my ego. The beginning of the climb was not good. It took an hour or so to get back to the rhythm of the previous day by connecting back. There were a lot more monks that day and one of them helped push me up. They offered some black dried fruits which stay in the mouth as you chew, more like a chewing gum. The climbing was steep and it seemed endless. It makes one realize the strength of Grace ever so more than anything else. With that Grace, I was able to cross the Dolma pass and the sight of Gauri Kund was overwhelming and refreshing. I did spend a few minutes on top of the pass taking in the whole place. The place feels like a surreal place in a good way. This is true with most of the sites out there. At the end of that day, I had to crash into a bed and got some shut eye.

The third day's walking was comparatively easy. I never really realized that we had reached the end of the path - everyone thought it was the halfway point. The journey back to Kathmandu was also most enjoyable with all the tales of Mohanji as told by Devadasji. On the last day, we went to the Pashupatinath temple again. It took a while to get back to the routine of life. There was this floating sensation for a couple of weeks. Even while writing this, the whole body is in a vibratory mode.

Let Mohanji, who made this possible, help us sail through life towards the final merger. Special and heartfelt thanks to all the organizers who bore the heavy responsibility of organizing this trip. Thank You.

The Journey Has Only Begun

- Aviral Srivastava -

I NEEDED A MONUMENTAL push to pen my travel narrative. After procrastinating for forty days, I had a dream about Mohanji, got nudged during meditation and here I am typing away.

6.45 am, 8 Aug: I walked towards the boarding gate at Mumbai airport, thinking about the day's office work in Delhi and the flight to Nepal next morning. And yikes! I realised then that I had forgotten my passport back in my Mumbai apartment.

After five minutes of indecision, I boarded the flight anyway. And spent the whole day arranging for my passport's journey from Mumbai to Delhi. I had the parcel shipped to Delhi in my driver's name so that he could collect it. Arrgh, he didn't have an ID and the cargo personnel refused to release the parcel to me. After much personally pleading at the cargo office, I finally got my passport at 1 am - just ten hours before the flight to Nepal!

I was sure I would be among the youngest in the trek cohort. It was already hard to explain to my colleagues why a 25-year old wanted leave for an expensive pilgrimage (I named it 'an exotic trek to Tibet and a trip around Kailash'). At the airport, I met three wonderful Kailash veterans – Jayeeta, Anjali and Rima Dee- who pampered me throughout the trip!

Kathmandu was luxurious, and I resisted the urge to go shopping with the favourable foreign exchange rate. At the Pashupatinath temple, I got to feed animals along with Mohanji.

Mohanji randomly stopped an old, poor stranger and offered him money. The stranger smiled back and gratefully accepted the money. I so KNEW that there was more to that simple act, but kept silent - Mohanji would have playfully parried any questions.

The floating idol in the Budhanilkantha Temple presented a unique optical illusion - the top view of the idol was reflected in the lake as if the idol were present on both sides of the water surface!

I landed in China at 15000 ft in flip-flops and a raincoat - no gloves, jackets or headgear. Soon, I was losing count of the number of people lecturing me! Slightly anxious, I did the Consciousness *Kriya*, hoping it would boost my immunity! And I saw a visual of Mohanji with his third eye blazing. I could feel urges surfacing and dissolving.

I was looking at several nights of fitful oxygen-less sleep. I had banked on my youth to get me through, but my lungs were simply neglecting to breathe at night!

I forgot to breathe again when we went on my first ever helicopter ride. I panicked as there had been no safety briefing (I wanted to know where the parachute was!). Rima Dee calmed and reassured me throughout the trip. I felt so pampered! The helicopter ride was awe-inspiring. When the ground beneath suddenly gives way to a valley, you feel a lurch in your stomach but you forget to panic: the mind chatter has long ceased as you soak in the visuals.

Imagine the serene waters of a white sand beach, long untouched by civilization. The rejuvenating sweetness of the fresh water from an oasis. Cold that cuts like icy barbed wires. A waterbed, springy as a mattress. Combine these visuals and you get Manasarovar. The Manasarovar dip was a once-in-a-lifetime opportunity. The water was freezing but a few steps in, my voice tenor changed and I was on autopilot. Mohanji's eyes were glazed and it was clear he was in another dimension. Outside the lake, Mohanji commented that several faces were visible on Kailash, especially of Lord Hanuman. He remarked that we were surrounded by several deities who had ensured our smooth journey throughout.

A day before the trek, I sought Mohanji's advice on some doubts floating in my head. His response was crisp yet gentle,

"Stop fluttering like a butterfly. Focus on the activity in front of you. You can do so much."

Trekking up high altitude is really humbling. The wind blew in my face, yet my lungs craved oxygen. I dragged my feet using climbing sticks, only to be overtaken time and again, by Tibetan grandmas whistling as they lugged several pounds of baggage.

With Grace, I managed to walk the entire 12 km first phase of the parikrama despite a splitting headache that had me reeling whenever I stood up or sat down. I relented and popped a Crocin pill. With every step, my curiosity grew - will I see more miracles? I did.

We were escorted by a Graceful white bird, flying 20 feet above in a zigzag manner, exactly in sync with our trekking path. I saw this bird again at the end of the day's journey at the resthouse, along with a rainbow.

I had no energy in the morning of the second day. Uncannily, Prashant spotted me and directed me to Mohanji who gave me a *rudraksha mala*. I hugged Mohanji and asked him for strength. He replied, "Don't worry, I am with you."

I climbed up a pony for the first mile. In my defense, there was a lot of horse manure on the ground and maneuvering around it would have drained me! I was one of the fortunate few who climbed down to Gauri Kund later that day. It was pristine and the water tasted ethereal. Throughout the 20+ kms that day, I was chanting *Om Namah Shivaya*. At one corner, I felt an instinctive urge to chant the Vishnu mantra *Om Namo Bhagavate Vasudevaya* instead. Twenty seconds later, I see a huge silhouette of Shesh Naag (the canopy of Lord Vishnu) on a mountain.

I completed the *parikrama* - gripping my *rudraksha mala* at every stumble and corner - with 49 km on foot and 1 km on pony. That 1 km pinched a little - I had wanted to join the 'elite' group who completed the entire trip on foot. In hindsight, it was a mere mindgame and I am grateful that my ego didn't get the opportunity to delusion itself over an achievement that was clearly the work of powers beyond its knowing.

The fun wasn't over yet. A few of us were stranded at Hilsa due to helicopter delay. And that night turned out to the best in the trip. Warren, Devadasji and Raksha swapped stories about Mohanji and Swami Bhakthananda, spiritual tidbits and endless jokes about my nose that had literally melted due to sunburn! During one of the intense spiritual discussions, I even saw the silhouette of goddess Saraswati in the clouds. There was an outburst of Rajas within me. I realised then that the mountains had worked their magic on me. For over a year, I had struggled with down-spiraling ambition and motivation. That night gave me closure, and I felt a return of the old ambition and drive.

I am the guy who stares blankly as others recount visions and premonitions in the experience-sharings after meditation. Nevertheless, this trip was laced with surreal experiences. The scenery without, was nothing compared to the spiritual rebooting that occurred within. Over the next month, it felt a little clumsy to go back to business as usual, with vivid memories of another world. Life will never be the same and yet, the journey has only begun!

Kailash - Heart To Heart

- Harpreet Wasir -

As I sat down by myself one day, a sudden thought came to mind from nowhere. I made it my phone status promptly. It was thus: "You will always be guided to be at the right place at the right time for the right person till the right time."

This one sentence sums up how I was to meet Mohanji and finally how I landed up at mighty Kailash. Now to share this in a bit expanded way.

I may please be pardoned if some thoughts I share sound gruesome to the reader.

As a cardiac surgeon my life has revolved around opening chests, operating while at peak adrenaline surges, breaking out in a sweat when a heart decides to stop pumping and praying for any miracle to happen for its revival, and then just wiping off the sweat when all goes well. Imagine a life like this for twenty years, and going almost non-stop. Vacations, time-off or breaks only came in the form of meetings or conferences.

Aha, but here I was - packing my stuff to visit Mt. Kailash and Manasarovar, about which I had only an iota of knowledge. As Mohanji had said to me: "Doctor, you are married to your work and you had to be brought out for a bit." I may have had very few meetings with Mohanji, but in probably the second meeting two years ago, he told me that I needed to go to Kailash.

To me, going to Kailash meant a pilgrimage to a holy place

somewhere deep in the mountains. That's all. It was about six months before the actual trip during a meeting with Mohanji that he confirmed my participation in the Kailash team through the organizers.

It had all begun the night when I had told Mohanji that it would never be possible for me to get ten days off, and that too for a spiritual journey. I could never get days off, least of all telling my department colleagues and those at home that I was set to go to Kailash.

All he said to me was to explain to all of them clearly my plan, and leave the rest to him. It was quite an intimidating task for me to open my mouth in front of my boss asking for permission.

Surely it must have been the flow of Grace that arranged this trip for me. What followed was almost unbelievable to my mind. There was not even a single word of protest, nor even a bit of resistance in granting me leave, and that too when my request was made at the peak work period. Right from financing, purchasing, ticketing, planning, flights, stays etc., the flow was so smooth that I did not feel any hurdles at any step.

This was the first understanding of what everyone was saying about Kailash, i.e. it was a calling, nothing else. Awareness slowly began to creep in, from understanding all the events that were opening one door after another, at each step towards Kailash. I started to understand what Mohanji always kept repeating: "AWARENESS! AWARENESS! And AWARENESS!" I was just in his consciousness, understanding and growing in awareness. How else could a layman like me with total ignorance of what was ahead, make this journey of a lifetime?

Glimmerings of understanding were revealed at every stage. Knowledge about what was in store for me, came from the most unexpected people. These included my ward boys, servants, drivers, the chemist, my gardener, shopkeepers and many strangers who just held my hand on learning about the impending journey to Kailash. And really, the least acknowledgement was from the so-called educated, intelligent men and women who had travelled the world. This made me realize that the Grace that falls on people is independent of wealth and status. The final understanding of what I was in for, came after I read the book 'Kailash with Mohanji', which gave me goose pimples many a time.

The final realization of the Grace upon me, came on the day when I was to leave New Delhi for Kathmandu. I had an operation scheduled, a single open-heart case which I thought would be over by noon, and thus I would have the rest of the day free for packing etc. I would leave home by midnight to board an early morning flight to Kathmandu. At 11 am, I was informed that I had one more case which was a second-time heart surgery, normally taking 8-10 hours. This case was to start at 4 pm. By no means could I have gotten out of the operation, let alone pack my stuff and leave by midnight. I was in a total fix as my work was my priority, and the trip all on my mind. I had no option but to text Mohanji. I informed him that I was to go for an unexpected long case with all time constraints and just needed my focus. No more details were shared. Immediately came the reply: "I am with you." With this in mind and nothing else, I started operating.

To my utmost surprise the surgery finished in less than 5 hours and I was home by 9 pm. The impossible had been made possible. To me, this was the beginning of Kailash. A realization of how Grace works and how things happen in its presence.

At 6:30 next morning I found myself sitting in an upgraded business class seat - most unexpected again. This surely must have been Kailash calling.

Still, the realization of Kailash had not dawned upon me completely. What I was in for I knew not. On reaching Kathmandu, I sat down to the first *satsang* and heard the disclosure in which Mohanji shared Kailash with all. I was like a blank slate, totally void of thought. A person like me whose brain waves were active even during sleep was finding himself in that state. I must have been only in his awareness, dimly conscious that something had already started working on me, and that the divine plan was slowly unfolding. I had no expectations, and any desires kept dropping off one by one.

I was meeting new people, and hearing about the experiences of those for whom this would be the second trip. If on one hand I felt like a kindergarten child, on the other hand I was subconsciously preparing myself for something which would be the turning point of my life on a totally different plane and consciousness level.

More than visiting and seeing Kailash in its physical form, it was the emotional and physiological impact it was making on me. A transformational experience, which was at that time totally beyond my belief system. To be a part of a group of more than 80 pilgrims and workers gave a feeling of oneness, since all were under the wing of an evolved guide, Mohanji. Whenever I saw him, his physical form spoke something yet his ethereal form came to me as a protector and a guide always saying, "God Bless You, I am here for you."

A heightened sensitivity to all experiences and happenings had set in, which for sure seemed beyond the norm. It began to dawn on me that the seeds for Kailash had been sown not days, weeks, months or years ago, but perhaps in past lifetimes. By now I no more thought of it as a pilgrimage to Kailash, but as Shiva's call to come home, to return to the place where I have always belonged. It was a father's call to welcome his son back home. This thought so overwhelmed me, at times I felt that even if I had to turn back at any point I would still feel totally contented and fulfilled. My Kailash trip seemed fulfilled at the mere thought that it was purely through Shiva's permission that I was where I was finding myself now. Just to be selected for this transformational trip was enough of a feeling of adoption by a Guru and Guide. Now it did not matter how many lifetimes it would take for liberation - because for sure liberation was assured with being allowed to walk the trail of Kailash.

I became aware of the synchronicities, and of unusual events occurring more and more often. Getting to the right bus, finding the perfect seat and getting spontaneous answers to any thought or questions, all these were becoming more frequent.

With my surrender happening naturally, also came more acceptance of situations leading to more awareness. It seemed as if people were saying out aloud what I was thinking. I was in some kind of a flow. At other times I experienced total silence amidst all the crowd and noise, totally blanked out. At other times I found myself just folding my hands, prostrating with complete humility and peace and just thanking Him for all He was doing. I started feeling deep stillness, quietness and blankness from within. For me it was a state of Shiva Silence. I had no needs or desires, nor was I anticipating any kind of divine experience which many pilgrims spoke about and discussed. Now and then I asked myself: what if I don't see or hear any experience, then what? Immediately came the answer, "You have been given everything, you have been given Kailash. Take as much as you can." All I could do was to seek the blessings of all Gurus, Masters and finally of Kailash itself.

I am not sure it will be appropriate to speak about personal experiences both physical and mental, since to differentiate these from the games of the mind would be very difficult. Yet I am completely sure that during the *parikrama,* my porter in the form of a woman who often comforted me by holding my hand in all the most difficult terrains was none other than the Divine Mother herself. This I have realized today. Though I did not know much about the Saints, Masters and various Guru forms, when I saw Kailash I realized what they were all about and what was presenting itself to me.

Kailash had my entire consciousness submerged within itself. I had nothing left on me and even within me as I stood in front of the mighty Kailash. At all moments I felt that this was all I had in the form of any named relationship only leading me to the Power of Purity.

The sense of Mohanji's constant presence even in his physical absence, was absolutely evident. All throughout the *parikrama* I knew I was being carried all the way. By the end of the last leg all I could say was, "Thank You God", for making me realize more that you are there, were always there and will always be there.

It has been three weeks since I returned. The drill of work and physicality of the worldly vices are there again. The only thing that has changed permanently is an ever-growing and everlasting awareness, along with a permanent shift in attitude - that of total surrender to His Will and the constant feeling of a protector always being present as a guide giving directions. There is also present the intelligent awareness to identify them. This is not a one-stop destination but an ongoing journey, the start and end of which only God knows.

What is good and correct is only what will happen in any physical or mental form. It seems that the first wait may be over, partially or fully. I don't want to think.

This call and journey gave answers to all deep-rooted questions and for me Mohanji was the one who carried me to the destination, to this abode, Shiva's abode.

I am one with Him, I am Him and He is the Doer as always.

No amount of writing or sharing can ever completely express this journey.

For me this was a call of a lifetime and for a lifetime.

A Journey Of A Lifetime

- Jay Jeyaseelan -

It was in March 2010 that we began learning the *Sri Rudram*. Since that day, we have been chanting it every Friday evening with our Sai family. It is our beloved Swami, Sri Sathya Sai Baba, who has sown the seed of Mount Kailash in this lifetime. In 2013, Swami introduced Mohanji to us through our dear Vijay and his family.

As much as I wanted to join the Kailash trip in 2014, due to family commitments my family traveled to California and then to Toronto that year. However, my thoughts were with the Kailash *yatra*.

While we were in the US, I received a text from Vijay, who was in Kailash at that time saying that Mohanji would be going to Toronto right after the Kailash trip. What joy! Mohanji's stay in Toronto would be coinciding with our time in Toronto. My wife Shyama and I were over the moon and had never expected to see Mohanji in Canada. We couldn't believe our luck. We met Mohanji at Niagara and spent the whole day with him. He told us about the Kailash trip and that he would be going back one more time to do the Inner Kora. Both of us were overjoyed to hear that from Mohanji and straight away we asked him humbly whether he would take us along. The Master smiled and said, "You come, I will take care of you." What love he showed, I still remember those words!

On the 31st of July 2016, I drove to Skanda Vale in the morning and brought back Swami Brahmananda, Swami Govinda and Swami Karunananda to our home. It was a long drive, 4 hours to get to Skanda Vale and then another 4 hours to get back to London. We had a small *bhajan* session with the *swamis* and the kids at home. That *bhajan* session with the Swamis gave us the blessings and were an auspicious start to our epic *yatra* to Kailash. We drove the *swamis* to London's Heathrow airport to see them off to Badrinath.

On the following Sunday, the 7th of August 2016, we left London Heathrow with some of the other pilgrims from UK. We met Mohanji at Delhi airport just before boarding the plane to Kathmandu. He gave me a hug and with a big smile said, "Good to see you." Just seeing Mohanji and being in His presence is something special, no words can express the joy that I felt.

August 10th - Wednesday – travel to Nepalgunj

In the morning we went to the Pashupatinath temple. It was an excellent experience. The priest allowed a special *darshan* of the main Pashupatinath Shiva *moorthy* for Mohanji. Mohanji asked me to join him. After the *darshan*, Mohanji went and broke coconuts (hitting the coconut on a stone). He did nine coconuts and then gave the others one coconut each. I couldn't break my coconut in half on the first hit and it took several attempts. Mohanji must have felt my disappointment. After a few more coconuts He smiled at me and gave me the last one. This time it broke in half on the first hit. Mohanji smiled and asked, "Are you happy now, president?" He takes care of all of us fulfilling our little wishes. All my gratitude to Mohanji and to our beloved Swami Sri Sathya Sai baba. There were many times in my life when I have asked Swami why He never gave me a chance to touch his feet or be next to His physical body - I now see Swami in Mohanji. Thank you my beloved Swami, I see YOU in Mohanji.

In the afternoon we flew to Nepalgunj and arrived at about 7 pm. On the way to the hotel, we chanted *Sri Rudram* on the bus. The group was in good spirits and high energy. All instructions about the next day's trip were given to us after dinner. We were placed in two groups. Mohanji and the three *swamis* with a few others were in the first group that would leave the hotel at 6am and the rest were to leave at 7am.

August 11th - Thursday – travel to Taklakot

Due to bad weather in Simikot, Mohanji's group only left the hotel at 7.30am. While we were waiting at the hotel for our turn, we chanted Sri Rudram and sang *bhajans*. Some other pilgrims joined in and a few of them meditated and created positive energy. Eventually we arrived at Nepalgunj airport at about 11am. After two hours we took the small 17-seater flight to Simikot. Many pilgrims from our group were still waiting at Simikot to get the helicopter to Hilsa. The helicopters only carried 5 or 6 people at a time based on the weight of people. We waited another 3 hours for our turn. Simikot is almost 3000m high. Shyama and I started to feel altitude sickness. We were the last group and got on the helicopter at about 6pm. In fact, they were going to leave 18 of us behind in Simikot but with Mohanji's Grace, we all made it to Hilsa. Crossed the Nepal and China border, we went to the Chinese immigration. There was a long wait there too. Eventually, we arrived at the guest house in Taklakot. By this time I had developed a severe headache and little while later, I felt sick. Mohanji gave me some dry fruits to eat. The sherpas served dinner after an hour. We were extremely tired and went to bed without changing our clothes. All I could chant was *Om Namah Shivaya*.

August 12th - Friday – rest day

Today was a rest day at Taklakot. We went out to do a bit of shopping with others. We had a *satsang* with Mohanji in the afternoon. He explained the significance of having dips in Lake Manasarovar.

August 13 - Saturday - dip at Lake Manasarovar

All of us were very excited. An important day in our lifetime. We left Taklakot about 10.00am. The bus stopped after 40 minutes at Lake Rakshastal where Ravana from the epic Ramayana had a dip. Then we drove another hour or so and stopped at an information centre before leaving for Manasarovar. After another hour on a very rough track, we could see the east face of Mt. Kailash. The skies were blue and with the sun shining, it was a perfect day to do the dip. I was really trying hard to control my emotions. I felt as if my body were on a different planet. Mohanji went into the water first. We followed him. It was COLD. Mohanji had his first dip. Soon after I followed suit. A dip for my soul, in front of my Guru. I poured a little bit of water on Him. By now all the pilgrims were inside the lake and were pouring water on Mohanji. Mohanji was shivering. For the first time I saw Devi looking concerned about her husband's health. I suppose we all want to pour water on our Guru not realising that His physical body will have to endure it. However, the Master let His physical body go through pain for us, only so that His devotees fulfill their desires – what unconditional LOVE!

I did dips for all my ancestors, family members, my Sai friends, Harrow West Sai centre members, for my Gurus and for the entire world. Suddenly I saw Devi standing in front of me. I felt the presence of Mother Parvathi and she poured water on me, and I did the same. The immense amount of *shakti* I received was something I will never forget.

Mohanji was standing at the bank of the lake and making sure all finished their dips and came out safely. As we came out, he asked us to pour water on a Shirdi Sai statue left at the edge of the lake. I came out of the water and took *pada namaskaram*. I couldn't have asked for more. At this point I was shivering. I bet my bones would have made lots of noise.

We then sat down to chant the *Sri Rudram*. As we continued, my body started to warm up. All my energy and mind were fully surrendered to Lord Shiva. I have no words to express that feeling. Nothing but pure oneness with Lord Shiva.

Then Mohanji and Swamis Brahmananda, Govinda and Karunananda started the *havan*. We had idols of Ganesha, Shirdi Baba, a *lingam* from Pashupatinath temple, and a carving of an *Aum* on a stone (this was donated to Skanda Vale Swamis by Swami Muralikrishna) at the front of the *havan kund*. We all joined in and chanted the mantras. Mohanji was leading the mantras and invoked the gods one by one. As it happened we saw Lord Ganesha and Hanumanji in the clouds. My soul must surely have done some good deed in the past to witness that wonderful scene. As we chanted the *Mrityunjaya mantra*, Swamis gave the offerings which they brought from Skanda Vale. At the end the chanting intensified and the *poornaahuti* was offered by Mohanji. I still can't find words to express my feelings. You needed to be there to feel the magical moments!

Again, the sherpas kindly prepared food for us. After the meal, we continued with the Manasarovar *parikrama*. My heart was filled with gratitude to Mohanji for taking care of us and to Lord Shiva for pouring His Grace on us.

We stayed at Darchen overnight in a newly-built guesthouse. The team was in good spirits and the energy level was high. However, Mohanji didn't join us for dinner as He must have cleansed a lot of our bad energy during the dip and the *havan* and that must have taken a big toll on His physical body.

August 14 - Sunday - first day of parikrama

After breakfast, we left Darchen for Yam Dwar. Porter and pony were allocated to us via a lottery system. All set, we started walking. The energy was high, the Grace was pouring, and I was trying hard to control my tears! At Yam Dwar, we went around three times and then through the gate. Walked slowly, step by step chanting *Om Namah Shivaya* and *Om Sri Sathya Sai Shivaya Namaha*. We kept on moving, being with Lord Shiva and His consciousness. There were no emotions, just emptiness now. I paid my gratitude to Lord Shiva and the west side of Mt Kailash. After almost 5 hours we came to the North face of Mt Kailash. What a view! You need to be with Lord Shiva to enjoy the feeling, a feeling that I had never experienced before in my entire life. I sat down on a flat rock and closed my eyes. I was taken to a place where I could only see golden light. There were lots of beings, all gold in colour and running back and forth. I had a bird's eye view. I enjoyed watching them. After 15 minutes or so I felt the cold and opened my eyes to see the north face still shining in front of a blue sky! What an experience. Returning to my room, I could see Mt Kailash through the window. A little while later Vijay came and invited us to chant the *Sri Rudram*. As we started chanting, I felt the energy going through me and giving me more strength to chant louder and louder and at the same time enjoy the oneness with Lord Shiva.

Though I tried to have dinner, I was not able to because of altitude sickness, and went to bed without eating. The toilet facilities didn't help either. Had a very rough night.

August 15- Monday - Second day of parikrama

I drank a cup of ginger tea, but even the tea didn't want to stay inside my body. Could not eat or drink anything. Sat in my room and prayed to Lord Shiva and Mohanji to get me through the rest of the *parikrama*. I felt really weak wondering whether I would be able to continue. The porter came and asked me whether I was going up to Dolma La Pass. Not sure where I got the energy from but I said YES. Came down and saw Mohanji standing at the entrance saying goodbye to the pilgrims. He put his hand on my chest and said, "Do well president, I know you will." That gave me the strength to continue.

With His blessing, I started day 2. I hadn't heard Shyama talk for two days now. Struggling to breathe, all I wanted now was to stay with her for the rest of the day, especially going up to Dolma La Pass and then walking down the steep hill. I couldn't walk so I decided to use the horse. With Mohanji's blessings, both of our horses stayed together and walked up Dolma La Pass. As we ascended uphill into the clouds, the Kailash Mountain vanished slowly from view, but all I could say was *Om Namah Shivaya*, being with Lord Shiva and HIS consciousness. We reached Dolma La Pass in 3 hours.

From the top of Dolma La Pass, looking down, we saw the majestic Gauri Kund. What a view! We stayed there for a little while, saying prayers to Mother Gauri. Though I wanted to go down to the lake and get some water, that didn't happen.

Shyama and I slowly made our way down the steep hill. We made every step with great difficulty. My mind was blank, no thoughts at all. Looking back, I have no idea how I managed to come almost 4km down a steep hill. Eventually, we came to a tea hut and met our porters. After a 10-minute break, we resumed our journey. It was a long trek. The horses walked very elegantly with the bells on them making charming sounds. I just enjoyed the walk and paid my respects to Lord Shiva. Eventually, we reached our overnight stay at Zutulphuk.

August 16 – Tuesday - Third day of parikrama

It was a very pleasant morning and we started the day very early. My energy was high and I felt that I could walk that day. It was dark when we started but after a while, the sun greeted us with a beautiful sunrise. Walking about an hour we came to a narrow path at the edge of a deep valley. All pilgrims walk from here to the end as it is too dangerous to go horseback. Shyama and I walked slowly enjoying the morning sunlight and the amazing view of the valley. After an hour's walk, we got to the end. We made it. We all made it. All of us were so happy and hugged each other with big smiles of gratitude.

Lord Shiva and Mohanji were with us throughout these three days, their presence evident in many places and they saved us from many dangerous situations. Our *koti pranams* and heartfelt gratitude to you Lord Shiva and Mohanji. Without your abundant love and Grace we couldn't have done this epic *yatra*.

After bidding goodbye to our sherpas, we took a bus trip to Darchen and then to Taklakot. Passing through the Chinese immigration office and crossing the bridge, we got to Hilsa. There was again a long wait for the helicopter journey. One by one, we managed to send most of the pilgrims to Simikot. While waiting for the helicopter, we chanted *Sri Rudram* to give energy and protection to the Inner Kora pilgrims. Due to bad weather 13 of us were left behind in Hilsa to stay overnight.

Yet again, Mohanji showered His Grace on us. The conditions were so bad but none of us complained or fussed about it. We stayed up late, sharing our experiences and discussed many topics. I had an amazing time and felt the oneness with the group.

August 17 - Wednesday

After a nice and simple breakfast we waited for a helicopter to take us to Simikot. The helicopters started flying but none for us, for almost another two hour wait. We kept calm and started to chant Mohanji's *Gayatri*. What compassion from the Master - he sent not one but three helicopters at the same time to pick all 13 of us. We all came to Simikot safely. From Simikot, we took the 17-seater plane to Nepalgunj and then to Kathmandu. Reached the Crown Plaza hotel late evening.

August 18 - Thursday

It was a rest day at Kathmandu. Some of us went back to the Pashupatinath temple too. I had feeling of completion of the *yatra* on visiting the temple again. After a beautiful *darshan* we chanted *Sri Rudram* sending the powerful energy to the pilgrims who were doing the Inner Kora.

August 19 - Friday

Yohan, Vignesh anna, Shyama and I went to Sri Sathya Sai Baba's ashram in Bengaluru from Kathmandu. We stayed there four nights and returned to the UK on 24th of August. The peace and tranquility at Prasanthi Nilayam helped me absorb the Kailash energy and look within.

I offer my sincere gratitude to our beloved Guru Mohanji and His organising team for making this once in a lifetime trip possible.

An All-Encompassing Feeling

- Priya Maharaj -

In January 2016 I attended my first Power of Purity meditation and from that moment felt a deep connection with Mohanji. For many years I had wanted to go on the Mount Kailash pilgrimage and when I found out that Mohanji was hosting a pilgrimage to Mount Kailash – everything came together.

I needed to go on this journey, it was meant for me to embark on a pilgrimage of a lifetime to the abode of Lord Shiva with our dearest Mohanji.

After many years of yearning to go to Mount Kailash, and then months of planning for the trip, finally the time arrived for most members from the South Africa group to leave for Mount Kailash. During the months leading up to the ultimate journey, while preparing myself physically, mentally and emotionally, I told myself that I would not have any expectations from the pilgrimage. It is in Lord Shiva and my Gurus' (Sathya Sai Baba and Mohanji) hands - there is a reason why I am going and they know the experience I am going to have. It was futile to think that I was in control of this journey.

I received a lot of well wishes and blessings from my family and friends before I left South Africa. I made a sash and got my loved ones to write their names on it, and I wrote names of people that I wanted to carry with me to Mount Kailash.

When I arrived in Kathmandu, the only thing I wished for was to see Mohanji. The first and last time I saw Mohanji was in April 2016 in South Africa. When Mohanji arrived, and I went down to see him while he was having dinner, he told me that I had lost weight. I confirmed with Mohanji that I hadn't but later realized he was talking about my karmic baggage! Over the months while preparing for my Mount Kailash pilgrimage, Mohanji had been working on me through meditations and healing to get me ready for the pilgrimage.

As pilgrims started to arrive at the hotel over the next two days, we had the opportunity to do yoga in the morning with Devi Mohan and thereafter we went to two temples in Kathmandu, the Swayambhunath temple and Boudhanath temple. Sharing this experience with other pilgrims and Mohanji was amazing.

The next day we went to the Pashupatinath temple and the Budhanilkantha temple. At the Pashupatinath temple the queues were too long to go pray in front of the *Shiva lingam*, so I went around the temple 3 times. While waiting for the other pilgrims, a security guard called over Nameshri Chetty. Milu Ferreira and I followed her – we had the opportunity to view the *Shiva lingam* inside the temple and pray. I felt so blessed and the priest inside the temple gave me a coconut. While leaving the temple we had the opportunity to feed the birds and cows with Mohanji.

Our next stop was the Budhanilkantha temple - the sleeping Vishnu temple. While praying and going around the Vishnu, I thought I was imagining that the sleeping Vishnu was breathing. I checked with Warren de Beer, a fellow South African and we both agreed that we were seeing the same thing. We stood and watched this for about 5 minutes in complete awe. Thereafter we had to rush back to the hotel to collect our items and start our journey to Kailash.

From the moment we left, I could feel the excitement build up within me – I was finally going to Mount Kailash! I remember the day we spent at Taklakot to acclimatize to the high altitude. We did group Kriya with the pilgrims from other parts of the world. Thereafter we played the *Shiva Kavacham*, which was so powerful

An All-Encompassing Feeling

and electric. I had a vision of Mohanji clearing the negative energy around me so I could commence the pilgrimage. That evening Mohanji said to me, "Maharaj, you will enjoy it, don't worry and don't forget to take dips in Manasarovar for your ancestors and all your family." That evening I reached another level of excitement and could not contain my emotions. I felt this abundance of gratitude: how did I get so lucky to share this experience with such a divine being, Mohanji? The next day as we started our journey to Manasarovar, the air was charged – everyone was so excited and cheerful. We were blessed to have Mohanji and Devi ride in our bus, and as we got closer to our destination, Mohanji said, "Look, our first sight of Kailash." The tears started to stream down my face uncontrollably - there are no words to describe the feeling when you see Kailash for the first time.

When we got to Manasarovar, it was time to take our dip. Mohanji had entered the water first and then the rest of us followed. When I went to Mohanji to do *abhisheka* for him, I could not believe what I saw. Mohanji was in an expanded state in Shiva form – he was in full Shiva consciousness. As I poured water on Mohanji and chanted *Om Namah Shivaya*, I was overwhelmed with emotions – I was doing *abhisheka* to Lord Shiva himself. Thereafter, Mohanji poured water on me and I could feel something physically leave my body. I didn't think that I would stay in the water for so long, more than 15 minutes. I took so many dips - for my ancestors, family and friends. Later I saw Mohanji at the shoreline and went immediately to him and did *pada pooja*.

Once everyone had completed their dips, Mohanji and the *swamis* from Skanda Vale in the UK did *homa* on the banks of Manasarovar with Mount Kailash in full view and all pilgrims had the opportunity to participate in the *homa*. There was such calmness and stillness while doing the *homa*, as if the Gods were watching over us – I felt complete. I then did my chanting and my *Kriya* which was the best feeling ever. From the age of eight, I have chanted *Om Nama Shivaya* (108 times) every morning and on that day I got to do my chanting at such an auspicious place, with Lord

Shiva's abode in full view. At Manasarovar, we also got to see the beautiful golden ducks and birds.

That night after taking my dips in Mansarovar, I had the most beautiful dream which confirmed my journey and the reason I was on this pilgrimage.

Day one of *parikrama* was here. I didn't have any real concerns or issues and was just floating. Once we arrived at the start point, I went to take blessings from Mohanji and he just gave me a hug and the most beautiful smile. As I walked away, like a little girl I threw Mohanji a kiss and like a father with unconditional love, he put his hands to his lips and blew me a kiss too. In my heart I knew that I would be safe and that Mohanji was going to be with me every step of the way throughout this journey. Even when I had to choose my porter, he picked me first by throwing a stone on my bag and came to speak to me. I was confused, I knew I had to pick a number to get a porter. Lo and behold, the number that I had picked was the number that belonged to the same porter who had thrown the stone on my bag. It was as if he was meant to be with me on this journey.

The first day of *parikrama* was beautiful and divine. I chanted *Om Namah Shivaya* with every step I took and when I got tired I chanted the *Maha Mrityunjaya Mantra* followed by *Om Namah Shivaya*. The energy and vibration of this beautiful mystical place was enthralling - I could feel Lord Shiva all around. When I saw beautiful birds in the sky, I wondered if they really were saints taking on forms of birds.

Just before arriving at our accommodation, the view of Mount Kailash was breathtaking. I stood and prayed for more than half an hour, looking at this beautiful mountain. I could feel Lord Shiva deep within me and all around me. There was nothing more beautiful than Mount Kailash – I was completely drawn in. That night all I could think of was Mount Kailash - I felt blessed, I felt humbled; I felt Lord Shiva. That same night one of our fellow South Africans got really sick and I spent most of the night trying to help her. Though I had a thought about how I was going to complete the next day's *parikrama*, which was to be the most challenging

An All-Encompassing Feeling

one, I reassured myself that Lord Shiva and Mohanji would take care of me.

The next morning when I took blessings from Mohanji, he told me, "Priya, take it slow today." And I listened whole-heartedly. What a beautiful day it was, and even though Dolma la Pass challenged me mentally, physically and emotionally, I was perfectly fine. When I saw Gauri Kund my heart started to beat a lot faster, I could not believe what I was feeling. Before my porter could say anything I started my tracks down Gauri Kund. I had to go and nothing was going to stop me. I reached Gauri Kund and I fell to my knees praying to the lake. I offered water, I drank some water and I said a prayer of gratitude to the Mother.

When I collected my water, I realized that I was all alone at Gauri Kund and could see everyone at the top walking by. Before I knew it there was a porter who had come to collect water, and he insisted that I go back with him. With every 5 steps I took I ran out of breath. I prayed to Lord Shiva and Mohanji and before I knew it I was half way up Gauri Kund. The porter never left my side, he waited with me, and every time I stopped, he stopped. When I reached the top I sat on a rock to try to catch my breath. Yohan, another pilgrim from UK, came to me offering me water and sweets. Once I calmed down and settled my breathing, I started my journey again. Having gone to Gauri Kund was absolutely amazing, and I know in my heart that it was Mohanji who helped me up Gauri Kund. I felt so blessed to be able to collect the Gauri Kund water, which is so sacred and precious. While on my journey I saw four dogs - three black ones and one golden one. When I checked with other pilgrims, they had also seen these dogs which followed us from the time we started with day 2 of the *parikrama* until we reached our accommodation. Later Mohanji confirmed that they were Dattatreya's dogs with us, seeing that Mohanji wasn't physically with us because he and a few other pilgrims had started on their journey to the Inner Kora of Mount Kailash that day.

When I reached the accommodation on the second day of *parikrama*, I was so overwhelmed that I could not stop crying. I released a lot of emotions that day and felt much lighter - I felt different. While going through these emotions, I could hear a few pilgrims calling for me to come outside. Two beautiful rainbows had appeared and lit up the sky. I knew that was a gift from Mohanji to say to all pilgrims, "You did it, well done." That night I had a dream that Lord Shiva was touching my third eye and Mohanji and Sathya Sai Baba watching over. I woke up that morning with a feeling of such calmness.

The third day of *parikrama* was as if I floated and bounced to the end. It was beautiful and serene. I thought to myself this is how I picture heaven to look like. When I got to the end, I hugged my fellow pilgrims, we laughed and cried and were so happy to have completed the pilgrimage of a lifetime. I went onto my knees to thank Mother Earth for allowing me to walk on this sacred ground and prayed to Lord Shiva for lovingly welcoming me to his abode with open arms. The tears rolled down my face uncontrollably – I cried tears of joy, tears of gratitude, tears of release and cried some more because I didn't think that I would complete this beautiful journey. I felt my heart *chakra* open up completely exuding immense gratitude. A few South Africans and I took our sashes and tied it to the rocks at the end of the *parikrama* – we had completed our journey to this sacred abode, carrying loved ones with us.

Thereafter we left to collect our luggage at Darchen and then drove to the Chinese border (Friendship Bridge). We crossed the bridge and spent time waiting for our helicopter to take us from Hilsa to Simikot. It started to get cloudy, and when 6 of us took the helicopter, halfway into our journey it started to rain. While in the helicopter I was chanting and all I could see was Mohanji's eyes and Sathya Sai Baba on the mountains. I kept these visions to myself. When we got to Simikot, the weather got progressively worse. Loshini Naidoo asked me if I saw the faces on the mountains. Then I confessed what I saw. My Gurus had been watching over us every step of the way until we landed in Simikot. The helicopter after us was the last one to come through. Fellow pilgrims had to spend the night at Hilsa and the rest of us stayed at Simikot.

The next day we started to chant for the weather to improve.

An All-Encompassing Feeling

Suddenly the skies cleared up and half an hour later, the rest of the pilgrims arrived from Hilsa. The two chartered flights were able to come to Simikot to take us back to Nepalgunj.

When we arrived at Kathmandu I was in a daze, trying to take in all that I experienced. We shared stories and experiences with other pilgrims and while I was there I prayed so hard to see Mohanji before I could leave for South Africa. I knew once I got Mohanji's blessings my pilgrimage would be complete. On the day we were leaving Kathmandu, two hours before we were to leave the hotel, Mohanji and the rest of the Inner Kora pilgrims arrived. I screamed with delight, Mohanji was here! Sitting at the table, while Mohanji was eating, a few of us shared our experiences with him. He said that he had done his best to fulfill all our wishes. I said, "Babaji, you fulfilled my wishes tenfold, there are no words to thank you enough." Mohanji was so tired but he still had time for us, he gave *Shaktipat* to all of us who were leaving that day. My pilgrimage was complete. I had got blessings from Mohanji before I left for South Africa.

There are no words to describe my Mount Kailash journey, it was all about feeling Mount Kailash. This feeling I shall treasure for the rest of my life.

I got to meet the most beautiful souls on this journey. The tour company was amazing, trying to accommodate our every need. Rajesh, DB and Sumit, I am so grateful to you for all that you did – my pilgrimage was blissful, it was everything and more. And to my dearest loving Mohanji, how do I ever thank you . . .

Outer Kora Experiences

- Rakshita Ananth -

With humble pranams and surrender at my guru Mohanji's feet, I begin to write my experiences during the Kailash Yatra of 2016. I am always his instrument and he writes the experiences through me.

Ever since my childhood, even before I knew of the word spirituality, the Himalayas have always been my dream destination. I was fascinated by the very thought of them. Though I had never been serious about it, I had this secret dream of running away to the Himalayas into the world of saints and never come back to this noisy world. As I grew up, due to the concepts that people had built into me about being spiritual, being a woman I considered myself not so eligible to even think about stepping at the foot of the Himalayas. But it always remained my secret dream.

After my first meeting with Mohanji in December 2015, it is Mohanji's Grace that he uncovered this dream and made it a reality today. When my husband asked me about my thoughts of joining Mohanji's group to Kailash, something inside me told me, that "This is the purpose of my birth." To be in the presence of my Master and in a very sacred place – Mt. Kailash. I readily accepted, however with the fears about physical limitations like: will I be able to climb, am I eligible, am I spiritual enough, will it just end as a dream, will my visa application be accepted, will there be a decline of visa due to health requirements etc. Too many thoughts which this monkey mind didn't want to stop.

I have to mention here that in a practical world, I am not physically fit enough for such tasks. I have multiple uterine fibroids that require me to be surviving on at least 5 pain pills a day, at least 15 days a month. Added to it is my ACL reconstruction surgery from eight years ago, which still gives me trouble while walking. I usually speak to Shirdi Baba like I speak to a friend, about anything and everything. After meeting Mohanji, I do the same with him, most of the times in silence. For me Shirdi Baba and Mohanji are not different. So they knew my fears. My Kailash journey commenced months before the actual journey began. Things started unwinding slowly after I signed up for this journey to the Land of Gods.

First was my job. Due to multiple organizational restructuring, things weren't going well at work. So I quit. Though it put a lot of pressure in the short term, when I look back now, I realize that I badly needed that resting period due to the physical pain I was undergoing through the health issues. When I contacted Baba (I prefer referring to Mohanji as Baba) in May 2016, he asked me to go to an orthopathy clinic in Kerala. I made my own decision that I would do it after my Kailash journey as I would then have more time to relax and rest.

In June 2016, I was mostly on bed rest due to mounting pains. I was so worried about the *parikrama* that I was unable to continue with walking and yoga practices. I contacted Baba again and he asked me to leave for Kerala immediately. I gave him a long explanation with all my logic as to why it made sense to do it after Kailash. The second message came immediately: "I think you should go now." His words were my command. With a month and half left for the *yatra*, I packed my bags and left for Kerala the very next day. All the while I had read about Baba speaking on 'going with the flow', 'surrender' and 'being spontaneous'. I got to experience this first hand on that day.

It was so sudden that I had to cancel my pre-booked tickets, book a fresh set of tickets by almost paying double the price. We (my husband and I) had previously planned that we would travel together, meet a few friends from another country during a stopover and do some shopping before heading home. Now all that had changed. My ego mind was telling me that such things wouldn't have happened if I hadn't contacted Mohanji. What a silly mind! Who was I trying to defend? Who was I trying to win over? To whom am I trying to explain? I was both laughing and crying at the same time for such a thought. I was crying because my ego mind couldn't execute its plan and was severely hurt. My logic didn't work with him . . . ha ha. I was laughing because of the realization of my ego, and that the real me wants to accept the guru's words as a command.

I left for Kerala, staying there for almost sixteen days. I was also able to gather information that Mohanji stayed in the clinic a year ago and Swami Bhakthananda had also stayed in the clinic a few months ago, which gave me immense joy. It is indeed a blessing to be in a place where my master and his *parambhakt* had breathed/stayed/walked.

This clinic specializes in fasting as a cure for many diseases. I fasted on water for four days, on tender coconut, juice and water for another four days, and on fruits, vegetables and juices for almost another five days. I never thought I could possibly survive for so many days without eating, what we commonly consider real (or cooked) food. When I was fasting, I suddenly remembered my conversation with Baba during our first meeting. I had told him that I was fond of food, and that it was my weakness. Coming out of the fast, I never had the lust for food. In fact, fasting was easier than eating. Eating made me feel dull and sick. I realized that Baba was silently working on my weaknesses.

I had a relapse of abdominal pain while I was at the clinic. Because I was fasting and not allowed to take any pain pills, I had to bear it all. I was crying out to Baba for having put me in such a helpless situation. I was crying, looking at a plain wall in front of me and was able to see Shirdi Baba's face in the wall. The face remained there all through my stay. Knowing that he was there

Outer Kora Experiences

with me felt good. Though that did not ease my pain, I was able to endure it knowing there must have been a reason for going through the pain.

With about fifteen days left before the *yatra*, I planned every day, walking for almost 6-7 kms a day, practicing silence, observing myself, listening to the *Nirvana Shatakam* etc. I usually walked around a Lakshmi temple in Bangalore. I prayed every day, "My Kailash is right here right now and every step that I take is towards Kailash and that Mother would help me with enough strength always." I sometimes saw a dog walking in front of me for some time, when I felt tired and not so energetic. Sighting the dog would give me strength and joy as I felt he was my master's servant helping me.

I read half of the book 'Kailash with Mohanji' but stopped reading as my mind started expecting miracles. Every night I humbly prayed to Mohanji telling him that I was not expecting anything and happy to go with the flow. I also prayed for a couple of my wishes to come true. 1. I wanted to be able to press Baba's holy feet 2. To do a *parikrama* around him before starting for Mt. Kailash as he is my Kailash.

I had a dream where Baba offered me an opportunity to press his holy feet. I was so much in tears for that is an instant recognition to a devotee. He also hugged me and said, "You are very pure and I am so happy about it." I realized that the pure me doesn't need anything. The real me doesn't have any requirements in life. It is the body and the mind that I am wearing that is behind the emotions and sensations. If only I were able to remember these at all times, it would be the greatest blessing. I was, and still continue to be amazed at how much my guru works on me. The ones mentioned here are only a few such instances.

With so many similar experiences nearing the journey, I was clear about one thing, NO EXPECTATIONS whatsoever and that Baba would take care of everything. But I always prayed to Baba to give me enough strength to WALK the *parikrama* and that he would allow me to do a *parikrama* around him as HE IS MY KAILASH, MY SHIVA, MY GURU, FATHER AND MY

EVERYTHING. Doing a *parikrama* around HIM is equal to doing a *parikrama* around Mt. Kailash.

With constant updates from the Kailash yatra family in the WhatsApp group, I was so happy to learn that Mohanji had arrived at the hotel in Kathmandu, and that he would already be there when we reached the hotel. I got to meet him only during the evening *satsang* on the day we arrived. I was thrilled to be in his presence once again after our meeting in Dec 2015.

Day 1: We visited the Pashupatinath temple, a very old huge temple with a four-faced *shivalinga* as the main deity. Most of us had an opportunity to feed the cows there. For some reason, I felt that it was some '*devata*' in the form of cow as her movements were unusual for a cow. She responded to prayers and gave equal opportunity to all those who fed her. It was a beautiful sight to see how she pleased everyone. A few of us met a *Naga Baba* inside the temple. He blessed each one of us and was the only person among other *sadhus* who did not ask for money. Realizing that he did not take money from anyone, I went to him and got blessed once again. He put his hand on my head and blessed me both times. While walking back to the bus, an old man called me towards him. I walked past ignoring him thinking that he was asking for money. But my intuition guided me to turn back and when I did, he blessed me and gave me a *tulsi* leaf as *prasad*. I wanted to ask Mohanji who those *Naga Babas* were, but refrained as it didn't really matter, for is it not the same consciousness that projects through various identities?

Day 2: We reached Nepalgunj. Baba, during breakfast blessed and gave me postcard-sized pictures of Bhagavan Nityananda of Ganeshpuri and of Swami Vasudevan of Vajreshwari.

Day 3: We reached Simikot and travelled to Hilsa by helicopter. It was on this day that we (my husband and I) got a chance to speak to Baba. It was my husband's star birthday as per the Hindu almanac, and so I had gifted him an *Eka mukhi rudraksha*. We got it blessed by Baba. He hugged both of us and we were in tears. We had nothing to say or ask but the tears were flowing. I will cherish that moment forever. Being in the presence of the Guru, one needs nothing else in life. The mere presence is enough, because unconditional love is in the air. I also expressed that I would like to do a *parikrama* around him. He told me to do it after the dip in Manasarovar.

On the same day we crossed Nepal border and reached Taklakot. In the evening, there was a *satsang*, with Baba explaining the importance of this journey and how we should approach this yatra. Right from the moment I stepped into the presence of Baba, my mind went very quiet. I felt as if it had been taken over by Baba and except for a few necessary thoughts, it was blank. It was quite surprising to have this monkey mind be silent. It was a great relief and a wonderful feeling. Most of us were in tears during this *satsang* as we all felt the Grace of Guru and the blessings of our ancestors that brought us together to undertake this great journey. Most of us showed the first signs of altitude sickness on this day by either having headaches, insomnia, feeling weak etc. I had all - headache, insomnia and sore throat.

Day 4: This day was a day of rest and acclimatization. I had signs of the common cold and was beginning to feel nasal blocks, congestion and difficulty breathing, alongside headaches due to altitude. In the evening after dinner, during a quiet time, I went to Baba, took his blessings and wept my heart out. I prayed that my devotion only increases towards him and shall never wander away from this path. I also expressed my wish to press his feet and he offered me the greatest blessing ever. I was all smiles while pressing his lotus feet and was looking at him speaking to others. I felt I could spend my entire life like this – just looking at him, sitting by his feet and pressing his feet. I told Baba that he offered this blessing to me in my dreams. He immediately answered, "That was not enough for you, so I had to complete it in person now. See what all I have to do." This was the best day of my life.

Day 5: We arrived at Lake Manasarovar. We followed Baba when he entered the lake. All of us broke down into tears of joy/satisfaction/cleansing/emotions (whatever we wanted to call it) the moment we stepped into the lake. In the view of Mt. Kailash, in Lord Shiva's (Mohanji's) presence, in Mother's lap (Lake Manasarovar), this energy was very different. I have no words to express what I witnessed. We had the opportunity of a lifetime in performing *abhisheka* to Mohanji. He was clearly in trance with his RED eyes fixed on Kailash while his physical body was shivering due to the weather and water. It was very much visible that he was not in this dimension.

As Baba advised, I took the first dip for myself surrendering everything at the feet of Mt. Kailash, the second dip for the Guru Parampara, and for the third dip, I called upon all my ancestors who gathered to take a dip with me for cleansing off our lifetimes of karma. I took many more dips for the living, nonliving, Mt. Kailash, for Mother Ganga, for the deities I worship, etc. I did not count the number of dips, but felt I had released all the known/unknown baggage from many lifetimes.

As soon as I emerged from the lake, I saw Baba standing looking at Kailash. I surrendered at his feet. He blessed me and asked me to perform *abhisheka* to Shirdi Baba's idol. At first nothing went into my ears, and he had to repeat it for me. I did as he said with the holy water, then came back and circumambulated Baba, praying that I was doing my Kailash *parikrama* 'now and here' for he is my Kailash, he is my Shiva, he is my Guru and everything to me. I didn't count the number of rounds, but felt so blessed and relieved to be able to complete the *parikramas* around him. He was in deep trance with his eyes fixed on Kailash when I completed my *parikrama*.

While we were arriving by bus to Manasarovar, I had seen six pairs of eyes in the clouds, either looking at me, or looking at the lake or looking at the bus in which Baba was travelling. One set of eyes was clearly Shirdi Baba's and he was looking at me. The others I do not know. After the dip, I asked Baba about those eyes. He acknowledged and explained to me that they were celestial beings looking over us. It was indeed a great experience.

This was followed by a *homa* (fire ritual) performed by Mohanji and three other *swamijis* from Skanda Vale. I felt very sick and couldn't participate in the *homa* for long. I was down with cold, headache and fever, which Mohanji attributed to the cleansing of karma.

Day 6: This was the first day of *parikrama*. I absolutely had no strength due to the altitude sickness. Moreover my nose was completely blocked and I could hardly breathe. I had had absolutely no sleep too due to all the above reasons. I had no confidence to even begin the *parikrama*. I surrendered all my thoughts to Baba and reached Yam Dwar, from where we would begin the *parikrama*. While at Yam Dwar, when others were talking about leaving a piece of cloth or their belonging as a symbol of leaving something behind and being born new, I had an intuitive guidance to leave my body consciousness behind and walk ahead as a soul. I did the same.

I walked the *parikrama* for approximately 30 minutes and every step was very heavy. I was the last person to walk, it was cold, I couldn't breathe and had absolutely no strength. I finally gave up my ego 'to walk the entire *parikrama*' and surrendered to the situation. Going with the flow was the only means and I climbed on top of the pony and completed my first day. During a break midway, I expressed to Baba about the suffering of the horse carrying us. Baba explained that half the karma will go the horse. The reply was satisfying for all the pains the poor beings undergo for us. Upon reaching Dirapuk, I took blessings from Baba and had a chance to be in his presence for a few minutes. (We both were the first to reach Dirapuk from our group, where we had the closest view of majestic Kailash). Baba showed me the 'M' on Kailash. I said that I was able to see another face nearby. Baba said, "That is Hanumanji meditating." He also showed me Garuda in the sky. I was happy for the presence of Lord Vishnu in the form of Garuda. But nothing excited me more than the presence of my master. I was overjoyed to be in the presence of my Guru, my gigantic Kailash forever, in front of the Majestic Kailash.

As we progressed to the night, I was becoming much weaker. I could hardly take a step and had lost all will power to do the *parikrama* Day 2. I bowed down to Kailash for underestimating the journey and Mt. Kailash itself. A couple of pilgrims were being sent back the next morning to base camp Darchen due to their health conditions. I was also contemplating going back. My condition was such that I was shivering with six layers of clothing (two layers of thermals, two layers of t-shirt, two jackets). I could not even tie my shoelaces. Even removing the gloves or wearing them felt like a humongous task. I was coughing, my nostrils were blocked, my chest congested and I was barely breathing. Here, I express my humble gratitude to Preethi, Madhu, Tina and my husband for taking care of me, bringing me food and special mention to Preethi for the very timely help of putting on two more layers of socks and boots.

With too many thoughts about continuing my *parikrama* further, I surrendered at the feet of Baba to help me. I was even prepared to go back if it was HIS WILL. I played the *Shiva Kavacham* by Mohanji and lay in bed helpless. After an hour, I felt a bit better and warm. I removed one layer and tried resting.

Day 7: Day 2 *Parikrama*: Due to cold weather, altitude and my chest congestion, I couldn't sleep the whole night. I kept coughing, moving and sitting in the bed. When we were called for breakfast, I decided that I would do whatever Baba says and not have any second thoughts about it. After my breakfast, I had *darshan* of Baba. I took his blessings and cried hugging him to give me strength. He said, "I bless you, I am with you." Those were the words I wanted to hear. I took it as the command to proceed and hopped on to the horse. Climbing the Dolma La Pass was difficult even for the porter and the horse who were very much acclimatized to the altitude and used to climbing such steep climbs. If I were to make it by foot, I wouldn't have completed the parikrama, which was very evident. I was in so much gratitude for the horse and porter for helping me out and blessed the horse with more strength throughout the journey. I kept chanting '*Om Namah Shivaya*' throughout my journey on the horse.

We had to climb down by foot from the peaks of Dolma La Pass. The view of Gauri Kund was refreshing. I had no strength to climb down Gauri Kund and so I prayed to Mother to bless me with her nectar (Holy water). It was a steep and slippery climb down. Half way through, with porter and pony nowhere to be found, I held onto my trekking poles on either side, as Lord Shiva on one side and Mohanji on the other, chanting Mohanji's *Gayatri* all through my way.

Somehow I lost my way and was on an alternative path which was very very steep and slippery. I was stranded midway unable to take the next step. I had no strength to climb all the way up and change to the right path, from where my husband was waving his hand. I was chanting Mohanji's *Gayatri* to help me climb down. Suddenly from nowhere, a teenage boy appeared, took my hand and helped me take the next few steps. Meanwhile one of the organizers found me stranded and helped me all the way down. At one very steep step, my toe nail hit the edge of the boot very hard and it caused a lot of pain. (After our return to Melbourne, I noticed that I had a black blood clot on my toe nail. It still exists in dark red colour at the time of writing this. I took a picture of it and was telling my husband that perhaps this was the only physical proof that I really completed the *parikrama* in Mt. Kailash. Else it still feels like a dream). I had tears in my eyes for it was Mohanji who had come in the form of a teenage boy and the organizer to help me climb down. His words, "I am with you" lingered in my ears for he had kept his promise. I surrendered at the feet of the organizer saying, he is my Shiva who came to my rescue. Were it not for him, I wouldn't have reached Zuthulphuk in full form. It still feels like a dream that I was able to complete day 2 for all the health issues I had during the morning hours.

Having completed the second day with so much of Grace visible during every step, we had a mini *satsang* with our roomies in Zuthulphuk. Many people opened up and shared their experiences with Mohanji with moist eyes and we listened with awe. One of the roomies offered the Gauri Kund water, as an answer to my prayer to Mother. We slept with contented hearts, looking forward to the next and last day of *parikrama*.

Day 8: Day 3 of *parikrama*: I felt a little better today, the altitude being more tolerable and knowing that the difficult day was past. I still had difficulty breathing due to cold and cough. But it was manageable. Because we had to reach Nepal border as soon as possible, we left early that day. I took the horse for three quarters of the distance. The last quarter, I walked with so much energy. Reached the end of parikrama, where we would be picked by our bus and taken to our base camp. Most of us or all those who I spoke to, felt it was like a miracle that we really completed the *parikrama*.

The descending journey was very quick. We reached our base camp, had lunch and left for Taklakot. We picked our bags, reached the China immigration and reached Hilsa (Nepal border). Because the weather was bad and the helicopter services to Simikot stop by 6.30 pm, 14 of us were held back at Hilsa. Though the place had the bare minimum comfort like no electricity, 9 people sharing one small room, 40-50 people sharing one functional toilet, water seeping from toilet into the room and wetting the beds where the men slept, it was also one of the best nights we had. No one had any complaints.

We shared a lot of jokes, making comments about each other, had a mini *satsang* of sorts with each of us sharing our experiences and connection with Mohanji, miracles that he had performed and miracles that we heard of. Stories about Swami Bhaktananda, his connection with Mohanji, how he became his *parambhakt* etc. were also shared. It was very evident that Baba is beyond physical dimension and he exists everywhere as a consciousness. He is available to us at all times of need. I felt like he was a part of the conversation and has been witnessing all our chats/experiences. It is a wonderful feeling.

Day 9: At the first sound of a chopper arriving, we all jumped into packing our bags to take the ride, only to learn that it was not ours. Also we kept receiving information that the weather condition was bad at Simikot that the helicopter services could be cancelled any time. After waiting for a couple of hours in uncertainty, we started chanting Mohanji's *Gayatri* to get us to Simikot safely. After just 15-20 minutes of intense chanting, we saw 3 choppers in total arriving one after the other and all fourteen of us were picked up at one go. On the way I saw huge mountains and all of them represented "M", letting us know of his Grace. At

Simikot, we joined the other group who left the previous day. We all travelled together to Nepalgunj. It was surprising to know that all other flights after ours were cancelled due to bad weather. We felt blessed for the Grace: his magic hands were on this too and made sure we all reached safely. We had smooth travel from here on and reached Kathmandu on the same day at night.

Day 10: Bidding goodbye to the M family was one of the most difficult things. We all left wanting to meet up with this family once again for a different cause. Some of us extended our stay in Kathmandu for a couple more days. It being a full moon day, my husband and I decided to visit the Pashupatinath temple in the evening (a small urge to meet those *Naga Babas* again). The temple was very crowded as they had *bhog* for full moon day and there was *aarthi* done for Baramati River. We couldn't find those Babas anywhere inside. As we came out of the temple, we heard sounds of bells, conch and *damaru*. We had an amazing *darshan* of an *Aghori Baba* with his disciples doing pooja to *trishul* (pyre) and singing *aarthi* songs. We waited until the *aarthi* was over and prostrated at the feet of the *Aghori Baba*. He blessed us with sacred ashes from the pyre. It was at the end that I came to know that he belonged to the Dattatreya (Nath) tradition. I was in heaps of joy at learning this for it meant that it was indeed Baba who had given us such a blessing.

Day 11: Ananth left for Melbourne by a different flight while I was still in Kathmandu. Deep inside, I had a small desire to meet Baba, if the Inner Kora team would be back before I left for Melbourne. Though they were supposed to arrive two days later, my intuition kept telling me that they would arrive the next day. Around evening, I got the message from the Inner Kora team through WhatsApp that they would be reaching Kathmandu the next day, but not sure of the time. With my flight late in the night, I prayed that I meet Baba as a completion of my Kailash journey and that he would fulfill my wish.

Day 12: I packed my bags around noon and awaited the message from the Inner Kora team on their arrival. When they were at Nepalgunj, my heart jumped with joy that they would be in Kathmandu in a few hours. We (Warren from SA team and I) went to the Hotel Soaltee awaiting their arrival. When I saw Baba entering the hotel, I ran to him, sought his blessing and hugged him tight. He fulfilled my wish. My *parikrama* was completed only then. Meeting the other members of the Inner Kora team felt great as we missed them from Day 2 of our *parikrama*. A few of us had this great blessing of being with Baba for a couple more hours while he had his lunch. He acknowledged to all of us that he kept his word and did what he promised. He looked at me and said, "I know you weren't sure you would complete the *parikrama*, but I did what I said." The Inner Kora team then explained how difficult their journey had been and how Baba's Grace had saved them at every step. We all listened with awe when the team explained how almost each of their steps was a life and death situation. I also had a shaktipaat blessing from Mohanji along with the SA group. I left the hotel feeling blissful and contented at meeting him.

With my mind still in Kailash, there are a few takeaways from this trip:

1. Throughout my journey, I kept my faith intact, reminding myself of Baba's words, "If your faith is taller than Kailash, you will be able to complete the journey". It was indeed very true. Mt. Kailash is possible only through faith and Grace.

2. All of us felt that it is HE who walked the entire journey for us and it was impossible for us otherwise.

3. With only 40% of people completing the *parikrama* every year, our group has over 90% success rate, which was only possible because of Mohanji.

4. No matter how much your preparation, Kailash will test your faith. Surrender is the only means to survive in the Land of Gods.

5. It is impossible to understand or fit Baba into the frames. He is beyond physical dimensions and logical understanding. It is purely through faith and

surrender that one will be able to feel at least a glimpse of what he really is. What he does behind the scenes and how much we are blessed is something that we cannot even comprehend with our little brains.

6. In the midst of tall mountains reaching up to the sky, we are not even the size of a mustard seed. It is a constant reminder that nature is bigger and more powerful than us. Respect Mother Nature.
7. When your desires are pure, non-material and selfless, the master comes down to fulfill it.
8. Mohanji says, you need not come to me, I come to you. I realized this all the way.
9. With Baba's blessing I got to experience fasting and realized that we do not need so much food to live.
10. Surrender everything at the Lord's feet for HE knows. I am truly blessed.

Gratitude

- Shyama Jayaseelan -

Mohanji visited Canada after the 2014 Kailash yatra and our family was blessed to see and spend time with Him there. It was an unexpected gift and we were very happy. At that time we had asked Mohanji if we could go to Kailash with Him on the next *yatra*. Mohanji replied saying it could happen, and all that was needed was Lord Shiva's Grace.

Just as Mohanji said, with Lord Shiva's Grace, everything fell into place smoothly. Taking time off work, the children going off to Canada, our cats being looked after by my parents, and with no health issues ourselves, our trip was being taken care of by divine hands.

We had dropped the three *swamis* from Skanda Vale at Heathrow the week before our departure. It was a privilege to spend time with them before our trip. A week later, we too left from Heathrow along with a few others travelling from the UK. We were all so excited to be part of what was going to be the sacred trip of a lifetime. We met Mohanji and some of the other *yatris* in Delhi and flew to Kathmandu.

Visiting the Buddhist and Hindu temples with Mohanji was amazing. Being in His presence anywhere is so wonderful, and I was cherishing every moment. At the famous Pashupatinath temple, a holy man covered in ashes and long matted hair suddenly walked up to me and placing his hand on my head, blessed me beautifully. I felt as if it was Lord Shiva Himself, with fierce eyes and *jata mudi*!

The flights to Nepalgunj and Simikot were fairly quick. From Simikot to Hilsa, the helicopter rides meant waiting for hours. Although tired, everyone was in good spirit and we were sharing some of our experiences with Mohanji. I was one of the last to take the helicopter to Hilsa. The beauty of the mountains and valleys was breathtaking. However, for someone who does not like heights, it was a time spent in prayers! Then we crossed the China border and took a coach to Taklakot. It was late night when we got there and Mohanji gave us all dried fruit and nuts, while waiting for dinner to be made.

After a day of rest, we went to Manasarovar for our first *darshan* of Kailash. Before the trip, I was praying to Mohanji that I should be able to touch His feet in the sacred waters of Manasarovar. Not only was my wish granted, I was able to do *abhisheka* to him as well by pouring a little water on Him. After doing my offerings and a few dips, I had the additional blessing of Mohanji pouring water on my head three times too! I felt so much joy and humility at such amazing Grace from our wonderful Guru. We chanted the *Rudram* at the banks of Manasarovar, facing Mount Kailash. What a privilege!

We all did *abhisheka* to Mohanji's idol of Shirdi Sai. Mohanji and the three *swamis* did a beautiful *havan*, in which we all were able to take part as well. The clouds near Kailash took on divine shapes during the *havan*. Until the time of leaving Manasarovar, I was able to cope with the high altitude. By the time we got to Darchen, the lack of oxygen was making me quite ill. I was breathless and my heart rate was pretty high. With poor appetite, it was a struggle to eat anything too. The next day, on the first day of *parikrama*, we chose our porter/pony and went through Yam Dwar. After walking for just a few minutes, I felt too ill to continue. I took the pony, feeling quite sad as I had wanted to do the *parikrama* on foot as much as possible. Suddenly one of the many dogs we saw, started to trot next to my pony, keeping me company for nearly an hour. I felt cheered by his company. Halfway through, I stopped at the tea house for a rest, and Mohanji who was there too, asked how I was. It was great to see Him and we also had *prasad* from His food. The *darshan* of Kailash on this first day was truly wonderful. That evening we chanted *Rudram*, with Kailash so very near us, bathing us with divine energy!

Before beginning the *parikrama* on the second day, Mohanji gave me a hug and said "Bless you". His loving blessing gave me the strength to complete the hardest day of our journey. After climbing up the Dolma La Pass, we saw Gauri Kund below us. How beautiful to see the waters where Ma Parvati bathes! The stay that night was at Zithulphuk, in another guest house. The third day of *parikrama* was the easiest. We set off in the darkness before dawn broke, and as the sun arose, the beauty of the majestic mountains, valleys and rivers kept us enthralled. I had seen a few small birds and animals along the way, but was really surprised to see a cream/gold colour dog amongst all the darker ones. She was so beautiful!

What joy it was to meet up with everyone at the end. As I stood chatting with the other pilgrims, a little bird decided to sit on my head for a few seconds. I would like to think that it was a little pat on the head by Mohanji saying, 'well done you made it', but I think she may have perhaps wanted my woolly hat for her nest!

Our trip back from Kailash was also eventful. Physically, I was feeling better as we travelled to lower altitudes. Thirteen from the group had to stay back in Hilsa due to bad weather. That night was so joyous. We passed it in chanting, praying and sharing experiences. Despite the small difficulties during the trip, with the Grace of Lord Shiva, Mohanji and the Masters, our *yatra* was completed with so much love, blessings and divine Grace. The stillness and innocence of Lord Shiva was truly felt in the presence of Kailash. I was filled with gratitude, devotion and surrender during the whole trip, especially during the three days of *parikrama*.

My heartfelt gratitude to all my beautiful companions for their endless love and support. The support of the sherpas, porters and ponies was such a blessing. I have no words to express my gratitude to Mohanji for His love, compassion and blessings. I offer my loving and humble *pranams* at His lotus feet.

The Journey Of My Life

- Vesna Bogdanov Štark -

I THOUGHT IT WAS impossible. It happened though.
Travelling to another part of the world.
So many books where Kathmandu is mentioned. So many spiritual seekers who come to this city and continue their journey further, most often to the Himalayas. It seems that this place for many people represents an entrance door to further their spiritual journey. We set off on this journey as well.

We arrive at a magnificent hotel surrounded by the park of one's dreams. What a city! What to say? Three million inhabitants, and no traffic lights. Yet everything goes smoothly. They respect each other and do not abuse each other's trust. We go to a huge temple complex including the Vishnu Temple. We feed the animals. Cremation of the dead near the bank of the river. Meditation with sadhus in a small temple.

Another hotel, and tonight I sleep in a room with strangers. Why am I separated from our small group from Serbia? The answer to this question comes soon. I share the room with two wonderful women, one of them being Riana from South Africa. She helps me pack only the necessary things in an organised manner and leave the unnecessary ballast behind, and she also gives me some golden tips. I am very grateful for all that.

Flights on board small planes and helicopters follow. In my heart I have already been flying for a long time, now I fly with my body as well. Magnificent scenery! The Himalayas! We land among the ruins with a couple of small houses nearby where you may have a rest. Our bodies start reacting to the sudden change of altitude. Mohanji is with us and his very presence makes our acclimatisation easier. We are all here. We proceed.

Crossing from Nepal to Tibet along the suspension bridge which swings in the wind above the troubled waters flowing through the canyon. The scene resembles the one from the Indiana Jones series. Colorful prayer flags are fluttering along the bridge adding to the beauty of the scenery.

Then follows a day of rest – acclimatisation. Many people have minor or major problems. We drag ourselves along the corridors and barely manage to climb the stairs. We help each other.

Mohanji and Devi's energy is surrounding us. Devi tirelessly goes from one person to another, and the resulting changes are incredible. I had the opportunity to experience the effect of it. "How pure you are," says Devi to me. Thank you. It means a lot to me.

Satsang. Mohanji gives us instructions and tips about our inner ritual bath at the sacred lake Manasarovar. The following night is very difficult for some of us.

Morning. We continue our journey. What scenery! The colours! The play of sunlight and shadow is quite different here. Everything seems unreal! Marvellous! Lake Rakshastal. Steep descent. Prayer rocks and wind-dishevelled ribbons. Smiling faces. Taking photos to document the memories. We continue our journey.

We see Mount Kailash for the first time! Partially wrapped in clouds it rises above Manasarovar Lake.

We come to the bank of the sacred Manasarovar Lake! Everything happens fast.

Mohanji enters the icy-cold lake and makes it accessible to us. However, during the first dip my body is so shocked with the coldness that I take a deep breath and reflexively gulp some quantity of water. Excitement. Here I am! Here and now! C'mon, pull yourself together. A look at Mohanji and the people around me. I pull myself together and continue with the dips... Mohanji's blessing... My heart rules over my mind!

We are warming up on the bank of this majestic lake. Warm sand. The sun. The whole of Mount Kailash is now clearly visible overlooking the landscape.

Only now do I realise that the two Indians from our group are still in the lake. They took 108 dips?!! Is that even possible?

A small statue of Babaji is in the lake. We wash him with sacred water! What a feeling! As if he were here with us!

Homa. A great ritual. Setting up fire... Prayers... Mantras... We are all united here...

We slowly pack our things, walk around the lake that offers unforgettable images and impressions because of which we are going to carry this holy and majestic experience forever in our hearts.

We start the *kora* around the divine, remarkable, unique, marvelous, simply unreal sacred Mount Kailash! Lord Shiva resides here!

That morning we gather to get our sherpas and mountain horses. Right in front of me a ritual is being carried out by the sherpas who shout and crack jokes, before they let us pick a slip of paper out of a hat with a name of a "lucky winner" on it!

So I get a young sherpa and a beautiful white little horse. I promise myself that I shall go on foot for as long as I am able to, but also that I will carefully consider my age and how tired I might feel. I notice the huge gap between my rapid-fire temperament, and the unavoidable slow pace with frequent rest breaks. In addition, a sherpa who keeps asking me to climb the horse. Eventually I do it. How things would have developed had I not complied, I will never know.

A part of the route I trek beside Mohanji. In this bliss, I am overwhelmed by the huge amount of love, happiness and gratitude, and can sense the positive vibrations of this landscape of extraordinary beauty. The mountains surrounding us are impressive, each of them with different structure, colour and shape. A small stream formed of snow melting from the mountain tops, accompanies us along our way.

The vibes are unbelievable. Each moment that one's eyes meets someone else's is precious and full of understanding, most often accompanied by a smile. These are people I have never seen before, from all parts of the world, and yet such a feeling of closeness.

All around us in the mountains one can see the images of faces carved into the rocks.

And then, suddenly, a huge, imposing Kailash, so close, yet so far away.

I cannot believe that we are going to spend a night in such a place, at the foot of the mountain! What a view! All-black rock, the northern side covered with snow.

Our whole team is in the room! Night falls. I wake up very early before dawn, with the words, 'Have you come here to sleep?' ringing in my head! I sit up and start meditating, and since that moment everything in a way becomes different and easier.

In the morning we continue our trip. More out of habit I mount my horse and continue the journey. When after some time I get off the horse and start to walk again, matching my step with the *Om Namah Shivaya* mantra, I feel as if I am flying! Since that moment, that very day and the following day my legs seem to carry me of their own accord. Or maybe I only got acclimatised to the altitude at that point? It doesn't matter. I have a feeling of something carrying me and I move fast. At a magnificent pace. As if I were flying!

I come to the end of the route and the gathering place. Only a few of us have arrived. We congratulate one another with gleaming smiles. We did it! We are all here. Taking pictures. We say goodbye to our sherpas and beautiful horses, who are in a stampede, and shouting merrily, start down the valley. In front of us there is a huge plain, still in shadow, surrounded with the mountains bathing in the sunshine.

We wonder - how is that part of our group who separated from us to travel closer to the majestic Kailash mountain, feeling now?

They had told us the climb would be difficult and gruelling. So we send them lots of positive energy.

We are leaving...

Again we go through a magnificent landscape. The lakes are immense, they resemble the sea. All around are mountains bathing in majestic sunrays which seem to be falling at unusual angles, emphasizing the slopes and turning them into the most beautiful masterpiece of Nature.

We return to the same hotel in which we had roamed about at snail's speed when we first arrived. Now we run skipping up the stairs! Is it possible? Maybe if we had gotten more time to acclimatise, a day or two...

The journey continues... The places are now familiar to us...

Helicopter again. I know! The feeling and the image resemble my former but frequent dreams in which I would fly all night long. I muse - how much time would be needed, and could we at all pass the places we fly through, if there were no helicopters?

We land. The weather changes. It is cloudy and the visibility poor. No helicopters and planes are flying any more. We stay put. We are not supposed to sleep here. It starts raining and mud is everywhere.

A vehicle comes soon to take us through a poor, yet very vivid place. Where are we going? Around us we see slums in a very poor state. The environment is not a promising one. But then... we arrive at a beautiful, large house which is in fact a hotel. Bravo to the people who organised the travel!! Nothing can faze them. Thirteen of us in a large, nice room in the attic! We are chatting merrily and happily, and after a warm and delicious meal we drift into quiet sleep.

The morning resembles the evening, the weather rainy and gloomy. We gather in the covered part of the yard and chant mantras...

The sky clears up. We continue our journey. A plane... a bus...

Kathmandu. The same hotel and the same room. A wonderful bathroom! Taking a shower. The following day we scatter and everyone travels back to his own destination. We make arrangements to visit the Buddha Temple and walk around the city, because our flight isn't until the evening.

Morning. Breakfast. The return to our rooms. A question: "You wouldn't like to return?" Suddenly I burst into uncontrollable tears . . . I can't stop . . . I stay in the hotel . . . I am crying for a long, long time. A return to the so-called civilisation! To the Western world burdened with aggression, alienation, anxiety, recklessness, arrogance, misunderstanding, insincerity, breakneck speed and way of life, depletion of natural resources . . . Wars and violence, how much they affect me emotionally! It all hurts me unbearably! I have the same feeling actress Milla Jovovich had while watching a brief history of mankind in the film 'The Fifth Element'.

Such a wonderful planet, yet what its people are like!

A woman enters my hotel room saying that I should not worry, that I am in a safe place and that I may stay there as long as I need to. She brings me a box of tissues and leaves me alone. Thank you. It takes me a long time to calm down.

Reflections . . . .

Now after much time had passed I feel that I have changed. Somehow I am better able to manage getting away from certain situations, viewing them more objectively. A recognisable impulse, the unnecessary one, has grown weaker, followed by a desirable solution. I surprise myself with my positive and good reactions. I view things with a different perspective. I am calm. Happy and satisfied. Around me are people who I love. Those who have given me support. I am thankful for all them, but first of all I am thankful for my husband.

Thank you, Mohanji!

Kailash And Badrinath – My Experiences

- Vidya Rajagopalan -

I KNEW THAT MOHANJI would be making a trip to Kailash in 2016 and while it is always my desire to be with him on any pilgrimage or retreat, little did I think that I would actually make this one!! I have attended retreats previously and consider myself very fortunate to have spent some time with Father thus. This association has brought about changes from within. I have become more aware of my feelings and also started appreciating more often the many blessings in life. I have heard Mohanji (or Father, as he is affectionately called), often say, "Catch the thread of life", and am beginning to understand what that means, after my most recent trip to Kailash and Badrinath!

My brother and sister-in-law had plans to go on this epic journey and while I did love the idea, I was very doubtful if I could do it. During a Skype *satsang*, Rajesh (Kamath) suggested I submit my application and let things take their course. Though I did and was approved, I had not discussed the details at home. I silently prayed for everything to work out.

I attended the retreat at Yogaville, VA in April 2016. There, I heard about the trip to Badrinath too and requested Father to bless me with this trip in August. He said none could go unless 'He' wills it and asked me to chant *Om Namah Shivaya* 500,000 times. I was

Kailash And Badrinath – My Experiences

also blessed with *Kriya* initiation during this trip to Yogaville. I started chanting in earnest and also tried to keep up with *Kriya* practice.

We started some renovation work around the house and I remember trying to squeeze in time to do the *Kriya* and chanting. During these months, there were two instances when there were small fire accidents, both in the *puja* area and one directly in front of Mohanji's picture. I had a feeling these were blessings taking away larger problems and then happened to read Arpana's blog, where the very small fire in her house indeed prevented a larger accident from happening, and this was explained by Mohanji himself. Content in this knowledge, I continued to chant and go for brisk walks in preparation for the longer journey in August!

Buying Hiking shoes

It was time to buy hiking boots and it took a while to understand the requirements since the trek would be in terrain and weather that I had no idea about! The Kailash team was very helpful. Listening to the long audio recording discussing everything from shoes and socks to layers of clothing and snack ideas, I realized this was going to be a tough trip. None of the shoes I tried on seemed to fit. Either they were too expensive or the right size was out of stock. I was trying to find the time to shop for shoes in the midst of home renovations, remember? Just when I was getting frustrated, my brother suggested an online site and even picked a few shoes for me to try out. What a blessing this turned out to be! I picked out two shoes, tried them on and chose a comfortable one, all from home, because this was a mail order website! I was so thankful for this experience.

My flight to India

Time rolled by and I was trying to book tickets for the trip. I was fervently praying for budget pricing, since I was planning to take my children to India too. I was able to find a good deal via Turkish

Airlines and I booked my tickets. My parents graciously agreed to take care of my kids while I undertook this pilgrimage. There was a Skype *satsang* planned with Father on the Sunday before Wednesday, the day I was to leave for India. It also turned out that now there was political turmoil in Turkey, and I began wondering about its repercussions on my layover in Istanbul.

The *satsang* was beautiful as always. Towards the end, I was able to talk to Mohanji. I sought his blessings and also mentioned my flight via Turkish Airlines. He immediately asked me to look for alternative routes and added that they would have to refund my flight cost, if the flight were to be canceled. Right after the *satsang* ended, I looked at the news and sure enough FAA (Federal Aviation Authority, USA) had grounded all Turkish Air flights into USA until September! I started looking for safer alternatives and booked my ticket with Air India. I was hoping to get a refund of the Turkish Airlines tickets soon. It was a sum of about USD 3000! A couple of weeks passed by, and I received an email confirmation from the Airlines. The actual refund came a few weeks later, just after my trip to Kailash was completed! What is fascinating is that my flight was scheduled for July 20, 2016 at 11.55 pm. That was the last day Turkish Airlines was refunding tickets. FAA lifted its ban, and flights from July 21st onwards via Turkish Airlines did not receive a refund. Thus my refund was processed because of a 5 minute difference in flight departure time! Isn't this a miracle?

My trip to Badrinath

I reached India and soon left for Delhi to make our onward journey to Badrinath. Our visit to Haridwar, a dip in Har Ki Pauri, bus trips with the three *swamis* from Skanda Vale, UK, filled with *bhajans* and friendly interaction with fellow group members were indeed memorable. We reached Pipalkoti and halted for the night. That's when we learned from Mamu (Mr. Narinder Rohmetra, affectionately called Mamu by all) that there had been landslides along the route and that the bus we had traveled in could not take us all the way to Badrinath. We would have to trek a short distance and reach Badrinath via jeeps from there on.

When I came to know that Father was already in Badrinath, waiting for us, I packed my backpack with enthusiasm and we left the next morning. As expected, there was a short stretch that we had to hike. There were shooting stones and a stretch of road was covered with water! Our shoes and socks were drenched, but we walked across. The sights all around were beautiful, and so was the jeep ride to Badrinath. We reached the hotel and saw Mohanji! I was filled with immense joy!

Later that evening we visited the temple. We walked across a bridge over the fast-moving and loud Alakananda River. The entire place felt magical. As the bus/jeep climbed up the hills, I felt I could hear the mountains hum '*Om*', but in the temple it was even more powerful! Mohanji said that we should soak in the energy of the place and do as many *parikramas* as we could. My aunt Usha and I decided to do 108 and I consider it a blessing to have completed it!

In the temple, when I first stood in front of Lord Badri Vishaal, I felt an intense draw and connection. It was so powerful and hard to explain in words, that I did not even notice Father entering. But Father being Father asked me to stay where I was and continue my *darshan*. There were hardly any pilgrims in the temple and our group was the only one! Perhaps the landslides made it difficult for buses to ply. But I have come to realize that every temple visit with Father fills us with inexplicable satisfaction and the experience is enhanced manifold! The next day we were to participate in the early morning puja when Lord Badri Vishaal is adorned with clothes and jewels and crown (*mukut*). While we waited to be ushered in, Father chanted the *Vishnu Sahasranama* and we joined in. There was a light rain as if to bless us, signifying acceptance of our prayer! We spent three hours inside the temple in front of the Lord, chanted *Vishnu Sahasranama* and watched the *abhisheka* and *alankara*. Divine bliss and a blessing!

We came out of the temple and saw Father talking to someone near the *havankund*. Soon, we sat down around the *havan kund* and assisted by a priest, Mohanji was performing a *Vishnu*

Sahasranama homa! And I was sitting right next to him, along with many others and placing offerings in the *kund*! Blessed again!

After this we met the Rawal – chief priest of the temple and received *prasad* from him. We were able to see a sketch of Lord Badri Vishaal with four arms. At the temple I had not been able to see this clearly. The Rawal always hails from Kerala, as was laid down by Sri Adi Shankaracharya some centuries ago. I learnt about how Shankaracharya retrieved the Badri Vishaal idol from Narad Kund and established the *pooja vidhi* (procedures). The reason I mention this is that I realized how Saivite and Vaishnavite energies merge for our greater good!

The same day, we had the good fortune of climbing up to Charan Paduka, the place where Lord Vishnu meditated as a young boy and where his feet are engraved on a rock. As we climbed up the mountain with Father, the hum of '*Om*' could be heard and the sight of the indigenous Indian cows and calves (which are shorter than other breeds) grazing happily is one that I will cherish. He gave some fruit to the cows and I did too. There is a small shrine near a rock on which are carved Lord Vishnu's feet. We placed our forehead on it and prayed. Mohanji asked us to chant the Sanskrit *shloka*.

> '*kaayena vaachaa manasendriyairvaa, budhyaatmanaa vaa prakrutesvabhaavaath,*
>
> *karomi yadhyat sakalam parasmai shriman Narayanaa yeti samarpayaami.*'

It means that whatever we do using our sense organs and other faculties, we offer everything at the lotus feet of Lord Narayana. As I sat around enjoying the experience, Mohanji commented, "If you stay much longer, you will not want to go back to USA!" And of course that was true. I felt that the mountains had an indescribable charm; words fail to capture the pure joy I felt there. This was followed by a visit to Hanuman Baba and his small temple of Hanumanji and Lord Shiva and then we descended the hill. As we did, we saw Hanumanji's face in the mountains, in the midst of the rocks and the greenery! The bath in the thermal springs of Tapta Kund is purifying and I was able to do this on two days! We were also blessed with *darshan* of *aarti* at night, when all ornaments are removed and the Lord is covered with a clean white *dhoti*. Every *darshan* was intense and I feel blessed to have been there.

The next morning we began our descent from Badrinath, the mountains still humming the '*Om*' I had heard on the way up. The entire region is called Dev Bhoomi – land of the Devas and that is indeed true. The majestic Ganga winds down the entire stretch of the road and views were incredibly picturesque! We were forced to halt for a while because a stretch of road that had been destroyed by a landslide, was being relayed! Some of us walked up to see the construction and noticed the thin stretch of road left behind after a large chunk had fallen off into the valley below. Those seated along the window recalled that many a time they had seen themselves at the very edge of level ground, as the bus traversed the narrow roads; in other words, the bus was only just about staying on the road!

We halted for the night and enjoyed a *satsang* that evening. The next day we traveled further, stopping at Devprayag where the rivers Alakananda and Bhagirathi merge and the Ganga is formed. The confluence of the two rivers is a sight fit for the Gods (*Devas*) and is rightly called Devprayag. There is another significance to it, I learnt – that it was symbolic of the meeting of the *ida* and *pingala naadis*, according to Yoga Shastra. It is a blessing to merely look at the *prayag* or confluence, and I was fortunate enough to also be able to take a dip and also offer prayers to the gods and my ancestors in the water, with the help of a priest in the area.

The next stop was at the ashram of the Late Swami Purshottamananda. His disciple, Swami Chaitanyananda, who managed the ashram was very old and had great affection for Mohanji. We took a dip in the Ganga which flows along the ashram and sought the Swamiji's blessings. The Ashram also has Vasishta and Arundhati *guhas* (caves). Since it was the monsoon season, there was a lot of water in the river and we could not visit the Arundhati cave. But we did sit down for a while in meditation inside the Vasishta Guha. The cave has *shivalingas* and is very quiet. It was a calm and serene environment and I meditated for a while. The ashram is quite close to Rishikesh and we next visited the Shivananda Ashram at Rishikesh. We meditated at the huge prayer hall and were fortunate to take the blessings of an old *swami* there. We also went down to the *ghat*. It was closed, so we could only see the Ganga, now a wide and calm river, gently flowing along, much in contrast to the Ganga we had seen while coming down the hills!

Complete with *bhajans*, the bus journey was memorable. We reached Haridwar and later left for New Delhi. I left the place a tad sad that the trip to Badrinath was over, but then was also looking forward to our Kailash trip next!!!

Journey to Kailash

Our journey to Kailash was from Delhi via various cities/towns in Nepal - Kathmandu, Nepalgunj, Simikot, Hilsa and finally across the border to Taklakot/Purang, Tibet! It was exciting to arrive at Kathmandu and drive through the streets to the lovely hotel.

It was August 9th, 2016. All of us had assembled in the large hall to meet together for the first time and understand what the journey would entail. Father spoke about previous experiences and explained the significance of the *yatra*. It was heartening when he added that Shiva had blessed us and given permission. "Go into silence to experience the stillness", was his message. This was followed by a briefing by the tour organizer, Kailash Trek Pvt. Ltd. The chief tour guide had visited Kailash 57 times and had even completed the Inner Kora four times. He had some practical tips for all of us.

The next morning, we visited the Pashupatinath and Budhanilkantha temples. We had darshan of Lord Pashupatinath and also prayed at the other *sannidhis* in the temple. The Bagmati river flows near the temple and in hopes of spiritual salvation, people cremate loved ones nearby. We also saw some people performing the last rites and rituals on the *ghats*. We joyfully fed

Kailash And Badrinath – My Experiences

grains to pigeons and cows along with Father and then hurriedly left for Budhanilkantha, since we were to leave for Nepalgunj later that afternoon. The temple is located outside the city amidst mountains. It was a picturesque day with beautiful clouds. Lord Vishnu lay on Adisesha (the serpent) with His *shankha* (conch), *chakra* (discus), *gadha* (mace) and *Padma* (lotus) in a pool of water and I was praying to him for safe completion of the trip, when I received a call. Surprised, I spoke and found that it was from the tour organizer regarding my passport for Chinese visa processing! They needed it immediately and here I was, at the temple far away from the hotel where he was! I fervently prayed to Lord Vishnu that all should go well. We prayed at the altar for Mahalakshmi next. The priest gave us *teertha* or holy water and blessed us saying '*shubh yatra*'. We hurriedly returned to the hotel and I handed in the passport and photos to the tour organizer. Later, I learned that my visa had been processed as a 'special' case!

We reached Nepalgunj that afternoon and it was an 18-seater aircraft! I have had a long standing fear of flying in very small planes but I think I overcame that during this flight! It was a smooth ride. Our trip to Simikot and then to Hilsa was to be the next day. We all reached Simikot and next was the helicopter ride to Hilsa. These are remote, hilly towns in Nepal and I enjoyed the beauty of the mountains as we moved along from one place to another.

Helicopter ride

We seated ourselves in the helicopter. It was a beautiful ride, breathtaking scenery and a chopper ride was something I had always wished for! We were flying between mountains, which were densely covered by trees with rivers and streams winding through them. Some of these streams were still frozen and the mountain air was crisp and cool. As we flew further, the mountains started to look more barren and there was even a slight drizzle. We took a few photographs.

Suddenly, I felt the urge to chant Mohanji's *Gayatri* and since

Warren was right next to me, I requested him to join in. We chanted Mohanji's *Gayatri* and as I continued to chant, I could feel tears flowing down and I visualized Mohanji's closed eyes. It felt like the weather was now windy and I wondered if this urge to chant was Mohanji's way of protecting us! Soon we landed and headed to the guest house, where we were welcomed with cups of tea. We were all asked to cover our head, ears and chest. We did and as we drank tea we were laughing and took pictures. Warren even commented that Mohanji must be nearby and since we were so happy, we must be in his aura! And it turned out true. We went into the building and I was delighted to see Father with a few others in a room. Then he smilingly asked me the question, "How was the helicopter ride?" Of course he knew the answer to it! I could only thank him for the experience! I touched his feet and he hugged me. A laughter fest followed, while we waited for the others to arrive and it continued through our lunch session, when we ate our fill of *rotis*, rice and vegetables.

Mohanji healing with Deviji

A little later Deviji came in and I was blessed enough to have Mohanji Healing done by her. As I was waiting she narrated the story of how she had healed a prematurely born baby. Doctors could not medically intervene any further and at that stage Deviji performed Mohanji healing on the baby for about 5 minutes. She explained that since a baby has no ego, it took in all the energy and soon slept peacefully. The parents cried in joy and the father of the baby did the recording of the first Power of Purity meditation.

As Deviji performed the healing on me and worked on all chakras, I could feel a surge of energy flowing in, and saw Shirdi Sai Baba's face and eyes, Mohanji with his eyes closed in meditation and a little later even the *Vishwaroopa* of Lord Vishnu and Mohanji's expanded form! When she completed the healing, she advised me to rest for a while in order to absorb the energy. I did and realized that although I was aware of happenings around me, it was all quite hazy! I rested for quite some time until it was time to leave for Taklakot or Purang, Tibet.

Taklakot

We crossed the river and were in Tibet. There was sparse vegetation all along but a gurgling river flowed by, and there were clumps of bamboo trees on its banks. These and a few greenhouses with a few flowering plants in them filled the otherwise cold barren landscape. It was a beautiful cold desert with snow-capped mountains. We completed immigration and headed to the hotel.

By now we were at 13205 feet and the effects of altitude sickness were showing. My heart was pounding loudly and merely moving around was a task in itself! I asked for priority room allotment and as I was lifting my bag to go towards the hotel room, Mohanji came by and said, "I am right next to you", and proceeded to tell me how to get to the room. When someone tried to help me with my bag, he said, "She is carrying her own karma. Let it be. " It was much later that it dawned on me that though this was his first time at this hotel too, he knew how I should walk to my room!!! I went up to the room and then came downstairs for dinner. Dinner and in general food is very essential to provide the energy to counter altitude sickness. Mohanji stressed on the need to eat and even sent volunteers looking for those that had missed dinner!

The next day was reserved for getting used to the place, weather, altitude and the journey in itself! Mohanji explained the importance of visiting Kailash, where he stressed the need to settle differences with everyone we knew before embarking on this journey. Kailash he said, brings out the real person within us! In the holy Manasarovar Lake we were to take at least 3 dips, one for ourselves, one for our *kula devata* and *ishta devatas* and one for our ancestors.

An interesting talk by Swami Brahmananda of Skanda Vale UK, and later by Sumit, who has accompanied Father on all Kailash trips, were the other highlights of the morning. Swami Brahmananda spoke about the need for being spiritual and the necessity to go within and reflect. He also said that he saw many similarities between his Guru Subramanian Swami and Mohanji. Sumit's narration of his experiences during the *parikrama* and also the difficult descent and ascent to Gauri Kund were very inspiring.

We went out to the market to buy some gloves, sun hats, trekking poles etc. We rested that afternoon and came down for a group *Kriya* session followed by listening to the *Shiva Kavach*. The headache that had been bothering me disappeared after these! This was followed by another impromptu *satsang* with Mohanji and I felt that every word spoken gave direction to my life!

The next morning we got into the buses to take a dip in the holy Manasarovar. The bus ride to Rakshastal and Manasarovar lakes was filled with beautiful sights. The salt water Lake Rakshastal, although very beautiful, true to its name has no vegetation or fish/aquatic life in it. We did not even see birds flying around in that area! The name literally translates to Abode of Demons and is said to be where Ravana prayed to Lord Shiva. We took many pictures there and proceeded further for a dip in the sacred Manasarovar, which is said to have been created by Lord Brahma and is near Mount Kailash. Father had mentioned that further into the lake, the sand feels rubbery under our feet and this is because of the presence of Adisesha who is the *asana* or seat for Lord Vishnu. He added that the energy of Lord Vishnu could also be felt there, besides of course that of Lord Shiva!

We reached the shores of Manasarovar and were spellbound by the serenity of the place. It was a beautiful landscape no doubt, clear blue water and lovely blue skies, but it was also a tranquil atmosphere and the sanctity of the place started sinking in, as we looked beyond to Mount Kailash! *Om Namah Shivaya*! We walked further into the water and the first feeling was indeed of extreme coldness. However I looked ahead to see that Father was already in the water taking dips. Holding onto a few others near me, I moved along. I began taking dips in the cold water while gazing at Kailash with folded hands, and chanting *Om Namah Shivaya*. After the first three dips, I must say I did not feel the cold anymore! I was

Kailash And Badrinath – My Experiences

blessed enough to pour some water on Mohanji and also received his blessing in return. I took 9 dips in all, and that included dips for my *kula devata*, *ishta devata*, my ancestors, my parents, my husband, children, in-laws, all relatives and friends. I was in the lake where the celestials themselves come every morning for their daily dip! These waters were near Mount Kailash. Could I ask for more or feel more blessed, I wondered? I am eternally grateful for the sublime, divine experience.

Slowly I made my way to the shores of the lake and we quickly changed into dry clothes in temporary tents erected by the tour organizers. Mohanji had advised that we were protected as long as we were in the water, but had to take precautions once we were back on the shore. We then filled our containers with the holy water, and dipped the malas that we had bought into the lake. We also collected some small pebbles to place at *pooja* altars at home, which is said to be auspicious.

Next, Father had planned to conduct a *havan* with the *swamis* from Skandavale on the shore. The *havan* was intense and we had an opportunity to submit offerings in the *havankund*. All deities were invoked and as the *havan* proceeded, cloud formations indicating acceptance by the gods could be seen. Some saw a cloud in the shape of a spoon and also in the shape of Ganesha! There was also chanting of the *Rudram* by some in the group. I also had the opportunity to pour Manasarovar water on a small idol of Shirdi Sai Baba. The tour organizers prepared lunch right there and we ate lunch on the shores of Manasarovar! Indeed it was a blessed morning.

However, soon I noticed that I was starting to develop a headache, probably from being out in the sun at that altitude of 15000 feet above sea level. I noticed that while I had been comfortable in large, open spaces and the outside, I felt very claustrophobic and suffocated in the hotel room. We were all going about our tasks very very slowly and many of us had varying symptoms of altitude sickness. We did not have much of an appetite, and eating and drinking was just only to help us move on!

That night I felt even more difficulty in breathing and somewhere in the middle of the night I felt like I could not take the suffocation anymore and prayed fervently to Lord Venkateshwara (who is my *ishta devata*) that He help me complete the Kailash Manasarovar journey successfully. I had a doctor from the USA, Dr. Nirmala, as my roommate and within minutes of my prayer, she woke up and asked if I was doing well! I told her I had trouble breathing and she immediately gave me an air puff medication that instantly helped me breathe better! This was nothing short of a miracle! I slept for a little bit and with renewed energy and enthusiasm and most importantly, faith in God and Guru, left for Day 1 of Kailash *parikrama*.

We reached the large open ground where we would be assigned our pony and porter. As I stood in line, I noticed Father a little further up. He was with the group that was to go for Inner *parikrama* of Kailash. I heard that he was not feeling too well and went up to enquire. He said he was feeling better now, but that his sickness was from helping many others who were very sick. In other words he had taken on their discomforts! What can I say? Grace and compassion is obvious at every step of the journey! I sought his blessings and we moved on.

Our first stop was at Yam Dwar (temple of Yama, the Lord of Death), where we enter the small temple, leave behind one of our belongings, and walk out without looking back. We then circumambulate the temple 3 times. The belief is that we enter a new life once we come out of the temple. I left a handkerchief behind and we proceeded on our journey which was estimated at a few hours and the plan was to halt for the night at Dirapuk. I was glad to be on the pony and things seemed quite alright initially. My porter was a young man named Loh-Se, friendly and ready to help me climb up and down the pony.

The trek was filled with beautiful sights and we even saw Mount Kailash at some points. Many others in the group were fit enough to walk and were taking pictures of the majestic mountains and babbling brooks along the way. I shared with my porter some nuts and chocolates that I had carried along and even some of the food the tour organizers had packed for us. At that altitude I did not

Kailash And Badrinath – My Experiences

have much of an appetite and I ate and drank just to have some energy to move on.

We reached the guesthouse and it was a blessed sight – the north face of holy Kailash was right in front of us! The letter 'M' (for Mohanji) and the face of Lord Hanuman could be clearly seen on the face of the mountain! I was elated at this sight, as were the others in the group. We were glad we could see it as long as we were in the guest house! However, slowly weakness began to set in, and soon I could not even climb the stairs. The night passed somehow, and in the morning we set out for the most difficult part of the journey.

I sat on the pony and felt very thankful for it, because I was certain I could not walk up the hill. The climb uphill was quite steep and I was trying hard to hold onto the pony. But every now and then Loh-Se would ask me to dismount in order to adjust the saddle and my seat and tighten it. Every such dismount and mount was becoming difficult and I kept praying that I should keep at it and complete the *parikrama*. I had unusual weariness.

The sights along the way were incredibly wonderful. The highest point in Dolma La Pass is about 22000 feet above sea level. As I neared that point, my porter told me that I had to complete the trek downhill by foot, since the pony could not carry someone down the mountain. It was also time to feed the pony. I started walking using my trekking pole for support. One of the other porters held my hand and led me down the path. He had a *japa mala* and kept chanting as he walked. Soon I saw the divine Gauri Kund. It is the lake where Mother Parvati bathes and is said to be the place where Lord Ganesha was first created! The beauty of the lake has to be seen and cannot be explained in words! The clear glistening water is a beautiful aquamarine color. It lay about 1000 feet below the path and although I would have loved to sip some of the water from the *kund*, I knew that I was not physically fit for it. I bowed to Maa Parvati and continued walking.

After a little while, the porter decided to walk ahead and I managed to drag myself along. I felt like I was tottering along! I had lost my bottle of water and was not strong enough to carry much food, but in the Kailash *parikrama*, help comes just when it is needed the most. Along the path, my group members offered water and encouraging words to keep me going. Yohan even gave me gingko biloba for more energy!

Towards the very end, I was coming down the steepest section of the hill, when I suddenly slipped. But miraculously, I did not fall because someone held my hand, just in time! It was a person from the Kailash Trek organizing team and I had never seen him along the path. He supported me and brought me down to the base, where I met my brother. I could see my pony and porter waiting for me and a little ahead was the resting point, a hotel!

As I sat down at the bench, munching some goodies given by others in the group, I knew for certain that I made the trek because of the pure Grace of my Guru and of course, the Almighty God. I am abundantly grateful for it. The total distance covered on Day 2 was about 22 km. I reached the guest house at Dzultripuk and slept for a while. I woke up and no longer felt weary and tired! I was even able to eat with pleasure. There was nothing more that I wanted. But that evening, one of the tour organizers offered Gauri Kund water in bottles that they had filled up. So the desire to sip the holy water from the *kund* and carry some for my family, was also satisfied.

The next morning, we woke up early and looked at the clear, star-studded sky in the midst of beautiful mountains. It was a beautiful sight, one we very rarely see in our daily lives. We had to traverse only a few kilometers. I set out on my pony with Loh-Se and soon reached the point from where we had to walk along. The rising sun and the flowing river provided a picture-perfect setting. All along the *parikrama*, I saw colorful Tibetan flags fluttering in the wind and mounds of stones. The prayer flags have auspicious symbols and mantras on them, and the belief is that with the help of the wind, they spread good vibes and happiness all around. It is also a practice among Buddhists to stack small stones along paths. I saw some Tibetans doing *parikrama* by prostration. The devout complete the parikrama, not by pony or even by foot, but by prostrating! The person held two small planks in his hands, and had a few extra layers of padding around his knees. He prostrated, lifted himself up, walked up to where his head touched the ground and again prostrated! Such a journey is supposed to take around three weeks and I could only marvel at the unwavering faith and steely determination of the Tibetan Buddhists! A little later, we reached the end of the *parikrama* route and it was a jubilant atmosphere. We were thankful to have completed the *parikrama* successfully and took pictures.

We retraced our route back to Kathmandu, Nepal. But on the journey from Hilsa to Simikot, Nepal, our group split and some of our group members, mainly the organizing volunteers, stayed back at Hilsa while the rest of us were in Simikot. The next morning we were told that the helicopters would fly only if the weather was conducive. So the group at Simikot decided to sing *bhajans* and pray for good weather. We sang *bhajans* for a while and soon the skies cleared! That meant that the helicopters would bring the remaining group to Simikot. The next challenge was to reach Nepalgunj, since the plane to Nepalgunj from Simikot could take only 18 and our group consisted of around 66 members. With a group as large as ours, it was no mean feat to make this trip as planned. We later learnt that our group was the last one whose visa had been approved by the Chinese authorities! Blessings and more blessings had helped us in this journey!

After we returned to Mumbai, we felt drained of energy and went about our tasks slowly, even though we had no altitude sickness to cope with anymore! I was told this was common - our bodies were trying to cope with the increased energy dose from the epic trip.

Soon I started noticing some changes in my life. I had clarity of thought, felt more confident and was able to speak my mind with ease. I have always valued a career and also tried hard to make a successful one. However, that had proved to be an elusive dream and I did not have much success in that aspect of my life. This had been bothering me for years, but after the Kailash and Badrinath trip, as time passed by, this extreme urge has all but died down. I had secured a job in early 2016 and Father had said that he brought it to me. It was a good position and lasted a few months. It also made me realize how many duties I had been taking care of at home, when I did not work full-time. In other words, I realized my worth in the household and that is a blessing in itself! It also gave me the income that came in handy for the Kailash and Badrinath trip. I can say that today I am happier and able to look at the brighter side of things more easily. I have learnt to be grateful for many things. The trip reminded me of the basic needs of life. Since my return, as I interact with others, many of my friends have remarked that I sound very different and think this change is for the better!

As I reflect and write this, I feel a great sense of satisfaction. But I know that I was a part of this magnificent journey only due to the blessings of Mohanji. From boarding the plane to India from the USA, to the wonderful darshan of Lord Badri Vishaal at Badrinath, to sitting down on the pony during the Kailash *parikrama*, to walking down the steep hill in the last part of the *parikrama*, the blessings of the Gods and my Guru are evident.

Pranaam! I am eternally grateful for this wonderful trip to Badrinath and Kailash Manasarovar and consider it a blessing beyond measure. My deepest gratitude to all those who helped me be a part of this journey. Thank you all!

We Are Complete

- Yohan Pathmanathan -

On hearing in February 2016 that Mohanji was taking a group on a *yatra* (pilgrimage) to Kailash, an inner calling arose in my soul. Although my application was accepted, I had to withdraw due to issues with work. In June 2016, I was asked to leave the company by my line manager, and my brother Vijay then suggested the trip to Kailash. After discussing with the family, a plan was set up for me to travel for two months in India covering Badrinath, Kailash and Prasanthi Nilayam ashram. Because of having to move houses, there was very little time left for preparation. I only managed to get about twenty hours of training before departing London on 31 July. A 7-day acclimatisation trip to Badrinath with Mohanji at 3200m above sea level was the first part of the journey about which I have written separately.

My key places for the Kailash Yatra:

1. Pashupatinath Temple in Nepal
2. Manasarovar Lake in China
3. Kailash - a 55km *parikrama* over 3 days in China
4. Presence of Mohanji

Pashupatinath

Pashupatinath is a Hindu temple with the deity as Lord Shiva in a five-headed form. The fifth head was visible to my third eye and was about 50ft high when viewing the sanctum sanctorum from behind the golden Nandi at the top of the temple steps. It was glowing in golden light and showering this golden light in and around the sanctum sanctorum. My gratitude to brother Rajesh K from UK. It was my heart's desire to have darshan of all 4 faces from North, South, East and West. Rajesh suddenly appeared and said, "Let's go!" Most of the priests were operating in silence. One priest looked up and on our making eye contact his eyes emitted golden light. We were in communion via the 3rd eye for some time afterwards. The energy was not of this world, and I felt Lord Shiva covering me with an invisible cloak of protection.

While going around the 184 *shivalingam* shrine I could feel the presence of my family and ancestors on a soul level. After completing this, I saw a sadhu giving blessings. Usually I stay well way but his energy was different. After blessing, he asked for money. So I offered Rs100. He then said he had no money. I then showed him what I had in my pocket. He wanted the Rs 500 note and for some unknown reason I knew it was meant for him. He blessed me again with the note in his hand, touching the top of my head. Somehow that made me feel fulfilled. It was meant to be.

The flight from Nepalgunj to Simikot, then via helicopter to Hilsa (crossing from Tibet into China) and then on to Purang (Taklakot), due to logistics, meant that some of us had not eaten since breakfast and it was now 11pm. Mohanji on hearing this, said this was not good because of hypoxia and that we should eat immediately. He personally, and like a loving father, gave us some dried fruits and I am grateful to the Serbian and South African groups for providing this.

Perfect elimination in the morning. The next day Mohanji said, "Eat well." In the evening before retiring, Mohanji touched my tummy at the dining table and I felt energy enter. I went to the toilet eight times during the night!! Next morning when greeting Mohanji at breakfast, he laughed and said, "Totally empty." I laughed, saying, "Yes, you know!"

Manasarovar Lake

What an honour to be here. As I first stepped into the sacred water, I froze. It's beyond cold. I walked over the stones and hobbled over to Mohanji to receive his blessings. As I approached, I saw the energy of Shiva flowing through Mohanji. His eyes are bloodshot red and he connects to my eyes. 'Shiva' (Mohanji) throws water 3 times and it feels like icicles going through my aura and my face. I could not breathe. I turned away to catch my breath.

Before the first dip, I asked for permission to dip and for Shiva to make me pure enough. The next dip I asked for all my negativity to be washed away. I then invited my mother, father, family and all ancestors to be present on a soul level. We completed and dipped together. I then saw bubbles of white orb lights disappear into ether. Then further dips of gratitude followed for Mohanji, Shiva, mother Parvathi, members of Harrow West Sai Centre (HWSC) and so on, until a voice inside commanded, "Stop - you are complete." The water was clear and fresh to drink as I offered my ablutions.

Again, there was the feeling of what an honour it was to be here in this ethereal lake, where the gods and celestial beings themselves visit. After collecting some water, I wanted a stone to take back. As I walked in the sacred lake, the inner voice said, "This is the stone for you." My mind inquired and thought, "Really, but it's so dirty." "This is the stone for you", comes the reply. So I took the stone and washed it in the holy lake. Later I noticed the stone resembled the shape of Mount Kailash . . . what Grace!

Kailash Parikrama

Darchen was the final stop before the Parikarma and one night given for acclimatisation. The air was thin and I found it difficult to breathe. To make matters worse I could not find my duffle bag.

After 90 minutes of walking up and down and complaining to the organising team and sherpas, I was losing my patience. The bag was returned after the person realised it was not theirs. Relieved and annoyed, I crashed out on the bed, exhausted. This was the second time my bag had been sent to the wrong room!! Immense gratitude to Rianna and for the homeopathic altitude remedy with added oxygen (Coca).

That night, the most unpleasant dreams of me killing people and fighting arose and I chant *Om Namah Shivaya, Om Namah Shivaya*. I could not understand where these were coming from and why, but as I accepted them, they gradually stopped. What a night of darkness and negativity!

The next day the porter with pony was chosen at random. It was a father and son team and Rashilaben was chosen for the father. I was not surprised given that I was the reason or inspiration for her coming to Kailash. The 3-day, 55km *parikrama* began. At Yam Dwar, I saw Mohanji after my first round. On the third round, I went inside, tied my red tee-shirt and rang the bell. I left my old life behind, becoming open to a new life. I felt Kailash - a rock poured out the frequency of love and I stood still to absorb it.

After walking for a bit, I met Jay. He told me that I had another 14km to walk according to his iPhone. The mind kicked in - 'you better use the pony (horse), tomorrow is the toughest day'. The pony was somewhat uncomfortable. *Om Namah Shivaya. Om Namah Shivaya.* Keep eating and drinking. *Om Namah Shivaya.*

With the glimpses of Kailash, I also could make out images of entities on the mount. I saw what appeared to be the third eye on Kailash. We arrived at the first stop, Dirapuk. Ahh, the beauty of Kailash, what a sight, what a feeling! I also noticed the other energy centres to the left. I wanted to run closer to Kailash, but could barely breathe. I wanted to meditate but it was difficult because of the cold. I sensed the presence of many many beings, not of this world. Some from the time of Egypt and Lemuria, and many others. Kailash seemed full of aliens. I was feeling weak and tired and was grateful for some more coca from Rianna. Vijay came in saying, " Let's chant *Rudram*, what an opportunity with Kailash right there!". Internally my mind screamed, "NO, are you mad, you can barely breathe!" The inner voice directed, "One for the UK group." So we chanted the *Sri Rudram*. After the first *anuvaka*, I could feel the energy inside. Mohanji appears, lying down and unwell. I used the energy being generated by the chanting to heal. Streams of Golden light from my hands and fingertips enter every part of Mohanji - physical, bones, nerves, cells etc. I've never seen such power flow, and am so grateful to be an instrument, to serve and to witness this. This is just a fraction of the power of the *Sri Rudram*, *Om Namah Shivaya*.

That night I had an amazing dream - I was in a celestial green crystalline garden. We are playing, and I see Jay and some other members of HWSC. What magical joy, fun and laughter. Later I ask where this place is. 'Gopis with Krishna' comes the reply.

Day 2: the Dolma la Pass and saying farewell to the Inner Kora group. My mind screamed, "What am I doing, why am I here, I must be bonkers etc.." I was filled with doubt, as if not knowing why I was there. I saw Mohanji, we hugged, he said, "I love you, I love you." I replied saying, "I love you too." *Om Namah Shivaya*, let's do it. My gratitude to Riana for some more coca and to Chai, Bridget, Dhanya for the Chinese ginseng. No Diamox required.

I saw the head of Hanuman on Mount Kailash. I look closer, is this an alien? No energy to take a picture - the lack of oxygen was forcing the mind into stillness.

The body was feeling dead. *Om Namah Shivaya* reverberates within. My horse was struggling and the new porter (a young boy) was not happy with my position. I didn't look down due to my fear of heights. The front legs of the horse buckled - *Om Namah Shivaya*. The porter was really unhappy. I saw others fall off their horses, but through the Grace of Shiva and Mohanji, they were safe. Finally we made it over Dolma la Pass. The descent was by foot. The vertigo completely disappeared at seeing the beautiful Gauri Kund. I wanted to go down but would I have enough energy to come back up? Rashilaben too wanted to go. We sat together in meditation. The energy did not feel right to go down together. I sent out a silent prayer for some sacred water. I spotted small golden orbs dancing on the lake and offered my gratitude to those celestial beings.

We made it down with a few slips and help from a sherpa. Along the way someone was selling some Gauri Kund water, and my prayer was fulfilled. I saw a stone roll out of nowhere in front of me and picked it up. The energy was wonderful. I placed the stone to my forehead. A majestic golden triangle/mountain appeared in my third eye. I became very still and silent within. No thoughts. I asked if I could take the stone with me, but no - it belonged there, so I placed the stone back on the ground.

I was back on the horse and there was another 14km to get to the next stop. I saw a black mountain in front, not sure if it was Kailash. It was enchanting. As we got closer, we saw a number of beings on the mountain faces. One had a long white beard and felt like one of the *saptarishis*. His eyes emitted a constant beam of golden laser light which entered my third eye. Whatever is for my highest good let it be. This continued for 15 to 20 minutes. My head felt hollow, with a tunnel from my third eye to the back of my head. I silently bowed in immense gratitude to the *saptarishi*.

The porters told us that the horses needed to eat and that we should walk the rest of the way as it was not far. Not far turned out to be several kilometers!! I silently watched the churning in Rashilaben. We got to the next stopover, Zuthulphuk. The conditions were not great - welcome to the stables!! I felt things crawling up my leg as I slept. I looked underneath and saw sand and below the mattress was damp. Nothing I could have changed, so just accepting it I then fell asleep.

Day 3: Reflecting in the morning that the journey had been relatively smooth with only two more hours until the final completion at Chongdo. The porters and horses were told to be ready by 6am. It was now 8am and Rashilaben and I were the last ones remaining. We decided to walk and were grateful to the sherpas for carrying our bags. The porters and horses catch up after about 45 minutes. I decided to mount the horse and continued to chant *Om Namah Shivaya*. The porter was told to be quick. My porter was trying his best, but the horse really did not want to,

We Are Complete

especially with 100kg on its back! We crossed a small bridge and the porter boy was getting more frustrated with the horse.

I saw a single black and brown dog approach and walk to the side of the open grass. I sensed that something was not right. The porter got a rope and hit the horse in the rear for the first time. I felt the horse jerk. The porter went to hit the horse again, but I put out my left hand and shouted for him to stop. He ignored me and hit the horse again. I saw my body flying up in the air. A white light enveloped my right arm and shoulder and then I crashed to the ground. I felt shooting pains all the way up my right arm. I was thinking, "This is it!! I've probably broken or shattered my bones in many places." I checked my arm and the porter boy was dusting me and asking me to mount the horse quickly (before his father and sherpas caught up). No, stop! I was not going to mount the horse. His father saw what had happened, and came running and shouting. While he fixed the saddle, the sherpas checked my arm. Although the shooting pains continued for five more hours, my arm and shoulder were perfectly fine. I felt immense gratitude to Lord Shiva and Mohanji for protecting me. I felt as if a large part of my karma was wiped out in the fall. Even more surprising is my complete non-reaction, in not scolding or even getting angry with the porter boy. I blessed the horse and its fearlessness.

We completed the *parikrama*, headed for Hilsa and the plan was to get everyone back to Simikot by helicopter that night. Somehow I knew that I would be staying in Hilsa, which did happen and along with twelve others. What a wonderful *satsang* up until 1am! The talk about spirits and then Warren's experience in the middle of the night will make us laugh for years to come!

With the Grace of Shiva and Mohanji we caught up with the group in Simikot and we all made it to Gauri Kund that day. Many groups had not moved for several days, so just a one day's delay, was truly a miracle and divine Grace.

After flying to Bangalore via Delhi and coming to Prasanthi Nilayam ashram in Puttaparthi, the 'morphine' of Grace wore off. Pain within the inside left ankle and foot continued after more than two weeks. My body felt as if it had aged by five years. The daily ayurvedic massages, steam and *shirodhara* are helping.

Some concluding thoughts . . .

It's been a few months since the Kailash trip, but I still have no idea why I went there! Writing this has been extremely difficult as the mind wants to forget.

I now have an overwhelming urge to return back to the power of my soul, the real self. There are moments where I go beyond the mind. Through Swami's (Sri Sathya Sai Baba) Grace I get deeper into stillness day by day. The energy flow from his samadhi in Sai Kulwant Hall is tremendous. I yearn for the self, my soul, to return back home, to live from the self and not this false 'I'.

Kailash is within.

I am an alien in the sense that my being is beyond Mother Earth and originates from a source not of this earth.

I have moments of no thought, stillness, and real peace beyond the mind. Inside, I cry within: "I am my soul, sorry for ignoring you for all this time, I am now ready to go back home, I am self."

My immense gratitude to Lord Shiva & Mohanji; the organising team; the sherpas, the group; the horse and porter; to Kailash; to all the Masters and beings for your love, help, protection and guidance.

To my ancestors, we are complete.

For my Karma, thank you for the lessons.

To Kailash, we are complete.

Badrinath Acclimatisation Yatra

One of the most sacred and powerful metaphysical experiences of my life . . .

The Badrinath acclimatisation turned out to be a powerful *yatra* (pilgrimage) with Mohanji, the *swamis* from Skanda Vale Ashram in Wales, and a group of wonderful souls.

Initially I thought Badrinath was one of the power centres of

We Are Complete

Lord Shiva and was eager to visit. While travelling with the group from Delhi, I learned this was actually the abode of Lord Vishnu. Deep inside I was wondering why I was going on spiritual level.

The coach journey was long, but time passed easily with lovely *bhajans*, amazing scenery and chanting of *'Om Jai Mohana Badri Vishal'*. I witnessed a large purple ellipse with a vertical column of white light going through the centre. It was huge. It was Lord Vishnu in an energy pattern I had not seen before.

Due to many landslides along the way, we had to take our belongings on foot as the road was impassable for about 2 km. I heard the sound of rocks tumbling down, and for the first time saw 'shooting stones'. We are nothing compared to the power of nature and this was the first time I felt genuinely scared on the trip. Just one hit and this mortal body would be no more. As I crossed with a friend, we heard the rocks starting to fall again but Mamu shouted for us to keep going and not stop. I felt an energy surge within, placed my hand on the shoulder of the friend in front of me. "Don't look up, quick, keep going." I felt the protection of the divine, and apologised for my doubting mind. The water from the flowing streams refreshed the soles of my feet and luckily my trainer shoes dried out in the next three days. The air was thinner, colder and full of *prana*. As we arrived at the Snow Cross Hotel in Badrinath, I had the craving for sugar as my body started to shiver. The pack of polos was a treat, followed by some snacks bought by my roommate (thank you).

Mohanji and team organised an *abhisheka* on 4th Aug 2016 and we left the hotel to bathe in the Tapt Kund at 3.40am and caught up with the rest of the group. The water was very hot and it took about five minutes for the body to get used to the temperature. Mohanji told us that the first dip should be for ourselves, the next dip for our parents and the third dip for our ancestors. I invited my entire line of ancestors to be present and to dip with me. I could feel their presence and requested that all differences and karma be resolved and we all dipped together. I then offered all my impurities and asked to become a healing instrument for the divine and golden light flows through and surrounding my hands. We then offered water to Mohanji, and I was filled with gratitude for all he has done in my life. It is truly an honour to serve a realised Master who has taken the duty of taking me to liberation. My gratitude to Sri Sathya Sai Baba for sending me to Mohanji and all the countless masters. After drinking the water, I felt refreshed and filled with light within.

As we sat in the sanctum sanctorum of Sri Badrinath Vishal I asked the inner question - what is so special about the place? The reply came for within. I, Narayana, incarnated as an ordinary man to meditate here. In my foolishness I then asked if I could have the experience of this meditation. Don't pay attention to the *abhiseka*, close your eyes - was the reply. I then felt a golden ball of light in my forehead and energy start to fill my entire being. My body started to shake. I could feel the light in my cells and the golden ball expanding in my third eye. I was burning within. The power of the sun was expanding within the centre of my brain. I opened my eyes to see the wonderful *abhisheka* and the various deities. How truly blessed we are, I thought that we are in the very place the Divine had sat to meditate. The voice within kept urging to close the eyes and go deeper within. I tried but my body could not cope with these higher frequencies. I apologised. "Take rest and come back later on today" - was the reply.

When I returned, I was asked to walk around the temple and not to meditate. The energy was magnetic, strong and deeply purifying. I thanked Lord Vishnu for revealing his face with a conch in his third eye on the Nar-Narayana Mountain the previous day. The frequencies of golden light continued to flow.

I placed my forehead at the back of the sanctum's outer wall. I was completely empty. A void in the third eye started expanding so I stepped to the side and balanced with one hand touching the back of the sanctum. The energy flow was incredible and beyond description. I was timeless, I was nothing, I was filled with golden light. My cells were shaking within. I then continued to walk around the temple, filled with eternal gratitude and floating in divine love. I offered my entire being for reprogramming. The Lord knows what is for my highest good.

The next day, we again dipped in the sacred hot steaming waters of the Tapt Kund. My gratitude to Lord Agni for meditating here at the feet of Lord Badri and providing an everlasting flow of hot water. My ancestors, my son, wife, family, relatives were here on a soul level. What Grace, what love! We all surrendered in our own ways. After walking around, a strong feeling of wanting to meditate was arising within. But where? Then one of the saints in the temple pointed to a place where Mohanji was sitting in meditation. What synchronicity!

Later, a friend saw me and was very excited. She explained that originally Shiva and Parvathi used to live here before Lord Narayana, and the *yatra* is incomplete without a visit to the small Shiva temple. Also she explained the story of how Vishnu appeared as an adorable baby and how the feet are engraved in the stone. I was privileged to chant the *mrityunjaya mantra* inside and the energy was intense. *Om Namah Shivaya*! It felt as if the energies from both the Narayana and Nar-Narayana mountains were flowing through with further cleansing.

Also she explained there are a number of *shilas* or stones where Sage Narada, Garuda, and Sage Vashistha had meditated. After touching some of these stones, the *yatra* was complete. My gratitude to Mohanji, the team, all the masters, Adi Sankaracharya, and the group for making this a reality. A powerful shift has indeed occurred in my entire being. I bow down in complete reverence to Lord Badri. Jai Shri Badri Vishal!

Let it all go

- Milica Bulatovic -

My Kailash experience started few months before I arrived to Tibet. I had deep experiences of walking on this sacred path and these experiences brought a lot of new awareness, slowly preparing me for the ultimate journey. I felt being called as well and that most of the time that I was there already

I was blessed to start the trip with a visit to Badrinath with Mohanji where a small group of people gathered from around the world. We were all looked after by an incredibly loving and caring Mamu. He treated us all like we were his children. It was incredible to watch him deal with so many unpredictable issues that arose all the time with love and care.

We travelled long on the bus through roads that were just cleared from dangerous landslides just minutes before we got there. It was a bumpy ride, but we were so happy to be in that bus that it did not bother us for a second. After 3 days we arrived and we were greeted by Baba (Mohanji)! It was so heart warming to arrive at Badrinath and be welcomed by Baba!

The tempo became even faster and we hardly had time to sleep but that did not matter to anyone. We went to Vishnu temple as we arrived and entered such amazing energy field of calm, love and peace. What a special place it is! You slip into silence so easily.

As I was about to start walking around the Ashram, Baba came

Let it all go

and called me to come with Him to show me each deity and asked me to put my third eye at the back of the temple, which I did right after Him, which was an experience by itself! This trip together with Kailash trip offered me so many small and huge blessings that I cannot count or even recall all of them. The only thing was that we were always on the go, so there was no time to contemplate at all. You experience and you move to another one. The next day we went for a dip in hot water under the temple, Tapt Kund. It is said that water comes from Lord Vishnu's feet. We were up at 2:30 am and walked through Badrinath in darkness, but so many people were up already doing their sadhana.

Water was so hot that it felt like daggers piercing your legs, but we all persevered and got as many dips as possible. After that, we were treated to a rare private Maha puja with abishekam and aarti in the temple as it was Thursday. Our group was seated in the center for the few hours of puja. Energy was electric. Time disappeared and we were blessed many times. We also met many saints that approached Baba and after lunch a small group went up the mountain to seek blessings of Lord Vishnu's foot imprint known as Charan Paduka. We all stopped at a small Hanuman temple that stands on its own and were welcomed by the Swami who lives there. Later he invited all of us for tea and that was a real treat!

We had to leave Badrinath early as weather was not stable and we did not want to put our Kailash trip into jeopardy, but little did we know what treats Baba had in store for us.

On the way to Rishikesh, we went to Vashishta Cave. We got welcomed by Head Saint, Swami Chaitanyananda and received his blessings. He was so happy to see our Baba, who introduced all of us to Swami. I felt so happy, just as a small child traveling with Baba as He decided to share a few places that were special to him.

After meeting Swami, we all went for dips in Ma Ganga by the Ashram. I felt a call from The Sacred Ganga for months before this, but at that moment did not think about it; actually my mind felt empty. As I walked in, I felt a tremendous power envelop me.

I clearly heard a voice say "Let it all go!" At that same moment, I started crying, but there was no sadness. I did not even take a dip yet. I was only standing in the water to my waist. I felt being embraced, but could not stop crying, I was receiving so much love, so much acceptance of my being. It felt so gentle. I cried, but there was no suffering, there was more of reverence, like the most loving Mother enveloped me with tremendous love that completes you and also takes away all that is not needed so gently that cannot be described by words. I stood in the water not able to move much, but somehow got to Baba who poured water over me. I know that it was all His Grace and I did not need to go to Him for cleansing as he had done it already. He was my mother, my father, my all at that moment. The love that I felt is indescribable in words. It is love that completes you. I felt that there is nothing else that exists, but that love.

I did not want to leave this precious river; I had heard its call a month before I became it. Same happened when I experienced a call from Kailash. Then when you physically go there, if you do not allow your physical body to distract you, you just merge with the energy that these sacred places provide. Only later I found out that remains of beloved Swami Vasudevan were consigned to Mother Ganga and I got to witness it. Baba knows how I wanted to meet him, but it was not necessary and I know it was not a coincidence that I was there that day! What a sacred day!

In a blog about Swami Vasudevan that I read after this experience and just before I finished writing it, Baba wrote that if you want to experience real love, you have to meet such people. I feel that day I experienced real love. Everyone went to the cave to meditate long before me, I just stood in awe next to the river that gave me all! But it was not just the Sacred River, it was the exact moment in time met with Baba's Grace. I was in a bubble of love for a few hours after that. I literally felt expanded into bubbles of air. I felt reborn and like every cell of my body was buzzing with new renewed energy.

I went into the cave and it was pitch dark, not one place to sit, but as I stood there, I saw Baba sitting in front of Shiva linga. I felt

Let it all go

that my third eye opened and could see Baba disappearing in form and becoming invisible. I also saw a beautiful blue light coming out of His third eye and connecting to Shiva Linga in front. It felt like I was in a sci-fi movie, but I know that Devi witnessed a few times something similar, so I accepted it and found a small spot to sit on and meditate. Silence was so deep. Such stillness. Then people came and started chanting outside and Baba performed abhishekam on Linga and let us all do it. I was again one of the last ones, but experience was blissful again.

As I poured water over Shiva Linga, I felt water being poured over me. It was an incredible experience.

After I got out, I stood and watched Ma Ganga flow and felt like I was flowing with her, I did not know that at that moment so much was still leaving me. I somehow got to the bus and floated in these loving energies that were still around me.

We arrived at Rishikesh and went to the Sivananda Ashram.

Wow, to finish such a day at such a special place! Energy is so beautiful there. We also got blessed by Swami and as I entered and kneeled in front of him, he chanted a mantra and blessed me. He was Swami Govindananda who told Baba many years ago to feed the children of this world and He would be taken care of. I believe that is how Ammucare started and then ACT that is a big part of my life.

And there I was in front of them both. It was a humbling experience and I felt such deep gratitude and still do!

After that we went and sat next to River Ganga, and I just slipped into silence. I just felt deep peace and flow and power of the sacred river and felt blessed beyond words! We reached the hotel in Haridwar late and went for dinner. I had a deep urge to say thank you to Baba and I went to His table and did so. I did not expect what was to happen next. He told me that he had washed hundreds of lifetimes of mine today! I was stunned. Baba said it will all be better from now on. He asked me how do I feel? I tried my best to explain what I felt, but I could see He was looking right through me and he knew much better than I did, how I really am.

The next day I got sick and each approaching day towards Kailash, I was getting worse. My physical body was still shedding and letting go. The day came when we were traveling to Kathmandu, luckily I was with Baba and Devi on the same flight, so I did not care much about my physical body. Baba kept checking on me and asking how I am. That was enough medicine for me. The next 2 days in Kathmandu, I spent in bed. As everyone was cheerfully arriving, I was getting worse, so blocked and coughing. Devi gave me healing and some insight into what was going on, but my body stayed the same. I knew that cleansing I was going through is meaningful and necessary, but fear started creeping in that I might not get to travel further.

Day arrived of our flight to Nepalgunj. I was in a small 18 seater plane, separated from most of the group and really scared of flying, so blocked as last time I did, I got permanent buzzing in my ears and still have permanent damage to my ears. So I had to face my fear. I was in excruciating pain during flight like someone was stubbing my ears. I could not hear anyone when we landed in 40 degrees heat. Just saw people open their mouth and no sound...

We were told we will go in a different hotel, just our group, and we will not see Baba. I felt scared as we had another flight in the morning. I also developed running stomach for 3 days as I could not help myself get into fear that I might not see Kailash. I do not remember the last time I felt fear, not since I met Baba. However, it was a test, one of the many I had to face over the last few months. Even with all that, I carried on walking one step at a time and without knowing where I will reach. Lots of people offered their help and it was lovely to be around such caring people.

The next morning, I got up and went to the airport where I heard another small plane awaited us, it was very hot, I did not eat and was just about to pass out, that same second Mohanji walked through the door along with Devi. I will never forget that moment. He looked at me and said to come with him. Devi assisted me as well. We went into a separate room with Aircon and comfortable seats and private toilet which is luxury in that part of the world. He asked how I was and let me sit close to him. Baba gave me a bracelet He was wearing and Devi started with healing on me. He also told me I will be fine.

Our plane was postponed for a few hours and in those few hours, I recuperated. I started eating and settled down into peace again.

Once we boarded the plane, I was right behind Baba. Even though I was still very blocked, there was no ear pressure, no pain during flight which is a miracle by itself. As soon as we landed, a helicopter was ready for us and I got into the first one with Baba behind me, even when it was planned for Him to be in another one. I felt so looked after and blessed again. I had a severe headache, but as Baba tapped me on my head during the flight, pain started going away. We arrived at the border of Nepal and China and were kindly given a room at a guest house in Hilsa to use with some beds as we would be waiting for 6 hours for the rest of the group to arrive as the helicopter could take 6 people at a time.

Baba was with us all the time and made us laugh for hours. We were already in high altitude and had a chance to rest and laugh and adjust for 6 hours before the trip commenced again. It was one of the best days of my life! Baba took me in and looked after me the whole day! Then the time arrived to cross the border and there was silence as each year people get turned away from entering China, Tibet for silly little reasons. This time it all went smoothly and everyone got through. Even after all these travels from early morning till late at night, I was getting better. That day Baba told me that I would be fine after the dip in Manasarovar and that I would be flying up Dolma La Pass. That was all I needed to hear!

Next day we arrived at Manasarovar Lake. I was so happy to be there and see Kailash! Baba did not wait much and went into the lake before most people were out of the bus. I found myself right behind him and ready to go in. I was a bit scared the day before as to how to go in such cold water sick, but when I arrived, I just followed Baba without one thought in my head. I did not feel much cold. I just focused on following Baba's footsteps. Baba took first dip and I was behind him and got the opportunity to pour water over Him and followed His lead and took the first dip.

The first dip is incredible, it shocks you, it transforms you in one split second. I carried on as long as I can remember who I was taking dips for and then Baba started leaving and I followed. Just before He went out, He poured water over few people and me. We all got an opportunity to do abhishekam on Shirdi Sai Baba's Murti also in the lake. I felt so blissfully happy after I came out! Something shifted in me. My illness was fading away. Sacred water of Ganga brought on cleansing and sacred water healed me. After the Manasarovar dip, I was healthy again, coughing healed completely. Even weather changed and it became sunny and pleasant. I felt happy as a child can be.

And so the day arrived of Kailash Yatra! As people started getting unwell because of altitude, I started getting better! First day was bliss! I was so happy I made it, I was literally skipping half of the way from joy. Also, the beauty of the surroundings was incredible watched constantly by Kailash above us along with the most amazing people. I had planned to walk with Riana, DB, Hanumatananda and few others on and off, I did not think it would have been possible, but it happened! Also I was right behind Baba at Yama Dwar as we circled it 3 times and left our old lives behind. It was a perfect start to amazing Yatra.

During the day, my Sherpa went ahead as he tried to get me on the horse so many times, but I would not hear of it, so he gave up and left with all my food and water, even money.

I had nothing with me, but at the exact time when I could not manage without water, a friend would show up and get me a bottle. If I felt that I needed food, friends would come and stop and offer food. Towards the end, I was getting rapidly tired and really wished that my Sherpa would show up as I was struggling. Just one kilometer from our stop for the night, he was waiting for me. I do not know if I would have managed to walk that bit, but even that

Let it all go

was taken care of. I finally got on my pony and reached the resting place safely.

The first night was at a place looking at Kailash, but it was also the most difficult night for most. I felt the heaviness that was in the air. People battled, vomited, some had hallucinations, some shaking with fever, and so much more. I was fine, but felt that heaviness as rain and wind were raging outside the whole night. I do not think anyone slept. I got up very early, washed my face in darkness, had breakfast and got ready to leave for the second day. As I was waiting for my Sherpa, Baba and Devi came to greet us and give us encouragement. It was great as everyone going to the Inner Kora came and we could say goodbyes.

My Sherpa came and we started going up the Dolma La Pass. I had to use a pony for climbing up. I just knew my body was not up to it, but my pony went so fast and we left everyone behind. I felt we were up so fast and the next moment Gauri Kund was in front of me. It is so breathtakingly beautiful. The color is magical and energy is incredible. Out of nowhere, one man showed up and asked if I had a bottle as he could bring me water from Gauri Kund. Interestingly I just finished drinking water from my bottle and gave it to him. He ran down and came up so fast like it was nothing, but it is very steep and we are on an altitude of 5800 m. So I received a bottle of very sacred water without even voicing my wish.

Then the steep going down part came and I had no thoughts. I just put one foot in front of the other and that day I spent mostly walking on my own, not like the first day. It was a total contrast. Everything was grey and very dark. Mountains were dark grey, nobody around. Second part of the day was like a new day altogether. Again complete contrast. Sun came out, scenery was beautiful again with river running close, but again nobody around me. I walked as much as I could and occasionally used the pony. Had food with locals at one tent and was very aware of my physical body and discomfort and then suddenly I felt something huge leave me energetically. It was triggered by me getting upset with my Sherpa as he was pushing to go on the horse or walk faster and all I wanted was to be left alone to walk at my own pace. Then I realized he was here for a reason, he was given to me for a specific reason. As I realized that, I felt anger leave me and so much more with it. After that I felt much better and could walk till the next resting point for the night.

As we reached our place of rest for the night, we were blessed by a double rainbow. Scenery was beautiful. Big contrast from the rest of Tibet we saw; it was completely barren. In the morning, I was up early again, had breakfast and was ready to leave, but my Sherpa had other plans.

I waited over 1.5 hours for him watching everyone leave. We also had a time constraint of 3 hours, and I was determined to walk all the way. So I was getting angry.

I was upset to have a schedule even in Kailash that my Sherpa was late and so on. As he arrived, I started walking in front and actually left him behind like we switched our pace, usually he was in hurry and walking too fast, but not today. It was still pitch dark, but I had a lamp and there was only one way to go.

After some time, I simply decided that I will not allow my physical body and my emotions to influence this special pilgrimage and as I decided that again, I felt something huge shift in me and energetically release. I felt my heart chakra expand and from that moment on, I felt I was flying, not walking. My pace became even faster and did not have to stop much, maybe 2 short times. Soon I saw the end of the road. I got emotional as words came to me, 'I did it!' However, I corrected myself fast, Baba you make my every wish come true!

I really felt that no part of me finished this Yatra and that it was all Mohanji's Grace. We often say it, but now I had truly experienced it!

I realized that it is very physically demanding, but same like in everyday life, we must not let our physicality get to us. It is only the outside layer of us. When we start feeling places instead of seeing them, when we experience them instead of visiting them, you get in touch with another realm of you.

After Kailash, I felt so expanded. I felt I did not have a physical

Let it all go

body. I felt I was existing in another realm. From the beginning when I felt the call, I knew that Kailash is within, but when you physically go there and experience it so close you get such strength within. You almost become it and as Baba said Kailash keeps on giving. I feel inner strength, clarity, determination to overcome or achieve whatever the task is in front of me, I never felt before like this. I feel like there is a mountain within. I feel reborn.

Also when you completely surrender and trust, everything just flows and you are completely taken care of. There were so many things that happened during both trips that just showed me how well looked after I was. I had a few issues during and after parikrama, but if you do not resist, it all gets taken care of. The more you flow and have no resistance that comes from your mind at a place of such power, true miracles are possible. Now I can say that I know for sure Baba it was all your Grace as what I experienced was not possible by this body of mine. This whole year was about complete surrender for me, and it is so rewarding, so much letting go of who you are not and coming home to who you really are. I was in safest hands possible! Thank you Baba, love you deeply!

Always grateful and at your feet!

PS; As I took some time to send this testimonial, all along I knew something was missing and was not happy with it, but did not know what. So I left it and also got very busy and just knew that the missing part wouldcome to me. And so it happened! As weeks progressed after Kailash, I started receiving much clearer guidance from my Guru. I felt more and more of merger and I was guided so clearly to my state of being and gently led away from my state of doing. I was a big doer in my life, always in constant action. Imagine what a change for me. In the state of being, I clearly hear guidance and I am constantly inspired. Inspired to share everything that comes my way, to flow and in that flow to be of more service. However now, there is no separation, service became me or I became service.

I feel that there is no more doing as I effortlessly slip into this state of being and inspiration. I do not get upset much and if I do it is a good lesson that is learnt fast and let go with gratitude. Nothing deeply disturbs me. It really feels like I am flowing like a river, maybe do get stopped for a bit by some obstacle, but get to flow soon again.

Not A Soul Goes Untouched

- Nameshri Chetty -

"**K**AILASH AGAIN? WAS the question many asked me and frankly in my still times, I asked myself, Why ?? Divine has a different journey for us beyond our wildest imagination . . .

I had been to Kailash before in 2014 with Mohanji, but I had forgotten the tangible difficulties that came with it. All I knew was that I needed to go back. My meeting Mohanji in itself is a testament to Grace and how He is so connected to us even though we do not know who Mohanji is.

PASHUPATINATH TEMPLE

Grace flowed from the beginning. Like we know it is extremely busy there, so if you are lucky to be in stillness even for a moment then wow!, . . . Well whilst going around the temple and trying to go to the main Mandir, I was pushed and decided to join others in the group, let me tell you, I boiled it down to "it is what it is" (just so that you know I am not learned in many of our scriptures. I learn from others, so I accepted that my presence there alone was amazing), only to have the security guard call me alone to come and stand in front of the Mandir. As I walked up the stairs alone, he ushered all the people out and gave me the Grace to stand in front alone for a few moments, pure Grace. I was unaware of the magnitude of the interaction as later I was told that this temple holds the head of all the Jyotir Lingams.

On going to the Vishnu temple thereafter, we were asked to come into the Goddess Temple which is a little temple above - such Grace as we were on a tight schedule and seeing that we had a flight to catch that was leaving for Nepalgunj.

Helicopter to Hilsa

We reached a small town called Simikot. Here we were told that we were going to take a helicopter across to the border post called Hilltake. Divinity decided to Grace us with rain and wind, so we all waited patiently for the weather to be appropriate for small groups of us to travel to the border post. On this note, I would like to say that many other groups were stranded in Nepalgunj due to the weather. We were the fourth lot to reach the border post of China. There we saw Mohanji waiting for all his Yatris to arrive. We were lovingly welcomed by Mohanji who embraced each and everyone of us with a playful and loving embrace. He was waiting patiently with loving and protective concern to make sure that all were there prior to leaving for the border post. We crossed over a very wobbly bridge, trust me it was just that, without any hassle from the very rigid Chinese military.

Taklakot

Then we reach Taklakot where we were going to acclimatize, already people were looking a bit worse for wear. It was still good that day. We were told we were heading to Manasarovar after one day of full acclimatization. The next morning, I was down due to acclimatization, we had a beautiful satsang with Mohanji and Devi, basking in gratitude and teachings. Devi selflessly offered herself to all who needed healing. She was always busy from morning to the very, very early hours of the morning. Usually, I never thought that I would use her as I am normally in control and I do not like to bother others, but this was not one of those times. I had to surrender that I was not in control. As Devi and I sat, goose bumps totally took over my entire being as we were in each other's space. Before I go any further, I would like to share an experience I had with Devi in India the year prior. I had met Devi shortly during my Kailash trip in 2014. In 2015, whilst doing eye gazing with Devi, we both went down to ours knees with tears in our eyes as she was the Divine Mother herself ,such love, purity, and strength radiated from her that we connected on soul levels. Devi had relayed to me that I had grown spiritually as many chakras were open and active. Seeing that I have been doing healing and have been working on my spiritual growth, I knew there were radical changes; however, she asked me to ask Mohanji to tell me about it. How would I get a chance to chat with Him as He was always busy, nevertheless, I saw a chance and went for it. I was still in severe pain and discomfort. Upon getting Mohanji's attention, I gently took Him aside and told Him my dilemma and as usual He joked and said it was a blessing to be born a woman. I told him what Devi had said and His response was rest tonight. It was already after 1 am and both Mohanji and Devi were still helping others. So I did rest. I must say I felt as if my entire being was taken over by something else. At breakfast that morning, as Mohanji walked in the room and whilst all were greeting him and showing respects, He greeted me by touching the lower end of my back. Mohanji has never done that before to me. He definitely knew that I needed some physical affirmation of my spiritual growth.

Lake Manasarovar

As we drove to Manasarovar, the heavens opened its gates with showers of blessing, but knowing Mohanji, we were not afraid that we were going in for the dip. Although I was unable to go in, it made no difference to me as I was still present. I cried as we saw Kailash in the background. Mohanji went in the lake giving respects and gratitude to the Divine Goddess (Manasarovar) and Mahadev (Kailash), thereafter all went in. I stood and watched with tears in my eyes and total gratitude for being there. I had asked Mitesh and Milu to take a dip for me so I was covered, but I also knew that Mohanji would have had me in His space. I could see all doing abhishekam for Him and taking in the sheer sacred divinity of the moment. As He was coming out of the lake still in Shiva state and totally immersed in consciousness, I was privileged to do the last abishekam for Him. I stood there in total surrender (still get goose bumps thinking and feeling that moment) and offered my gratitude to Mahadev for Him then to take the last dip before returning to His human form. Just being there, standing in front of Kailash and Lake Manasarovar, one becomes humbled by the sheer magnitude of the Divine. Although many have read literature about it and have heard stories about it, being there and feeling it and breathing each moment is something that words fail to explain.

We were blessed to have Mohanji say that we will be doing the sacred homa with the help of the Swamis from Skandavale. We were encompassed in total devotion to the Divine in all forms. We left for the hotel that lay at the foot of Kailash.

Darchen

The morning after, prior to leaving for our first day of the parikrama, we met at the eating area. There were many that were fighting their inner battles and upon seeing this, something came over me. I am normally a very reserved individual, but I was lead by a force that said extend your hand and help those that need it. So I took heed and offered healing to a few that needed it... it seemed so natural. I was fully present knowing that my natural gifts were to be used. I remembered Devi telling me that I will see an exponential growth in my way forward if I allow it. Now thinking back, Mohanji gave me that wakeup call in Taklakot.

Day One

The first day started already on a high, so I was ready to take on the bliss of Kailash. As we drove towards the drop off point, my doubts of why Kailash was totally gone, I was in true beauty and Mahadev's Grace. What more could I feel! We were allocated porters. The porter that was allocated to me seemed caring and ready to take on Kailash with me. As we were getting to know our porter and pony, saddling up as you would say, I was given the Rudraksha malas which were for the group, to take along so that Mohanji could hand them over to each Yatri. I felt it was a huge responsibility as Mohanji had blessed it for each one in Manasarovar and accepted the duty. As we started to walk, I felt Mahadev's energy as the goose bumps and love filled my eyes with tears of pure bliss. On the first sight of Kailash, I knew I was home; I dropped to my knees and took in all that is Shiva.

As my porter and I walked, (he told me that we have to get the fawn of the pony at the top of Dolma La pass not realizing what this meant) merrily chanting Shiva's name and Mohanji's name, we found Mohanji in front of us. I greeted Mohanji and at that point, my porter decided that I should go on the pony. Mohanji, true to His nature, helped me on and I rode alongside Him for a bit taking in Kailash and Mohanji's Grace, only to say I knew why I was given the duty of taking the malas as Mohanji would bless it whilst doing his own Yatra.

During our chat, Mohanji asked me if I went through Yam Dwar. I had not discussed this with anyone, but I had brought my sacred marriage thread, my wedding bangles, and a few other pieces that I wore when I took the vow of marriage. I had set the intention to leave all that behind and of course Mohanji knew; all He just wanted to affirm was that I was good in carrying out my duties.

As I continued my journey on the first leg of the parikrama, I was enchanted by the presence of Kailash as if it was the first time. The beauty of Kailash is something totally unique, one sees many different types of terrain from arid, luscious, wet to rocky.

It would also be a symbol of the different phases that one goes through different terrains of life. There are sprawling mats of green untainted grass fed by flowing crystal streams protected by majestic mountains. The air feels different as well as if every part of your being is being energized with new life.

When I reached the rest point for the first day, Mohanji was there to greet each and every Yatri. This in itself showed His love, respect, and concern for each of His followers. As we waited for all to arrive, Mohanji showed us the M on Kailash. Mohanji said that Bhagavan was glad to see us and was giving us His blessings for our journey. After all made it to base camp in high spirits, we retired for the night.

Day Two

As we were leaving for the second day, the toughest day of the Yatra, Mohanji came to send us off. He gave each one a Mala and a few words of inspiration. His words are still so clear to me, "YOU KNOW WHAT TO DO." The second day was intense. Although Mohanji was not physically with us, His presence was felt. On reaching Dolma La pass, my porter left me to fetch the fawn, so I was alone only to have 3 black dogs and one golden dog follow me throughout . . . such Grace as they waited for me to walk and then they walked.

I was alone without any assistance, but I walked in pure amazement as everything seemed as I was experiencing it for the first time. Maybe the way my eyes saw it was different, but every step I took seemed wow. I had never been here before, although I was there 2 years ago. Although you come in a group, this is a lone journey. Many do not see one another until base camp. You walk alone facing your true self without any cover-ups. As I walked this downhill single file path, for the first time I was amazed by how present I was breathing in each breath of Kailash. The beauty of Gauri Kund reflected pure feminine love. All I can say is that always be open to new possibilities of seeing things differently as I was shedding many of layers of my personality. I saw everything so differently. WOW! As I approached the bottom of the pass, there I saw my porter with mother and baby waiting patiently for me.

It was so beautiful having a baby and mother with us, every time the baby wanted to suckle, we waited. When the mom could not smell her, she called for her and we waited. It made me think of my own life. During that time I realized the patience and love she had for her baby and then I realized that I did the same thing in my personal life, but never acknowledged it as I was busy living. Seeing that relationship of mother and child, it showed me my duty or the profoundness of being a mother. On reaching base camp that evening, the dogs left and we saw two beautiful rainbows. We all decided that it was Grace welcoming us in as we managed to finish the hardest day. WE ALL WERE IMMERSED IN PURE GRACE.

Day Three

The last day was filled with me strolling, feeling the earth, and soaking in the air of Kailash. I made a few Lingams along the way and physically felt the earth with my hands. As everything is so full of divinity, one wants to use all of one's senses, JUST TO BE. I felt like a different person whilst there, being fully present for all that Kailash had to offer. I could have been one of the few that finished last, but I was happy to take the time to feel the earth and embrace the immense presence of the Divine.

My Words

Whilst on this magical carpet of Grace, I realized that this journey was different for me as I released a lot of my baggage that was holding me back. When I say that, I mean I had not released all the emotions of my past. In certain moments, mainly at night I felt the pain and cried. I physically felt the sorrow and betrayal that I had gone through from my past (trust me it was at times scary for me as it was me feeling these emotions or rather the depth of them for the first time). Whilst going through my traumatic past, I did not allow myself to feel the intensity of the hurt as I believed in being strong for my children and others, but this time Kailash said, "Feel every cell of your body, release every bit that does not serve you." Just imagine - I could feel every cell of my being, feel and release what was stored . . . scary, but grateful, as it was about time.

After Kailash

The experiences did not stop there. On arriving home I was not the person that had left. I started having experiences with Ascended Masters, Mohanji, Lord Shiva, Divine Goddess, Shirdi Sai and even Kailash to name a few. For two solid weeks I was in communication with all be it in my waking state or dream state I looked and felt tired.

I normally host the first week meditation in Johannesburg and that weekend after the meditation one of the devotees noticed a Lord Ganesha that appeared on the wall. In days to come the Ganesha grew bigger and became luminous only to notice on the other side of the wall Mother Parvati and Lord Shiva, Hanuman and Shirdi Sai forms appeared. In Kathmandu, Mohanji had told me that he had removed a lot of obstacles from my path and lo and behold I got physical proof

The days that followed, I embraced myself in a whole new light as I was given the push from Mohanji not to be shy and be who I truly am. I started seeing the true beauty of life and felt so much lighter. I became more aware of life itself that I was and still am on a natural high. When Mohanji says he is with you trust me he is.

Mere Mahadev (My Mahadev), I surrender graciously and humbly at your feet, for you are the beginning and end of all that is and is not

Aum Namah Shivaya

- Rashila Pankhania -

For many, many years, my husband and I had been attempting to organise a *yatra* to the beautiful and divine Kailash. Due to various reasons outside of our control, our once in a lifetime trip never quite managed to materialise. We were, however, content in the knowledge that it was obviously not meant to be for us - in this lifetime at least. By divine chance, I happened to hear about the very same trip being planned by none other than Mohanji himself! Both my husband and I were so excited when we heard, that we filled in our applications forms as quickly as we could and once they were submitted, we did the only thing we could do – pray and pray that we were picked for this once in a lifetime experience.

We were picked! From then on, there was not much for us to do, the Kailash Planning team organised the whole trip superbly - all the arrangements and preparations for the trip were taken care for us - all my husband and I had to do was our *sadhana* and pack our winter warmers!

One of the highlights of the trip for me was reaching the sacred Lake Manasarovar. We arrived about midday, the atmosphere calm and tranquil and the sun shining allowing us to have the first *darshan* of Kailash. My husband and I walked into the lake side by side. The water was freezing but we took no notice. Tears rolled down our cheeks, and instead of feeling the cold water lapping our bodies, we felt a deep sense of gratitude. We felt totally blessed and also a huge relief - after all the years of praying, it had finally happened.

The experience of being immersed in the holy waters was incredible, after how many lifetimes was this made possible? Despite the subzero temperatures, I took multiple dips for my family, friends and ancestors to purify our bodies and souls. I felt so blessed and kept thanking Mahadev and my ancestors for the opportunity.

Once we had finished our dips, I went over to Mohanji, as I wanted to do *abhisheka* to him like the others were doing. However, he was freezing and literally shaking so he started to leave the lake and I knew either it was now or never, so I seized the opportunity and quickly did *abhisheka* to him, (which turned out to be more of splash than anything else!) As soon as I did it, I realised it was a mistake. Mohanji turned around and looked at me with piercing eyes and I quickly apologised to him in my mind for being thoughtless! However, a Master like Mohanji does not get aggravated. He instead returned the gesture, and splashed me back; blessing me as he lovingly poured the holy water over my head! Overwhelmed by the love and compassion, I once more submerged myself under the water and offered my humble *pranams* at his feet.

No one could have prepared me for what was going to happen next. The following day we began the *parikrama* (the path surrounding Kailash). I was struggling to breathe with the altitude taking its toll. With Kailash to my right, I channeled my energy towards it. As soon as I did this, I could feel a huge sensation in my chest. I felt my entire heart expand and I witnessed a pink/pale blue light envelop over my whole chest. I was swept away and it was a total out-of-body experience.

My mind became very still and I could not think about anything, but just chanted *Aum Namah Shivaya*. I felt so privileged to be walking on this sacred ground.

I had walked about 8 km and it was physically exhausting. My pace was becoming slower and slower so the last 4 km my porter insisted I get on the pony as it would take another 2 hours at the speed I was walking. With no energy left, I complied.

That night, as I tried to fall asleep, the divine experience continued. I saw a bright white light appear behind my eyes, which then evolved into what looked to be Mohanji's eyes and then again, it reverted to this pure white light. The energy emanating was so strong that I could not take it. I sat up and put my feet onto the ground to ground the energy to Mother Earth but this didn't help much so I went outside for some fresh air. The views were breathtaking, with Kailash shining in the moonlight in total silence. It was just Kailash and I. How I wish to be back there now.

The next day we set off for Dolma la Pass and the experience was so peaceful. I could hear the occasional chatter, and the sound of the river but no other noise. When I reached Dolma la Pass I wanted initially to walk down to Gauri Kund but had no guide or porter to take me. I apologised to Gauri Ma and asked for her forgiveness at not being able to come down. A local devotee, seeing my disappointment, came to the rescue. He had just been down to Gauri Kund and had collected the holy water. With Her Grace, even if I could not physically go down to the place where Gauri Ma had bathed, I was fortunate enough to be given the water by the devotee. It is such faith that allows dreams to come true.

The third and final day had arrived. We started the walk early in the morning and it was much easier than the last two days. I finished the *parikrama* and even though I was the last one to finish, I knew it was not a race but with His Grace, I had made it to the finish line.

On reflection, when I was at Kailash, I was connected with the Source and had a deep feeling of contentment and at the same time felt detached. Nothing mattered and I was able to surrender to Him.

I am very grateful and blessed to have undertaken this journey with such wonderful, kind souls and to have had Mohanji who guided and guarded us all throughout the journey.

It was truly a wonderful experience where I received more than I had ever imagined I would. I can only say a 'thank you' to my ancestors, my parents, the Kailash team, Mohanji and Bhola Nath for allowing me to step on the sacred soil of Kailash.

Someone mentioned on the pilgrimage that the full benefits of Kailash would be seen and felt in the months to come. I can say that it has started . . . .

Journey To Kailash

- Tina Arya -

It was January of 2014 and I had moved to Singapore a few months ago from US. One night, I was reading up information on ancient Hinduism online and suddenly I heard a voice in my head, 'KAILASH MANSAROVAR'. I started searching online and read up as much as I could with fascination for next one hour. I thought that I would like to go there someday. Fast forward to May, 2014, my friend Saisha told me about her meeting with a living Master, Mohanji. I was awed as I listened to her and prayed to Sai Baba that I would get to meet Mohanji too. I was blessed with an opportunity to be in His presence when I went to attend a Retreat with Mohanji in India in October, 2014. Around that time I came to know from Saisha that Mohanji travels to Kailash with his devotees. I was beyond excited . . . I could hardly believe that a thought that appeared out of nowhere (did it?) had the power of becoming reality due to Baba's Grace. When I look back, I realize that it was none other than Guru Mandala that whispered in my ear that night and I had a deep longing to be able to visit the Holy land of Kailash.

My story of Kailash is one of countless blessings and Grace of Father (I address Mohanji as Father) and deep faith and gratitude that grew as my journey to Kailash started in 2014. I moved back to US in the summer of 2015 (Kailash with Mohanji trip did not take place in 2015 due to the massive earthquake in Nepal in May,

2015 and damage to the roads from Nepal to China/Tibet) and settled in our home in the next couple of months. There were many hurdles from the time 'Kailash with Mohanji 2016' trip was announced. I was in the middle of getting my US citizenship, which is a long drawn process, but it came through just in time in May, 2016 with Mohanji's Grace. I was finally all set to embark on this journey of a lifetime. My parents arrived from India in June so they could take care of my 14 year old son when I was away. There was so much excitement in anticipation of the trip and it was building up every day. My tickets to New Delhi and Kathmandu were booked. We received the itinerary and a list to help us pack for the trip and I started shopping for items on the list. I was also looking forward to once again meeting Father and many family members from Mohanji family. As I was preparing for the trip, I started hearing from friends and acquaintances about the tough and dangerous journey, high altitude sickness and how many people can't complete it. My parents were worried for me but I told them that I was going with Mohanji and I knew that He would take care of me. I never felt any fear and did not even have the desire to go through the detailed itinerary that was given to us, I had a deep faith that everything will work out fine.

Finally, the long awaited day was here and I flew to Delhi and stayed with Saisha and Manoj, next day Madhu and Preethi also arrived in Delhi and on 9th August, 2016 about 20 of us flew into Kathmandu. We were all so happy to meet some of our family members again and also to meet some new ones. I remember feeling that I was floating thru all this; there was no worry or stress. We reached the Hotel in Kathmandu and were surprised to meet Father in the lobby. There was a Satsang with Father in the evening; I was again overwhelmed with gratitude to have reached this point. Father emphasized the importance of faith and surrender on this journey. Next morning, we visited Pashupatinath Temple and Budhneelkantha Temple to seek blessings. The roads in Kathmandu were congested and we had to be back in the hotel for lunch and to pick up our bags to catch a flight to Nepalgunj by 2pm. It was nothing short of a miracle that we were able to make

Journey To Kailash

it to Kathmandu Airport in time. We stayed in Nepalgunj that night to catch early morning flight on an 18 seater small airplane to Simikot (a small village in the mountains in Nepal) and as soon as we landed, we were transferred to Hilsa by helicopters.

The helicopter flew between towering Himalaya Mountains and the pilot manoeuvred it between the narrow passages with extreme expertise. As I looked at the Himalayas I was filled with amazement and I could not help but notice how tiny and insignificant I was compared to the nature around me! That was a humbling moment and I was grateful to have experienced the unity with nature as well as a realization that I need to detach from my ego. All of us gathered in Hilsa and had delicious lunch prepared by the Sherpas travelling with our group. Some people were already experiencing shortness of breath and headaches. We crossed over to China on a suspension foot bridge and were given the group permit to travel to Manasarovar and Kailash. We stayed in Purang (altitude of about 14000 feet) that night and were feeling exhausted because of lack of oxygen. Nearly everyone had a headache. We found it difficult to take even a few slow steps without stopping for a few moments. Devi and a few other healers were giving healing to people in the group to support us. At dinner time, Father told us that we should all eat even if we were not hungry and should not miss any meals to avoid hypoxia or high altitude sickness. He really took care of us like a Father. It was very cold at night but we were told by Father to keep the windows open so that there was enough oxygen in our rooms. More and more people started feeling sick that night and next day, which was a rest day in Purang for acclimatization. I was so fortunate to receive Mai-Tri healing from Devi, I felt very tired after that and slept for about two hours until we were called for Satsang with Father. That day we were informed by Sumit how our group was the last group to get the permit for China/Tibet and after that Chinese embassy in Kathmandu was closed for 3 days and many group travelling to Kailash were stuck in Nepal. We had miraculously travelled all the way from Nepalgunj to Purang in a few hours without getting stuck anywhere and made it over to immigration in China well before 5pm; this was all Father's Grace.

He had ensured a smooth and timely transfer through different airports and immigration office in Purang.

Father talked about the importance of taking dips in Manasarovar on behalf of ancestors, family and friends as well. He talked about the spiritual significance of Kailash and many people started feeling the cleansing effect of His words and tears started flowing. I was overwhelmed with the enormity of blessings that I had been experiencing and wondered if I was eligible to receive all this, tears started flowing and I felt lighter. How blessed I was to have connected to Father in this life! I was feeling quite fine until this point except for a slight headache. Next day we got on to the coaches to go to Manasarovar. I felt so excited because Darshan of Kailash would soon be a reality. I had heard from many people that Manasarovar water is icy cold. Father stepped in first and people in the group followed Him. I put my foot in felt the cold water and wondered how I would take the dips. Right away, that thought was replaced by my faith in Father; I knew He would take care of everyone! We only had to hold on to Faith and Surrender! As I started wading through water, I was not so cold after all. After the first dip, I did not feel cold and felt cleansed and more energized with each dip. I felt a surge in energy after that. I became aware of each moment and felt completely at peace. My headache was gone and I could feel my entire body buzzing. Father performed a Homa on the banks of Manasarovar and I started feeling the thoughtless state. It was quite amazing and something I experienced so completely that I was not aware of it until later.

We moved to Darchen by evening. As I went into the dining hall that night I felt little breathless yet full of energy. I asked Sumit if it was possible to get sick now and he told me that we are in a very powerful place and we must watch our thoughts and keep them positive, as any negative thought will be easily energized. I went to bed around 1am and woke up at 3am feeling sick and completely drained, I took some homeopathic medicine for nausea given by Spomenka and slept again. I woke up at 6am to see my roommates, Ami and Marina packing their backpacks for the parikrama. I had a very bad headache and did not have energy to sit up in bed. I asked them for an energy bar and electrolytes and Ami gave me a tablet for headache. I was now panicking as I knew that I could not even stand, leave alone pack and go for the Parikrama. I told Ami that I needed help; I just wanted to go at any cost. I started praying to Baba for help. Ami went searching for organizers and after some time one guide came to check my oxygen level. He told me that I could sleep for 1/2 hour and then I will be fine and sure enough I got out of the bed in 1/2 hour and packed. I feel Baba came in the form of that guide to bless me because in 30 minutes I started feeling better. I still had a splitting headache and I luckily boarded the same coach as Madhu, Preethi and Preethi's Maama, Maami. They gave an oil to put on my temples and also to inhale and my headache got better. We got off the coach near Yam Dwar to line up for porter and pony. I drank some juice out of a box while waiting in line and was going to throw the empty box away when I heard Father tell me to walk slowly. I was so happy to see Him, I went to seek His blessings and He told me, " Bless you! Don't worry, I am with you. You will complete the parikrama!" He always knows our thoughts and fears and takes care of us. I was so grateful for His unconditional love and blessings.

I started the Parikrama on the pony but within 5 minutes wanted to walk as I felt I had the energy to walk. I was chanting Om Namah Shivaya and walking. Around lunch time, I started feeling very tired and I saw Dhanya having the pack lunch so I stopped to have lunch with her. I told her that I had started feeling sick again, she pointed towards Kailash and asked me to look at the images that looked like faces carved in the rocks and she said those are Gods. As I connected to Kailash, I had a surge of energy and started feeling better right away. What an amazing blessing from Almighty! Many a times, while walking I could see myself moving but did not feel I was making any effort, only my chanting existed. It was a beautiful experience of oneness with Kailash. Father's Grace was carrying me forward and I walked most of the way, using the pony only to rest for short periods. I reached Deraphuk and rested before having dinner. Many people were sick and everyone was tired, the healers and doctors in our group were going from room to room checking on everyone and giving healing and medicines to people who were not well.

Next morning, I again met Father before starting the Parikrama and He blessed me again. I could not have asked for more! The Parikrama on day two was the toughest as we had to climb to Dolma La (19,200 feet) and walk 22 km. I had the faith that I would have no trouble as He had blessed me. I started on foot and sat on the pony to take breaks. Going uphill was very tough, we had to stop every few steps to breathe. The path leading to Dolma La was really narrow and the ponies were slipping at times. Getting on top of Dolma La was exhilarating, we stopped there for a minute and prayed to Goddess Dolma, I looked at Kailash and Gauri kund and prayed for my family and friends and I realized that I had not thought of anyone in the last 40 hours or so. I was amazed how being in the Holy land of Kailash had helped me stay rooted in the moment and become aware of silence within. I felt another rush of energy as I breathed deeply and started downhill, moving over boulders and then steep downhill narrow path. My porter had taken the pony thru another route which was longer. There were a few times that I felt I could slip and fall and local people appeared out of nowhere to hold my hand and help me. I saw many people being helped and I understand from that these are Shiv Ganas helping people complete the Parikrama. I finally reached the Tea house where my porter was waiting, I had some lunch with him and he insisted that I sit on the pony for some time as we had to cover a long distance. I sat for about 10 minutes and decided to walk again. I was slowing him down so he told me that he was going to feed the pony around one of the hills and very soon he disappeared from my sight. I was walking alone for some time and started getting worried as I could not see anyone from our group. I walked for 3 hours and just when I would start feeling scared because there was no one in sight, a black sheep dog or a local group would walk with me. Father said that Shiv Gana come in different forms to help us on this sacred journey. I was getting tired and my water was also finished, my porter was carrying the backpack that had more water and I started feeling desperate.

I wondered if he had already reached the guest house and I would have to walk all the way on my own. I started praying to Baba and just as I turned around a hillock, I saw my porter resting with the pony grazing nearby. We reached the guesthouse and it rained that evening but not before everyone from our group had made it to the guesthouse. Another blessing from Father! It rained again at night too but stopped well before we started on the last day of Parikrama around 6.30 am. It was still dark and I finished around 9am. We all cheered as more people completed. We were all tired yet excited. I was feeling little sad that I would be moving from there soon.

Being in the high energy field of Kailash had helped me connect to my inner true self and experience silence. I am eternally grateful to dearest Father for blessing me so I could hear that call to Kailash and also for taking me there and being with me every step of the way. The experiences are unparalleled and totally unexpected and yet it's faith and surrender that helped me on this journey.

Glossary Of Terms

Aarti: A Hindu religious ritual of worship, a part of puja, in which light from wicks soaked in ghee (purified butter) or camphor is offered to one or more deities. Aartis also refer to songs sung in praise of the deity, when lamps are being offered.

Abhishekam: Auspicious bath for a deity.

Amrit: Celestial nectar

Avadhutha, avadhoota: A type of mystic or saint who is beyond egoic-consciousness or duality. Such a person is held to be pure 'consciousness' in human form.

Avatar: incarnation

Babaji: The immortal yogi of the Kriya Yoga tradition referred to as Mahavatar Baba in the book, 'Autobiography of Yogi' by Sri Paramahansa Yogananda.

Bade Babaji: Bhagavan Nityananda of Ganeshpuri.

Bhaav, bhaav: State of being, a subjective becoming, state of mind; often translated as feeling, emotion, mood, devotional state of mind.

Bhai: Brother

Brahma Muhurt: Hours before dawn (between 3a.m. to 6 a.m.) considered most auspicious and pure.

Glossary Of Terms

Brahmin: The priestly caste in Hinduism or people who engaged in attaining the highest spiritual knowledge

Dakshina: Offering (usually in form of money or other material)

Damaru: Small two-headed drum, used in Hinduism. Known to be an instrument of Lord Shiva

Darshan: Vision, sight, beholding

Datta, Dattatreya: Hindu deity encompassing the trinity of Brahma, Vishnu and Shiva, collectively known as Trimurti.

Dharma: Duty

Dhyana: Meditation

Ganesh: Hindu God with elephant's head, widely revered as the Remover of Obstacles and more generally as Lord of Beginnings and Lord of Obstacles. Son of Shiva and Parvati.

Garuda: A large, mythical bird or bird-like creature that appears in both Hindu and Buddhist mythologies; usually the vehicle (vahana) of God Vishnu

Hanuman, Hanumanji: A Hindu deity, who was an ardent devotee of Rama according to the Hindu legends, central character in the Indian epic Ramayana. Also called the 'monkey God' and considered to be an incarnation of the Lord Shiva.

Jal: Water

Kailashpati: Referred to Lord Shiva. The one who resides in Kailash

Kailash Yatra: Pilgrimage to Kailash

Lakshmi: Hindu Goddess of wealth, prosperity (both material

and spiritual), fortune, and the embodiment of beauty. She is the consort of the God Vishnu

Leela: Divine play

Loka: Sanskrit word for "world". In Hindu mythology it takes a specific meaning related to cosmology. Also used for a plane of beings or plane of consciousness.

Mahabharata: Indian epic

Mahamrityunjaya mantra: A verse from Vedas addressed to Lord Shiva.

Nagas, Naag devtas: Higher celestial entities operating in the form of snakes.

Nandi: The white bull on which Lord Siva rides.

Pandit, pundit, Panditji: The Hindu variant, a broad term for teacher or priest in the ancient and contemporary Indian context. The 'ji' suffix is added to the words as a gesture of respect.

Parabrahma: The Father, the Supreme God.

Parabrahman: Literally, 'that which is beyond Brahman'; the self-Enduring, Eternal, Self-Sufficient Cause of all causes, The Essence of everything in the Cosmos.

Paramahamsa: Literally, "Supreme swan," and symbolizes spiritual discrimination; to be in divine ecstasy and simultaneously to be actively wakeful is the paramahansa state; Paramahansa is a sanyasi of the highest level of spiritual development in which union with ultimate reality is attained.

Parikrama: Circumambulation, walking or going around a deity/temple/mountain etc.

Glossary Of Terms

Puja: A process and ritual of worshipping the deity, God or Guru.

Puja thali: A plate in which ingredients of pooja re kept.

Rama: The epic hero, Hindu deity and seventh incarnation of Lord Vishnu in Hinduism; Rama's life and journey is one of perfect adherence to dharma despite harsh tests of life and time. He is pictured as the ideal man and the perfect human.

Rudraksha: Seeds from a tree sacred to Shiva, often strung as beads for malas

Sadguru: true Master

Sadhana: Spiritual practices

Sai, Sai baba, Baba: A great Sadguru who is respected and worshipped by all religions. Incarnation of Dattatreya and part of Navanath tradition. He is also considered as an incarnation of Lord Shiva. Some may refer to the Sanskrit term "Sakshat Eshwar" or the divine. The honorific "Baba" means "father; grandfather; old man; sir" in Indo-Aryan languages. Thus Sai Baba denotes "holy father", "saintly father".

Samagri: Utensils and material collectively required for havan

Samsara: Universe, daily household routine

Sapta rishis: Seven sages mentioned in the Vedas, Vashista, Bharadvaja, Jamadagni, Gautama, Atri, Visvamitra, and Agastya.

Satsang: Spiritual gathering or getting together to discuss and understand spiritual knowledge and practices.

Shaktipat: From Shakti – "(psychic) energy" – and pat, "to fall") refers in Hinduism to the conferring of spiritual "energy" upon one person by another; transmitted with a sacred word or mantra, or by a look, thought or touch – the last usually to the head or forehead of the recipient – Shaktipat in considered an act of Grace on the part of the guru or the divine.

Shaivic (energy): Energy of Lord Shiva

Shiva: A major Hindu deity, and is the Destroyer or Transformer among the Hindu Trinity of Gods.

Shivling/Shiva Linga: The lingam (also, linga, ling, Shiva linga, Shiv ling, linga, meaning "mark", "sign", "gender", "phallus", "inference" or "eternal procreative germ") is a representation of the Hindu deity Shiva used for worship in temples.

Shivoham: Shivoham, Shivoham sat chit Anandohum. A mantra meaning 'I am That' or 'I am Shiva'. It expresses the inner experience of knowing oneself as the pure unbounded all-pervading consciousness.

Sushumna, Ida, Pingala: Channels (nadis) through which, in traditional Indian medicine and spiritual science, the energies of the subtle body are said to flow. They connect at special points of intensity called chakras. Energy meridians along the spine.

Siddha: In Tamil means "one who is accomplished" and refers to perfected Masters who, according to Hindu belief, have transcended the ahamkara(ego or I-maker), have subdued their minds to be subservient to their Awareness, and have transformed their bodies (composed mainly of dense Rajo-tama gunas)into a different kind of body dominated by sattva.

Trishul: A type of Indian trident. The word means "three spear", also weapon of Lord Shiva

Vahana: Vehicle, Gods have their own vehicles, like Garuda for Vishnu

Vishnu: Second of the Hindu trinity, governs the aspect of

preservation and sustenance of the universe, so he is called "Preserver of the universe".

Vaishnavic (energy): Energy of Lord Vishnu

Yagna, havan: A ritual of sacrifice (also "worship, prayer, praise, offering and oblation, sacrifice", derived from the practices in Vedic times. Any ritual in which making offering into a consecrated fire is the primary action. The words homa/homam and havan are interchangeable with the word Yajna.

Yatri: Pilgrim.

Tantra: A type of spiritual practice

Tandava dance: dance of lord Shiva

Made in United States
Troutdale, OR
08/11/2023

11982748R00300